Susan Calmens

Florence
and Tuscany

Sheila Hale

D0885126

Prentice Hall Travel

New York • London • Toronto • Sydney • Tokyo • Singapore

THE AMERICAN EXPRESS ® TRAVEL GUIDES

Published in the United States by
Prentice Hall General Reference
A division of Simon & Schuster, Inc.
15 Columbus Circle
New York, NY 10023

PRENTICE HALL and colophon are
registered trademarks of Simon &
Schuster, Inc.

First published in the United
Kingdom by Mitchell Beazley
International Ltd, Michelin House
81 Fulham Road, London SW3 6RB

Edited, designed and produced by
Castle House Press, Llantrisant,
Mid Glamorgan CF7 8EU, Wales

First published 1983 as *The American
Express Pocket Guide to Florence and
Tuscany.* Second edition 1987,
reprinted 1987. Third edition 1990.
This edition, revised and updated,
published 1992.

The author wishes to thank Burton
Anderson, Caroline Elam, Count
Roberto and Countess Maria Teresa
Guicciardini, J.R. Hale, Sally Hood,
Charles Hope, Nicos Pervanidis,
Nanni Ricci, Nicolai Rubinstein, Stella
Rudolph and Faith Heller Willinger.
The editor and publisher thank the
London office of the Italian State
Tourist Board and Sylvia Hughes-
Williams, Hilary Bird and Muriel and
Alf Jackson for their assistance during
the preparation of this edition.

The author and publishers are grateful
for permission to reprint the following
extracts: Phaidon Press Ltd (UK and
US) for the quotations from *Piero della
Francesca* by Kenneth Clark; John
Murray (UK) for the quotations from
Kenneth Clark's *The Other Half;* and
Laurence Pollinger Ltd and the Estate of
the late Mrs Frieda Lawrence Ravagli
(UK) and Viking Penguin Inc. (US) for
the quotation from *Aaron's Rod* by
D.H. Lawrence.

FOR THE SERIES:
General Editor:
 David Townsend Jones
Map Editor: David Haslam
Indexer: Hilary Bird
Cover design: Roger Walton Studio

FOR THIS EDITION:
Edited on desktop by:
 Eileen Townsend Jones
Illustrators:
 Sylvia Hughes-Williams, Jeremy
 Ford (David Lewis Artists), Illustra
 Design Ltd, Illustrated Arts
Art editor:
 Eileen Townsend Jones
Gazetteer: Anne Evans
Cover photo: David Usill/Mantis Studio

FOR MITCHELL BEAZLEY:
Art Director: Tim Foster
Managing Editor: Alison Starling
Production: Sarah Schuman

PRODUCTION CREDITS:
Maps by Lovell Johns, Oxford,
 England
Typeset in Garamond and
 News Gothic
Desktop layout in Ventura
 Publisher
Linotronic output by
 Tradespools Limited, Frome,
 England

Contents

Culture, history and background

Basic information

Shopping

Words and phrases

Maps

How to use this book

Few guidelines are needed to understand how this book works:

- For the general organization of the book, see CONTENTS on the pages preceding this one.
- Wherever appropriate, chapters and sections are arranged alphabetically, with headings appearing in **CAPITALS.**
- Often these headings are followed by location and practical information printed in *italics.*
- As you turn the pages, you will find subject headers, similar to those used in telephone directories, printed in CAPITALS in the top corner of each page.
- If you still cannot find what you need, check in the comprehensive and exhaustively cross-referenced INDEX at the back of the book.
- Following the index, a LIST OF STREET NAMES provides map references for all roads and streets mentioned in the book that are located within the areas covered by the main city maps.

CROSS-REFERENCES

These are printed in SMALL CAPITALS, referring you to other sections or alphabetical entries in the book. Care has been taken to ensure that such cross-references are self-explanatory. Often, page references are also given, although their excessive use would be intrusive and ugly.

FLOORS

We use the European convention in this book: "ground floor" means the floor at ground level (called by Americans the "first floor").

KEY TO MAP SYMBOLS

FLORENCE CITY: MAPS 1-4

- Place of Interest or Important Building
- Built-up Area
- Park
- Cemetery
- † Church
- ✡ Synagogue
- ⊞ Hospital
- *i* Information Office
- ✉ Post Office
- Ө Police Station
- ☎ Parking Lot / Garage
- → One-way Street

FLORENCE ENVIRONS: MAPS 5-6

- ═○═ Autostrada (with access point)
- ═══ Main Road / 4-Lane Highway
- ━━━ Other Main Road
- ──── Secondary Road
- ──── Minor Road
- SS73 Road Number
- ═══ Railway
- ▪ Place of Interest
- Built-up Area
- Park
- ✦ Airfield
- † Church
- ⚘ Viewpoint

KEY TO SYMBOLS

☎	Telephone	⬛	Meal obligatory
Tx	Telex		Residential terms available
Fx	Facsimile (fax)		Secure garage
★	Recommended sight		Quiet hotel
☆	Worth a detour	⬍	Elevator
♣	Good value	♿	Facilities for disabled
i	Tourist information		people
⬅	Parking	▢	TV in each room
▥	Building of architectural		Telephone in each room
	interest		Dogs not allowed
†	Church or cathedral		Garden
▣	Free entrance		Swimming pool
▨	Entrance fee payable		Good beach nearby
▪	Entrance expensive		Good view
▨	Photography forbidden		Tennis
✗	Guided tour		Golf
▣	Cafeteria		Riding
✳	Special interest for children		Fishing
☜	Hotel		Conference facilities
▦	Luxury hotel	▽	Bar
▢	Cheap		Restaurant
▨	Inexpensive		Simple restaurant
▧	Moderately priced		Luxury restaurant
▨	Expensive	▭	A la carte available
▨	Very expensive		Set (fixed-price) menu
▦	Air conditioning		available
AE	American Express		Good wines
▣	Diners Club		Open-air dining
▣	MasterCard/Eurocard	●	Disco dancing
VISA	Visa	♫	Live music

HOTEL AND RESTAURANT PRICE CATEGORIES

These are denoted by the symbols ▢ (cheap), ▨ (inexpensive), ▧ (moderately priced), ▨ (expensive) and ▨ (very expensive). They correspond approximately to the following actual local prices, which give a guideline **at the time of printing**. Naturally, prices tend to rise, but, with a few exceptions, hotels and restaurants will remain in the same price category. Prices are usually lower outside Florence. Breakfast, which is often not included in the room price, costs an extra Ł15,000–30,000.

Price categories	Corresponding to approximate prices for **hotels** *double room with bath and breakfast (single not much cheaper)*	for **restaurants** *meal for one with service, tax and house wine*
(Lire: Ł)		
▨ very expensive	Ł400,000–600,000	over Ł100,000
▨ expensive	Ł275,000–400,000	Ł60,000–100,000
▧ moderately priced	Ł150,000–275,000	Ł40,000–60,000
▨ inexpensive	Ł75,000–150,000	Ł25,000–40,000
▢ cheap	under Ł75,000	under Ł25,000

About the author

Born in New York, **Sheila Hale** has lived in Italy and England since 1962. She is a contributor to a number of American and British newspapers and magazines, and her books include *Verona,* published by Taurus Parke in 1991, and, in this series, the widely admired *American Express Venice.*

   Burton Anderson, author of the award-winning *Wine Atlas of Italy* (Mitchell Beazley), contributed the chapter titled *Tuscan wines.*

A message from the series editor

In redesigning *American Express Florence and Tuscany* we aimed to make this revised and updated edition simple and instinctive to use, like all its sister volumes in our new, larger paperback format.

   The hallmarks of the relaunched series are clear, classic typography, confidence in fine travel writing for its own sake, and faith in our readers' innate intelligence to find their way around the books without heavy-handed signposting by editors.

   Readers with anything less than 20:20 vision will doubtless also enjoy the larger, clearer type, and can now dispense with the mythical magnifying glasses we never issued free with the old pocket guide series.

   Many months of concentrated work by author **Sheila Hale** and her editor have been dedicated to ensuring that this edition is as accurate and up to date as it possibly can be at the moment it goes to press. But time and change are forever the enemies, and in between editions we very much appreciate it when you, our readers, keep us informed of changes that you discover.

   As ever, I am indebted to all the many readers who wrote during the preparation of this edition. Please remember that your feedback is extremely important to our efforts to tailor the series to the very distinctive tastes and requirements of our sophisticated international readership.

   Send your comments to me at Mitchell Beazley International Ltd, Michelin House, 81 Fulham Road, London SW3 6RB; or, in the US, c/o American Express Travel Guides, Prentice Hall Travel, 15 Columbus Circle, New York, NY 10023.

David Townsend Jones

Florence
and Tuscany

Tuscans in Tuscany

Tuscans quite properly regard themselves as the most civilized of Italians. They speak the purest Italian, they have a long and distinguished cultural ancestry, they created the first Renaissance. They will also admit to being the least cosmopolitan of Italians and the most afflicted with *campanilismo*, the Italian word for provincialism, which means, in the literal sense, excessive attachment to everything within sight of one's native bell tower.

Florence, the little city that helped to transform Western European civilization and which still possesses many of its supreme artistic achievements, is capital of a region that is predominantly rural. That harmonious trio, the vine, the olive and the cypress, climbs up to the walls of many Tuscan towns and villages and slips into the conversation of the most sophisticated city dwellers. "They argue endlessly about *language*," observed the French writer Stendhal, who understood the Tuscan character better than most foreigners; "they argue no less about the price of various oils."

They are in fact an argumentative and factious people; lack of consensus has been their undoing in the past and causes trouble even today. Nowadays, they argue also about the tourists, who are drawn to Florence in ever-increasing numbers. Some see mass tourism as a gold mine, others as an affliction: organizations exist both to promote and to discourage it. They argue about the traffic: some would ban all motor traffic permanently from central Florence; others, the shopkeepers in particular, would prefer a motorized free-for-all.

But the most serious and difficult argument is about the conflict between a long and weighty past that must be honored, whose monuments, most would agree, must be preserved, and the requirements of a modern-minded people who enjoy change and need new buildings, new roads. And so in the 1990s the arguments continue about whether or not to raise a brand new city, *Firenze Nuova,* to the west of the historic center, and whether or not to permit long-haul international flights to land at the domestic airport of Perètola.

Tuscans neither romanticize their countryside nor do they create artificial barriers between city and country. The landscaped garden was a short-lived fashion borrowed from England in the 19thC. If you come across an ornamental tree or herbaceous border in a suburban garden, the chances are that it was planted not by a native but by a homesick foreigner, probably English-born.

Two-thirds of mainland Tuscany is hilly, one-fifth mountainous, one-tenth plain. The cultivated land is extraordinarily productive thanks to naturally fertile soil and an abundance of both sunshine and rain. Farming in modern Tuscany is nevertheless not without its problems. Methods have changed drastically in the last 30 years: the picturesque white oxen that once pulled the plows have been replaced by machines in all but the most remote areas; the feudal *mezzadria* system, or share-cropping, began to die out in the 1960s. Nevertheless, although social reformers have disapproved of it since the 18thC, and the practice is now discouraged by law, it has not yet been satisfactorily replaced and still occurs widely. The cost of agricultural labor today makes the wonderful Tuscan olive oil nearly as expensive as the liquid green-gold it resembles. In the industrialized vineyards beyond Pontassieve and above Siena, disease-proof concrete vine supports have proliferated like tombstones. Elsewhere, wine growers, suffering the consequences of over-production, have turned their fields over to such easily grown crops as tobacco and sunflowers.

Such changes are esthetically regrettable, but they have not fundamentally altered the appearance of a landscape that has been ordered over centuries by collaboration between man and nature. Tuscans have imposed their own character on their countryside: their methods are conservative, enlightened but motivated by a not unnatural desire to make a profit. Industrial development, and the agricultural use of modern chemicals, have in places taken their toll on the ecological balance. Nevertheless, Tuscany still looks, as Goethe noticed almost 200 years ago, the way Italy ought to look, and promotes a sense of well-being in most Northern Europeans.

The countryside still shelters a profusion of rare wild flowers, butterflies, birds and indigenous animals. The *macchia*, the dense Mediterranean scrub characteristic of the Tuscan coast, is now officially protected in designated areas, where it acts as a sanctuary for migrating birds, roebuck, deer, partridge and wild boar. In the wild mountains on the Umbrian border you may still sometimes hear the lethal moan of a wolf or the cough of the hoopoe. Some of the noble mountain forests of fir and beech have been maintained by monastic foundations for centuries. Elsewhere the woods are protected by their very utility. The chestnut trees, which attain magnificent proportions on the lower mountain slopes, produce chestnuts for flour; the beech trees that grow at high altitudes shed mast on which pigs are grazed; pine trees produce pine nuts; and the scented yellow *ginestra* is used to make brooms. In late summer and fall the forest floor is a treasure trove of luscious mushrooms and white truffles.

Below the surface of this productive landscape is a wealth of minerals, mineral springs and building materials. The soil of Elba contains 150 different minerals, and its iron mines produce much of Italy's total requirement. The hills that form a ridge running toward the coast from just below Siena are called the Colline Metallifere, after the copper, zinc and lead they contain. Monte Amiata is one of the major sources of mercury in the world, and half a million tons of Carrara marble are quarried each year from the Apuan Alps. Then there are the colored marbles — red from the Maremma, dark green from Prato, yellow from the Montagnola hills west of Siena, which have supplied the festive dressing for many great Tuscan churches.

Tuscan towns are made out of the Tuscan countryside. No one town or village or city is like another, because the shape, color and texture of each is determined by the contours and building materials of its particular site. Siena is built of burnt-Siena bricks from the clay hummocks found to its southeast, Cortona is a brown sandstone city, Volterra is honeyed limestone, and Florence is gray-brown *pietra forte*.

Tuscans themselves are, as they were in the Renaissance, hardworking, inventive and commercially tough-minded. If you visit a busy, well-kept town such as Prato or Arezzo, you will see the consequences of modern prosperity, negative as well as positive. The center may be clogged with tourist motorbuses, the old walls may have been torn down to make way for highways with factories and industrial suburbs beyond. And the days when you could live in Tuscany for next to nothing or buy an abandoned farmhouse for a song are over.

But before complaining about Tuscan commercialism, do remember that it was the unprecedented success of Tuscan commercialism that fueled and paid for the Renaissance art and architecture that you may have come to admire. Remember too that despite their native commercialism — and their factiousness — Tuscans have preserved their beautiful landscape and historic centers far more conscientiously than have most countries.

The traveller who has gone to Italy to study the tactile values
of Giotto, or the corruption of the Papacy, may return
remembering nothing but the blue sky and the men and women
who live under it.
(E.M. Forster, *A Room with a View*, 1908)

Culture, history and background

Landmarks in Tuscan history

ETRUSCAN, ROMAN AND EARLY CHRISTIAN TUSCANY
8th-4thC BC: Area called Etruria after the Etruscans, the most ancient of the indigenous Italian tribes, skillful artisans and seafaring tradesmen.
6thC BC: Etruscan civilization reached from Po valley to Bay of Naples; federation of autonomous kingdoms or "lucomonies" included Arezzo, Cortona, Chiusi, Fiesole, Populonia, Roselle, Vetulonia, Volterra. **351BC**: Etruria annexed by Rome.

3rd-2ndCBC: Roman roads (the Aurelia, Clodia, Cassia and Flaminia) built across Etruria; Roman colonies included Ansedonia, Fiesole, Roselle and Volterra. **91BC**: Roman citizenship extended to Etruscans, whose cultural identity was gradually absorbed.

570AD: Tuscany occupied by the Lombards, a Germanic people, whose dukes ruled from Lucca. **774AD**: Tuscany annexed to Charlemagne's empire and administered, still from Lucca, by a succession of imperial margraves. The countryside was held by feudal landlords, lay and ecclesiastic; the Benedictine Abbadia S. Salvatore was the most powerful of the religious foundations.

THE HIGH MIDDLE AGES:
THE COMMUNES AND THE GROWTH OF FLORENTINE POWER
11thC: First crusade opened trade with eastern markets and stimulated religious feeling; city life revived with formation of new class of merchants and artisans. Reforming religious orders founded at Vallombrosa and Camaldoli. Powerful warlords, such as the Guidi, Aldobrandeschi and Malaspina, still held large tracts of country in fee.

1115: Countess Matilda, the last of the Germanic margraves, died, leaving her lands to the Pope. With Papacy and Holy Roman Empire locked in conflict, the nascent Tuscan cities asserted their independence; experimental republican governments were administered from public buildings fortified against the unrepresented majority and jealous feudal landowners. From the end of the 12thC, a magistrate or *podestà,* usually a foreigner, was responsible for law and order. The most prosperous early communes were Arezzo, Florence, Pisa, Pistoia and Siena; a strong economy developed, based on commerce, especially the cloth trade, and banking.

1125: Florence took Fiesole, the first, most violent conquest in the gradual takeover of Tuscany.

1215: Tuscan participation in long-standing conflict between Pope and Emperor was sparked off by a feud between the Buondelmonti and Amadei clans, according to legend. The words "Guelf" and "Ghibelline," for supporters of the Pope and Emperor respectively, were not used for several decades. By 1266 the Guelfs prevailed in Florence, with the two main factions after 1300 named the "Blacks" and the "Whites."

1293: The Ordinances of Justice consolidated the political power of the major guilds, excluding the nobility from government.

1338: The chronicler Villani recorded Florence's population as 90,000. It was Europe's richest city. The Palazzo Vecchio, the churches of S. Maria Novella and S. Croce had been built, and the Duomo begun. Internal politics in the merchant oligarchy were chronically unstable. Dante's comparison of his native city to a sick woman tossing and turning in her bed, searching in any direction for rest and relief, still held.

1342: First of the Florentine bankruptcies after King Edward III of England defaulted on large debts. To reconcile civil factions, a foreigner, Walter of Brienne, Duke of Athens, was granted executive authority, but was expelled within the year.

1348: The Black Death killed off more than one-third of the population of Tuscany. **1378**: Armed uprising in Florence of the *ciompi,* the lowest-paid employees in the wool industry, seeking guild representation. After initial concessions, the result was a tightening of the merchant oligarchy.

1384: Arezzo fell to Florence, which, although at war with Milan and Naples, continued its imperial expansion, gaining Montepulciano (1390), Pisa, the great prize (1406), Cortona (1411) and Livorno (1421). Chroniclers increasingly referred not to Tuscany but to the "Florentine Empire."

THE EARLY RENAISSANCE:
THE MEDICI AND THE FLORENTINE CITY STATE

1434: After a brief exile, Cosimo de' Medici, from a rich business family, became unofficial leader of Florence, initiating a period of unprecedented stability, prosperity and achievement. **1469**: Lorenzo the Magnificent, although only 20, was called upon to take charge of the city after the brief reign of Piero, Cosimo's son.

1478: Francesco and Jacopo Pazzi, encouraged by Pope Sixtus IV, made an ill-judged bid for power by plotting the assassination of Lorenzo and his brother Giuliano at High Mass in the Duomo. Giuliano was stabbed to death; Lorenzo escaped. The Pazzi family and its supporters were exiled or executed with the enthusiastic backing of the Florentine public. Sixtus served an interdict on Florence and excommunicated Lorenzo. **1492**: Death of Lorenzo.

1494: Charles VIII of France invaded Italy, took rebellious Pisa under his protection and entered Florence. The Medici were expelled and Florence governed according to a new, broader-based republican constitution supported by Savonarola, Dominican prior of S. Marco and a puritanical preacher. Some 3,000 citizens were enfranchised.

1498: Savonarola burned at the stake in the Piazza della Signoria as a heretic, with the connivance of the Borgia Pope, Alexander VI. **1502**: The democratic constitution proved an inefficient instrument at a time of unremitting war. Piero Soderini was elected head of government for life.

1503-4: Leonardo and Michelangelo commissioned to fresco the walls of the council chamber of the republic with representation of past Florentine victories; unfortunately neither work has survived. **1509**: Reconquest of Pisa.

THE HIGH RENAISSANCE: THE TUSCAN GRAND DUCHY

1512: The Medici were reinstated as leaders of Florence, and their control subsequently fortified by two Medici Popes, Giovanni as Pope Leo X, and Giulio as Pope Clement VII. **1525**: Accademia degli Intronati, the first of the modern literary academies, founded in Siena. **1527**: As imperial mercenaries sacked Rome, Florence again expelled the Medici and reinvoked the Savonarolan republican constitution.

1530: Florence besieged by imperial forces. Alessandro de' Medici installed as head of the defeated republic. **1531**: Alessandro created first Duke of Florence. **1532**: First (posthumous) publication of Machiavelli's *The Prince*. **1537**: Cosimo I, from a lateral branch of the Medici family, created Duke of Florence, after assassination of Alessandro. He ruled until 1574.

1555-9: Florentine conquest of Siena and its territories. The concept of Etruria was revived to emphasize the cultural and political unity of Cosimo's enlarged empire. **1563**: The Accademia del Disegno, the first fine arts academy in Europe, founded with Cosimo I as its patron. **1569**: Cosimo I created Grand Duke of Tuscany by Pope Pius V. Of the six grand dukes who succeeded Cosimo, only his grandson Ferdinand I (reigned 1587-1609) inherited his gift for leadership.

1582: The Accademia della Crusca, a scholarly body responsible for the purity of the Tuscan language, began work on a definitive Italian dictionary. **1589**: Galileo demonstrated the first principles of dynamics at Pisa. **1593**: The free port of Livorno, established by Cosimo I, was opened to all immigrants.

TUSCANY UNDER THE LORRAINE, THE RISORGIMENTO AND UNIFICATION OF ITALY

1610: Galileo discovered the satellites of Jupiter, the "Medicean Planets," and was made court mathematician to Cosimo II.

1737: Gian Gastone, the last of the Medici, died without an heir; the Tuscan grand duchy passed to the house of Lorraine, under whose enlightened rule Tuscany became known as a liberal oasis in a Europe that suffered from despotic and inefficient governments. Administrative procedures and religious foundations were reformed and rationalized; agricultural improvements included draining swampy coastal plains and the Valdichiana. **1753**: The Accademia dei Georgofili was founded and supported an agricultural economy.

1799-1814: The Lorraine were exiled during the Napoleonic occupation of Tuscany.

1815: Restoration of Ferdinand III of Lorraine, who continued to implement progressive policies. The Congress of Vienna ceded Monte Argentario, Piombino and Elba to Tuscany. Lucca and Massa Carrara were still separate duchies. **1847**: Lucca ceded to Tuscany.

1848: Uprisings spearheaded by middle-class radicals. Leopold II retired to Gaeta but was recalled in a year. **1860**: Tuscany voted to be annexed to the united Italy emerging from the wars. The following year, a United Kingdom of Italy was officially proclaimed. **1865-71**: Florence capital of Italy. Part of the old city rebuilt as Piazza della Repubblica.

TUSCANY IN THE 20TH CENTURY

1944: German bombs destroyed Por S. Maria, Ponte Santa Trìnita and Borgo San Jacopo. Outside Florence the most severe war damage was inflicted on Grosseto, Livorno, Pisa and along the "Gothic Line" from the Versilia through the Mugello into Romagna.

1966: Florence suffered its most severe flood in recorded history. The low-lying Santa Croce area was the worst affected. Some 1,000 paintings and 500 sculptures were damaged or destroyed. **1992**: Tuscany is now one of the most prosperous Italian regions, thanks mainly to the development of light industry and tourism.

The Renaissance

The first writer to popularize the idea that art was reborn in central Italy shortly after 1300 was Giorgio Vasari in his *Lives,* first published in 1550 at the end of the period he was describing. According to Vasari's anthropomorphic chronology, each art had its own life cycle: in painting Giotto was the representative genius of vigorous youth, Masaccio of early maturity, Michelangelo and Leonardo of perfected prime. Vasari contended that with these late Renaissance masters, art, hitherto devoted to reproducing the appearance of the real world, had finally triumphed over nature and become its own master.

It was not, however, until the publication of the French historian Jules Michelet's *La Renaissance* in 1855 that the word "renaissance" was applied not only to art but to an entire historic period. Michelet was, in fact, describing 16thC France; but five years later Jacob Burckhardt picked up the term and attached it to the spirit of Italian history from 1300-1550. And there, dazzlingly and maddeningly, it has stuck ever since.

The word is out of favor with modern historians. They argue that all period labels are misleading because history is a continuum, not a series of neatly packed "ages," and that this particular label is worse than most because it refers to the activities of an unrepresentative elite minority.

A common reaction to all clinical historiography of the Renaissance is rather like that experienced by the character in E.M. Forster's novel *Where Angels Fear to Tread*. He was forced to think of a dentist operating among the medieval towers of a Tuscan hill town, and found it painful and disgusting to accept "False teeth and laughing gas and the tilting chair at a place which knew . . . the Renaissance, all fighting and beauty!" The Renaissance is a sensitive subject because it contains the roots of our own civilization; yet we do need the dentist-historians because it is also one of the most complex of historic periods.

Fighting and beauty, yes, but also crises within municipalities, wars between city states, invasion from without. Deference to the ideas and achievements of ancient Rome and Greece set standards that stimulated every form of thought and practical endeavor. Through the weight of investment, the technique of business practice and the geographical reach of commerce, capitalism emerged in something very like its modern form.

If to these developments we add transformation in the arts — music and literature as well as painting, sculpture and architecture — then we have a revolution. But a revolution cannot last for 250 years. So we use a label: the Renaissance. Modified, the label came to describe the outward flow from Italy: the English Renaissance, the French Renaissance, and so forth. Inwardly, however, the pulse rate had certainly been set by Tuscany.

All Florentine work of the finest kind — Luca della Robbia's, Ghiberti's, Donatello's, Filippo Lippi's, Botticelli's, Fra Angelico's — is absolutely pure Etruscan, merely changing its subjects, and representing the Virgin instead of Athena, and Christ instead of Jupiter.
(Ruskin, *Mornings in Florence*, 1889)

Who's who

The following list of biographies is the author's personal selection, and introduces the leading artists that were at work in Tuscany during the 13th-17th centuries.

Alberti, Leon Battista *(1404-72)*
Influential Renaissance architect, theoretician and scholar.
Ammannati, Bartolomeo *(1511-92)*
Florentine sculptor and architect influenced by MICHELANGELO.
Andrea del Sarto *(1486-1531)*
"Flawless painter" of the early Florentine High Renaissance.
Angelico, Fra Giovanni *(active c.1418-55)*
Dominican monk and Renaissance painter.
Arnolfo di Cambio *(before 1245-c.1302)*
Gothic architect and sculptor, a pupil of NICOLA PISANO.
Baccio d'Agnolo *(1462-1543)*
Florentine Renaissance architect and woodcarver. His son **Giuliano** (1491-1555) was a fine Mannerist architect.
Baldovinetti, Alesso *(c.1426-99)*
Florentine Renaissance painter and mosaicist.
Bartolommeo della Porta, Fra *(1472/5-1517)*
A leading painter of the Florentine High Renaissance.
Beccafumi, Domenico *(c.1486-1551)*
The outstanding Sienese Mannerist painter and sculptor.
Botticelli, Sandro *(1445-1510)*
The greatest linear painter of the Florentine Renaissance.
Bronzino (Agnolo Allori) *(1503-72)*
Florentine Mannerist painter, a polished portraitist.
Brunelleschi, Filippo *(1377-1446)*
The creator of Florentine Renaissance architecture.
Buontalenti, Bernardo *(1531-1608)*
Florentine Mannerist architect to the Medici grand dukes.
Castagno, Andrea del *(active c. 1442, died 1457)*
Renaissance painter strongly influenced by DONATELLO.
Cellini, Benvenuto *(1500-71)*
Florentine sculptor, goldsmith and autobiographer.
Cimabue, Giovanni *(c.1240-?1302)*
Florentine painter and mosaicist who may have taught GIOTTO.
Civitali, Matteo *(1436-1501)*
The most important Renaissance sculptor of Lucca.
Cronaca (Simone del Pollaiuolo) *(1457-1508)*
Florentine architect and stonemason.
Daddi, Bernardo *(c.1290-c.1348)*
Florentine painter influenced by GIOTTO and the LORENZETTI.
Della Robbia, Luca *(1400-82)*
Sculptor who invented a method of applying vitreous glazes to terra cotta. Nephew **Andrea** (1424-1525) and sons **Giovanni** (1464-c.1529) and **Girolamo** (1488-1556) continued the family workshop.

Desiderio da Settignano *(1428-64)*
Renaissance sculptor of delicate reliefs and portrait busts.
Donatello *(1386-1466)*
The greatest Italian sculptor of the early Renaissance.
Duccio di Buoninsegna *(active 1278, died 1318/19)*
The greatest and most influential of early Sienese painters.
Ferri, Ciro *(1620/34-89)*
Baroque painter, PIETRO DA CORTONA's most important pupil.
Francesco di Giorgio Martini *(1439-1502)*
Sienese architect, military engineer, sculptor and painter.
Gaddi, Agnolo *(active c.1370, died 1396)*
Florentine painter, son of TADDEO.
Gaddi, Taddeo *(active c.1325, died 1366)*
GIOTTO's most important disciple.
Ghiberti, Lorenzo *(1378-1455)*
Florentine early Renaissance bronze sculptor.
Ghirlandaio, Domenico *(1449-94)*
Florentine Renaissance painter, a teacher of MICHELANGELO, and master of a large studio run with his brother **Davide** (1452-1525) and son **Ridolfo** (1483-1561).
Giambologna (Jean Boulogne) *(1524-1608)*
Flemish-born court sculptor to the Medici.
Giotto di Bondone *(1267/77-1337)*
The first great innovatory genius of Florentine painting.
Giovanni da San Giovanni *(1592-1636)*
Tuscan Baroque painter of frescoes in Florence and Rome.
Giovanni di Paolo *(1403-82/3)*
A leading 15thC Sienese painter working in 14thC style.
Gozzoli, Benozzo *(c.1421-97)*
Florentine narrative painter, a pupil of ANGELICO.
Guido da Siena *(active mid-13thC)*
Founder of the Sienese school of painting.
Leonardo da Vinci *(1452-1519)*
One of the greatest figures in the history of Western art, with an apparently limitless power and range of intellect. Engineer, anatomist, sculptor, architect and creator, with MICHELANGELO and RAPHAEL, of the High Renaissance style of painting.
Lippi, Filippino *(1457-1504)*
Son of Filippo and distinguished quasi-Mannerist painter.
Lippi, Fra Filippo *(active c.1432, died 1469)*
Florentine Renaissance painter; disciple of MASACCIO.
Lorenzetti, Ambrogio *(active 1319-47)* and **Pietro** *(active 1320-45)*
The Sienese Lorenzetti brothers worked in a style that synthesized the prevailing Florentine and Sienese schools.
Maiano, Benedetto da *(1442-97)*
Florentine Renaissance sculptor, especially of fine reliefs. His brother GIULIANO (1432-90) was an architect.
Margaritone d'Arezzo *(active mid-13thC)*
One of the earliest Italian painters to sign his work.

20

Martini, Simone *(active c.1315, died 1344)*
The leading Sienese exponent of International Gothic painting.
Masaccio *(1401-c.1428)*
A founder of Florentine Renaissance painting.
Michelangelo Buonarroti *(1475-1564)*
Painter, architect, poet and sculptor of deeply expressive human figures.
Michelozzo di Bartolomeo *(1396-1472)*
Cosimo de' Medici's favorite architect.
Mino da Fiesole *(1429-84)*
Florentine Renaissance sculptor in marble.
Nanni di Banco *(c.1384-1421)*
Late Gothic-early Renaissance Florentine sculptor.
Orcagna, Andrea (Andrea di Cione) *(active c.1343, died 1368)*
The greatest mid-14thC Florentine painter, sculptor and architect.
Piero della Francesca *(1410/20-92)*
One of the outstanding Tuscan painters and theorists.
Piero di Cosimo *(1462-1521)*
Idiosyncratic Florentine painter of mythological subjects.
Pietro da Cortona *(1596-1669)*
Painter and architect; a founder of Roman High Baroque.
Pisano, Andrea *(c.1290-1348)*
Sculptor known for the bronze S doors of Florence Baptistry.
Pisano, Giovanni *(c.1245-c.1315)* and **Nicola** *(c.1223-c.1284)*
Nicola and his son Giovanni created modern figure sculpture.
Poccetti, Bernardino Barbatelli *(before 1548-1612)*
Florentine painter, the leading master of *sgraffiti.*
Pollaiuolo, Antonio *(c.1432-98)* and **Piero** *(c.1441-96)*
Florentine painters, sculptors, engravers and goldsmiths. **Antonio**, one of the great draftsmen of the Renaissance, is considered the more talented of the brothers.
Pontormo, Jacopo Carucci *(1494-1556)*
Deeply religious painter and one of the creators of Mannerism.
Quercia, Jacopo della *(1374-1438)*
The greatest Sienese sculptor of the early Renaissance.
Raphael *(1483-1520)*
Umbrian pioneer of High Renaissance painting.
Rossellino, Antonio *(1427-79)* and **Bernardo** *(1409-64)*
Brothers whose sculpture exemplifies the "sweet style" of the Florentine Renaissance. BERNARDO worked also as an architect.
Rosso Fiorentino *(1495-1540)*
A founder of Mannerism; important religious painter.
Salviati, Francesco (or Cecchino) *(1510-63)*
Florentine Mannerist painter and friend of VASARI.
Sangallo
Florentine family of architects. **Giuliano** (c.1443-1516), a follower of BRUNELLESCHI, was Lorenzo the Magnificent's favorite architect. His brother **Antonio the Elder** (c.1453-1534) introduced the Roman High

Renaissance style to provincial Tuscany. Both were military architects, as was their nephew **Antonio the Younger** (1483-1546).
Sansovino, Andrea *(c.1460-1529)*
High Renaissance sculptor in terra cotta and marble.
Sansovino, Jacopo *(1486-1570)*
Andrea's pupil and namesake and city architect of Venice.
Sassetta (Stefano di Giovanni) *(c.1423-50)*
The most important early 15thC Sienese painter.
Signorelli, Luca *(c.1441/50-1523)*
Tuscan painter; an influence on MICHELANGELO.
Silvani, Gherardo *(1579-1675)*
One of the best High Baroque architects outside Rome.
Sodoma *(1477-1549)*
Interpreter to Siena of LEONARDO's style of painting.
Spinello Aretino *(active 1373, died 1410/11)*
Narrative painter in the style of GIOTTO.
Starnina, Gherardo *(c.1354-before 1413)*
Florentine painter, a modest anticipator of UCCELLO.
Tacca, Pietro *(1577-1640)*
Sculptor to the Medici grand dukes after GIAMBOLOGNA.
Tino di Camaino *(c.1285-1337)*
Sienese sculptor who also worked in Pisa, Florence and Naples.
Tribolo *(1500-50)*
Florentine sculptor and designer of gardens.
Uccello, Paolo *(1387-1475)*
Florentine Renaissance painter famous as a perspectivist.
Vasari, Giorgio *(1511-74)*
Architect, painter and author of the first history of art.
Vecchietta *(1412-80)*
Sienese sculptor, painter and architect.
Verrocchio, Andrea del *(1435-88)*
Painter, goldsmith and the leading bronze sculptor of his day.
Volterrano *(1611-89)*
Tuscan Baroque painter influenced by PIETRO DA CORTONA.

My soul, affected by the very notion of being in Florence, and by the proximity of those great men, was already in a state of trance. Absorbed in the contemplation of sublime beauty, I could perceive its very essence close at hand; I could, as it were, feel the stuff of it beneath my fingertips. I had attained to that supreme degree of sensibility where the divine intimations of art merge with the impassioned sensuality of emotion.
(Stendhal, *Rome, Naples and Florence*, 1817)

Tuscan architecture

For a fuller explanation of architectural and art terms used throughout this book, see the GLOSSARY on page 32.

ETRUSCAN
Although few non-mortuary buildings survive, there is evidence to suggest Etruscan origins for the atrium, the central courtyard of the Roman house, and a remarkable similarity between the Etruscan villa type and that of 15thC Florentine palaces. The Tuscan order was characterized by plain rounded columns and capitals. The Etruscan urn (pictured

left), in the shape of a house, provides rare evidence about the domestic architecture of the period.

Sections of city walls built with huge irregular blocks remain at Volterra, Cortona and other Tuscan towns. Outside the walls, rock-cut underground tombs were constructed.

For suggested driving tours encompassing Etruscan sites and other remains, see ROUTE 4 on pages 62-63. The Florence Archeological Museum provides a good

Etruscan urn in the shape of a house (6th-3rdC BC).

introduction to the subject. Some books about the Etruscans are recommended on page 35.

ROMAN
The Romans, superb engineers, developed the Tuscan arch as a central structural element, the Classical Orders being used mainly for decoration. They were master town-planners, and the most complete city remains are at Fiesole, Roselle and Cosa (now called Ansedonia), one of the earliest and most extensive colonies, which is still under excavation. Ruins of patrician villas can be seen on Elba, Giannutri and near Porto Santo Stefano.

ROMANESQUE *(11th-12thC)*
The most influential single building was the Duomo at Pisa. Its tiers of open arcades, a mixture of Lombard and Oriental stylistic elements, were imitated in country churches and at

Duomo, Pisa. Begun in 1064. The tiered facade was added in the 12thC.

23

Carrara, Pistoia, Prato and Lucca. Florentine churches — the Baptistry, Santi Apostoli, San Miniato (pictured on page 121) — remained more strictly within the Classical tradition; the Collegiata at Empoli marks the western limit of the Florentine influence. The Benedictine Abbey of Sant'Antimo, built in local alabaster but in a style imported from northern Italy, is one of the most incandescently lovely religious buildings in Italy.

Medieval towns bristled with defense towers; those of San Gimignano and Monteriggioni are the best preserved.

GOTHIC *(13th-14thC)*

Gothic architecture was first introduced into Italy by the French Cistercians, who built San Galgano around 1218. A native variation of the Burgundian model emerged first in Florence, with the preaching churches of Santa Maria Novella (illustrated on page 117) and Santa Croce, and reached its noblest expression there with Arnolfo di Cambio's Duomo. The two loveliest Gothic structures in Florence are the Loggia

dei Lanzi and the church of Orsanmichele (illustrated on page 97), which was also originally a loggia. Civic buildings were conceived as fortresses: the Palazzo della Signoria in central Florence is the most imposing of these republican strongholds, and the Palazzo Pubblico at SIENA is without question the most graceful.

Loggia dei Lanzi, Piazza della Signoria, Florence. Built from 1376-82.

RENAISSANCE *(15thC)*

The innovative genius of Brunelleschi (1377-1446) was nourished first by Florentine Romanesque church architecture, later by Byzantine and Classical Roman engineering principles. His Innocenti loggia in Florence is the first building of the Renaissance, and his cupola of the city's Duomo its outstanding engineering achievement. Brunelleschi's architectural style reached its maturity in Florence with the Pazzi Chapel and Santo Spirito.

Of equal caliber but less influential in the Florence of his own day was the Genoese architect Leon Battista Alberti, whose Rucellai Palace (illus-

Innocenti loggia, Florence.

trated on page 103) and Chapel are elegant and scholarly restatements of Classical themes, and whose facade of Santa Maria Novella was later imitated all over Italy.

Michelozzo's Medici Palace in Florence remained the prototype for domestic building in Tuscany through the 16thC; there are fine Renaissance palaces at Pienza and Montepulciano. Perhaps the most magnificent of all Medici villas is Giuliano da Sangallo's symmetrical POGGIO A CAIANO (see illustration), with its Classical arcaded basement.

HIGH RENAISSANCE AND MANNERIST *(16thC)*

The initiative passed to Rome. Michelangelo's first architectural works, the Laurentian Library and New Sacristy at Florence's San Lorenzo, were Medici commissions, built after he had worked for some years in Rome. His dynamic flouting of Classical order and constructional principles provided inspiration for the later Florentine Mannerist architects, Ammannati and Buontalenti.

Michelangelo's **Laurentian Library steps** (1550s), San Lorenzo, Florence.

The classicizing influence of the Roman High Renaissance style, founded by Bramante, is most evident in Antonio da Sangallo the Elder's domed church of San Biagio at Montepulciano, with a Greek cross plan.

Two 16thC Medici villas near Florence, Artimino and Petraia, were built by Buontalenti for Ferdinand I, and Giuliano di Baccio d'Agnolo's Palazzo Campana at Colle di Val d'Elsa shows Mannerist architecture at its most elegant.

San Biagio, Montepulciano (built 1518-45), designed by Antonio da Sangallo the elder.

BAROQUE AND NEOCLASSICAL *(17th-18thC)*

The swirling theatricality of the Baroque was created in Rome, but Florence boasts some fine church facades: G. Silvani's San Gaetano is the most beautiful, and Ferdinando Ruggieri's San Firenze the largest and boldest. The master of Italian Baroque, Bernini, added the Chigi Chapel to the Duomo in Siena. Interesting palaces in Florence include the *trompe*

San Gaetano, Florence (1648).

l'oeil Cartelloni in Via S. Antonino, the Capponi in Via G. Capponi, and the Corsini on the Lungarno Corsini.

MODERN *(19th-20thC)*

The Mercato Centrale at S. Lorenzo (1874, restored and enlarged 1980), designed by Giuseppe Mengoni, architect of the famous Milan Galleria, is an exhilarating example of the use of cast-iron. The synagogue (1882), one of the first modern Jewish temples to be built in Italy, has a dignified exoticism that sets it apart from the prevailing historicism of the late 19thC.

There are some pleasing Art Nouveau houses in Florence, notably the elegant Villino Broggi-Alinari *(Via Scipione Ammirato 99)*. But the Tuscan capital of Art Nouveau is Viareggio, where the sea front is lined with splendid hotels.

Central Station, Florence (1935).

P.L. Nervi's stadium (1931) at Campo di Marte is an ingenious and, for its date, daring application of reinforced concrete; and the S.M. Novella (Central) Station (1935) was one of the earliest rationalist buildings in Italy. Distinguished post-World War II buildings are thinner on the ground in Florence, although the apartment block at Via Guicciardini 26 (1957) and the racecourse (1967) in the Cascine are successful.

With the unique exception of one or two townships
in the Low Countries, Florence bids fair to be acclaimed
the cleanest city in the universe;
and undoubtedly she is to be numbered among the most elegant.
Her Graeco-Gothic architecture has all the clean finish
and the consummate artistry of a perfect miniature.
(Stendhal, *Rome, Naples and Florence,* 1817)

Tuscan painting

For a fuller explanation of art and architectural terms used throughout this book, see the GLOSSARY on page 32.

ETRUSCAN
The only Etruscan painted tombs now in Tuscany are in the Florence Archeological Museum and at Chiusi.

THE BYZANTINE MANNER *(12th-13thC)*
Each center developed the so-called Byzantine Manner in its own way, as one can see from the many painted crosses in Tuscan churches. Panel paintings of other subjects are now more usually in museums, although Bonaventura Berlinghieri's *St Francis* has been left in San Francesco, Pescia. Other Tuscan masters were Giunta Pisano and the St Martin Master, represented at the Museo Nazionale at Pisa, Margaritone d'Arezzo in Arezzo, and Guido da Siena.

Toward the end of the 13thC, iconic stylization began to give way to the more vigorous monumentality of Cimabue and the Gothic grace and humanity of the Sienese master Duccio. Cimabue's famous *Crucifixion* is in the S. Croce Museum, Florence; he is also represented in the Uffizi and at S. Domenico, Arezzo, and mosaics he worked on are in the Florence Baptistry and Pisa Duomo.

Duccio is on show in his home town in the Museo dell'Opera Duomo and Pinacoteca Nazionale, and at S. Francesco in Grosseto and at the Uffizi.

GIOTTESQUE REALISM AND INTERNATIONAL GOTHIC *(14thC)*
At the turn of the 13thC, Giotto introduced a new kind of painting, which represented solid forms placed in three-dimensional space and conveyed the humanity of its subjects. His example determined the course of Florentine painting through the High Renaissance. His principal works in Florence are in the Bardi and Peruzzi Chapels of S. Croce and in the Uffizi.

Two schools dominated Tuscan painting: Giottesque Realism from Florence, and the International Gothic from Siena. Giotto's successors include Taddeo Gaddi, Bernardo Daddi, Giottino, Agnolo Gaddi and Spinello Aretino: they refined his settings, but never quite matched his psychological power. Two notable Florentine painters who rejected Giotto's example and worked within the graceful but two-dimensional Gothic tradition were Andrea Orcagna and Lorenzo Monaco. In Florence, 14thC painting is best represented in the churches of S. Croce and S.M. Novella.

The great Tuscan interpreter of the International Gothic was the Sienese master Simone Martini, whose major works are in the Palazzo Pubblico and Pinacoteca Nazionale at Siena, the Museo Nazionale in Pisa, and the Uffizi. Along with the Horne Museum, Florence, these galleries also house works of the Sienese Lorenzetti brothers, Pietro and Ambrogio, who combined elements from both styles.

THE RENAISSANCE *(15thC)*

The astonishing story of Florentine *quattrocento* painting is best told in the Uffizi, where portable works from the Medici collections and Tuscan churches are arranged chronologically, enabling one to follow the various innovations, preoccupations and influences: perspective, light, anatomy, Neo-Platonic and Christian symbolism, and the first contact with Flemish Realism.

Fortunately, more masterpieces have remained outside this didactic sanctuary than can be listed here. They include, in Florence, the Brancacci Chapel Masaccios, the Medici Palace Gozzoli cycle, the S. Apollonia Castagnos, the S. Marco Angelicos, the S.M. Novella Uccellos, and the Ghirlandaios in Ognissanti, S.M. Novella and S. Trìnita.

The greatest masterpieces outside Florence are the Piero della Francescas at San Francesco, Arezzo, in the little church at Monterchi and, at Sansepolcro, the *Misericordia* altarpiece and *Resurrection.* Filippo Lippi's outstanding works are the lovely frescoes in the Prato Duomo. The Museo Diocesano in Cortona possesses one major Angelico and a number of Signorellis. There are delightful narrative cycles at San Gimignano by Ghirlandaio in the Collegiata and Gozzoli in San Agostino.

HIGH RENAISSANCE AND MANNERIST *(16thC)*

Florence lost its artistic supremacy. The two greatest Tuscan geniuses, Michelangelo and Leonardo, left Tuscany after the first few years of the century. Only one painting by Michelangelo and three by Leonardo remain in Tuscany, all in the Uffizi, where there are also fine works by other 16thC masters such as Andrea del Sarto and the early Mannerists.

The disturbing, highly intellectual style later called Mannerism was the last original Florentine contribution to mainstream Italian painting. The leading Tuscan Mannerist painters were Rosso Fiorentino, Pontormo, Bronzino, Salviati, Sodoma and Beccafumi.

The richest collection of 16thC paintings in Tuscany is at Florence in the Pitti's Palatine Gallery, where Cristofano Allori's ravishing *Judith* sums up many of the achievements of the century, and where masters from other Italian centers compete for attention with Florentines, including Andrea del Sarto, Fra Bartolommeo and the Mannerists.

At Arezzo, Vasari decorated his own house with allegorical frescoes, which have a freshness and charm lacking in his official work. The great Pontormos outside Florence can be seen within a day. They are in S. Michele at Carmignano, at the Certosa Pinacoteca, Galluzzo, and at Poggio a Caiano. The Rossos are farther flung and are to be found at the Galleria, Arezzo; at S. Lorenzo, Sansepolcro; and one of his most stirring works, the *Deposition,* is housed in the Galleria Pittorica at Volterra.

BAROQUE AND ROCOCO *(17th-18thC)*

The Baroque, like the Gothic, was a style that Florentine artists never embraced wholeheartedly. The most splendid Baroque decorations are in the Pitti Palace, where the first rooms of the Palatine Gallery were frescoed by Pietro da Cortona, and in the ground-floor rooms of the Argenti Museum by A. M. Colonna and Giovanni da S. Giovanni.

The Florentine Rococo painters were not original but cannot be ignored. Their decorations, mainly frescoes, can be seen in many churches, notably San Firenze, the Badia and Ognissanti.

NINETEENTH AND TWENTIETH CENTURY

The Pitti Gallery of Modern Art displays a vast collection of 19thC academic paintings. Several rooms there are devoted to the Tuscan school, known as the "Macchiaioli" after their Impressionistic "blotted" paintings, which reacted against the academic style. Also in Florence, the Alberto della Ragione Collection in the Piazza della Signoria contains some interesting 20thC figurative pictures by Tuscan artists.

At Livorno, the Museo Civico possesses several works by Modigliani, who was born there, and by the Macchiaioli, for whom the town was a major center. The Futurist Gino Severini was born in Cortona, where a room in the Museo dell'Accademia Etrusca is devoted to his life and work. Prato has an exciting new purpose-built museum of modern art.

Etruscan art remains in its own Italian valleys, of the Arno and upper Tiber, in one unbroken series of work, from the seventh century before Christ, to this hour, when the country whitewasher still scratches his plaster in Etruscan patterns.
(Ruskin, *Mornings in Florence*, 1889)

Tuscan sculpture

ETRUSCAN

Etruscan sculpture was broadly Greek-based, but more vigorous and less rational in character. The finest examples in Tuscany are in the Florence Archeological Museum, but exceptional pieces do remain at Chiusi, Cortona and Volterra, and the museum at Grosseto is a beautifully organized introduction to the subject. See ROUTE 4 in TOURS.

ROMAN

Roman humanism led to a new emphasis on portraiture, and the Uffizi possesses one of the most distinguished collections of Roman busts in the world. The sarcophagi in the Pisa Camposanto affected the new sculptural art created by the Pisani in the 13th-14thC, and Roman columns and capitals were often incorporated into Romanesque churches.

ROMANESQUE

Romanesque figure sculpture developed relatively late in Tuscany. In Florence the work is mainly decorative, with Classical or Oriental motifs, as illustrated in San Miniato and the Baptistry.

Pisa emerged as the leading center in the late 12thC and produced the first named Tuscan sculptors: Guglielmo, whose ornate style is demonstrated in the decorations of the Pisa Duomo and Baptistry; and Bonanno, famous for the bronze doors of the Pisa Duomo. Followers of the Lombard Master Antelmi worked in Arezzo, the Casentino, Massa Marittima and Volterra. The wealth of Romanesque sculpture at Pistoia includes the more austere and highly individual work of Gruamonte.

THE PISANI AND THE GOTHIC

Nicola Pisano and his son Giovanni (active 1258-1314) created a realistic and expressive figure style that looks modern even today. Their four famous pulpits in Tuscany are in the Pisa Duomo and Baptistry, the Siena Duomo and in the church of Sant'Andrea at Pistoia. Giovanni also carved the figures for the facade of the Siena Duomo, which have now been removed to the Museo dell'Duomo, as well as a Madonna in the Pisa Duomo and a Madonna and Child in the Prato Duomo. They and their immediate successors, Andrea and Nino Pisano, and Tino da Camaiano, established Pisa and Siena as the most active centers, although Andrea is best known for the first doors of the Florence Baptistry. Tino's works are scattered, but well represented in the Duomos of Pisa and Siena and the Bardini Museum, Florence.

The exquisite relief of carvings of another Sienese sculptor, Goro di Gregorio, on the tomb of St Cerbone in the Massa Marittima Duomo, demonstrate the continuing influence of illuminated manuscripts on Gothic sculpture despite the example of the Pisani. The most important Florentine Gothic sculptors were Andrea Orcagna, whose principal works are the relief carvings of the Orsanmichele Tabernacle in Florence, and Nanni di Banco, whose sinuous relief of the *Assumption* over the Porta della Mandorla of the Florence Duomo and the Classical *Four*

Crowned Saints on the facade of Orsanmichele point gently but firmly toward the dawning Renaissance.

RENAISSANCE *(15thC)*
The richest collection of Renaissance sculpture is in the Florence Bargello, where, among many key pieces, are the Donatello and Verrocchio *Davids,* and works by the Della Robbias, Desiderio da Settignano, Antonio Pollaiuolo and Antonio Rossellino, demonstrating the variety of interpretations of the ideals and proportion of Classical sculpture. The two best places in Florence to study the evolution of Florentine sculpture from Gothic to Renaissance are the exteriors of the Baptistry and Orsanmichele, although most of the original sculptures have been removed to museums, with copies occupying their original positions. Lorenzo Ghiberti's first set of Baptistry doors, on the N, are still late Gothic; the second set, on the E, are fully of the Renaissance. Ghiberti is represented on the facade of Orsanmichele, as is the transitional work of Nanni di Bianco. Donatello's St George predella, the earliest example of perspective in relief carving, has now followed the St George into the Bargello.

Donatello, who infused feeling and tension into Classical forms, was the dominant genius of 15thC sculpture. To appreciate his full range, one must visit the Duomo Museum and the churches of Santa Croce and San Lorenzo, as well as the Bargello.

The greatest master outside Florence was the Sienese Jacopo della Quercia whose animated works in Siena include the original carvings from the Fonte Gaia in the Palazzo Pubblico.

RENAISSANCE *(16thC)*
The Florentine Michelangelo held that sculpture was the highest art form, and his work in this medium has an unprecedented expressive range. Important works in Florence include his first carvings in the Casa Buonarroti and his last in the Duomo Museum, as well as the *David* and *Slaves* in the Accademia and the Medici Tombs in San Lorenzo.

Michelangelo's overpowering genius has caused his contemporaries and Mannerist successors to be seen in an unfair light in the eyes of posterity. A recently arranged room in the Bargello is designed to show his influence on, as well as the individual talents of, Andrea Sansovino, Vincenzo Rossi, Vincenzo Danti, Giambologna and, most impressive, Benvenuto Cellini. Outside Florence, the most exciting works are Domenico Beccafumi's uncharacteristically restrained eight bronze angels in the Siena Duomo.

BAROQUE AND ROCOCO *(17th-18thC)*
The ivories in Florence's Argenti Museum express all the inherent fantastication of the Baroque and Rococo spirit, and Ferdinando Tacca's tomb sculptures in the San Lorenzo Cappella dei Principi convey its authoritative courtliness. The greatest Baroque sculpture was created, and mostly remains, in Rome, although there are some Berninis in the

31

Glossary of architecture and art

Aedicule Niche framed by columns
Ambo Early form of pulpit
Archivolt Continuous molding around a door or window
Atrium Central room or court of pre-Christian house; forecourt of early Christian church
Baldacchino Canopy, usually over altar, throne, etc.
Basilica Rectangular Roman civic hall; early Christian church of similar structure
Bottega Artist's workshop
Campanile Bell tower
Camposanto Cemetery
Caryatid Carved female figure used as column
Chiaroscuro (Heightened) light and shade effects in painting
Ciborium Altar canopy; casket for the Host
Crossing Space in church at intersection of chancel, nave and transepts
Diptych Work of art on two hinged panels
Entablature The part of a Classical order above the columns consisting of architrave, frieze and cornice
Ex-voto Work of art offered in fulfilment of a vow
Fresco Technique of painting onto wet plaster on a wall
Herm Sculpted male nude or bust on tapered pillar

Intarsia Inlay of wood
Loggia Gallery or balcony open on at least one side
Lunette Semicircular surface or panel, often painted or carved
Misericord Ledge or bracket projecting from pew or stall
Ogival Of a double-curved line, both concave and convex
Piano nobile Main floor of house, usually raised
Pieve Parish church
Pietà Representation of the Virgin lamenting over the dead Christ
Pietradura Mosaic of semiprecious stone
Predella One or more small paintings attached to the bottom of an altarpiece
Putto Plump, naked child, often winged, in works of art
Scagliola Plaster-work polished to resemble marble
Sgraffiti Designs scratched into glaze to reveal base color
Sinopia Preparatory drawing made beneath a fresco
Stucco Light, reinforced plaster
Tondo Circular painting or sculpture
Transept Transverse arms of a cruciform church
Tribune Raised area of gallery in a church; the apse of a basilica
Triptych Work of art on three hinged panels

Bargello, Florence and the Siena Duomo. The Florentine Pietro Tacca, sculptor to the grand dukes, produced a number of notable works including the lovable and much-patted Porcellino Fountain in the Florence Mercato Nuovo, and the strange, wicked fountains in Santissima Annunziata. His four Moors at Livorno are strenuous but empty of meaning. G. B. Foggini, one of the most prolific Florentine Baroque artists, both as sculptor and architect, is increasingly admired, especially for his decorative stucco reliefs in the Brancacci Chapel and Santissima Annunziata.

NINETEENTH AND TWENTIETH CENTURY

There is a revival of interest in early 19thC sculptor Lorenzo Bartolini, whose work has a smoothly accomplished feel. There are works by

Marino Marini in his native Pistoia and at Florence in the Alberto della Ragione Collection in the Piazza della Signoria and in the new Marini Museum next to the Rucellai Chapel.

Tuscany and literature

The great period of Tuscan literature began prodigiously, with three writers whose words have since been the chief shaping influence on the Italian language. Dante (1265-1321) was hounded out of his native Florence in 1302 into an exile during which he wrote the greatest work in the language, the *Divine Comedy,* a comprehensive vision of this and the next world. He signed himself "Dante Alighieri, a Florentine by birth but not by character," and his love-hate feelings for the beautiful city that ejected him are especially pungent in the first two parts of the poem, *Inferno* and *Purgatorio* . Spiritualized love is represented by the figure of Dante's Beatrice.

Laura was the love of Italy's second greatest poet, Petrarch, born in Arezzo in 1304 to a father who had been exiled in the same purge as Dante. A good translation conveys the meticulous delicacy of his vastly influential love sonnets. His close friend Boccaccio, born in Certaldo in 1313, is the third of the 14thC Tuscan triumvirate. His *Decameron* starts with a description of Florence during the Black Death of 1348.

The next burst of Tuscan vernacular literary talent came late in the 15thC with the subtle, polished poetry of Pulci, Poliziano and Lorenzo de' Medici; little has been worthily translated into English. Thereafter it was chiefly in prose that Tuscans of genius expressed themselves. Machiavelli's brief *The Prince* (written 1513) still retains the incandescence of its conviction that politics is not about morals but about getting things done, and the *Maxims* of his friend Guicciardini (1483-1540) conveys the realistic appraisal of human affairs that Tuscans have prided themselves on ever since. *Storia d'Italia,* Guicciardini's account of the wars and crises of 1492-1534, has been called the most important work to have issued from an Italian mind.

The poems of Michelangelo, unusually troubled and ecstatic for the period, offer a balancing vision not only of his work but also of his times, as does the marvelously picaresque and direct self-revelation of Cellini's *Autobiography* (1558).

It was a scientist, Galileo (1564-1642), who was to be the last great writer of Tuscan prose. Since his *Dialogue Concerning the Two Chief World Systems* and *The Two New Sciences,* Tuscany has contributed little to the mainstream of Italian literature, apart from two exceptional 20thC Florentine novels: Aldo Palazzeschi's *Sorelle Materassi* (1934), about genteel poverty in a Florentine suburb, and Vasco Pratolini's *Cronache di Poveri Amanti* (1947), a picture of working-class life in Santa Croce.

In the early 19thC, Tuscany began to play a different literary role. Florence, the city that had exiled its own greatest geniuses, was now capital of a region which Shelley, in his famous letter to Medwin of 1820,

33

described as the "paradise of exiles." Dostoevsky (1821-81) was one of these literary exiles, but mostly they were British or American, often taking refuge in Tuscany because the living was cheap, the climate healthy and the peace and order of its landscape and depth of its history cast a spell on the foreign imagination.

Many writers discovered in Tuscany their ideal working environment. Mark Twain, working on *Pudd'nhead Wilson* in Settignano in the 1890s, claimed he had written more in four months than he could in two years at home. Henry James pronounced the atmosphere of Florence better for mental concentration than Venice. D. H. Lawrence wrote *Lady Chatterley's Lover* (1928) sitting on the grass outside his villa at Scandicci, inspired, so his friends said, by contact with a sympathetic alien culture. Shelley, Nathaniel Hawthorne, James Fenimore Cooper and Arnold Bennett all enjoyed productive visits to Florence.

Yet the many foreign poets and novelists who have attempted to write *about* Tuscany have generally failed. Elizabeth Barrett Browning's long verse polemics about the Risorgimento (1847-61), and George Eliot's novel *Romola* (1863) about Renaissance Florence, are among the most ambitious and most unreadable efforts. William Dean Howells' *Indian Summer* (1886) is one of the more delightful of novels set in Tuscany; Anatole France's satire *Le Lys Rouge* (1894) is perhaps the sharpest and funniest; E.M. Forster's *Where Angels Fear to Tread* (1905) and *A Room with a View* (1908) are the ones that are still widely read. John Mortimer's *A Summer's Lease* (1988) is amusing about life in modern Chiantishire.

Much of this fiction takes place within the foreign community, a large various group of cultivated aliens given to making crucial excursions into a landscape where the senses and intellects of the repressed Northern European may open and flower. Italians, when they appear at all, are often lazy opportunists or forces of nature. Stendhal (1783-1842) was unusual for being a foreigner who really did wish to understand how Tuscans of all classes lived and thought. The others, even those passionate "Italophiles" the Brownings, didn't often meet real Italians, and their fictional treatments of Tuscany suffer from what Charles Greville, writing about Florentine society in 1830, described as "no foundation of natives."

The only novelist to turn the Florentine foreign community into the subject of truly great literature was Henry James (1843-1916). Although *Portrait of a Lady* is partly set in Florence, James generally did not wish to be regarded as one of the crowd of "local" novelists, and would disguise or sublimate his source material. Nevertheless, there is something of Florence in most of his Italian novels, and many of his characters are based in whole or part on Florentine acquaintances. *The Aspern Papers* is a good example — although set in Venice, it was inspired by the story of Jane Clairmont, mother of Byron's daughter Allegra and step-sister of Mary Shelley, who spent her old age in voluntary exile in Florence in possession of many of Shelley's papers. James' concern with the experience of exile and the meeting of cultures gives us perhaps the truest impression of Florence as a paradise of exiles. And although his treatment of this subject has never been bettered by a non-Italian writer, his influence is evident in the best of the recent Italian novels set in

Tuscany, *Happy Ending* (1991), by Francesca Duranti, who is often described as "the Italian Henry James."

Suggestions for further reading

GUIDEBOOKS

The *Blue Guide to Florence* is art-historically reliable and is updated regularly. Eve Borsook's *Companion Guide to Florence* is readable, learned and full of fascinating detail, but Klaus Zimmermanns' *Florence and Tuscany* (English translation 1986) is easier to use for on-the-spot reference. The Touring Club Italiano *Firenze e Dintorni* (1974) and *Toscana* (1974) are detailed but out of date; new editions are due in the 1990s. Jonathan Keates' *Tuscany* (1988) is stylishly written, by an experienced and enthusiastic Italophile.

HISTORY AND ART HISTORY

Giorgio Vasari's *Lives of the Painters, Sculptors and Architects* (1550) is still the essential basis of the art history; the best selective edition, in two volumes, is in Penguin, edited by George Bull. The most comprehensive and lavishly illustrated modern book about Renaissance art is the massive 2-volume *The Art of Florence* (1991) by G. Andres, J. Hunisak, and R. Turner. Numerous books about the inscrutable Etruscans include George Dennis' *Cities and Cemeteries of Etruria*, written in the 19thC and now out of print, and Michael Grant's *The Etruscans* (1980). Gene Adam Brucker's *Florence 1138-1737* (1983) is authoritative as well as beautifully written and illustrated. Iris Origo's classic *The Merchant of Prato* (1957) is about a businessman who lived on the eve of the Renaissance. J.R. Hale's *Florence and the Medici* (1977) is the clearest account of how and why the Medici took control; Harold Acton's *The Last Medici* closes the story. Judith Hook's *Siena* is the best short account of the history and the art.

MEMOIRS AND IMPRESSIONS

Books about the Anglo-American passion for Tuscany include Paul R. Baker's *The Fortunate Pilgrims: Americans in Italy 1800-1860* (1964), Olive Hamilton's *Paradise of Exiles: Tuscany and the British* (1974) and Giuliana Artom Treves' *The Golden Ring: The Anglo-Florentines 1847-1862* (1956).

Accounts of Florence and Tuscany as it was earlier in this century can make fascinating reading. E.H. Hutton's books explore the area before and after World War I. Iris Origo's *War in Val d'Orcia* is a rivetting account of World War II, as is Eric Newby's *Love and War in the Apennines*. Read also Iris Origo's autobiography *Images and Shadows*. Alan Moorehead's *The Villa Diana* and Mary McCarthy's *The Stones of Florence* are about Tuscany in the late 1940s and 1950s. If you read Italian you will be uncomfortably amused by Curzio Malaparte's brilliant analysis of the Tuscan character, *Maladetti Toscani* (1964).

Basic information

Before you go

DOCUMENTS REQUIRED
For **citizens of the US and British Commonwealth**, a **passport** is the only document required for visits not exceeding 3 months. For **citizens of the EC**, a **Visitor Card** will suffice. For longer visits, and for most other nationals, a **visa** must be obtained in advance in the country of departure. **Vaccination certificates** are not normally required, but if you are traveling from the Middle East, Far East, South America or Africa, you should check when buying your ticket.

To drive a car in Italy, you do not need an international driver's license; a **valid driver's license**, accompanied by a **translation** (obtainable from **CIT, ACI** or the Italian Tourist Office in the country of origin) is all that is required. If you are bringing your car into the country, you must carry the **vehicle registration document** (logbook) and an **insurance certificate** or **international green card**, and display a **national identity sticker**.

TRAVEL AND MEDICAL INSURANCE
It is advisable to travel with an **insurance policy** that covers loss of deposits paid to airlines, hotels and tour operators, and the cost of dealing with emergency requirements, such as special tickets home and extra nights in a hotel.

Travelers from EC countries are entitled to all free health services available to Italians, but should still take out insurance to cover cancellation fees, loss of personal possessions and emergency expenses incurred for medical reasons. All other nationals should take out travel and medical insurance. **Travelers from the US** should always consult their own insurance company for advice when going abroad.

The **IAMAT** (International Association for Medical Assistance to Travelers) has a list of English-speaking doctors who will call, for a low fixed fee. There are member hospitals and doctors throughout the world, including numerous centers in Italy and one in Florence. Membership is free. For further information, write to **IAMAT** (*417 Center St., Lewiston, NY 14092, USA*).

UK nationals entitled to full **UK benefits** should obtain form E111 by filling in form CM1 from leaflet SA30, *Medical Treatment During Visits Abroad,* obtainable from local health offices before leaving. If medical aid is required, the form should be presented to the nearest office of the

INAM *(Istituto Nazionale per l'Assicurazione contro le Malattie),* which will issue a certificate confirming your right to treatment and give you a list of doctors, dentists and clinics to consult, all of which are within the INAM scheme. Without the form you will have to pay and then reclaim the full costs.

MONEY
The **monetary unit** is the lira (plural lire, for which the symbol is Ł). There are coins for 50, 100, 200 and 500 lire, and notes for 1,000, 2,000, 5,000, 10,000, 50,000 and 100,000 lire. There are no **restrictions** on other currencies or travelers checks taken into the country, but if you intend exporting more than Ł1 million-worth of any currency exceeding the money that you have imported, you should complete form V2 at customs on entry.

Carry **cash** in small amounts only. **Travelers checks** issued by all major companies are widely recognized. Make sure you read the instructions included with your travelers checks. It is important to note separately the serial numbers of your checks and the telephone number to call in case of loss. Specialist travelers check companies such as **American Express** provide extensive local refund facilities through their own offices or agents. **Eurocheque Encashment Card** holders can cash personal checks in most banks, and there are machines that exchange foreign bills for lire. The **principal cards accepted** in Florence and increasingly in provincial Tuscany are American Express, Diners Club, Mastercard (Eurocard) and Visa.

American Express has a **MoneyGram** ® money transfer service that makes it possible to wire money worldwide in just minutes, from any American Express Travel Service Office. This service is available to all customers and is not limited to American Express Card members. See USEFUL ADDRESSES on page 44.

CUSTOMS
The completion of the European Single Market takes place at the end of 1992. Under the Single Market arrangements due from January 1, 1993, travelers between EC countries need only make a declaration to Customs for prohibited or restricted goods. Limits on duty- and tax-paid goods purchased within the EC will end after 1992, although there will be certain higher limits on tobacco goods and alcoholic drinks, designed to prevent unfair commercial exploitation of the new arrangements.

These new higher limits will be: **Tobacco** — 800 cigarettes *plus* 400 cigarillos *plus* 200 cigars *plus* 1kg tobacco; **Alcohol** — 10 liters of liquor (spirits) *or* 20 liters fortified wine *plus* 90 liters wine (not more than 60 percent sparkling) *plus* 110 liters beer.

Limits that apply within the EC until the end of 1992 only are widely publicized in duty-free shops and at ports, airports and international crossing-points. All allowances apply to travelers aged 17 and over.

The EC decision is that duty- and tax-free shopping will continue until July 1999, based on what is referred to as a "vendor control system." What this appears to mean is that no duty or tax will be charged within the appropriate stores, but prices charged for goods on sale will be up to the store management. Our best advice is: be on your guard.

Travelers from countries outside the EC will still have to declare any goods in excess of the Customs allowances. If you are in any doubt at all, inquire before you depart.

When returning, you can export up to £1 million-worth of goods. The export of antiques and modern art objects is restricted; apply to the Export Department of the Italian Ministry of Education.

ITALIAN TOURIST OFFICES

UK   Italian State Tourist Office (ISTO), 1, Princes St., London W1R 8AY ☎(071) 408 1254 [Fx](071) 493 6695

USA   Italian Government Travel Office (ENIT), 630, 5th Ave., Suite 1565, New York, NY 10111 ☎(212) 245 4822 [Fx](212)245 4822

There are also offices in **Chicago** (*☎(312) 644 0990* [Fx]*644 3019)* and **San Francisco** (*☎(415) 392 6206* [Fx]*392 6852)*, and in **Montréal** (*☎(514) 866 7667* [Fx]*392 1429)*.

GETTING THERE

By air   The main Tuscan airport is **Pisa**, which receives European and domestic flights. More convenient for Florence is **Perètola**, which is only about 10 minutes from the city center, but takes only domestic and European short-haul flights. (The restaurant at Perètola ([□]) is excellent.) Some European flights arrive at **Bologna**, some 70km to the N of Florence.

Passengers returning to Pisa by train can now check in, 20 minutes before the scheduled train departure time, at the British Airways and Alitalia air terminal at Florence Central station, on track (platform) 5. Passengers from outside Europe will have to make a transfer stop or fly direct to Milan or Rome. An hourly train, using the *linea direttissima,* takes 2 hours from Rome.

By train   The two main trans-European trains to Florence are the *Palatino* from Paris (couchettes and sleeping cars only) and the *Italia Express* from London stopping at Lille, Strasbourg, Basel, Milan and Bologna. Both carry first- and second-class passengers, and reservations are obligatory.

By car   Two superhighways (autostrade) enter Tuscany from the N: the **A12** along the coast from France via Genoa, and the **A1** across the Apennines from Bologna.

CLIMATE

The weather in Florence is more variable than in most Italian cities. The temperature ranges from a brisk average of 5.8°C (42°F) in December, January and February to a sticky 25°C (77°F) in late July and August. It can rain at any time of the year but rarely for prolonged periods in summer. The wettest months are January, late November, October and April, in that order. On the SW coast, winters are generally much milder.

CLOTHES

Be sure to pack one comfortable pair of shoes for sightseeing. In summertime, wearing light, loose clothing is essential for comfort. In spring and fall you should bring a sweater or light coat and an umbrella. In winter you will need full protection as it can become cold, particularly at night. Florentines are justly famous for their sense of fashion, but their style is extremely understated. Informal day clothes will take you virtually anywhere. Italian men do tend to wear ties on most occasions, but there is no rule about wearing ties in restaurants. Evening dress is rarely seen these days except in private houses.

GENERAL DELIVERY (POSTE RESTANTE)

Correspondence marked *Fermo Posta*, plus the name of the town and province, will be held at the central post office. A small charge is payable on collection; you must show your passport for **identification**.

Getting around

FROM THE AIRPORT TO FLORENCE

At Pisa, incoming and departing flights are served by direct **trains** to and from Florence Central station at S. Maria Novella; the journey takes about 1 hour. **Taxis** are available, of course, but they are expensive.

BUSES

City and intercity buses are cheap and efficient. In Florence the city lines, run by the **ATAF** bus company (☎ *56501)*, are explained in the Yellow Pages telephone directory. One ticket is good for up to 70 minutes' travel. For most buses, **tickets** much be purchased in advance from bars or tobacconists, in the form of a *biglietto semplice* (one-way/single ticket) or a *biglietto multiplo* (book of 11 tickets). There are also new buses that accept exact change only; these are marked by a hand holding a coin.

RAIL SERVICES

The Florence Central station at Santa Maria Novella *(map 1 B3)* is one of the busiest and best connected in central Italy. The information office is open from 7am-10pm (☎ *278785)*. There are usually long lines at ticket counters, but American Express Card holders can buy their tickets from automatic machines. There are stations at or near all the provincial capitals. **Fares** are quite reasonable by European standards, but they do vary according to the speed and type of train. Trains are often very crowded, so it is wise to reserve in advance to be sure of a seat. Trains are classified as follows:

Inter-City (IC)   Fast trains running between the main Italian cities. A supplementary ticket is necessary and seat reservations can be obligatory.

Pendolino   First-class-only trains offer special services to travelers, and are faster than IC trains.

Euro City   Fast trains running between major Italian cities and other European countries. A supplementary ticket is necessary, and seat reservations are obligatory.

Espresso   Long-distance express trains stopping only at main stations, and carrying both first- and second-class passengers.

Diretto   Trains stopping at most stations; both classes.

Locale   2nd-class-only trains stopping at all stations.

TAXIS

Taxis do not usually respond to being hailed, but it is worth trying. There are taxi stands in many of the main squares of Florence, but you will be lucky to find a taxi waiting anywhere. For **radio taxis** in Florence ☎4390 or 4798. Extra charges are made for this service, also for each piece of luggage, for journeys made between 10pm and 7am, and on Sunday and public holidays. The driver is not required to take you outside the city limits; if he does, the fare increases. Taxis are now so expensive that Florentines no longer tip unless the driver is particularly helpful, in which case give 10 percent.

GETTING AROUND BY CAR

Having a car in Tuscany is obviously a great advantage but be prepared to cope with Italian driving, which is skillfully aggressive. International **road signs** are in use and vehicles drive on the right; unless signposts indicate otherwise, cars must yield to traffic coming from the right. Carry a warning triangle (no longer compulsory but always advisable) and adjust the headlight beams of cars if coming from the UK.

The standard of the roads is variable, and road repairs on autostrade (superhighways), many of which are being widened or extended, can cause delays. **Tolls** payable on the autostrade can be a considerable expense, but this is partly compensated for by the high standard of such roads.

Gas stations often close between noon and 3pm and after 7pm. Maximum **speed limits** are 50kph (32mph) in built-up areas, 110kph (70mph) on country roads and 140kph (85mph) on autostrade. Heavy, **on-the-spot fines** are strictly enforced for breaking these limits.

Tourists who take their cars to Italy are entitled to **gasoline coupons** and **highway vouchers**. UK visitors can buy these through the **AA** and **RAC** motoring organizations, the tour operator **CIT** *(50 Conduit St., London W1* ☎ *(071) 434-3844)*, and at Italian frontier points from the **Italian Automobile Club** (**ACI**) — but not within Italy itself. They can be refunded only by the issuing office.

Florence is served by **autostrade** in four directions. They are: the **A1** running N to Bologna and SE to Rome via Arezzo and Chiusi; the **Florence-Siena link**; and the **A11** for Pistoia, Lucca, Pisa and the sea. The stretch of autostrada, **A12**, along the coast from Marina di Carrara to Livorno, will eventually be extended to Florence and Rome. For traffic information ☎(055) 577777.

It is wise to leave your car outside the historic city centers you are visiting. Most cities are provided with attended parking lots for this purpose. Many centers are now zoned against traffic; where traffic is allowed it is directed through one-way systems that can baffle even the natives.

The **ACI** will give free assistance to members of affiliated touring clubs such as the **AA**, **RAC** or **AAA**. US citizens can obtain the pamphlet *Offices to Serve you Abroad* from the AAA, listing all cities where members can be serviced.

RENTING A CAR

The major international **car rental companies** have branches in most cities and airports, and sometimes offer various reduced-rate schemes for cars reserved in advance and paid for outside Italy. Companies can arrange to have a car waiting for you at your point of arrival. Cars rented from local agencies are often still somewhat cheaper, but try to arrange for unlimited mileage: the charge per kilometer can be exorbitant. In Florence most car rental companies are located in Borgognissanti. One of the least expensive is **Italy by Car** *(Borgognissanti 134* ☎ *293021/287161).*

Basic **insurance** is normally included in the rental charge, with extra cover optional at fixed charges. Some companies require drivers to be **aged 21** or over, and most firms require a **deposit** equivalent to the estimated total cost of rental. **VAT** (IVA) will be added to the final bill.

BICYCLES AND MOTORCYCLES

Able-bodied Florentines increasingly move about the city on two wheels. For information about rentals see SPORTS on page 50.

GETTING AROUND ON FOOT

All Tuscan towns and cities, including Florence, are small enough to be seen on foot, and many have now created traffic-free zones *(zone pedonale)* in parts of their centers. In Florence, inessential traffic is now theoretically banned from the center for most of the day. Nevertheless, the motorcycles, taxis and private cars that defy the law are still a nuisance for pedestrians, especially along the *lungarni.* In Italy, as elsewhere in Europe, pedestrians have precedence over vehicles at uncontrolled zebra crossings.

Walking in rural Tuscany, where some of the prettiest landscape and monuments have been bypassed by the modern road network, is still a delight. See LEISURE IDEAS on page 52 for further information.

On-the-spot information

PUBLIC HOLIDAYS

January 1; Easter Monday; Liberation Day, April 25; Labor Day *(Festa del Lavoro)*, May 1; Assumption of the Virgin *(Ferragosto)*, August 15; All Saints Day *(Ognissanti)*, November 1; Conception of the Virgin Mary *(Immacolata)*, December 8; December 25 and 26. Shops, banks and offices close on these days. Feast days in honor of local patron saints are not official public holidays, but many shops close in Florence on the Feast of St John the Baptist, June 24.

TIME ZONES

Like most Western European countries, Italy is 1 hour ahead of Greenwich Mean Time in winter and 2 hours ahead in the summer. It is 6 hours ahead of US Eastern Standard Time and from 7-9 hours ahead of the other US time zones.

BANKS AND CURRENCY EXCHANGE

Banks are open Monday to Friday 8.30am-1.20pm and 3-4pm, and closed on Saturday, Sunday and national holidays. You will need your passport when cashing **travelers checks**. **Personal checks** may be cashed by Eurocheque Encashment Card holders, and **foreign bills** can be exchanged for lire in cash machines. Most hotels cash travelers checks, but the rate is less favorable than at a bank. Foreign exchanges *(cambio)* are open during office hours. **American Express** *(Via Guicciardini 49 ☎ 288751)* also has an exchange desk.

SHOPPING AND BUSINESS HOURS

Shops are normally open 9am-1pm and 3.30 or 4 to 7 or 7.30pm, although some in central Florence now stay open all day. Not all shops close on Sunday. In winter most shops in Florence close on Monday morning, except for food stores, which close on Wednesday afternoon. In summer some bigger stores close all day Saturday, but remain open on Monday morning.

POST AND TELEPHONE SERVICES

Stamps may be bought from tobacconists (indicated by a **T** sign) and hotels as well as at post offices. **Mailboxes** are red and are marked with the words *Poste* or *Lettere;* collections may be erratic outside towns. The **central post office** in Florence can be found at Via Pietrapiana 53-55 *(map 2 C5)*.

   Public telephones are found in post offices, tobacconists, bars and at some newsstands. To operate a public telephone, you will need 100-, 200- or 500-lire coins or a telephone card (5,000 and 10,000 lire). Some telephones are still operated by *gettone* (tokens). Telephone cards and tokens can be bought from tobacconists, bars and newsstands.

   Direct calls within Italy (dialing **0**) and international calls (dialing **00**) can be made from public, private and hotel telephones. Each province has its own **area code**; see TUSCANY A TO Z entries for codes.

The Florence code is **055**. Most hotels now have fax ([Fx]).

PUBLIC LAVATORIES (REST ROOMS)
In Florence there are pay WCs in the basement of the Palazzo della Signoria, off the courtyard of the Pitti and in the station. Otherwise, they hardly exist. Most of the larger bars have WCs, which may be used in exchange for the price of a coffee. *Signori* means "men" and *Signore* "women."

ELECTRIC CURRENT
Electricity in most places is 220V AC. The standard two-pronged plugs or adaptors can be purchased in most countries. **Tecnica Radio** *(Porta Rossa 39* ☎ *283184)* is a fully stocked electrical store in central Florence.

LAWS AND REGULATIONS
Never leave your vehicle registration book or rental agreement in your car. If the car is stolen or towed away, the police will not co-operate unless you can prove your right to drive it.

The wearing of car safety belts is now compulsory. Although widely ignored in the helter-skelter of traffic within the city, once on the *autostrade* even Italian drivers belt-up.

Speeding and illegal parking are more carefully controlled than they once were.

CUSTOMS AND ETIQUETTE
When visiting churches, it is important to remember that they are not museums and that it is offensive to interrupt services even in the cause of seeing a major masterpiece. It is acceptable for women to wear trousers; shoulders should be covered.

Tuscans pride themselves on their egalitarian manners. In restaurants and hotels, a friendly handshake and even the clumsiest effort to speak Italian will often work wonders. Children are welcome even in the smartest restaurants; indeed they often get better service than the adults.

At times, Italian friendliness can be rather a nuisance, particularly when directed toward women traveling on their own. A firm but court-eous rebuff *(Va via, per favore)* is the most effective way of dealing with such attentions, which are generally just playful and rarely sinister.

DISABLED TRAVELERS
Italian legislation regarding the adaptation of premises for the disabled is not enlightened. Many hotels are located in old buildings that are not equipped with elevators, but the **Italian State Tourist Office (ENIT)** issues an *Annuario Alberghi D'Italia,* which identifies suitable hotels for disabled visitors, using the wheelchair symbol.

Some major galleries, such as the UFFIZI, are accessible to wheelchairs, but many are not. Remember that marble floors can be hazardous for crutches or calipers and that cobbled streets are not ideal for wheelchairs. Most restaurants happily accommodate wheelchairs with advance notice.

43

For further information on travel in Europe, and details of tour operators specializing in tours for handicapped people, **US residents** should write to the **Travel Information Service** *(Moss Rehabilitation Hospital, 12th St. and Tabor Rd., Philadelphia, Pa. 19141)* or to **Mobility International USA** *(PO Box 3551, Eugene, Or. 97403)*.

UK visitors should write to **RADAR** *(25 Mortimer St., London W1N 8AB* ☎ *(071) 637-5400)*. For specific information, send off for the inexpensive *Access in Florence*: *(OUSA Office, Sherwood House, Sherwood Drive, Bletchley, Milton Keynes MK3 6AN* ☎ *(0908) 71131)*.

LOCAL PUBLICATIONS
The daily newspaper of Florence is *La Nazione*, but the "Cronaca Firenze" section of *La Repubblica* is livelier, and carries a useful weekly list of recommended restaurants. The free bimonthly magazine *Firenze Oggi/Florence Today,* available from tourist offices and many hotels, is written in Italian and English and contains useful local information.

TIPPING
In a restaurant, if service is not included on the bill, leave 15 percent; if service is included, a small note per person is an adequate supplement. A cinema or theater usher will also expect a tip. If a sacristan or custodian does you any special favors, such as opening parts of a church or museum that are normally closed, you should be more generous. Porters and hairdressers also deserve to receive small tips. Taxi drivers don't expect 10 percent, and it is normal for passengers simply to round the fare up.

Useful addresses

TOURIST INFORMATION
The tourist offices provide city maps, up-to-date information about Florence and the province of Florence, including museum opening hours, special events, and bus and train schedules. The **main tourist office** in Florence is at Via Manzoni 16, 50121 Firenze *(*☎ *2478141, map 2 C6)*. There are two smaller tourist offices at the Station and Via Cavour 1 *(map 2 C4)*. The other eight provincial capitals, Arezzo, Grosseto, Livorno, Lucca, Massa Carrara, Pisa, Pistoia and Siena, have their own tourist information offices.

American Express Travel Service *(Via Guicciardini 49* ☎ *288751, map 1 D3)* is a valuable source of information for any traveler in need of help, advice or emergency services.

RENTING A COTTAGE OR VILLA
Agriturist *(Piazza S. Firenze 3, 50122 Firenze* ☎ *287838, map 4 D4)* provides information about all aspects of rural Tuscany, from walking to renting farmhouses.

AIRLINE COMPANIES
Alitalia Lungarno Acciaioli 10-12, 50123 Firenze ☎263051/2/3, map **3**D3. Reservations ☎2788.
Also at Via Veneto 9/10, 50047 Prato ☎(0574) 29220/33220.
British Airways Via della Vigna Nuova 36-38, 50123 Firenze ☎218655, map **3**C2.
TWA Piazza S. Trìnita 1, 50123 Firenze ☎284691, map **4**D4.

AIRPORTS
Perètola Airport ☎(055) 3498
Pisa Airport ☎(050) 28088

AUTOMOBILE CLUB
Automobile Club d'Italia (ACI) ☎24861

POST OFFICES
Central Post Office (Posta Centrale) Via Pietrapiana 53-55 ☎212305, map **2**C5, and at Via Pellicceria ☎216122, map **3**C3.

TOUR OPERATORS IN FLORENCE
American Express Via Guicciardini 49 ☎288751, map **1**D3
CIT Via Cavour 56-59 ☎294306, map **2**B4

MAJOR LIBRARIES IN FLORENCE
Biblioteca Comunale Centrale Via S. Egidio 21 ☎282863, map **4**C5
Biblioteca Nazionale Centrale Piazza Cavalleggeri 1 ☎244441, map **2**D5
British Institute Library Lungarno Guicciardini 9 ☎284031, map **1**D3
French Institute Library Piazza Ognissanti 2 ☎298902, map **1**C3
German Institute Library Via Giusti 44 ☎2479161, map **2**C5
Vieusseux Library Palazzo Strozzi ☎215990, map **3**C3

MAJOR PLACES OF WORSHIP IN FLORENCE
St James's (American Episcopal Church) Via Rucellai 9 ☎294417, map **1**C2
St Mark's (Church of England) Via Maggio 16 ☎294764, map **1**D3
Synagogue Via L.C. Farini 4 ☎245251/2, map **2**C5

CONSULATES
Austria Via dei Servi 9 ☎215352, map **4**B5
Belgium Via dei Servi 28 ☎282094, map **4**B5
Denmark Via dei Servi 13 ☎211007, map **4**B5
France Piazza Ognissanti 2 ☎2302556, map **1**C3
Netherlands Via Cavour 81 ☎475249, map **2**B4

45

Emergency information

EMERGENCY SERVICES
For **Police**, **Ambulance** or **Fire** ☎113.
You will be asked which service you require.

HOSPITAL EMERGENCY (CASUALTY) DEPARTMENTS IN FLORENCE
Camerata   Via Piazzola 68 ☎575807
San Giovanni di Dio   Borgognissanti 20 ☎278751, map 3C1
Santa Maria Nuova-Careggi   Ponte Nuovo ☎27741, map 6C4

OTHER MEDICAL EMERGENCIES
If your complaint does not warrant an ambulance, telephone the *guardia medica* (doctor on call) (☎*(055) 477891*). A list of English-speaking doctors and dentists is published in *Firenze Oggi*. The police can also be telephoned on **49771**.

LATE-NIGHT PHARMACIES
Every *farmacia* (pharmacy) has the late-night roster displayed in its window. This information is also published in *La Nazione* and can be obtained by telephone (☎*110*).

AUTOMOBILE ACCIDENTS
• Call the police immediately.
• Do not admit liability or incriminate yourself.
• Ask any witness(es) to stay and give a statement.
• Remember to use your warning triangle.
• Exchange names, addresses, car details and insurance companies' names and addresses with the other driver(s).
• Remain to give your statement to the police.
• Report the accident to your insurance company.

Norway   Via Piana 8 ☎2280316
Spain   Piazza de'Saltarelli 1 ☎2398276, map 4D4
Sweden   Via della Scala 4 ☎296865, map 1C3
Switzerland   Piazzale Galileo 5 ☎222434, map 1F3
UK   Lungarno Corsini 2 ☎2841133, map 3D2
USA   Lungarno Amerigo Vespucci 38 ☎298276, map 3C1

CAR BREAKDOWNS

- Put on flashing hazard warning lights and place warning triangle 50m (55 yards) behind the car.
- ☎116 and tell the operator where you are, with plate number and type of car. The ACI will bring assistance.

LOST PASSPORT

If you lose your passport you should immediately report the loss to the police and contact your consulate (see pages 45-46) for emergency travel documents.

LOST TRAVELERS CHECKS

Notify the local police immediately, then follow the instructions provided with your travelers checks, or contact the issuing company's nearest office.

Contact your consulate (see pages 45-46 or American Express (see page 44) if you are stranded with no money.'

LOST PROPERTY

If you lose anything it may be handed in at the lost property office (☎(055) 367943). If you do not find it, report the loss to the local police, as many insurance companies will not recognize claims without a police report.

EMERGENCY PHRASES

Help! *Aiuto!*
There has been an accident. *C'è stato un incidente.*
Where is the nearest telephone/hospital? *Dov'è il telefone/l'ospedale più vicino?*
Call a doctor/ambulance. *Chiamate un dottore/un'ambulanza.*
Call the police. *Chiamate la polizia.*
I have lost my purse. *Ho perso la mia borsa.*

Accommodations

Tuscany is now one of Europe's most popular vacation spots. The days when Aldous Huxley described Tuscany as "under-bathroomed and over-monumented" are past: many of the habitable monuments — palaces, villas, hunting lodges, farmhouses, even whole villages — are

47

occupied by hotels that have been well and truly bathroomed. If you are traveling as the spirit takes you, without previous reservations, do not despise the commercial hotels and motels to be found on the outskirts of the larger Tuscan towns. Most are at the very least clean and reasonably efficient.

Opportunities for **self-catering** have increased, and there are many agencies that will help you find rented accommodations in rural Tuscany. They include **Agriturist** *(Piazza San Firenze 3, 50122 Firenze* ☎ *287838, map 4 D4),* which also specializes in inexpensive farmhouse bed-and-breakfast accommodations.

There are five official **categories of hotel**, indicated by one to five stars. Standards and prices are strictly controlled by the Regional Tourist Board. See also WHERE TO STAY IN FLORENCE on pages 146-153 for more details and recommendations. Hotels in Tuscany are included, town by town, in the TUSCANY A TO Z. For information about **camping** see page 51.

Eating in Tuscany

Two words Tuscans often use to describe good food are *genuino* and *sano* (healthy). Although the 20thC plague of international junk food has inevitably spread, along with mass tourism, to Tuscan cities, many *trattorie* still serve wholesome, robust, traditional food that is indeed genuine, as far as the ingredients and cooking methods are concerned, and healthy, according to modern dietary principles. Thick vegetable soups, simply cooked meat or fish, chewy unsalted bread and only one cheese, *pecorino,* may sound a monotonous regime. But when prepared according to ancient recipes, flavored with herbs and aromatic wood smoke and accompanied by a bottle of local wine, these dishes add up to one of the most satisfying cuisines in Europe.

It is basically a peasant cuisine; and success comes to only a very few of the restaurants that attempt to please (and profit from) tourists by using alien and complicated preparation methods. The best Tuscan restaurants are generally outside big cities, often in deeply rural areas, or behind doors that may not even be signed. You won't necessarily be offered a menu; the proprietor may simply tell you what has been prepared that day.

This guide tries to single out with the good value symbol (♥) the most reliable and unpretentious of such restaurants. However, there are now more and more rural restaurants that misuse this tradition, especially during the tourist season, by insisting on a long and expensive fixed menu *(menu de degustazione),* or by offering verbal temptations that may add up to an alarming bill. It is often wise to settle on a ceiling price before beginning your meal.

One of the culinary glories of Tuscany is, in Elizabeth David's words, "that remarkable *bistecca alla Fiorentina,* a vast steak, grilled over a wood fire, which, tender and aromatic, is a dish worth going some way to eat." The best Tuscan beef, from a local breed called *Chianina,* which should be eaten when less than 2 years old, is increasingly difficult to find. The citified way of presenting it is as a *gran' pezzo,* a roast sirloin.

The other great treat is the greeny-gold olive oil that Tuscans use lavishly in place of butter to flavor the ubiquitous *fagioli,* as well as fresh vegetables, salads, soups and bread; they even pour it over *pecorino* and bitter oranges. The flavor, color and consistency of Tuscan oils vary from one valley to another; but all are best eaten in winter, immediately after picking and harvesting. Those made from trees growing in the warmer micro-climates of the w coast are mild and smooth; those from the eastern regions of the Chianti have a sharp, peppery flavor that catches in the throat.

Many restaurants serve oil from their proprietors' own farm, or offer a selection of estate-bottled oils. You can also buy oil direct from wine-making estates. The olive trees have now recovered from the frost of 1985. But take care: there is a big difference between Extra Virgin Italian oil (a blend of oils from olives that may not have grown in Italy, let alone Tuscany) and oil made from olives grown on one estate. Bottled olive oil labeled *prodotto* (produced) as well as *imbottigliato* (bottled) is much more expensive than blended oil, but it is also infinitely more delicious. A law passed in early 1992 will permit some outstanding Italian oils to qualify, like wines, for a DOC (see TUSCAN WINES on pages 175-178). Most will be Tuscan.

Pasta is widely available, but it is not a Tuscan specialty and is often overcooked. The farinaceous staple is bread, which is rubbed with garlic, toasted (preferably over a wood fire) and dipped in olive oil to make *bruschetta* or *fettunta,* or crumbled with olive oil and onion to make the bread salad, *panzanella,* or used to thicken the excellent peasant soups, which vary from one area to another. There are some 100 varieties of *pecorino* cheese, which is taken as an early summer *antipasto* with young *fave* (broad beans).

The *autogrills* that serve the autostrade offer acceptable and sometimes superior meals. Some also sell wine at bargain prices.

There is no shortage of pizzerias, or of restaurants that serve pizzas as well as other fare. But the indigenous snack food — the *crostini,* salamis, and nourishing vegetable soups once eaten by peasants in the field — is more interesting, and can be eaten, standing up or at communal tables, in *fiaschetterie* or simple *osterie.* Some bars serve hot food, as well as sandwiches, filled rolls and pastries — all very good value if you don't sit down at a table; if you do, the price doubles or even triples. Breakfast at a bar is both cheaper and better than the dreary and over-priced continental breakfast offered by hotels.

Refer also to DINING OUT IN FLORENCE on page 155.

Sports

There is much in Tuscany besides sightseeing, as those with small children may be relieved to learn; and you can usually buy temporary membership of private sports clubs and organizations.

BICYCLING
Many parking lots provide bicycles free of charge for the first 2 hours. For information contact **Ciao & Basta** *(Costa dei Magnoli 24 ☎ 2342726).* Other **rental agencies** for bicycles and motorcycles are **Free Motor** *(Via Santa Monaca 6-8 ☎ 295102, map 1 D2),* **Motorent** *(Via San Zanobi 9 ☎ 490113, map 2 B4)* and **Sabra** *(Via Artisti 8 ☎ 576256).* **Federazione Ciclistica Italiana** *(Piazza della Stazione 2, 50123 Firenze ☎ 283926, map 1 B3)* is the organization for serious cyclists.

GOLF
18-hole courses open all year: at PUNTA ALA and at **Ugolino** *(Strada Chiantigiana 3, 50023 Impruneta ☎ 2301096, map 11 E6).*

GYMNASIUMS
Farfalla *(Via Montebello 36 ☎ 296040, map 1 C2);* **Gymnasium** *(Via Palazzuolo 49 ☎ 293308, map 3 C2);* **Manfredini** *(Via Cavour 106 ☎ 588302, map 4 A4);* **My Center 104** *(Via dei Bardi 19 ☎ 2342801, map 3 E3);* **Palestra Savasana** *(Via Jacopo da Diacceto 26 ☎ 287373, map 1 B2);* **La Palestra** *(Via La Farina 50 ☎ 2476363).*

HORSE-RACING AND TROTTING
There are two **racecourses** in the Cascine in Florence, with trotting races in summer and racing in winter. Information from **Centro Ippico Toscano Le Cascine** *(Via Vespucci 5 ☎ 372621).* There are also racecourses at San Rossore, MONTECATINI and PUNTA ALA, and trotting races are held near Follonica.

HORSEBACK RIDING
There are many opportunities to ride in rural Tuscany. Two recommended **equestrian centers** are at the **Badia Montescalari** *(Via Montescalari 129, La Panca, Figline Val d'Arno ☎ (055) 959596),* and in the Maremma at Poggialto, **Cupi** *(☎ (0565) 597126).*

HUNTING
A **hunting reserve,** near CAPALBIO, is open to foreigners.

ROWING
Rowing on the Arno is a popular sport. Information is available from **Società Canottieri Firenze** *(Lungarno de' Medici 8 ☎ 282130).*

SAILING
There are **tourist harbors** at Cala Galera, CASTIGLIONE DELLA PESCAIA,

ELBA, Giannutri, GIGLIO, PORT D'ERCOLE, PUNTA ALA, TALAMONE and VIAREG-GIO. Report to the *Capitaneria di Porto* (harbor master). A useful guide-book is *The Tyrrhenian Sea* by H. M. Denham (UK publisher John Murray).

SKIING
The best **skiing** is in the Apennines, at ABETONE, Cutigliano and S. Marcello Pistoiese. Nearer to Florence, in the Pratomagno hills, there are **winter sports facilities** at Consuma, STIA and VALLOMBROSA. Monte Amiata has some 20km (12 miles) of piste; its principal resort is ABBADIA SAN SALVATORE.

SWIMMING
Beaches vary from superb to squalid. The best sandy beaches are shown in the ORIENTATION MAP on pages 56-57. Below LIVORNO and on ELBA, the coast is mostly rocky with small sandy bays. Although there are some free beaches, those that provide facilities are fairly expensive. Most inland towns have well-maintained **public pools**: there are three in Florence, the **Piscine Bellariva** *(Lungarno Colombo 6, ☎677521);* **Piscine Costoli** *(Viale Paoli ☎669744);* **Piscine Pavoniere** *(Viale degli Olmi ☎367506).*

TENNIS
Public courts and **tennis clubs** are widespread. The **Circolo del Tennis** in the Cascine is not keen to take temporary members, but there are also good courts on the Campo di Marte. Information (also about skating and track and field) is obtainable from **Associazione Sportiva** *(Viale Michelangelo ☎6812686, map 2 E5).*

Leisure ideas

There are many ways to pass the time in Tuscany. The following leisure ideas give a broad sweep; for detailed information on what is on offer in your area, consult the local tourist office. See also SPORTS on the previous page and FLORENCE NIGHTLIFE on page 165.

CAMPING
Helpful organizations include the **Centro Nazionale Campeggiatori Stranieri** *(at exit 19 of Autostrada del Sole, Calenzano ☎(055) 882391);* **Campeggio Club Firenze e Toscana** *(Viale Guidoni 143 ☎419940);* **Club Alpino Italiano** *(Via del Proconsolo 10 ☎2340580, map 4 C5);* and **Touring Club Italiano** *(Viale S Lavagnini 6 ☎474192, map 2 A4).*

FISHING
Fishing is a popular sport even in Florence. The clear waters off the rocky southern coast are excellent for snorkeling, and underwater fish-

51

ing is allowed anywhere except in harbors. For fishing in most lakes and rivers, an inexpensive license is required, as is membership of the **Federazione Italiana della Pesca Sportiva** *(Via De' Neri 6, 50122 Firenze ☎ 214073, map 4 D5).*

GARDENS

Tuscany is richly endowed with great historic gardens, some regularly open to the public, especially around Florence, LUCCA and SIENA. Others may be visited through **Agriturist** *(Piazza S. Firenze 3 ☎ 287838, map 4 D4)*

Serious enthusiasts can join the rather exclusive **Garden Club of Florence** *(Palazzo Strozzi ☎ 282245, map 3 C3)* for tours in summer of gardens not otherwise open to visitors. See the INDEX for lists of Tuscan gardens and parks.

ITALIAN

Since the purest Italian is spoken in Tuscany, it is an ideal place to learn the language. Most of the schools will help enrolled students find accommodations. The many language schools in Florence include the **British Institute** *(Lungarno Guicciardini 9, 50123 ☎ 284031, map 3 D2)* and the **Centro Linguistico Italiano Dante Alighieri** *(Via de' Bardi 12, 50125 ☎ 2342984, map 3 E3).*

MUSIC

Florence is one of the musical capitals of Italy; the **Florence Maggio Musicale**, which runs throughout the summer, is a festival of international importance *(for information ☎ 2396954)*, as are the summer master classes in Siena at the **Accademia Musicale Chigiana**. LUCCA and PRATO are musically active too, and BARGA, Batignano, CORTONA, GARGONZA, MONTEPULCIANO, S. GIMIGNANO and TORRE DEL LAGO PUCCINI have summer festivals.

NATURE PARKS, RESERVES AND ZOOS

The Maremma is well supplied: see ANSEDONIA, MONTE ARGENTARIO and, especially, MONTI DELL'UCCELLINA. Other **reserves** are at Bolgheri, Cavriglia, Migliarino (near Pisa), Montecristo and Orechiella (Garfagnana). Some reserves can be entered only with permission, which is usually obtainable from the communal government offices nearest the site.

There are **zoos** at PISTOIA, POPPI, at Tirrenia near PISA, and a small one in Florence.

WALKING

Near Florence there is pleasant **country walking** in the Fiesolan hills and around Arcetri. There are marked **trails** through the protected forests at ABETONE, CAMALDOLI, LA VERNA and VALLOMBROSA. Maps showing **footpaths** are obtainable from **Istituto Geografico Militare** *(Viale Strozzi 14, Firenze, map 3 C3)*. Information about **mountain walking** can be obtained from **Club Alpino Italiano** *(Via Proconsolo 10, 50123 Firenze ☎ 2340580, map 4 C5).*

Planning and tours

When and where to go

May and September are ideal months to visit Florence: cool enough for vigorous sightseeing, summery enough for leisurely day trips into the hills. The countryside in May is radiant with wild flowers, scented with blossom and young grasses.

For the grand tourists of the 18th and 19thC, September marked the start of the Florence season, and a very sensible time it still is, a little warmer and drier than May, and less crowded than August, that most uncomfortable of months.

In fact, those who do not wish to share their vacation with what seems like half the world, should avoid Florence, a city ill-suited to mass tourism, in the week before and including Easter and from June through to the end of August. Overcrowding, as regular visitors know, can render the narrow medieval streets barely tolerable. However, if you must go in the high season, be sure to reserve a hotel in advance.

Whatever the season, the day will come when Florence may seem too much: too much art, too much noise in the narrow streets, a stony maze from which one longs to escape. This is the day to go to Siena, gently dreaming on its landlocked hills, or to Lucca, proud and independent in its star of intact fortifications. These are undoubtedly the two most likeable provincial capitals.

Pisa should be visited for its churches and pictures as well as for the famous cathedral complex. There is pre-Renaissance sculpture in Pisa, Prato and Pistoia; and there are Renaissance churches in Prato and near Cortona and Montepulciano that are as fine and important as anything in Florence. The Renaissance paintings that can stir the modern soul most profoundly are the Piero della Francescas in and near Arezzo.

Then there are the smaller hill towns, each with its own distinctive shape and character: San Gimignano still bristling with medieval watchtowers; windy Volterra; Romanesque-Gothic Massa Marittima; Pienza and Montepulciano like miniature Renaissance cities. In fact, there is hardly a town or village in Tuscany that is not worth visiting.

The Tuscan countryside is as elusive to the would-be categorizer as it is inspiring to native and visitor alike. Geographically there is no such thing as one Tuscany. Each of the valleys, mountains, plains and stretches of coast has its own beauty, and, as often as not, its own microclimate. The best-laid plan for visiting Tuscany is the one that leaves room for spontaneous exploration and personal discovery.

Calendar of events

More details of many of the events listed here can be found in the regional entries later in the book. See also PUBLIC HOLIDAYS on page 42.

JANUARY/FEBRUARY
‡ Viareggio. **Carnevale**. The most colorful of Tuscan carnivals, in the weeks before Lent, culminating on Shrove Tuesday. Masked processions, fireworks, and football matches.

MARCH
‡ Florence. Italian and international **high fashion collections** shown in the Sala Bianca of the Pitti Palace.

APRIL
‡ Easter Day. Florence. **Scoppio del Carro** (Explosion of the Cart). A cart laden with flowers and fireworks is drawn by three pairs of white oxen to the Duomo. At midday mass, during the Gloria, a firework rocket in the shape of a dove is lit at the high altar, and whizzes the length of the nave along a wire attached to the cart. ‡ Florence. **Crafts exhibition** is held at the Fortezza da Basso. Continues throughout May. ‡ Florence. **Flower display** in Piazza della Signoria and Uffizi. Through to June. ‡ Lucca. **Sacred music festival** in the churches. Lasts until late June.

MAY
‡ Florence. **Iris show** in Piazzale Michelangelo. The largest European collection of the symbolic "lily of Florence." ‡ May 20 or following Sunday. Massa Marittima. **Balestro del Girifalco** (Joust of the Falcon). Procession, flag-waving and crossbow shooting at mechanical falcon in Piazza d. Duomo, all in 15thC costume. Again in August. ‡ Mid-May to late June. Florence. **Maggio Musicale**. Opera, ballet and concerts.

JUNE
‡ Fiesole. **Summer festival**. Concerts, ballet, theater. Through to September. ‡ June 17. Pisa. **Regata di San Ranieri**. The buildings facing the Arno are illuminated with torches the evening before the boat race. ‡ June 24. Florence. **Feast of St John the Baptist**, patron saint of the city. Fireworks over the Arno from Piazzale Michelangelo. ‡ **Gioco del Calcio Storico**. The traditional rough football game in 16thC costume in Piazza della Signoria. ‡ June 28. Florence. Second **Gioco del Calcio Storico**.
‡ June 28. Pisa. **Gioco del Ponte**. Mock 16thC battle.

JULY
‡ July 2. Siena. **Palio**. The most serious of all historic spectacles. The bare-back horse race around the Piazza del Campo is fiercely contested. Before the event there are processions and rehearsals. Again in August. ‡ Siena. **Accademia Musicale Chigiana**. Music festival.

AUGUST

‡ Torre del Lago Puccini. **Festival of Puccini operas**. ‡ 2nd Sunday. Massa Marittima. **Balestro del Girifalco** (see MAY). ‡ August 15, Assumption Day. Florence. **Festa del Grillo**. Caged crickets are sold in the fair in the Cascine. ‡ August 15-16. Montepulciano. **Il Bruscello**. Folklore and song festival. ‡ Porto Santo Stefano. **Palio Marinaro**. Parade in the square and rowing race. ‡ August 16. Siena. Second **Palio** (see JULY).

SEPTEMBER

‡ 1st Sunday. Arezzo. **Giostra del Saracino**. Eight horsemen dressed in 13thC costume joust against a mechanical Saracen, in the Piazza Grande. ‡ 1st week. Greve. **Chianti Classico wine fair**. ‡ September 7. Florence. **Festa delle Rificolone** (Lantern Day). On the eve of the Nativity of the Virgin, children race through the streets carrying colored paper lanterns. The following evening, the Via dei Servi is lined with candy stalls and the children process carrying lanterns from the Duomo to SS. Annunziata. ‡ 2nd Sunday. Sansepolcro. **Palio della Balestra**. Crossbow competition in medieval costume. ‡ September 14. Lucca. **Festa della Santa Croce**. On Holy Cross Eve, a miraculous wooden effigy of Christ is carried from the cathedral to the church of S. Frediano and back. ‡ Florence. Alternate (odd) years. **Antiques fair** at Palazzo Strozzi. Through to November. ‡ September 28. Florence. On St Michael's Eve, at the **beginning of the hunting season**, hunting equipment and birds of every kind, ranging from hawks to owls, are sold at Porta Romana.

OCTOBER

‡ Prato. **Season opens at Teatro Metastasio**. The home company is one of the liveliest experimental theater groups in Italy. Continues until April. ‡ Florence. **Winter fashion collections** shown in Pitti. ‡ Mid-October. Impruneta. **Agricultural fair** of St Luke. ‡ Last Sunday. Montalcino. **Sagra del Tordo**. Traditional shooting and eating of thrushes.

NOVEMBER/DECEMBER

‡ Florence. Opening of **main concert season at Teatro Comunale**. November through mid-December. ‡ Florence. Opening of **opera season at Teatro Comunale**. December through mid-January.

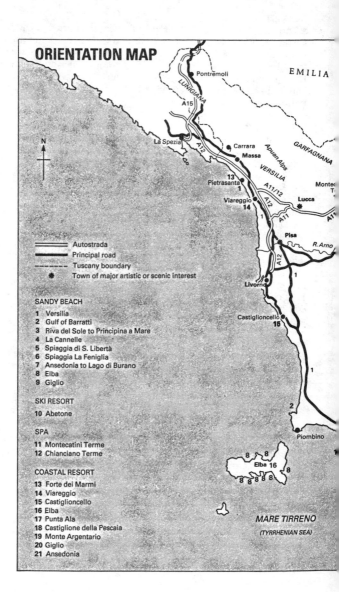

ORIENTATION MAP

Pontrèmoli

EMILIA

LUNIGIANA

A15

La Spezia

N

Carrara
Massa

Aquan Alps

GARFAGNANA

VERSILIA

13
Pietrasanta 1

A11/12

Monte
T

Viareggio
14

A12

A11

Lucca

1

Pisa

R. Arno

A12

1

Livorno

Castiglioncello
15

1

Autostrada
Principal road
Tuscany boundary
Town of major artistic or scenic interest

2

SANDY BEACH

1 Versilia
2 Gulf of Barratti
3 Riva del Sole to Principina a Mare
4 La Cannelle
5 Spiaggia di S. Libertà
6 Spiaggia La Feniglia
7 Ansedonia to Lago di Burano
8 Elba
9 Giglio

SKI RESORT

10 Abetone

SPA

11 Montecatini Terme
12 Chianciano Terme

Piombino

COASTAL RESORT

13 Forte dei Marmi
14 Viareggio
15 Castiglioncello
16 Elba
17 Punta Ala
18 Castiglione della Pescaia
19 Monte Argentario
20 Giglio
21 Ansedonia

8   8

Elba 16   8

8 8 8 8 8

MARE TIRRENO
(TYRRHENIAN SEA)

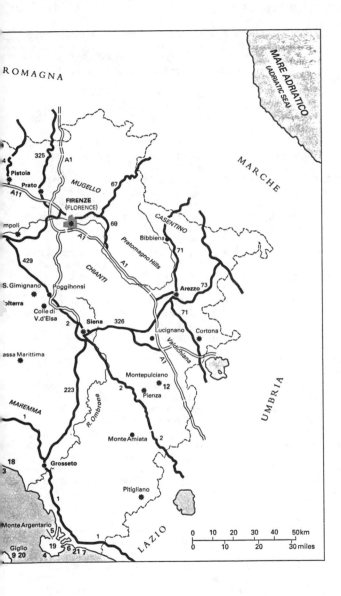

Area planners

Tuscany is one of the most geographically diverse of Italian regions, with a long coastline, mountains high enough for skiing, and hidden valleys. Each rural area has its own distinctive climate and landscape; the food and wine vary from one to another, and so does the character of the people.

THE CASENTINO. The remote upper valley of the Arno, to the N of Arezzo, enclosed by wooded mountains. The magnificent specimen forests of beech, fir and chestnut, and the green pastures where white oxen can still occasionally be seen, are loveliest in spring and remain cool even in high summer. The monastic sanctuaries of Camaldoli and La Verna are good bases for walking, picnicking, and gathering wild strawberries and mushrooms. Hotels are few and simple.

THE CHIANTI. The heart of Tuscany, and the landscape that matches many people's ideal of the way Italy ought to look, is now very fashionable with non-Italians, but still relatively unspoiled. Many old villas, castles, abbeys and farmhouses have been converted into hotels or residences, and others are now owned privately by foreigners. The area that originally gave its name to the wine has expanded over the centuries to include everywhere the wine is produced, which is now from a little to the N of Florence down to Siena. May is the most beautiful season.

THE GARFAGNANA. The landscape of the upper valley of the fast-flowing Serchio and the valleys of its tributaries is one of the most fascinating in Tuscany for the variety of climate and vegetation. The chilly marble peaks of the Apuan Alps contrast with the lower slopes of the Apennines, wooded with magnificent chestnuts and luxuriant vegetation, and the mild, humid air lower down. Lucca is just to the S, and Barga is the prettiest hill village.

THE MAREMMA. The word means coastal plain, but it is now most often associated with the province of Grosseto, including the coast known as the Costa d'Argento (between Alberese and Ansedonia), the promontory of Monte Argentario and, inland, the foothills of Monte Amiata. The Etruscan-red soil is wonderfully fertile, producing fruit, vegetables, grain, flowers and vines in colorful abundance. The many Etruscan sites remind one that the Maremma was probably more densely populated in the pre-Christian era than it is now. The natives, physically tough and independent-minded, regard themselves as the Wild Westerners of Tuscany; the local cowboys, less often seen than they were, are known as *butteri*. Apart from the Etruscan and Roman sites, you should at least visit Massa Marittima, Pitigliano and the nature reserve of Monti dell'Uccellina. Hotels are mostly basic, except on the coast, but there are some excellent country restaurants.

THE MUGELLO. In the early Renaissance, the Sieve river basin, the homeland of Giotto and the Medici, was considered to be the healthiest and most beautiful of the rural areas near Florence. More recently, its towns have suffered war damage and industrialization. Protected by the Apennines to the N and well-watered by mountain springs, the climate of this lovely gentle green valley is more temperate than that of the Arno.

THE VERSILIA. This coastal strip in northern Tuscany boasts the region's longest uninterrupted stretch of white sandy beach, and has an even, balmy climate with mild winters and light rainfall. Forte dei Marmi is fashionable with Italians; Viareggio's prime is past, but it still has a certain decaying period charm. Some of the other resorts are squalid. There are many hotels, some of which are excellent, and plenty of good fish restaurants.

Driving tours in Tuscany

The itineraries that follow offer suggestions for trips that might take anything from a day to a whole week.

ROUTE 1: PISA TO FLORENCE

Uninitiated visitors to Tuscany, automatically whisked from Pisa Airport to Florence, are often left with a dim impression of the intervening country, which does not reveal its treasures from the train or autostrada. Apart from four of the most artistically important Tuscan cities — Pisa itself, Lucca, Pistoia and Prato — this slower, more interesting itinerary embraces Romanesque churches, Medici villas, radiant mountain landscape, and good restaurants. It is well worth the luxury of a rented car. Anyone unfamiliar with the highlights of the trip could allow two or three days. Otherwise, a selective or partial section of the route could be followed as a day excursion from Florence by taking the autostrada as far as Pisa, Lucca or Pistoia and then returning along the suggested roads.

From PISA to LUCCA, you can choose between the low road, which tunnels under the montains and takes about 20 minutes, or the beautiful high road *(strada panoramica)*, which takes about 1 hour. The impressive aqueduct that you see as you leave Lucca was built in 1820-30. It carries water to the city from a spring near Capannori. From Lucca's Porta Elisa follow the SS435 for PESCIA, diverging from the Romanesque church of S. Gennaro and for COLLODI, on the left. After Pescia the road

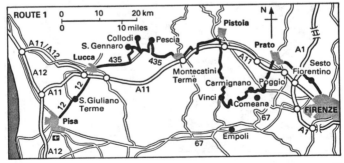

descends alongside River Pescia to MONTECATINI TERME. Heading now for PISTOIA, one passes the remains of medieval fortifications at Serravalle. Take the EMPOLI road from Pistoia's Porta Leonardo da Vinci; it winds over Monte Albano, commanding ravishing views of the Arno valley as it approaches VINCI through woodland and olive groves. From Vinci, fork left onto the pretty CARMIGNANO road, which runs for 16km (10 miles) along the s flank of the Albano mountains through pine woods, olives and the vineyards that produce some of the finest Tuscan wines, and past the Romanesque church of S. Giusto. The Medici villas of ARTIMINO and POGGIO A CAIANO are within 10km (6 miles) of Carmignano. PRATO is 8km (5 miles) N of Poggio a Caiano. Aiming now for Florence, eschew the autostrada and choose instead the Roman road along the base of the Calvana and Morello mountains, for SESTO FIORENTINO and CASTELLO.

ROUTE 2: THE CHIANTI

This short journey into the heart of Tuscany is one of the treats of a Florentine vacation. There are plenty of restaurants and hotels on and just off the route (see for example COLLE DI VAL D'ELSA, GAIOLE, GREVE, IMPRUNETA, MONTERIGGIONI, SAN CASCIANO, SAN GIMIGNANO and SIENA); and most wine growers will be happy to let you taste their produce and will sell wine and olive oil, beautifully packaged, by the bottle or cellarful. (See also TUSCAN WINES on pages 175-178 for suggestions.)

Visitors who want only one leisurely day's outing from Florence can simplify the itinerary by taking the Chiantigiana to Siena and returning to Florence on the SS2 or the autostrada. The whole circular tour can be made to fit into a busy day.

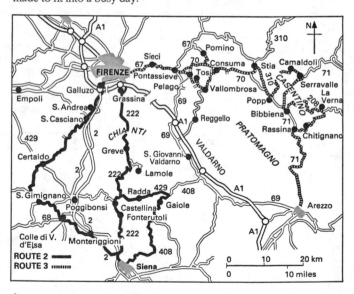

The starting point from Florence is Piazza F. Ferrucci. Take the 18thC wine road, the Strada Chiantigiana, SS222, the classic route into the Chianti, following the blue signs for Greve and Siena. After Grassina, the vista opens onto a hilly landscape punctuated by medieval towers. Shortly after passing the splendid Baroque Villa Ugolino, you are ushered by a large notice into the Chianti Classico wine zone.

The road now descends through spectacular landscape to GREVE. To the S, on the road for Lamole to the left, you can see in the distance the privately owned Renaissance Villa Vignamaggio, which appears in the background of an early drawing by Leonardo and where some romantics like to imagine the *Mona Lisa* was painted. At CASTELLINA you can turn left onto SS429 into the historic center of the Chianti for RADDA and GAIOLE, and then approach SIENA by the old Chiantigiana, SS408. Otherwise, continue S, via Fonterutoli toward Siena, which you will enter close to the station.

Return by way of the Via Cassia via the medieval hill villages of MONTERIGGIONI, COLLE DI VAL D'ELSA, SAN GIMIGNANO and CERTALDO. From Certaldo the road carries you NE across the Elsa and Pesa valleys for 23km (14 miles), past the castles of S. Maria Novella and Lucardo to SAN CASCIANO, at the end NW limit of the Classico zone. After GALLUZZO, one re-enters Florence by the PORTA ROMANA.

ROUTE 3: FLORENCE TO AREZZO BY THE PRATOMAGNO AND CASENTINO

The drive to VALLOMBROSA, less than an hour from Florence, constitutes a favorite Florentine family day outing. By allowing two days for this route to Arezzo you would have time also to visit the remoter monastic retreats of CAMALDOLI and LA VERNA.

From Florence, follow the SS67 along the N bank of the Arno, pausing at Sieci to admire the view of the Arno from the weir, and the church of S. Giovanni Battista a Remole, with its splendid Romanesque campanile. After crossing the Sieve at PONTASSIEVE, take the narrower road, SS70, signposted to Consuma, which climbs through vineyards and olive groves and soon passes the castle of Nipozzano on the left. Owned by the Frescobaldi family, its vineyards produce an outstanding Chianti Riserva.

Just past Borselli, a short detour to the left passes the Romanesque church of Tosina on the way to Pomino, another of the Frescobaldi properties, where the grapes for the excellent Pomino white wine are grown. Back on SS70, the road now climbs more steeply through beech, fir and pine woods toward Consuma. Just 1km ($\frac{5}{8}$ mile) before the village, a right turn leads to VALLOMBROSA, secluded in its dense beechwood on the eastern slope of Monte Secchieta.

Those who wish to return to Florence may vary the route by returning to Pontassieve via Tosi and Pelago. Otherwise, return to the SS70 and turn right toward Poppi, crossing the Pratomagno range through the Consuma pass. Descending into the Casentino you can see Monte Falterona, where the Arno has its source, on the left, and ahead the castle of POPPI, like a transplanted Palazzo Vecchio. Fork left 10km (6 miles) after Consuma for the castle of Romena, the Romanesque church of Romena on a parallel road, and STIA.

From there turn right onto the SS310 via Pratovecchio, where Paolo Uccello was born in 1397, and along the E bank of the Arno, past Campaldino, where Dante fought in the battle of 1289 against Arezzo, to POPPI. The road for the monastery and then the hermitage of CAMALDOLI is on the left just beyond Poppi.

Then descend via Serravalle onto SS71 to BIBBIENA, where a left turn onto the SS208 leads to the famous Franciscan sanctuary of LA VERNA high up in the mountains that separate the Arno and Tiber valleys. The road from La Verna via Chitignano, which rejoins the SS71 for Arezzo at Rassina, is rough in places but worth choosing for the views of the Pratomagno hills ahead as you descend. After Giovi, where the Arno curves away toward the W, you emerge from the Casentino into the suburbs of AREZZO.

The fast route to Arezzo is through the Valdarno by the autostrada A1. If time allows, this can be varied by leaving at Montevarchi or SANGIOVANNI VALDARNO and taking the so-called *strada di sette ponti* (the road of seven bridges) from which one can explore the hill villages and Romanesque churches in the foothills of the Pratomagno.

ROUTE 4: TRACKING DOWN THE ETRUSCANS

Traces of elusive and intriguing Etruscans remain all over Tuscany. The tourist who enjoys walking or riding, or who takes shortcuts along unpaved byroads, will sometimes discover tombs and trails that are not necessarily signposted or identified. But to appreciate the Etruscans' achievements in the arts and crafts one must also visit museums; there are some outstanding objects in the local museums on the following itineraries.

If you wish to test your interest in Etruscan sites before embarking on a longer journey, begin with FIESOLE, Comeana (see ARTIMINO) and SESTO FIORENTINO, which are all within easy reach of Florence.

Alternatively, if you are making an excursion to San Gimignano, go on to VOLTERRA, a lovely drive only 27km (17 miles) to the SW. The two densest concentrations of the major centers are in the Valdichiana and the Grosseto Maremma, and are most conveniently visited separately.

Route 4a) The Etruscan sites of eastern Tuscany

In the pre-Christian era when the River Chiana was navigable, the Etruscan cities of the Valdichiana were both prosperous and artistically sophisticated, thanks to their fertile farmlands, and to trade with other civilizations.

Start at AREZZO, the city Livy called the capital of the Etruscan people. Then take the SS71 for CORTONA, stopping just to the N of the city to see the tombs at Sodo. Have a look at the extraordinary bronze lamp in the Etruscan Academy in Cortona and, on the way S, visit the tomb near the station at Camucia.

The quickest way to CHIUSI, which has one of the most important Etruscan museums outside Florence, is by autostrada. Alternatively, take the SS71 along the shore of Lake Trasimeno. From Chiusi station, loop S

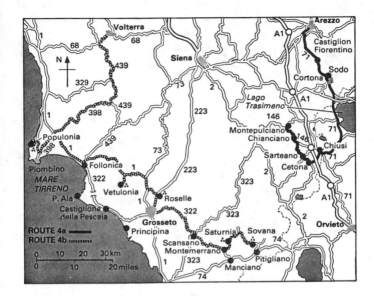

and then NW to visit the minor rural centers of Cetona, Sarteano, CHIAN-
CIANO and MONTEPULCIANO, all of which preserve interesting Etruscan
fragments. Perugia and Orvieto, outside Tuscany, are nearby.

Route 4b) The Etruscan sites of southwestern Tuscany
This is a much longer journey, requiring about three days, and it differs
in that many of the major sites were abandoned by later civilizations.
The necropoli are often in dense woods or cultivated fields, so wear
stout shoes and be prepared to take the car over unpaved roads.

Start at VOLTERRA, allowing at least half a day for the walls, gate,
necropoli and the museum, with its 600 funerary urns and miniature
votive bronzes. After perhaps spending the night here, POPULONIA, on the
coast, is a 1½-hour drive to the SW, and VETULONIA another hour farther on.
The second night could be spent on the coast at PUNTA ALA, CASTIGLIONE
DELLA PESCAIA or Principina a Mare. From Vetulonia continue along the
Aurelia (SS1) — but watch out, this is the most dangerous road in Tuscany
— and turn left after 15km (9 miles) for ROSELLE.

GROSSETO is 10km (6 miles) to the S and worth visiting for the material
excavated from Roselle, Vetulonia and other local Etruscan sites, featured
in the Archeological Museum. Now travel inland by the SS322 via Scansano to Montemerano, where you turn left for SATURNIA, and then SOVANA;
you might spend the third night in either. To complete a tour of the major
sites, journey S into Lazio, for Vulci, Tarquinia, Cervéteri and Veio.

ROUTE 5: FROM SIENA TO THE VALDICHIANA
This itinerary SE from Siena could be accomplished in one long day,

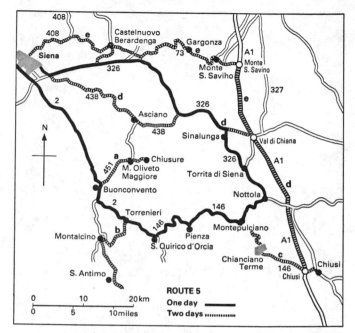

ROUTE 5
One day ▬▬▬▬
Two days ▪▪▪▪▪▪▪▪

but the variety and unfaltering beauty of the landscape of the *crete,* the Val d'Orcia and the Valdichiana, and the importance of the churches and hill towns, which include some of the finest examples of Renaissance architecture and town planning outside Florence, justify at least one overnight stop. Food and wine produced in this radiant countryside and served in the best of the restaurants is of exceptional quality.

One day   Leaving Siena from the Porta Romana, the Via Cassia, SS2, follows the River Arbia through a strange, furrowed landscape of infertile clay hummocks known as the *crete.* After Buonconvento, the Cassia begins to twist dramatically, and the view becomes more spacious, with MONTALCINO and MONTE AMIATA visible on the right. From SAN QUIRICO D'ORCIA, on its high plain overlooking the valleys of the Orcia and the Asso, take the SS146, which travels E to the Renaissance hill towns of PIENZA and MONTEPULCIANO.

Those who are returning to Siena should leave Montepulciano by the Porta al Prato, stopping briefly after 1km ($\frac{5}{8}$ mile) to admire the simple Mannerist facade of the church of S. Maria delle Grazie on the left, then proceeding N to Nottola, where you join the SS326 for Siena via Torrita di Siena and SINALUNGA.

Two days   Follow the route described above, and then make diversions to take in at least some if not all of the following excursions.

a)   At Buonconvento turn left on the SS451 for MONTE OLIVETO MAG-

GIORE. Then continue for another 2km ($1\frac{1}{4}$ miles) on the road for S. Giovanni d'Asso as far as lofty Chiusure, for the magnificent panorama of the moon-like landscape below. On the return drive to Buonconvento there are fine views of the *crete*, the Ombrone valley and MONTE AMIATA.

b) 10km (6 miles) S of Buonconvento, at Torrenieri, turn right for MONTALCINO. Then continue S into the Val d'Orcia for Sant'Antimo, set in an enchanted landscape of wheatfields, flickering olives and dark cypresses.

c) At MONTEPULCIANO, turn right and follow the SS146 for CHIANCIANO TERME; the old city can be seen high on the left as one approaches the modern spa. CHIUSI is a further 11km (7 miles) to the SE, by way of a beautiful undulating road running into the Valdichiana with the tributary of the River Chiana, the Astrone, with glimpses to the left of the lakes of Chiusi and Montepulciano.

d) Returning to Siena from Chiusi, take the autostrada A1 as far as the Valdichiana exit for SINALUNGA. Stay on the SS326 for 14km (9 miles), diverging for ASCIANO and then returning to Siena on the SS438 through the *crete*.

e) Alternatively, leave the A1 at the Monte S. Savino exit, following the SS73 to MONTE S. SAVINO, diverging briefly for GARGONZA on the right, then for CASTELNUOVO BERARDENGA on the eastern edge of the Chianti near the source of the Ombrone. Return to Siena either by the SS326 or by the old Chiantigiana road, SS408.

ROUTE 6: A DAY IN THE MUGELLO

In the days of the Grand Tour, travelers from the N crossed the Apennines into Tuscany by the Futa Pass and then continued along the Via Bolognese through the Mugello, making a last overnight stop at La Lastra before entering Florence through the Porta S. Gallo. That is still the most dramatic and scenic way to approach Florence — but it is

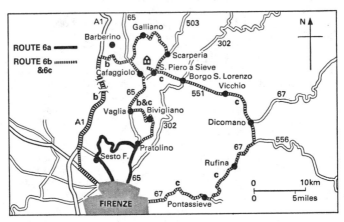

perhaps a little too slow for the modern tourist, and even too dramatic in winter, when the pass is often closed.

However, if you are driving in a southerly direction from Bologna on the autostrada A1, do follow part of this itinerary from the Barberino exit. Otherwise it is a day trip from Florence, which may be enjoyed in any or all of the three stages indicated, depending on the desired proportion of driving to sightseeing.

Route 6a)   This first short itinerary will be long enough for those who wish to visit the great gardens at CASTELLO. From Porta S. Gallo, cross the Mugnone by the Ponte Rosso into the Via Bolognese, which, once outside Florence, is now officially known as the SS65 della Futa. The road passes some of the grandest Renaissance villas in the environs of Florence. On the right, *(#120)*, is La Pietra, so called because it is near the old milestone from Porta S. Gallo.

Farther on the right is the Villa Salviati *(#156)*, a medieval castle reworked by Giuliano da Sangallo, where, in the 17thC, Jacopo Salviati was given the severed head of his mistress as a New Year's present from his wife. Past Montorsoli at Fontesecca, diverge to the left onto the panoramic road of the Colli Alti (high hills), which twists for 15km (9 miles) along the slopes of Monte Morello, passing Piazzale Leonardo da Vinci, which commands magnificent views of the Arno valley stretching out as far as the Chianti Mountains, to SESTO FIORENTINO, from whence you could return to Florence.

Route 6b)   Complete only the first 6km (4 miles) of the Colli Alti, as far as Piazzale Leonardo da Vinci. Returning to the SS65, continue N to PRATOLINO. For the convent of Monte Senario, a 13thC foundation remade in the late 16thC and worth visiting for its lofty situation, fork right from Pratolino. From Montesenario descend into the basin of the Mugello valley via BIVIGLIANO, rejoining the SS65 at Vaglia. Taking the left fork at the Novoli intersection, you pass, on the left, two of the earliest Medici villas, both of which were once fortified castles made into hunting lodges by Michelozzo for Cosimo il Vecchio: first Trebbio, then Cafaggiolo, where Poliziano spent the rainy winter of 1478-9 giving instruction to Lorenzo de' Medici's children.

To return to Florence rejoin the autostrada at Barberino.

Route 6c)   Otherwise take the SS551 from San Piero a Sieve to BORGO SAN LORENZO. The landscape visible from the road along this stretch is disfigured by industrial sprawl as far as Vicchio and Vespignano, after which the road follows the broad curve of the Sieve through gentle, cultivated country to Dicomano, Rufina, center of the smallest and choicest of the Chianti Putto zones, and PONTASSIEVE, where the Sieve joins the Arno. Turn W on the SS67 for Florence. The road follows the N bank of the Arno through industrial vineyards controlled by the Ruffino company, and passes many interesting country churches, of which the most notable are S. Giovanni Battista a Remole at Sieci and S. Andrea at Rovezzano, situated on the outskirts of Florence.

Florence (Firenze)
A to Z

Maps 1-4 (Florence streets) and **maps 5-6** (Florence environs) on pages 140-145
Postal code: 50100
Province: Firenze
Telephone area code: 055
Population: 422,000
i Via Manzoni 16 ☎2478141, map 2C6
See also: BASIC INFORMATION, pages 36-52

Florence is the most densely packed urban treasurehouse in Europe. If you were not detained by the profusion of artistic masterpieces it contains, you could walk across its historic center in half an hour. Only two of the sights recommended are beyond short walking distance of the Piazza della Signoria. It is, then, a city that can be explored according to the taste of the individual visitor.

> See where it lies before us in a sun-lighted valley, bright
> with the winding Arno, and shut in by swelling hills; its domes
> and towers and palaces rising from the rich country
> in a glittering heap, and shining in the sun like gold.
> (Charles Dickens, *Scenes From Italy,* 1846)

Although no one will be able to take in all that the city has to offer in one short visit — and it would be an exhausting waste of time to try — Florence does reveal its essential urban character to the visitor very quickly. Its narrow streets flanked by medieval and Renaissance palaces are, with very few exceptions, unspoiled as yet by modern architectural intrusions. Since the last building boom under the Medici grand dukes, the fabric of Florence has suffered only four drastic changes.

The first happened in the mid-19thC when Florence disastrously prepared itself for its brief period as Italy's capital by demolishing its old walls and part of its center to make way for the Viali and the Piazza della Repubblica. The second was the destruction toward the end of World War II of Ponte Santa Trìnita (subsequently reconstructed) and the areas to the N and S of the Ponte Vecchio. The third was the flood of 1966, the worst in the city's history. The fourth was the traffic, which from the early 1970s dominated Florence more cruelly than any of its tyrant-rulers, turning its beautiful squares into parking lots and roaring through its streets.

Now, although inessential motor-traffic is theoretically banned for most of the day from the center (the so-called *zona blu*) and parking is restricted, motorcycles, taxis, buses and those private cars prepared to risk breaking the law, continue to dominate and terrorize pedestrians. Florence remains the most densely motorized city in Italy, with a car owned by every two inhabitants; and removing the traffic from the center has had the effect of shifting the crush of cars, and the pollution, to the outskirts.

It is not, alas, a well-run city. The traffic is maddening, streets are dirty, the crime rate is rising; and excessive reliance on mass tourism has soured the tempers of a people long famous for their sharp tongues.

Fortunately there is probably no other major city in Europe from which escape is so easy and so delightful. Much of the lovely Tuscan countryside immediately to the s, e and n of the historic center has been consciously and courageously defended from the worst ravages of modern development, and can be reached easily, either on foot or by taking a short bus ride.

Two hints for visits to churches: take with you a good supply of small coins (₤100, 200 or 500), to operate the light-boxes without which many works of art cannot be viewed. When planning your visit, remember that in many churches, works of art are covered during the week before Easter, as a sign of mourning.

FINDING YOUR WAY ABOUT BY STREET NUMBERS
Street numbers in Florence are organized in two separate systems. **Black numbers** indicate **residential addresses** and **hotels**, and **commercial establishments**, including restaurants and shops, are given **red numbers**.

HOW TO USE THIS SECTION
Whether your stay in Florence is long or short, you may choose to follow the recommended walks. These lead you to acquire a general idea of the shape of the city, view its numerous palaces, cross over the bridge to investigate the Oltrarno and go beyond the boundary to the hills to the s.

In the pages that follow, Florence's sights are arranged alphabetically, using English or Italian names according to common English-speaking usage. The sights are classified by category on page 76.

Look for the ★ symbol against the most important sights and ✩ for those definitely worth a visit. Buildings of great architectural interest (𝕀𝕀𝕀) and outstanding views (≪≣) are also indicated. For a full explanation of symbols, see page 7.

If you only know the name of a museum, say, in English, and cannot find it in the following A-Z, try looking it up in the INDEX. Some lesser sights do not have their own entries but are included within other entries: look these up in the index too.

Bold type is generally employed to indicate outstanding buildings or other highlights. Occasionally it is used to single out other important features. Entries given without addresses and opening times are described more fully elsewhere: check the **cross-references**, which are in SMALL CAPITALS.

Walks in Florence

Sunday morning, when the maddening traffic is often calmer, is a good time for exploring Florence on foot.

WALK 1: GETTING TO KNOW FLORENCE
*Allow 30mins-1hr. Maps **3** & **4** on pages 142-143.*

On your first evening in Florence, an after-dinner stroll in the center, taking in the UFFIZI, PIAZZA DELLA SIGNORIA and DUOMO will make you at home in the dense cluster of the city's historic nucleus. Floodlighting touches even the most familiar monuments with fresh magic.

Start at Piazza SANTA TRÌNITA in order to enjoy the floodlit view of SAN MINIATO and the BELVEDERE from Ponte S. Trìnita, and to admire the recently installed lighting of the **Via Tornabuoni**. If you can resist window shopping, plunge into medieval Florence along Via delle Terme, named for the Roman baths that occupied this site, to the 14thC **Palazzo di Parte Guelfa** on the left. Turn right opposite it under Chiasso delle Misure and left into Borgo SANTI APOSTOLI, crossing Por S. Maria into Via Lambertesca, which brings you past Buontalenti's bizarre **Porta delle Suppliche** into Piazzale degli UFFIZI.

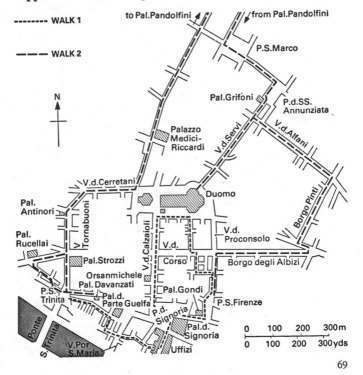

69

A left turn leads straight into PIAZZA DELLA SIGNORIA. Turn right around the N corner of the Palazzo Vecchio into Via dei Gondi and Piazza SAN FIRENZE, where the towers of the BADIA and BARGELLO rise with dignity beyond the Baroque extravaganza of the S. Firenze facade. Take the Via del Proconsolo, turning left after BADIA into Via Dante Alighieri. The Casa di Dante is a 19thC fiction made believable by the night lighting. Opposite is the Castegna tower, all that remains of the earliest seat of communal government.

Turn right into Via S. Margherita, left at the Corso and immediately right into Via dello Studio, where you will be rewarded with one of those astonishingly sudden views of Brunelleschi's Dome. The cathedral complex — campanile, Baptistry, DUOMO — reveals itself as you turn left along its s side. Third left is Via de' Calzaiuoli, which brings you past ORSANMICHELE back into the PIAZZA DELLA SIGNORIA.

WALK 2: A PALACE WALK
Allow 1-2hrs for each of three sections. Maps 3 & 4 on pages 142-143.
This is a walk devoted entirely to those domestic buildings that Italians rather grandly call palaces. It can be divided into three separate walks if you want to go slowly and thoroughly. It will take you, in roughly chronological order, past many of the most important Florentine palaces built for the merchants and bankers of the 14th-16thC.

Florentines being the least pretentious and most ironically humorous of Italians will often refer in conversation to a hut as a palazzo and a palazzo as a little house — which doesn't in the least mean that they are not proud of their palaces. A surprising number are still lived in by the descendants of their first owners; most are used as flats, restaurants, hotels, shops or offices. If you are not with a large party it is always worth ringing the bell and asking to see the courtyard. The 100 or so palaces built in Florence during the 15thC boom provided a model for the rest of Italy. In 15thC Tuscany there was no significant advance on the basic Florentine type except in PIENZA (see TUSCANY A TO Z). Nevertheless, there are certain practical or decorative additions to Florentine palaces that one encounters less often elsewhere.

The stone benches, or *muriccioli,* which run along the base of so many palaces, were a government-imposed condition of building permission. If you decide to rest and gossip on one of these public benches you will be exercising a civic right dear to the republican hearts of Renaissance Florentines. Machiavelli was shocked to find no *muriccioli* in Venice.

The projecting upper stories, supported on brackets known as *sporti,* were a device to grab more living space in a crowded city. Legislation against them generally failed.

The black and white decoration, or *sgraffiti,* on facades and in courtyards originated in the 15thC and was carried on through the 19thC. Two good 15thC examples not encountered on this walk are the **Coverelli** palace in Via dei Coverelli and the **Lanfredini** palace on Lungarno Guicciardini. The 16thC master of *sgraffiti* was Poccetti.

I. Start in the morning at the DAVANZATI, the best-preserved 14thC merchant's house in Florence. Next, to see what had happened to palace architecture a century later, cross the bottom of the Via Tornabuoni into Via del Parione; turn first right and immediately left into Via del Purgatorio, which brings you into the little piazza facing Alberti's RUCELLAI PALACE. Take the Via della Vigna Nuova back to the Via Tornabuoni, across which you see the STROZZI – later, larger and less refined than the Rucellai.

Go down the Tornabuoni to Piazza SANTA TRÌNITA. On its NE corner is the early 16thC **Bartolini Salimbeni**, the Roman-style palace thought by Florentines to look more like a church. Now look up the **Via Tornabuoni** for a minute before strolling up it. The palaces are 13th-16thC. At the top, partly closing the vista, is the **Antinori** palace, built in the 1460s by the Boni family who received permission to extend their site onto public land to provide this suitably elegant finish to the Via Tornabuoni.

Now press on to the Medici Palace by way of Via Rondinelli, right into Via de' Cerretani, and left along Borgo S. Lorenzo.

II. The MEDICI PALACE reopens at 3pm when the **Benozzo Gozzoli Chapel** is often less crowded than in the morning. Walk round the s side of the palace and turn right at the corner of the crenelated garden wall into **Via de' Ginori**, lined with good 13th-16thC palaces. The **Barbolani di Montauto** *(#9)* is an example of a 15thC palace modernized in the 16thC, with kneeling windows and herms. The **Palazzo Taddei** *(#19)* is a fine and typical early 16thC palace (1503) by Baccio d'Agnolo; Raphael lived here in 1505.

After crossing Via Guelfa, Via de' Ginori becomes **Via S. Gallo**. In the 16thC this was a street of churches, monasteries and high garden walls. It has a rather forlorn atmosphere now, but in the 18thC a carriage ride to the S. Gallo gate was *the* fashionable evening outing. On the left *(#25a)* is the severely beautiful portal, possibly designed by Michelangelo, of the **Monastery of S. Apollonia**. Farther along Via S. Gallo on the right *(#74)* is the **Pandolfini** palace (1520), designed by Raphael (who evidently thought the asymmetrical plan suitable for a large suburban site) and built by two members of the Sangallo family. The style of the palace is as Roman as the sympathies of its first owner, Giannozzo Pandolfini, Bishop of Troia, who records his gratitude to the Medici Popes for their help in acquiring the property in the inscription under the magnificent cornice.

If you turn right at the corner of the Pandolfini and right again into Via Cavour, you will soon come, on the right, to #57, the **Casino di S. Marco** (1574), built on the site of the Medici sculpture gardens by Buontalenti in his most bizarre, satirical vein. Francesco I had his alchemical laboratories here. The Casino is now the Court of Appeals, but, more to the point, if you happen to be thirsty there is a little bar off the inner courtyard to the left.

Turn right out of the Casino, left into **Piazza S. Marco**, and take Via Cesare Battisti into the northern corner of Piazza SANTISSIMA ANNUNZIATA. The rose-brick palace on the corner of Via dei Servi, a cavalier exception to the arcaded harmony of the square, is Ammannati's **Grifoni** palace. Its main entrance is in **Via dei Servi**, lined with grand-ducal palaces. Notice especially two on the right: #15, the **Niccolini** (1550), designed by Baccio d'Agnolo, with 19thC *sgraffiti;* and on Via Pucci, the **Pucci**

71

palace, ancestral home of the fashion designer, with a fine emblem of Leo X on this corner. Via dei Servi finishes at the DUOMO.

III. Alternatively, on leaving the Piazza SANTISSIMA ANNUNZIATA, take the first left off Via dei Servi into **Via degli Alfani**. On the right is a 1930s restoration of Brunelleschi's once-important **Rotonda di S. Maria degli Agnoli**. On the left *(#48)* is the **Giugni** palace (c.1577), one of Ammannati's best buildings. The courtyard, usually open, is remarkable for the alarming use of detached Classical elements. The Tuscan order was employed as a patriotic reference to the newly unified grand-ducal Tuscany. Notice the beautiful 16thC wooden gate.

Farther along, two simpler palaces on the left *(#34 and 32)* are also by Ammannati. The green dome you see ahead belongs to the synagogue. Second right is **Borgo Pinti**, which boasts 14th-16thC palaces. At #26, the house with the bust of *Cosimo I* over the door, Giambologna lived and died, and Pietro Tacca founded an academy.

At the bottom, as you pass under the Volta di S. Piero — the bar on the left serves rough wine and good ham sandwiches — you are crossing the second circle of walls into the 12thC city. Now turn right into **Borgo degli Albizi**, a street rich in good 16thC palaces. The **Altoviti** *(#18)* is known as Palazzo dei Visacci after the herm portraits of famous Florentines. Palazzo **Matteucci Ramirez di Montalvi** *(#26)* was built by Ammannati for a favorite of Cosimo I, whose emblem as Duke of Siena is over the door; there are remains of *sgraffiti* by Poccetti. The **Vitali** palace *(#28)* is also by Ammannati.

On the corner of Via del Proconsolo is the **Palazzo Nonfinito** (now housing the Institute of Anthropology), begun in 1593 by Buontalenti for Alessandro Strozzi but left unfinished. A left turn into Via del Proconsolo will bring you into Piazza SAN FIRENZE, where Giuliano da Sangallo's exemplary **Gondi** palace (1490-1520) is on your right opposite the S. Firenze facade. If you are in luck and have energy enough left to ring the bell at #2, you will be admitted into one of the most beautiful courtyards in Florence. You are now a minute's walk from the PIAZZA DELLA SIGNORIA and have earned a good dinner. If you choose to dine at **Cavallino** you will be overlooking the most famous Florentine palace of all.

WALK 3: THE OLTRARNO
Allow 1-2hrs. Maps 3 & 4 on pages 142-143.

This zig-zag route through the OLTRARNO will take you to its three important churches and past many of its most interesting palace facades. There are several expensive restaurants in and near the fashionable Borgo San Jacopo; those in the San Frediano quarter to the w are better value. Start off at about 3pm, when the churches begin to reopen, from Piazza SANTA FELÌCITA. The Medici dukes went home to the Pitti from this church by way of Vasari's aerial corridor, but you must make do with the Via Guicciardini, where the Machiavelli family once lived opposite the Guicciardini palace *(#15)*.

Passing the PITTI on your left, turn sharp right at Piazza SAN FELICE into **Via Maggio**, once the widest street in Europe and still the widest *(maggiore)* street on the Oltrarno. Palaces here are 14th-17thC, but most

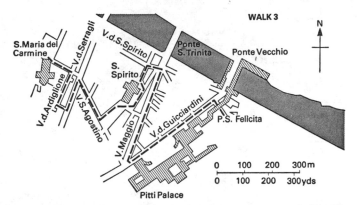

of the earlier ones were modernized in the grand-ducal period when Via Maggio was the best address in Florence. **Bianca Cappello's house** *(#26)* was remodeled in 1570-4 by Buontalenti for the Venetian mistress and future wife of Francesco I, who paid the bill. The Cappello emblem is over the rusticated doorway; the *sgraffiti* are by Poccetti. At the bottom of Via Maggio turn left into Via S. Spirito. On the right corner of Via dei Coverelli is **Palazzo Coverelli**, with good restored *sgraffiti.*

Turn left into Via dei Coverelli, bearing left around the apse and side of the church of SANTO SPIRITO. Imagine what the exterior would have looked like if Brunelleschi's unique plan had been carried out; he intended the 40 curved backs of the interior chapels to be expressed on the outside. A lively farmers' market takes place in the piazza on weekday mornings.

Crossing Piazza S. Spirito, turn right at its sw corner into Via S. Agostino. Where it crosses Via de' Serragli there is on the right a tabernacle (1427) by Lorenzo di Bicci. Turn left into Via de' Serragli and first right into Via dell'Ardiglione, which soon bends to the right along the side of a walled garden; from its gate there is a view of the apse of the CARMINE church. This is one of those Florentine streets where the bustle and noise of the city rarely seem to penetrate; it might have been this peaceful when Filippo Lippi was born in 1406 at #30. A left turn into Via S. Monaca brings you to the church entrance. If it is now late afternoon, Masaccio's frescoes might be as he intended them to be seen, lit by the setting sun.

WALK 4: TOWARD THE CHIANTI VIA ARCETRI OR SAN MINIATO

Allow a minimum of 1hr. Map 2E4-F5 on page 141.

The hills to the south of Florence are only a short walk from the Ponte Vecchio. This is a route that allows you to climb out of the city by a traffic-free path. From the Oltr'Arno foot of the bridge turn left into Via de'Bardi, which continues as Via S. Niccolò. These two streets are lined with some of the oldest palaces in the city and are now among its most exclusive addresses. From Via S. Niccolò turn right into Via S. Miniato

73

WALK 4

and through the Porta S. Miniato. Carry on straight up Via Monte alle Croci. This is the medieval road to the church of S. Miniato, described by Dante in Canto XII of the *Purgatorio* as climbing the hill "Where stands the church which dominates the well-run city." Take the first right into Via dell'Erta Canina, built for horse-drawn carriages and still mercifully free of motor traffic. A stiff, short climb is soon rewarded by a view of the lovely face of SAN MINIATO across an olive grove to your left.

When you reach the Viale Galileo Galilei you have several choices. You could turn left for San Miniato; or follow the signs to the right for ARCETRI and Pian dei Giullari, where you will find the restaurant **Omero**. Pian dei Giullari continues N of the Viale Galileo as **Via S.Leonardo**. This is the prettiest street in the environs of Florence, although traffic can make it an uncomfortable route for pedestrians. A plaque marks the house on the corner of the Viale where Tchaikovsky lived in 1878, "his music nourished by the soft hills of Tuscany." Ottone Rosai lived at #49; his paintings of Via S. Leonardo can be seen in the ALBERTO DELLA RAGIONE collection in PIAZZA DELLA SIGNORIA.

Otherwise, retrace your steps from the Viale back down the Erta Canina, enjoying the spectacular (and photogenic) views of the flank of SANTA CROCE, the DUOMO, its campanile and the tower of the Palazzo Vecchio.

OTHER IDEAS FOR WALKS

An alternative to the fourth walk might be along the stretch of city walls between the BELVEDERE and PORTA ROMANA.

For information about walking in the Tuscan countryside see LEISURE IDEAS on pages 49-52.

Sights and places of interest

Florence is so richly endowed with artistic treasures that the following guide is inevitably highly selective, and the use of stars (★ — recommended sight and ☆ — worth a visit) has been limited to the greatest and most famous only. This does not mean that they are all that is worth seeing. The city is packed with lesser-known museums, galleries, churches and private collections, which are essential to the specialist and which may charm and fascinate many independent-minded tourists.

Important recent restorations include the BRANCACCI CHAPEL, the Old and New Sacristies of SAN LORENZO and a number of paintings in the UFFIZI.

Most State museums are open mornings only Tuesday to Sunday, and are closed on Monday. But all opening hours can be subject to change. The tourist offices (see TOURIST INFORMATION, page 44) provide a list of current schedules. Churches, as usual in Italy, are generally open from approximately 7am to noon, and again in the afternoon from 3 or 4pm to 6 or 7pm.

ACCADEMIA (Galleria dell'Accademia) ★
Via Ricasoli 60 ☎*214375. Map 2B4* ■■ *★* *Open Tues-Sat 9am-2pm; Sun and holidays 9am-1pm. Closed Mon.*

In 1563, 70 leading Florentine artists founded the first Academy of Art in Europe. The organizing members were Vasari, Bronzino and Ammannati, and the president was Cosimo I. Thus academic art, like so many modern institutions, was a Florentine invention. First located at SANTISSIMA ANNUNZIATA, the Accademia was moved to Via Ricasoli 66 in 1764. This building, with its spacious 14thC loggia, is now the Florentine Art School and College.

The Accademia gallery nearby *(#60)* was founded in 1784 by Peter Leopold I, who donated a collection that was greatly enriched by works brought here from the suppressed religious orders in 1786 and 1808-10. Until World War I the Accademia possessed an outstanding collection of early Tuscan masterpieces, the best of which were transferred in 1913 to the UFFIZI. During the 1970s the display was reorganized and enlarged, in order to emphasize the link with the original Academy of Art, and new rooms housing 18th and 19thC academic paintings and sculptures, including hitherto neglected works by Lorenzo Bartolini, were opened in 1982.

Meanwhile, most visitors will come here, as they have for more than a century, to gaze up at Michelangelo's *David*.

ROOM I, SALA DEL COLOSSO: Dominated by Giambologna's model (c.1582) for the *Rape of the Sabines* in the Loggia dei Lanzi (see SIGNORIA). On the walls are 16thC paintings by Fra Bartolommeo, Perugino, Granacci, and others.

ROOM II, SALONE DI MICHELANGELO: Against the walls, which are hung with magnificent 16thC tapestries, are four of Michelangelo's unfinished *Slaves* (★) of c.1519-36, first meant for Pope Julius II's unrealized mausoleum in St Peter's in Rome (the Louvre possesses two other

75

Florence sights, classified by type

CHURCHES AND CHAPELS
Badia Fiorentina 🏛
Baptistry 🏛 ★
Brancacci Chapel ★
Carmine
Duomo 🏛 ★ «
Lo Scalzo 🏛
Medici Chapels
Ognissanti 🏛
Orsanmichele 🏛 ★
Pazzi Chapel 🏛 ★
Santissima Annuziata 🏛 ★
Santi Apostoli 🏛
Santa Croce 🏛 ★
San Felice 🏛
Santa Felìcita 🏛
San Firenze 🏛
San Gaetano 🏛
San Lorenzo 🏛 ★
San Marco
Santa Maria Maddalena dei
    Pazzi
Santa Maria Maggiore 🏛
Santa Maria Novella 🏛 ★
San Miniato al Monte 🏛 ★
San Niccolò 🏛
Santo Spirito 🏛 ★
Santo Stefano al Ponte 🏛
Santa Trìnita 🏛 ★

DISTRICTS AND SQUARES
Arcetri
Bellosguardo «
Oltramo
Pian dei Giullari

GALLERIES AND MUSEUMS
Accademia ★
Anthropoligical Museum 🏛
Antica Casa Fiorentina 🏛
Archeological Museum
Argenti Museum
Bardini Museum 🏛
Bargello (National Sculpture
    Museum) 🏛 ★
Castagno Museum ★

Corridoio
Corsini Gallery 🏛
"Firenze Com'era"
Fra Angelico Museum ★
Gallery of Modern Art
Horne Museum 🏛
Innocenti Gallery
Marino Marini Museum
Michelangelo Museum
Palatine Gallery ★
Raccolta d'Arte Moderna Alberto
    della Ragione
Sant'Apollonia 🏛 ★
San Salvi
Stibbert
Uffizi 🏛 ★

PALACES, TOWERS AND GATES
Belvedere 🏛 «
Davanzati Palace 🏛
Fortezza da Basso 🏛
Laurentian Library 🏛 ★
Medici Riccardi Palace 🏛
Palazzo della Signoria 🏛 ★
Pitti Palace 🏛 ★
Porta Romana
Porta San Frediano
Rucellai Palace 🏛 ★
Strozzi Palace 🏛
Torre di San Niccolò

PARKS AND GARDENS
Boboli Gardens
Botanical Garden
Le Cascine

SCIENCE AND TECHNOLOGY
Botanical Garden and Museum
Science Museum 🏛
Zoological Museum

VIEWPOINTS «
Bellosguardo
Belvedere 🏛
Piazzale Michelangelo
Ponte Vecchio ★

Slaves). The figures may represent the liberal arts enslaved by the death of their patron, Julius II. On the right wall are also the deeply expressive, unfinished *St Matthew* (before 1505), and the Palestrina *Pietà,* which is no longer attributed to Michelangelo. It was saved from export in 1940 and brought here from the Church of S. Rosalia di Palestrina in Rome.

> The *David* ... standing forward stripped and exposed
> and eternally half-shrinking, half-wishing to expose himself,
> he is the genius of Florence.
> (D.H. Lawrence, *Aaron's Rod,* 1922)

At the far end of the room, Michelangelo's *David* (★) dwarfs and astonishes the perpetual crowds. This tribune was specially built to receive the *David* when it was brought here from the Signoria in 1873. The statue was carved (1501-4) from a block of Carrara marble known as "the giant," which had been spoiled by Agostino di Duccio and abandoned in the courtyard of the Opera del Duomo. The *David* established Michelangelo's reputation as the leading sculptor of his day, and has remained the most potent of all symbols of Florentine republicanism. But it has not always been admired: William Hazlitt, one of the many early 19thC travelers to be irritated by Michelangelo's style, described it as looking "like an awkward overgrown actor at one of our minor theatres, without his clothes."

The other rooms are devoted to a study collection of 13th-18thC Florentine paintings, including, in the second of the three rooms to the right of the Salone di Michelangelo, Baldovinetti's important but ruined *Trinity with Saints.*

To the left of the Tribune, through a gallery of 16thC academic pictures, is the **Salone delle Toscani**, originally the women's ward of a hospital, now devoted to plaster models of works by Luigi Pampaloni and Lorenzo Bartolini, the two leading Neoclassical Tuscan sculptors, both of whom taught at the Accademia.

ANTHROPOLOGICAL MUSEUM (Museo Nazionale di Antropologia ed Etnologia) 🏛

Via del Proconsolo 12 ☎296449. Map 4C5 ▣ Open every Thurs-Sat and 3rd Sun of each month 9am-1pm. Closed July-Sept.

Opened in 1869, this was the first anthropological museum in Italy. The collection is displayed on the ground floor of the Palazzo Nonfinito (see WALK 2 on page 70) and is a fascinating documentation of ethnic custom and costume.

ANTICA CASA FIORENTINA, MUSEO DELL'   The House Museum of
Florence in the DAVANZATI PALACE.

ARCETRI AND PIAN DEI GIULLARI
Map 6E4. Bus #38.

Florence may be hot and crowded, but half an hour's walk s from the Ponte Vecchio will lift you into the cool, high heart of Tuscany. At #2 Pian dei Giullari is the **Astrophysical Observatory of Arcetri** with the first solar tower built in Europe (1872). Opposite the entrance is the Villa Capponi, with famous but private gardens. The **Torre del Gallo** is just to the E: this 19thC reconstruction was once owned by the antiquarian robber baron Stefano Bardini (see BARDINI MUSEUM). In the adjacent **Villa la Gallina** are Antonio del Pollaiuolo's **frescoes of nude dancers**: persistent or specialist visitors have been known to gain access by appointment.

Pian dei Giullari takes its name from the minstrels who entertained Florentine patricians here from the 12thC. Galileo died in the **Villa il Gioiello** *(#42)*. On #48 a plaque sentences to imprisonment anyone who dares to play any ball game within 200 yards of the monastery of S. Matteo in Arcetri.

In the Via S. Margherita a Montici, at the Villa Ravà *(#75)* Francesco Guicciardini wrote his histories of Italy between 1537-40. Farther on is the church of S. Margherita a Montici, commanding stupendous views of the Arno and Ema valleys. Inside are two 14thC panels by the Master of St Cecilia.

(See also WALK 4 on page 73.)

ARCHEOLOGICAL MUSEUM (Museo Archeologico) ★
Via della Colonna 36 ☎ *2478641. Map* **2B5** 🖼 ♣ *Open Tues-Sat 9am-2pm; Sun and holidays 9am-1pm. Closed Mon.*

To say that the Archeological Museum is of outstanding international importance may sound forbidding to the nonspecialist. In fact, every tourist will find much more here to delight the eye, stimulate the imagination and enrich further sightseeing in Florence and Tuscany. The Etruscan sculptures are an essential and fascinating grounding for those who intend to visit the sites; the Greek and Roman collections will deepen one's understanding of the Renaissance art they helped inspire.

Having suffered appalling damage from the 1966 flood, the museum still has an air of post-crisis impermanence. Many rooms are closed, others badly labeled, and all displays are subject to change, but the finest objects, of which only the highlights are mentioned here, have been brilliantly restored and are on public display.

GROUND FLOOR, ROOM I: François Vase (c.570BC), the earliest known Attic volute-krater, discovered in 1845 by Alexander François at Chiusi. Smashed by a member of staff of the museum into 638 pieces in 1900, the vase was restored in 1972.

ROOM II: Etruscan tomb sculpture (6th-5thC BC), from Chianciano and Chiusi.

FIRST FLOOR: The **Egyptian Collection** is in Rms I-VIII to the left of the stairs. It consists mainly of objects discovered in 1828-9, during a Franco-Tuscan expedition directed by Ippolito Rossellini and Jean François Champollion. The prize piece is the beautiful large **chariot** made of wood and bone that was found by Rossellini in a 14thC BC tomb at Thebes.

The **Etruscan, Greek and Roman Collection** is in the rooms to the right of the stairs and continues on the second floor. Etruscan tomb sculpture includes an *Urn in the Shape of an Etruscan House* (6th-3rdC

BC), no. 5539, from Chiusi, a rare piece of evidence about Etruscan architecture, worth bearing in mind when looking at 15thC Tuscan palaces. See the illustration on page 23. *Sarcophagus of the Fat Etruscan* (3rd-2ndC BC), no. 5482, from Chiusi, mentioned by Catullus.

The greatest Etruscan bronzes include *Wounded Chimera* (5thC BC), discovered at Arezzo in 1553 (the two left legs were restored by Cellini), and *The Orator* (c.4th or 3rdC BC), a funereal sculpture found near Trasimeno in 1566.

A small section of the ground floor, entered from Piazza SS. Annunziata, is reserved for special exhibitions. The garden and the topographical display charting the evolution of Etruscan culture have been closed for an indefinite period.

ARGENTI MUSEUM   Collection of *objets d'art* in the PITTI PALACE.

BADIA FIORENTINA ▥ †
Map 4C4.

The old Benedictine Abbey of Florence is the only church besides the Baptistry and S. Miniato to be mentioned by Dante, who tells us that he saw Beatrice at mass here and that the bell tower of the Badia gave Florence the hours. According to Vasari, the abbey, founded in 978, was enlarged by Arnolfo di Cambio, c.1285.

This 13thC building was reoriented and radically rebuilt in the 17thC, but the original apse can still be seen from the outside. The hexagonal Romanesque-Gothic **campanile** was completed in 1330. There is a striking view of it, with Giotto's tower of the Duomo behind, from Via Dante Alighieri.

The **interior** is best lit in the morning. The **portal** (1495) and **vestibule** leading to Via Dante Alighieri were designed by Benedetto da Rovezza. The noble Baroque **ceiling** is by Matteo Segaloni, architect of the 17thC church. Immediately to the left of the entrance is Filippino Lippi's restless masterpiece, *St Bernard's Vision of the Madonna* (c.1485). In the left transept can be found the late 15thC **monument to Count Ugo**, benefactor of the 10thC foundation, the masterpiece of Mino da Fiesole.

Two more Minos in the church are the *Madonna and Child with Sts Leonard and Laurence* (1464-70) to the right of the entrance, and the *Monument to Bernardo Giugni* (after 1466) in the right transept. The **Pandolfini Chapel** (1511) by Benedetto da Rovezzano is, alas, rarely open. Off it is the little chapel occupying the site of the church of S. Stefano, where Boccaccio delivered the first literary lecture, on the *Divine Comedy.*

Oranges were cultivated in the center of the large cloister (1439), attributed to Bernardo Rossellino. The tombs date from the 13thC onward. The early 15thC frescoes in the upper loggia of scenes from the life of St Bernard are by a follower of Uccello and Domenico Veneziano.

BAPTISTRY (Battistero)   The city's oldest building, and once its cathedral. See DUOMO.

79

BARDINI MUSEUM 🏛

Piazza de' Mozzi 1 ☎2342427. Map **4***F5* 🎫 ✗📷 *Open Mon-Tues, Thurs-Sat 9am-2pm; Sun and holidays 8am-1pm. Closed Wed.*

Stefano Bardini (1836-1922) was the leading Italian art dealer of his day, and by 1883 he had amassed a fortune more than large enough to build this palace. He tore down a 13thC church to create the site and, like the American robber barons of the period, incorporated architectural members from older buildings.

The first-floor windows are framed with the altars from a church in Pistoia. The cool, spacious **interior** is embellished throughout with ceilings, door surrounds and chimney pieces from other earlier buildings. Bardini's taste was almost boundlessly eclectic, and the collection includes, on the ground floor, sculptures and architectural decorations from the Etruscan period to the Baroque.

On the second floor there are pictures, furniture, ceramics, tapestries, musical instruments, arms and armor.

BARGELLO, NATIONAL SCULPTURE MUSEUM (Museo Nazionale) 🏛 ★

Via del Proconsolo 4 ☎210801. Map **4***C5* 🎫 *Open Tues-Sat 9am-2pm; Sun and holidays 9am-1pm. Closed Mon.*

There are a fair number of murderers in the National Sculpture Museum, of which the best known are Donatello's *David*, Verrocchio's *David*, Michelangelo's *Brutus* and Cellini's model for the *Perseus*. Thus Florentine Renaissance sculpture reflected the Florentine obsession with tyranny.

It is an ironic coincidence that during the turbulent period when these sculptures were created, the Bargello was the place where real murderers were tried and sentenced; and the message that crime doesn't pay even if committed in the name of freedom was advertised on the tower walls, frescoed with representations of the mutilated corpses of the condemned. The body of one of the Pazzi Conspirators was hung from a window, where Leonardo made a careful drawing of him, paying special attention to his clothes.

The Bargello was built around an earlier tower in 1255, just 5 years after the establishment of the new popular regime, as its first town hall. In 1261 under the *podestà*, or chief judiciary, it became the law court. The chief of police, or *bargello*, for whom the building is now named, first occupied the palace in 1574. The **Sculpture Museum**, the most important in Italy, has been here since 1859, and was enriched in 1888 by the Carrand Collection of small bronzes, ivories, enamels, goldsmiths' work and ceramics.

The **courtyard** is the most picturesque part of the palace. Its loggia and staircase are 14thC. Among the sculptures are Ammannati's figures from the fountain in the Boboli gardens. To the right of the entrance is the **sculpture gallery** (★) opened in 1975. Moving clockwise from the entrance one encounters, most notably: Michelangelo's *Bacchus* (c.1497), his first large free-standing sculpture, the *Pitti Tondo* (c.1504) and *Brutus* (c.1540), which possibly celebrates the assassination of Alessandro de' Medici; and Sansovino's *Bacchus*. There are also terra-cotta sketches by Michelangelo's followers and contemporaries. Works by Cellini include the **four bronze statues** and the relief panel of *Perseus Liberating Andromeda,* now brought here for safekeeping from the Loggia dei Lanzi; also his model for the *Perseus* — he boasts in his autobiography that Cosimo I doubted that anyone had the skill to enlarge it. Of the *Narcissus,* he tells us that a defective block of marble dictated the form. His larger-than-life portrait bust of *Cosimo I* (1557) was made, while he was perfecting his bronze technique for the *Perseus,* for the fortress Cosimo built at Portoferraio. You cannot very well ignore Giambologna's enormous, violent *Victory of Florence over Pisa* (1570), or the splendid *Honor Conquering Shame* (1561) and the **bronze reliefs** by Vincenzo Danti.

Beyond the courtyard are 14thC sculptural fragments, of which the finest piece is Tino di Camaino's *Madonna and Child.*

FIRST FLOOR: The open staircase leads to the **loggia,** with Giambologna's *Mercury* (c.1564) and bronze animals (c.1570) made for the Medici Villa at CASTELLO. On the right is the large **Salone del Consiglio Generale** (★). On the walls, notice especially the Madonnas by Luca della Robbia, Michelozzo and Agostino di Duccio; on the far wall, Donatello's *St George* (1416) with its original *predella,* which was the first Renaissance relief carving to achieve perspective, from the facade of ORSANMICHELE; and the two panels of *The Sacrifice of Isaac* by Brunelleschi and Ghiberti, which were competition entries for the second Baptistry doors.

> Donatello carved a statue of St George bearing arms and
> breathed life into it. From his head emanated the beauty of
> youth, courage and valour of arms, a vivacity proudly terrible,
> and a marvellous propensity to move within that stone.
> (Vasari, *Lives of the Artists,* 1550)

Among the free-standing sculptures by Donatello are the *Marzocco* (1420), the heraldic lion of Florence; *Cupid* (c.1430-40), described by Vasari as "dressed in a rather bizarre fashion"; and the polychrome terra-cotta *Bust of a Man,* probably Niccolò da Uzzano. Compare the swaying elegance of Donatello's early marble *David* (1408) with the late bronze *David* (c.1430), his most famous and titillating boy and the first free-standing nude of the Renaissance. Note also two sensitive busts by Desiderio da Settignano.

The 15th-17thC **majolicas** from the Carrand and Medici grand-ducal collections are of outstanding interest. The next rooms on this floor contain a large and heterogeneous collection of European and Islamic applied art, most of it from the **Carrand bequest** of 1888.

SALONE DEL PODESTÀ: This was the law court, frescoed during the brief reign of the Duke of Athens. Off the far end is the frescoed **Chapel of the Condemned** with fine intarsiate choir stalls (1493) and lectern (1490). Next is a room of metalwork, with Cellini's *Ganymede,* and another room devoted to 15th-16thC Italian majolicas.

SECOND FLOOR: At the top of the stairs is the Sala di Giovanni della Robbia where Giovanni Rustici's huge terra-cotta relief panel of *Christ* *and the Magdalen* demonstrates his superiority to Giovanni della Robbia. Bernini's bust of *Constanza Bonarelli* (★) is usually displayed in this room. This is Bernini's only portrait bust (he had a stormy love affair with the subject) and one of the most remarkable in the history of art. "It opens the history of modern portraiture in sculpture. All barriers have fallen: here is a woman of the people, neither beautiful nor heroized." (Rudolf Wittkower)

Off one end of the room is a display of arms and armor. Off the other, the Sala di Andrea della Robbia leads to the **Sala di Verrocchio** (★). In the center are Verrocchio's *David* (before 1476) and Antonio Pollaiuolo's small bronze masterpiece *Hercules and Anteus*. Among the works displayed on the walls are, clockwise from the entrance, the marble bust of *Battista Sforza, Duchess of Urbino* (1474-7) by Francesco Laurana, Verrocchio's *Bust of a Woman* and *Madonna and Child* (c.1480), and the bust of *Piero Mellini* (1474) by Benedetto da Maiano. Portrait busts and relief carvings by Mino da Fiesole include the tondo of the *Madonna and Child* (1481). Across the Sala di Andrea della Robbia is the **Sala dei Bronzetti** (★), containing the most important public collection of bronzes in Italy. The magnificent 16thC chimneypiece is by Benedetto da Rovezzano.

BELLOSGUARDO
Map 5D3. No bus connection ◁€

Bellosguardo is one of the nearest of the hill villages s of Florence. You can walk it in half an hour either from PORTA ROMANA or SAN FREDIANO, and will be rewarded for your stiff climb by views as ravishing as the word *bellosguardo* (fine view) suggests. Via Bellosguardo forks to either side of the piazza. On the w side is the Villa Belvedere al Saracino (1502) by Baccio d'Agnolo, and farther along the Via San Carlo is the Torre Montauto, where Hawthorne stayed. On the E side of the piazza is the park of Villa Ombrellino, where Alice Keppel, Edward VII's last mistress, lived from 1925 to her death in 1947. Her daughter, Violet Trefusis, also died at the Ombrellino.

The best views are from the garden of the **Hotel Torre di Bellosguardo** in Via Roti Michelozzi (see WHERE TO STAY).

In the piazza, a plaque records the most famous of the numerous foreign visitors who have lived in and around Bellosguardo. Aldous Huxley's short story, *The Rest Cure,* is about a neurotic Englishwoman staying here.

BELVEDERE (Forte di Belvedere) 血
Via S. Leonardo ☎ *2342822. Map 2E4* 回 ◁€ *Open summer 9am-8pm, winter 9am-5pm.*

Crowning the hill of S. Giorgio is the ruthlessly practical Belvedere fortress surrounding its elegant shoe-box-shaped Mannerist palace, both built by Buontalenti in 1590-5 for Grand Duke Ferdinand I. The terraces are now used for modern **sculpture exhibitions** (盟), which are only occasionally worthy of a setting commanding some of the most magnificent views of Florence and the surrounding hills and valleys. At the top of the Costa di S. Giorgio is the S. Giorgio gate (c.1260), reduced to about half its original height, embellished with a fresco of the *Madonna and Saints* by Bicci di Lorenzo. The relief carving of St George is a copy of the original now in the PALAZZO DELLA SIGNORIA.

Two of the most interesting buildings in the Costa di S. Giorgio are the splendid Baroque church of S. Giorgio, lately restored, modernized by G. B. Foggini in 1707, with a boudoir-like oval ceiling frescoed by Alessandro Gherardini, and the house *(#19)* where Galileo was visited by Ferdinand I.

BOBOLI GARDENS (Giardino di Boboli) ★
☎213440. Map 1E3 ▣ ▣ ♣ *Open 9am-before sunset, closed Mon. Main gate to left of Pitti: others not always open.*

"The most important if not the most pleasing of Tuscan pleasure gardens .... because the Boboli is a court garden, and not designed for private use." Thus Edith Wharton explained the curiously lowering effect the Boboli can have on one's spirits. At certain seasons, when roses ramble through the somber plantations of holly and cypress or when Florence is gilded with slanted light in fall, the Boboli would be a fine place for a gentle evening stroll. But as another American novelist, Mary McCarthy, has pointed out, this is just the time when the gates close. It is nevertheless visited by nearly 5 million people each year, which makes it the most frequented artistic attraction in Italy.

Eleanor of Toledo ordered gardens to be laid out behind the Pitti as soon as she and Cosimo I took possession in 1549. The original designer was Tribolo, who died before accomplishing the extraordinary technical feat of taming this wedge of steep quarry. Later alterations by Ammannati, Buontalenti and the Parigi gave the gardens their playful, grandiose complexity.

If you wander freely in the Boboli, the late Mannerist jokes will take you by surprise as they were intended to do. A more purposeful tour should include the following interests.

1. Statue of *Pietro Barbino Riding a Tortoise,* Cosimo I's favorite dwarf immortalized by Valerio Cioli. **2.** Buontalenti Grotto (1583-88), a serious joke about nature; the casts of Michelangelo's *Slaves* replace the originals, now in the ACCADEMIA, which were installed here for a time in the 16thC. Giambologna's *Venus* is in the third recess, not always open. **3.** The **Kaffeehaus** (1776), for a drink and fine views. **4.** The **Amphitheater**, "One of the triumphs of Italian garden architecture" (Edith Wharton). Built from 1618 by the Parigi for spectacular grand-ducal entertainments. **5. Neptune Fountain** (1565) by Stoldo Lorenzi. **6. Porcelain Museum** (Museo delle Porcellane) (*☎212557, visits by appointment),* a small but choice collection of French, Italian, Viennese and German porcelains, formerly exhibited in the Argenti Museum, has now been installed in the airy Casino del Cavaliere. Panoramic views to the s from the terrace. **7. Cypress Alley** (Viottolone), lined with statues of various periods, the most famous of which, toward the bottom, are the knowingly rustic 17thC groups of games. **8. The Isolotto** (1618) by A.

Parigi. The shallow pool, the tall box hedges and the pots of oranges and entwined trees on the island provide cooling relief. Rising from the fountain is a copy of Giambologna's *Oceanus* (the original is in the BARGELLO).

See also PITTI PALACE.

BOTANICAL GARDEN (Orto Botanico, Giardino dei Semplici)
Via Micheli 3 ☎ 2757401. Map 2B4 ▣ Open Mon, Wed, Fri 9am-noon.

In a stony city where most gardens are hidden behind high walls, this scholarly display of the vegetable heritage of Tuscany makes a refreshing change from art galleries and churches. It is also an excellent preparation for those who plan to visit rural Tuscany and would like to be able to identify the native trees and flowers.

The Giardino dei Semplici, as it was originally called because its first function was the cultivation of medicinal plants, was founded in 1545 by Cosimo I. The **Botanical Museum** *(Via La Pira 4 ☎ 2757462, open Mon-Fri 9am-noon)* may eventually be moved to a new science museum, the largest of its kind in Italy, in Via Circondaria.

BRANCACCI CHAPEL (Cappella Brancacci) ★
Piazza del Carmine. Map 1D2 ☎ 212331 ▣▣ Open Mon, Wed-Sat 10am-5pm; Sun, holidays 1-5pm; closed Tues. Entrance through the cloister on the right of the church of the Carmine.

Masolino and Masaccio's frescoes in the Brancacci chapel in the left transept of the Carmelite church are among the most important and influential landmarks of Western painting: the essential link between Giotto's Arena Chapel in Padua, the Piero della Francesca frescoes in the church of San Francesco in Arezzo and Michelangelo's Sistine Chapel.

They were commissioned in 1423 by Felice Brancacci, a rich and powerful patrician whose family were patrons of the chapel. Masolino and his much younger contemporary Masaccio collaborated on the frescoes, until Masaccio departed for Rome 4 or 5 years later leaving the project unfinished. Shortly afterwards, Felice Brancacci fell from favor and was exiled by Cosimo de' Medici. It was not until the 1480s that the cycle was restored and completed by Filippino Lippi, who followed Masaccio's style so closely here that it is not always easy to distinguish the work of the two artists.

A fire that destroyed most of the church in the late 18thC blackened and damaged the frescoes. The restoration carried out from 1984-88 has rendered them fully legible, unveiling previously invisible details and modeling, and revealing the airiness and clarity of the landscape backgrounds. Infilling and overpainting has been executed in tiny vertical stripes to distinguish it from the original paint.

Framed by the starting episodes of the Christian story, the *Temptation* and *Expulsion of Adam and Eve,* the redemptive power of Christ is represented with scenes from the life of St Peter, His spiritual heir and founder of His Church.

UPPER TIER, LEFT TO RIGHT: 1. *The Expulsion from the Garden,* by Masaccio, the first image in Renaissance painting to match the ex-

KEY 1 The Expulsion 2 The Tribute Money 3 St Peter Preaching 4 The Baptism of the Neophytes 5 The Healing of the Cripple and the Raising of Tabitha 6 The Temptation 7 St Paul Visits St Peter in Prison 8 The Raising of the Son of Theophilus and St Peter Enthroned 9 St Peter Healing the Sick with his Shadow 10 The Distribution of Alms and the Death of Ananias 11 The Disputation 12 St Peter Freed from Prison

pressive intensity of Giovanni Pisani's sculpted figures and probably inspired by his pulpits, particularly those in Pisa Cathedral. **2.** *The Tribute Money,* by Masaccio. Christ and the Apostles arrive in Capernaum. St Peter appears three times: in the central group, where Christ is saying, "Render unto Caesar the things that are Caesar's"; on the left catching the fish and extracting the coin; and on the right handing the tribute money to the tax collector. The head of Christ was painted by Masolino. **3.** *St Peter Preaching at Jerusalem,* by Masolino. **4.** *The Baptism of the Neophytes,* by Masaccio and ?Masolino. **5.** *The Healing of the Cripple and the Raising of Tabitha,* by Masolino, set against an intriguingly realistic evocation of the architecture and everyday life of *quattrocento* Florence. **6.** *The Temptation of Adam and Eve,* by Masolino, in a courtly Gothic style that is in striking contrast to the Masaccio *Expulsion* on the opposite wall.

85

LOWER TIER, LEFT TO RIGHT: 7. *St Paul Visits St Peter in Prison,* by Filippino Lippi in his most Masaccio-like style. **8.** *The Raising of the Son of Theophilus and St Peter Enthroned,* by Masaccio and Filippino Lippi. Theophilus was Prefect of Antioch. Here, St Peter resurrects his son, who has been dead for 14 years, and the people of Antioch, who are converted to Christianity by the miracle, build him a chair from which he can preach. The heads, by Filippino, are portraits of contemporary Florentines. **9.** *St Peter Healing the Sick with his Shadow,* by Masaccio. **10.** *The Distribution of Alms and the Death of Ananias,* by Masaccio. St Peter instructs the people to give up their possessions for redistribution to the needy. Ananias, who has retained a portion of his, is challenged by St Peter, and "gives up the ghost." **11.** *The Disputation with Simon Magus and the Crucifixion of Peter,* by Filippino Lippi. **12.** *St Peter Freed from Prison by an Angel,* by Filippino Lippi.

Elsewhere in the church of the Carmine, the **Corsini Chapel**, in the left transept, was built in 1675-83 by P. F. Silvani. The splendid relief sculptures (1675-91) on the walls and altar are by G. B. Foggini, and the cupola fresco of the *Apotheosis of S. Andrea Corsini* (1682) by Luca Giordano.

CARMINE   Carmelite church containing the BRANCACCI and Corsini Chapels.

CASA BUONARROTI   Built by Michelangelo's family after the artist's death; now the MICHELANGELO MUSEUM.

LE CASCINE
Map 5D3. Bus 17.

Surprisingly few tourists make use of Le Cascine, the shady park that runs for 3km (1¾ miles) along the N bank of the Arno W from Piazza Vittorio Veneto. Yet it is one of the very few places in the city where you can take the air undistracted by traffic and artistic masterpieces; and the private tennis club and swimming pool are open to foreign nonmembers. An open-air market is held, under the shadow of the poplar trees, every Tuesday morning.

Originally a dairy farm belonging to the Medici, the Cascine became the grand-ducal chase in the 17thC. Shelley composed his *Ode to the West Wind* while striding through the Cascine.

Later in the 19thC the park was so full of fashionable carriages that Charles Lever described it as being to the world of society "what the Bourse is to the world of trade."

CORRIDOIO ★
☎ 218341 ✗ take about 1hr, beginning at the UFFIZI: they must be reserved well in advance.

Vasari's aerial link between the PITTI PALACE and the UFFIZI, built as the Medici grand-dukes' private route across the Arno, is hung with a famous collection of artists' self-portraits. The ones to look out for are: Carlo Dolci, Rosalba Carriera, Annibale and Agostino Carracci, Salvator

Rosa, Rubens, Angelica Kauffmann, Joshua Reynolds, Jacques Louis David, Elisabeth Vigée Lebrun, Delacroix, Ingres and Beppe Ciardi.

CORSINI GALLERY ▥

Palazzo Corsini, Via del Parione 11 ☎218994. Map 3C2. Open by prior appointment.
The most important private collection in Florence, with works by Signorelli, Pontormo, Raphael, Rigaud and other Italian and European artists of the 15th-18thC.

The palace (1648-56) that gives its name to this stretch of the *lungarno* is by Pier Francesco Silvani and Antonio Ferri.

DAVANZATI PALACE AND ANTICA CASA FIORENTINA, MUSEO DELL'
(Florentine House Museum) ▥ ☆
Piazza Davanzati, Via Porta Rossa ☎216518. Map 3D3 ▨ ✦ Open Tues-Sat 9am-2pm; Sun 9am-1pm. Closed Mon.
The exterior of the Davanzati is the best-preserved of any mid-14thC palace in Florence. Inside, the House Museum offers a rare opportunity to explore an early palace interior and to learn about domestic life in 14th-16thC Florence. If George Eliot had known the Davanzati as it is today, *Romola* would have been a livelier novel. The house was built by the Davizzi family, who lived here for more than a century before selling to the historian Bernardo Davanzati in 1578. The interior was badly mishandled in the 19thC after the suicide by defenestration of the last Davanzati, but was rescued and accurately restored by Elia Volpi just after the turn of this century.

Architecturally the building is midway between a medieval defense tower and a Renaissance palace. Apart from the 16thC roof loggia, a replacement of the original battlements, and the Davanzati coat of arms placed here in the 16thC, the facade looks very much like the one you can see in Masolino's fresco of the *Resurrection of Tabitha* in the BRANCACCI CHAPEL.

The entrance loggia, initially used for important family celebrations, was converted into three wool shops by the end of the 15thC. These horizontal perches running across windows were used, as shown in the Brancacci fresco, for hanging out washing, or birdcages, and for festive drapes.

The interior is largely a reconstruction, and a very good one, by Volpi. The **courtyard staircase** is particularly worth noting as the only one of its type left in Florence. The well is an unusual luxury for a palace of this date; all five floors were served by a shaft that carried buckets of water upward by rope and pulley. Kitchens, as always in medieval palaces, were located on the top floor. The sanitary arrangements include lavatories, which you can see next to the bedrooms on the three upper floors. The house is unusual in having two *piani nobili*, on the second as well as the first floor.

Of the wall decorations, the most attractive and most complete is in the second-floor bedroom where a fresco cycle illustrates the medieval French poem *The Chatelaine of Vergi*.

DUOMO 🏛 † ★
☎ 294514. Map 4B4. Open Mon-Sat 10am-5.30pm.

The Piazza del Duomo is the crossroads of the city's busiest streets, the headquarters of its ancient voluntary ambulance service (the *Misericordia,* an original Red Cross) and a magnet for the modern tourist industry; but it is no place for a meditative cup of coffee. To appreciate the grandeur and significance of the Duomo and its attendant buildings you must first go away from it, glimpse its flagrant burst of color from the dark narrow city streets and take your coffee overlooking it from a rooftop or from the hills above, where you will see how disproportionately large the cathedral is in a small city.

> The cathedral and its belfry suggested the grotesque similitude of a huge architectural zebra and its keeper — the former with a coating or skin, consisting of alternate stripes of black and white marble, the latter exhibiting, on its exterior, all the colours of the rainbow, all the chequers of a gigantic harlequin! Is there no mitigation of the penalty due to this gothic and tasteless idea?
> (James Johnson MD, 1831)

The cathedral (Santa Maria del Fiore), clad in white marble from Carrara, green from Prato and pink from the Maremma, could hardly be more of a contrast with the plain brown understated city around it. Like the two sides of the Florentine character, one is measured, conservative, puritanical, the other excessive, innovating, festive; and both are dominated by the great cranium-shaped intelligence of Brunelleschi's dome — "rising above the skies, ample to cover with its shadow all the Tuscan people," wrote Leonbattista Alberti in 1436.

Arnolfo di Cambio was commissioned in 1296 to build a cathedral that would surpass anything produced by the ancient Romans and Greeks or by Florence's rivals the Pisans and Sienese. Work was interrupted by Arnolfo's death, began again in 1331, and after another pause resumed under the direction of Francesco Talenti from 1357-64. The nave was completed in 1380, the tribunes and the drum of the dome finished by 1418.

The problem then was how to raise a dome over a space 42m (138 feet) across and 55m (180 feet) above the ground. No dome of this size had been built since Antiquity, and various unlikely solutions were proposed before Brunelleschi, who had studied Classical building techniques in Rome, provided the answer. His dome, realized in 1436, was the supreme engineering feat of the Renaissance. The lantern was completed in 1461, after Brunelleschi's death; the gallery, on only one of the eight sides of the drum of the dome, was begun by Baccio d'Agnolo in 1506 but abandoned after Michelangelo called it "a cage for crickets."

The Neo-Gothic facade of the cathedral is a late 19thC interpretation of the original one. The apse is best viewed from the corner of Via Proconsolo and Via dell'Oriuolo. The s flank is the earliest section of the exterior, but the most beautiful of the doors, the **Porta della Mandorla**, is on the N nave. Above it is Nanni di Banco's lovely relief of the *Assumption of the Madonna* (1414-21).

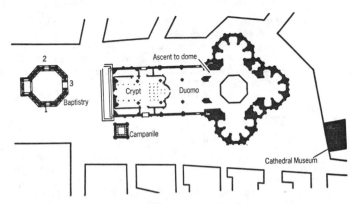

The cathedral interior, the fourth largest in the world, is all the more imposing for the sparseness of detailed decoration. There are only a few major works of art to distract from the sense of echoing space. In the left aisle of the nave are the two famous monuments to *condottieri* (mercenary commanders), which have been cited as examples of Florentine meanness because they imitate marble in *trompe l'oeil* fresco. Both have long since been transferred to canvas: the first, **Monument to Niccolò da Tolentino** (1456) by Castagno; the second, **Monument to Sir John Hawkwood** (1436) by Uccello. Just before the crossing is an interesting panel painting of *Dante Explaining the Divine Comedy* (1465) by Domenico di Michelino.

Access to the vast octagonal **crossing** and the three polygonal tribunes of the apse is barred to visitors when services are in progress. The interior dome is frescoed with a late 16thC *Last Judgement* by Vasari and Federico Zuccari that has been under restoration for years. Some experts argue that these frescoes should be removed in order to reveal more clearly Brunelleschi's structure.

The noble octagonal marble **choir enclosure** (1555) beneath the dome is by Bandinelli, as is the high altar, over which is a wooden **crucifix** (1495-7) by Benedetto da Maiano. The **bronze doors** to the New Sacristy are the only surviving work in this material designed by Luca della Robbia; they were cast by Michelozzo (1445-69). These doors were slammed on the Pazzi conspirators in 1478 after they had murdered Giuliano de' Medici, and Lorenzo de' Medici escaped through them. In the lunette above is Luca's terra-cotta *Resurrection* (1444). Michelangelo's *Pietà* from the left tribune is now in the Cathedral Museum.

Crypt (Santa Reparata) 🏛 ✝
☎ 2302885 🔳 *Open Mon-Sat 10am-5pm. Closed Sun; religious holidays.*

This crypt of the earlier cathedral, entered from the left aisle, was excavated in the 1960s. It contains the foundations of Roman and Romanesque buildings, a mosaic from the Paleo-Christian church, fragments of sculptures, frescoes and tombs. Here is also the tomb slab of Brunelleschi, the only Florentine to be buried in the Cathedral.

Ascent to dome lantern
☎ *and opening hours as for Crypt* ▦ ◀€

The ascent should not be attempted by anyone who suffers from vertigo, claustrophobia or weak legs; but those who can manage the stiff climb will be rewarded by a panoramic view and an increased understanding of Brunelleschi's constructional method, which involved the erection of two shells, one inside the other, with these maintenance stairs between.

Baptistry ▥ † ★
◨ *Open 1-6pm.*

Dante's "bel S. Giovanni," the Baptistry, is the oldest building in Florence, although it is not as old as Brunelleschi and his contemporaries liked to believe. In the early 15thC it was thought to have been the Roman temple of Mars, and it was a deeper influence on Tuscan Renaissance architecture than any real Classical building. Its date is still uncertain, but historians agree that it is not earlier than the 4th-5thC AD, and that it was probably built on the site of the old Roman praetorium. The green and white marble cladding belongs to the 11th-13thC, and the rectangular tribune was added in 1202. The Baptistry was the cathedral of Florence for a century before the completion of S. Reparata.

The gilded bronze Baptistry **doors** (★) chart the progress of sculptural style from Gothic to the Renaissance. The original reliefs are now being removed, after restoration, into the Cathedral Museum and replaced here by garish reproductions.

The chronological order of the doors is: **1. South gate**, from a wax model prepared in 1330 by Andrea Pisano. The 20 highest panels relate the story of John the Baptist; the eight below depict the cardinal and theological virtues. The Renaissance door surround is by Vittorio Ghiberti. Above the doors is the *Baptist and Salome* (1571), by Vincenzo Danti. **2. North gate** (1403-24) by Lorenzo Ghiberti and assistants. These are the doors resulting from the competition set in 1401. Brunelleschi's losing entry and Ghiberti's winner can be seen in the BARGELLO. The 20 highest panels illustrate scenes from the New Testament; below are the four *Evangelists* and four *Church Doctors*. Above the doors is *The Baptist between a Pharisee and a Levite* (1506-11), by G. F. Rustici, with advice from Leonardo. **3. East gate** (1425-52) by Lorenzo Ghiberti. Michelangelo called these doors "the gates of paradise," but the clumsy reproductions that have replaced the originals, now in the Cathedral Museum, are a disgrace to Florentine craftsmanship and taste. They opened a new artistic era when sculptural perspective replaced Gothic stylization. The doors are divided into ten panels with Old Testament scenes. The antique porphyry side columns were presented to Florence by Pisa in 1117 in gratitude for help in the conquest of the Balearic Islands. Above is the *Baptism of Christ*, started by A. Sansovino in 1502 and finished by V. Danti in 1564.

The exquisite Baptistry **interior** is more apparently Classical than the exterior and incorporates Roman columns and capitals. The 13thC mosaics in the vault, the *Last Judgment*, the *Creation*, the *Story of Joseph* and the *Baptist*, have never lost their magic despite five centuries of periodic restoration. The 13thC tessellated marble **pavement** around the font, representing the Zodiac, is unmatched in Florence except by a similar example in SAN MINIATO. 14thC Pisan reliefs have been applied to the 16thC font. To the right of the tribune is the **tomb of Cardinal Baldassare Coscia** (1421-7), the schismatic Pope John XXIII, by Donatello and Michelozzo.

Ascent of Campanile

▨ ✱ *Open summer 9am-7.30pm; winter 9am-5pm. Closed Easter; Christmas.*
The Campanile (★), built 1334-59, is known as "Giotto's Tower" although Giotto was responsible only for the first story. It was carried on after his death by Andrea Pisano until 1348 and completed by Francesco Talenti. The originals of the sculptural decorations are in the Cathedral Museum. The climb up to the bell tower is relatively easy and the views are spectacular.

Cathedral Museum (Museo dell' Opera del Duomo) ★

▨ *Piazza Duomo 9* ☎*2302885. Open Mon-Sat summer 9am-7.30pm; winter 9am-6pm. Closed Sun.*
The Cathedral Museum contains an accumulation of important works brought in over the last century from the Duomo, Baptistry and Campanile. The palace has been the administrative headquarters of the Duomo since the early 15thC. Michelangelo carved the *David* in the courtyard.

GROUND FLOOR: Sculptures from the 14thC cathedral facade, 16thC drawings of the unfinished facade, and 16th and 17thC models for a cathedral facade, Brunelleschi's death mask, the wooden model for his dome made for the 1418 competition, and tools that were used for its construction.

On the mezzanine is Michelangelo's *Pietà* (★), here for the duration of the restoration of the cathedral dome. Perhaps his most tragic religious sculpture, it was made (1550-c.53) for what he planned would be his own tomb. Vasari says the head of Nicodemus is a self-portrait. Dissatisfied with his unfinished work, he broke it up and gave parts away. They were pieced together in the 18thC.

FIRST FLOOR – SALA DELLE CANTORIE: Sit down and decide which of the two **choral galleries** (★) makes your heart sing more joyously. They were removed from the cathedral in the 17thC, stored away and forgotten until the 19thC. On the entrance wall is Luca della Robbia's (1431-8) with the original panels displayed below; opposite is Donatello's (1433-9). Underneath that is Donatello's stark, expressionistically penitent *Magdalen* (★), from 1435-5

The 16 statues by Donatello and others are from the bell tower's niches. The most startlingly realistic is Donatello's *Abakuk* (1434-6), known as "Lo Zuccone" ("Big Head").

SALA DELLE FORMELLE (★): The **relief panels** were brought here from the Campanile in the 1960s. The earliest are by Andrea Pisano, and were based on designs by Giotto. The series depicts man's spiritual progress by way of labor, art and the sacraments. "Read but once these inlaid jewels," wrote Ruskin, "and your hour's study will give you strength for all your life."

SALA DELL' ALTARE: Panels from the **Baptistry doors (★)** are displayed here after restoration. The **silver altar** from the Baptistry was begun in 1366, then labored over for a century by craftsmen and artists including Verrocchio and A. del Pollaiuolo.

ENGLISH CEMETERY (Cimitero Protestante)
Piazzale Donatello. Map 2B5 🔘

In this oval cemetery lie the remains of Protestants who died in Florence in the late 19thC. Many, like Elizabeth Barrett Browning, had come here from the chilly north to convalesce. Walter Savage Landor, Frances Trollope and Jean Vieusseux are among the famous foreigners buried here.

"FIRENZE COM'ERA" (Topographical Museum of "Florence as it was")
Via dell' Oriuolo 4 ☎ *298483. Map 4C5* 🔘 *Open Mon-Wed, Fri-Sat 9am-2pm; Sun and holidays 8am-1pm. Closed Thurs.*

The urban development of Florence from the 15th-19thC is traced in the vaulted rooms of this fascinating small museum with maps, topographical prints, plans, paintings and photographs. The largest of the maps of the 15thC city in the first room is a 19thC reproduction of the 1470 "Chain Map" (Carta della Catena); the original is on display in Berlin.

In the following rooms the delightful lunettes painted by Giusto Utens for the Villa Artimino record the appearance of grand-ducal villas and gardens at the end of the 16thC; and 18thC Florence comes alive with contemporary prints, notably by Giuseppe Zocchi, of churches, palaces and villas.

FORTEZZA DA BASSO 🏛
Viale Filippo Strozzi. Map 1B3 🔘 ✳ *Open for exhibitions and conferences.*

The largest historical monument in Florence and the most signposted, the Fortezza da Basso is now a traffic island ringed by the Viale Filippo Strozzi. The fortress was built in 1534-5 for Alessandro de' Medici, the first Duke of Florence.

Supported by Charles V, Alessandro's chief purpose was to cow the people of Florence into unquestioning obedience, by the erection of a citadel, as one contemporary historian described it, "whereby the citizens lost all hope of ever living in freedom." The design is by Antonio da Sangallo the Younger; the carved stones around the entrance depict the Medici emblem.

Within are a school, a restoration center, a barracks, and, since 1978, the **Crafts Exhibition and Merchandising Pavilion**, where some 30 exhibitions are held each year.

FOUNDLING HOSPITAL (Spedale degli Innocenti)
One of the inaugural buildings of the Renaissance. (See SANTISSIMA ANNUNZIATA.)

FRA ANGELICO MUSEUM (Museo dell' Angelico)
A collection of Fra Angelico's work, housed in SAN MARCO.

HORNE MUSEUM (Museo della Fondazione Horne) 𝕀𝕀𝕀
Via de' Benci 6 ☎244661. Map 4D5 ▨ *Open Mon-Sat 9am-1pm. Closed Sun.*
The two enduring achievements of the English art historian Herbert Percy Horne (1864-1916) were his pioneering work on Botticelli, then a still undervalued artist, and the collection he installed in this palace where he lived during the last few years of his life.

The palace was built in 1489 for the Corsi family. It resembles the later Guadagni palace in SANTO SPIRITO, and is also usually attributed to Il Cronaca. The Corsi were cloth merchants, and the design of their palace answered the requirements of their trade: a large cellar for dyeing vats, a sunny gallery over the courtyard portico for drying wool. The stone capitals, carved in the workshop of Andrea Sansovino, are among the finest in Florence.

The **museum** contains no major masterpieces. Horne was not a rich man, but he collected at a time when a keen and educated eye could spot real bargains, and there are many small treasures throughout the museum. These include pictures by Daddi, Pietro Lorenzetti, Filippo Lippi, Beccafumi, Dosso Dossi, and others; Renaissance furniture and majolica; and the pre-industrial domestic utensils that were among Horne's special interests.

LAURENTIAN LIBRARY (Biblioteca Medici-Laurenziana)   Library designed by Michelangelo in SAN LORENZO, epitomizing Mannerist architecture.

MEDICI CHAPELS (Cappelle Medicee)   The Medici commissioned some superb works of art for their own glorification, in these famous chapels in SAN LORENZO.

MEDICI RICCARDI PALACE 𝕀𝕀𝕀 ★
Via Cavour ☎217601. Map 4B4 ▣ *Open Mon-Tues, Thurs-Sat 9am-1pm, 3-5pm; Sun and holidays 9am-noon. Closed Wed.*
The palace building boom in 15thC Florence was made possible by the financial and fiscal policies of Cosimo il Vecchio, and his palace, built between 1444-64, was a prototype from which Florentine palace architecture rarely departed until the 16thC. The exterior of the palace is best seen from the corner of Via Cavour.

According to one story, Brunelleschi made a model for the Medici Palace that Cosimo rejected as being too elaborate. Brunelleschi flew into a rage and either smashed the model or sold it to Luca Pitti (see PITTI PALACE). Certainly Cosimo would not have wanted to build a family house that was too ostentatious; he was, after all, the unofficial leader of a supposedly republican government.

In the event it was Michelozzo, the loyal friend who had accompanied Cosimo into exile. who built the Medici Palace, a transitional mixture of medieval and Brunelleschian elements: biforate windows as in the Palazzo Vecchio, arranged symmetrically; graduated rustication, very heavy on the ground floor, entirely smooth at the top; the first *all' antica* palace cornice in Florence, but unsupported by architrave, frieze or columns. The crenelated garden wall carries the design back, with a jerk, into the

Middle Ages. These walled side gardens were attached to most new palaces in this area, but this is one of the few to have survived.

The ground-floor windows, enclosing what was originally a loggia, were designed by Michelangelo, and are the first appearance in Florence of the so-called "kneeling windows" that became such a common feature of 16thC palaces. The proportions of the palace were radically altered when the Riccardi, who brought it in 1659, added the seven northernmost windows on the Via Cavour.

The interior, much altered over the centuries, now houses the offices of the Prefecture. Vasari described the Medici Palace as the first to be built for domestic convenience but, inevitably, some of the great symbolic events of Florentine history took place in these rooms. It was here that Lorenzo the Magnificent, when only 21, accepted control of the government, "for in Florence one lives ill in the presence of wealth without power." Emperor Charles VIII was entertained here in 1494 and Charles V of France in 1536.

Uccello's *Battle of San Romano* hung in Lorenzo's bedroom. Donatello's *David* and *Judith* were both originally placed in the courtyard. *Judith,* the tyrant-slayer, was taken away to the SIGNORIA after the Medici were expelled in 1494, and was followed there 46 years later by Cosimo I, the tyrant in person. When Cosimo I moved out of the Medici's private palace and into the Palazzo della Signoria, republican government in Florence was irrevocably finished. Gradually, the old family palace was stripped of many Medici-commissioned works of art that are today among the greatest treasures of the city's museums and galleries.

Medici Chapel (Cappella di Benozzo Gozzoli) ✫
🖼 *Open Mon-Tues, Thurs-Sat 9am-noon, 3-5pm; Sun and holidays 9am-noon. Closed Wed.*
The Medici Chapel (✫) retained its treasures. Gozzoli's *Journey of the Magi* frescoes (1459), the artist's most popular and imaginative works, were commissioned by Piero de' Medici to commemorate his membership of the religious confraternity of the *Three Magi*. Around the walls, members of the Medici family process on horseback through a fairytale Tuscan landscape reminiscent of the Fiesolan hill of Vincigliata (see FIESOLE in TUSCANY).

In the first-floor **gallery**, reached by the second staircase on the right of the courtyard, is one of the most exhilarating and ridiculous sights in all Florence. It is Luca Giordano's ceiling fresco, the *Apotheosis of the Medici* (1683), commissioned by the Marchese Riccardi as a gesture of gratitude to the Medici whose palace his family had lately bought.

MICHELANGELO MUSEUM (Casa Buonarroti) ✫
Via Ghibellina 70 ☎ 241752. Map 4C5 ▇ Open 9.30am-1.30pm; closed Tues.
Michelangelo never actually lived here. The house was built on a plot of land he bought for his nephew and was later partly decorated in Michelangelo's honor by his grand-nephew Michelangelo the Younger.

GROUND FLOOR: The drawings are reproductions; the originals are sometimes shown on special occasions. The unfinished *Venus* and *Prisoner* statues are probably not by Michelangelo.

FIRST FLOOR: In the room to the left of the stairs are the two most interesting pieces in this museum. The *Madonna della Scala* (1490-2), Michelangelo's earliest known work, is extraordinarily prophetic in style, and like so many of his later works it is unfinished. Poliziano suggested the subject for the *Battle of the Centaurs* (1492), made while Michelangelo was attached to the Medici household; the artist's preoccupation with interlocking male figures began here. In the next room to the left are architectural sketches and the **wooden model for the facade of San Lorenzo** (1517), never carried out; the plain architecture, typical of his early period, was meant to be a setting for elaborate sculpture. Running along the left of the courtyard is the gallery frescoed in homage to Michelangelo by Baroque artists. In a room to the right of the stairs is the **wooden crucifix** from S. Spirito, first attributed to Michelangelo in 1962, although not all art historians agree on this point. In the next room is a **large model of a river god**, the only full-scale model by Michelangelo in existence.

OGNISSANTI ⌂ †
Piazza d'Ognissanti. Map 3C1. Refectory open Mon, Tues, Sat 9am-noon. Offering expected.

The church of Ognissanti was founded in the late 13thC by the Umiliati, the wool-weaving order that taught Florence the skill that was to be the basis of its prosperity. The building was made over completely in 1627 by the Franciscans. A complete restoration was carried out after the 1966 flood. The facade (1637) by Matteo Nigetti is one of the earliest appearances in Florence of the Baroque style. The slender campanile, very like that of SANTA MARIA NOVELLA but simpler, is 13th-14thC.

The interior is decorated in best-boudoir 17th-18thC Baroque style. On either side of the nave are two great frescoes of saints in their studies, both dating from c.1480 and both strongly influenced by the Flemish artist Jan van Eyck. Ghirlandaio's *St Jerome* (★) concentrates on realistic detail in contrast with Botticelli's impassioned and mystical *St Augustine's Vision of St Jerome* (★). On the ceiling, *St Francis in Glory* (1770) was frescoed by Giuseppe Romei.

Over the second altar on the right are the restored remains of Dom. Ghirlandaio's fresco, the *Madonna of Mercy Sheltering the Vespucci Family* (c. 1472), which gives the only authentic portrait of Simonetta Vespucci (whose funeral was held in this church in 1476), and a probable portrait of Amerigo Vespucci as a young boy.

In the sacristy, entered from the left transept, is a large School-of-Giotto *Crucifixion*, a *Crucifixion* by Taddeo Gaddi, and a fresco of the *Resurrection* attributed to Agnolo Gaddi (its sinopia can be seen in the refectory).

The entrance to the **cenacolo** (refectory museum) is to the left of the church and through the 16thC cloister, its lunettes frescoed with scenes from the life of St Francis by 17thC artists.

At the far end of the refectory Dom. Ghirlandaio's fresco of the *Last Supper* (1480) simulates real space. The sinopia is on the left wall.

OLTRARNO
Maps 3 & 4 and WALK 3 *(with map) on page 72.*

Although Florence is well served with bridges, any one of which is crossed in a minute, Florentines persist in referring to everything s of the Arno as the Oltrarno, or as the *Arno di là* (over there), as though it were still the suburb it used to be in the Middle Ages. The Oltrarno certainly has a very distinctive character, a far richer urban mix than you will find anywhere N of the Arno, in that part of the city Florentines call the *Arno di quà* (over here).

It is a working-class neighborhood amid which some of the oldest and wealthiest Florentine families have maintained palaces for centuries. Thus, some of the most fashionable restaurants and food stores are in and around Borgo San Jacopo, but you can just as easily choose your lunch from a market stall in Piazza SANTO SPIRITO or eat with students and craftsmen in any one of many cheap family-run trattorias. You can buy chic boutique clothes or antiques, or you can have your old shoes repaired in a hole-in-the-wall workshop.

It was a place of refuge for early Christians, and even after the 14thC walls embraced the Oltrarno and it became the S. Spirito Quarter of the enlarged city, it remained a place favored by outsiders and subversives. The nobles took their last stand here in 1343; here the signal was given for the Ciompi Uprising. Luca Pitti, a leading opponent of the Medici, chose to build his palace on this, or rather "that," side of the Arno.

In the 16thC, after Cosimo I made the PITTI *the* official ducal palace, the Oltrarno became the most fashionable address in Florence. The Via Maggio, which had been laid out in the 1250s as one of the earliest straight streets in Europe, was now lined with grand-ducal palaces and was linked to the Via Tornabuoni by Bartolomeo Ammannati's beautiful bridge of SANTA TRÌNITA.

ORSANMICHELE ▥ † ★
Via dei Calzaiuoli. Map 4C4.

The name Orsanmichele refers to an oratory, San Michele in Orto, which stood here in the 8thC. Later the site was occupied by a loggiaed grain market, famous for a miraculous image of the virgin painted on one of its pillars. The grain market burned down and was replaced by a grander loggia, which was used as an oratory and as a trading center by the guilds of Florence. This loggia, which is the basis of the present structure, was erected from 1337 by Francesco Talenti, Neri di Fioraventi and Benci di Cione.

> Orsanmichele... is the complete, unravaged child of the
> Renaissance. There more than anywhere one can feel the
> continuity of the Florentine spirit, with all its seriousness,
> its humanity and its unexpected love of beauty.
> (Kenneth Clark, *The Other Half*, 1977)

From 1380 the loggia was enclosed by Simone Talenti and used exclusively for religious worship. The two upper stories were added as warehouses for emergency supplies of grain. The decoration of the

church was supervised by the nearby Guelf organization, which delegated responsibility for each of the outside niches to a guild. Happily this decorative program, which was planned from 1339, did not actually get under way until the early 15thC when Florentine sculpture, after a dullish period, leapt forward into the innovatory age of Donatello and Ghiberti.

The original statues are gradually being removed, after restoration, into museums and are replaced here by reproductions. Donatello's *St George,* made for the smiths and armorers guild, is now in the BARGELLO, and his *St Louis,* made for the Guelfs, is in the SANTA CROCE museum.

E side (Via dei Calzaiuoli): Ghiberti's still-Gothic *John the Baptist* (1414-16) — the largest work in bronze to be made by that date; Verrocchio's *Doubting Thomas* (1466-83) and above it the ceramic medallion by Luca della Robbia (1463). **s side (Via dei Lamberti):** Donatello's *St Mark* (1411-12); the *Madonna of the Rose,* attributed to Piero di Giovanni Tedesco. **w side (Via dell' Arte della Lana):** Ghiberti's *St Matthew* (1419-22) and *St Stephen* (1428); Nanni di Banco's Gothic *St Eligius.* **N side (Via Orsanmichele):** Nanni di Banco's *Four Crowned Saints;* bronze copy of Donatello's marble *St George.*

INTERIOR: The odd but satisfying shape recalls the original secular function of the church. The pillars are frescoed with damaged and restored images of patron saints of the guilds. Orcagna's **tabernacle (★),** from 1348-59, one of the most beautiful Gothic aedicules in Italy, houses the miraculous image of the *Virgin* (1347), painted by Daddi.

The upper stories of the church, the **Saloni di Orsanmichele,** are entered through the restored 14thC palace of the Arte della Lana (Wool Guild) across a connecting bridge. There are splendid views from these imposing rooms, which were restored in the 1960s.

PALATINE GALLERY   Gallery in the PITTI PALACE with an outstanding collection of 16thC Italian paintings.

PALAZZO VECCHIO   See SIGNORIA, PALAZZO DELLA.

PAZZI CHAPEL   Brunelleschi's chapel in the cloister of SANTA CROCE.

PIAZZALE MICHELANGELO
Map **2E5** ◁⋿

Piazzale Michelangelo is the traditional orientation point for a vacation in Florence. The outlook over the city embraces some of the most celebrated and photographed views in the world. The **monument to Michelangelo** (1875) in the center of the piazzale is dominated by one of the city's two reproductions of Michelangelo's *David* (the original is in the ACCADEMIA).

97

If you place yourself at the center of the balustrade facing the Arno and above the tower of SAN NICCOLÒ, you will see, looking left to right across Florence, the bell tower of the PALAZZO DELLA SIGNORIA; the top of the tower of SANTA MARIA NOVELLA; the BADIA tower and immediately to its right the cupola of the SAN LORENZO Cappella dei Principi; the white marble tower of the DUOMO; Brunelleschi's dome; and, farther right, the minaret-like tower of SANTA CROCE; the green dome of the Synagogue; and the concrete tower of Nervi's stadium complex. In the distance, left to right, are the hills and valleys of northern Tuscany: see TUSCANY A TO Z for the hills behind PISTOIA and PRATO; the tower of Petraia at SESTO FIORENTINO; the three peaks of Monte Morello; and FIESOLE, with the hill of S. Francesco and the Mugnone valley to its left and Monte Céceri, Vincigliato, and SETTIGNANO to its right.

Farther right, on a clear spring day, you can see as far as VALLOMBROSA in the E. Back to Florence and moving to the far corner of the left balustrade and facing W, looking from the Arno southward, one can see the dome of SAN FREDIANO, the tower of SANTO SPIRITO, the silhouetted BELVEDERE and, dominating the view from the S, the Victorian crenelations of the restored Torre del Gallo on the hill of ARCETRI.

A staircase to the right of the restaurant **La Loggia** (see FLORENCE RESTAURANTS A TO Z) leads to **San Salvatore al Monte**, begun in 1499 following a design by Cronaca.

PITTI PALACE ▥ ★
Piazza dei Pitti. Map 1D3.

Luca Pitti's motive for erecting a building so unusually bold for mid-15thC Florence was partly a bid to outdo his political rival Cosimo de' Medici. When work began on the Pitti in the late 1450s, the more simply conceived MEDICI PALACE was nearing completion. The design of the Pitti is traditionally, but without evidence, attributed to Brunelleschi, and it is possible that the plans carried out by Luca Fancelli could have been those Brunelleschi supposedly submitted to Cosimo, who rejected them as too ostentatious.

Although the palace as left unfinished at Pitti's death in 1472 consisted of only the seven central bays of the present structure, both Machiavelli and Vasari commented on the unique size and splendor of the Pitti. Even now that the palace has been enlarged and altered, one can imagine the original impact of these lofty proportions, dramatically clad, like an Etruscan building, in huge, rough-hewn stone blocks. Nevertheless, the Pitti Palace, only one room deep and carved into the steep slope of its own quarry, must have been an uncomfortable living space for Pitti's impoverished heirs.

In 1549 the Pittis sold their palace to Eleanor of Toledo, Cosimo I's wife, and in May of the following year the Medici entourage moved in. Five years later, Vasari's CORRIDOIO was thrown across the Arno to connect the old palace, the Palazzo Vecchio (see SIGNORIA), with the new palace that was to be the grand-ducal and eventually royal residence for the next three centuries. Ammannati's extensions, the superb **courtyard** (★) and the wings toward the Boboli Gardens, were carried out between 1558-70.

Palatine Gallery (Galleria Palatina) ★
☎210323■ (ticket also valid for Appartamenti Monumentali). Open Tues-Sat 9am-2pm; Sun 9am-1pm. Closed Mon.

Try to allow the full morning for these two most important sections of the Pitti, the Palatine and Argenti. To reach the Palatine you must climb Ammannati's long, steep staircase to the first floor. The Palatine is famous for its great grand-ducal collection of 16thC paintings of which the supreme treasures are the Raphaels and Titians, mostly portraits; also of outstanding quality are the frescoes by Pietro da Cortona. The tiered arrangement, in keeping with the period of the rooms, is that of a 17thC princely collection; the works are thus placed for decorative effect and not, as in the Uffizi, according to date and school. Thanks to the splendid lighting, the good condition of the pictures and the impeccable taste and knowledge with which they are hung, it doesn't take long to accustom oneself to the lack of didactic guidance. Indeed, after the Palatine, the Uffizi seems dismayingly like a textbook.

From the vestibule one passes through two Neoclassical rooms to the Sala di Venere, where the gallery proper begins. On the ceiling: the bold **fresco allegory** (★) by Pietro da Cortona, which was commissioned by Ferdinand II and executed in 1641-2 with the help of Ciro Ferri, begins with the *Ideal Prince Being Torn from the Arms of Venus;* the cycle continues through the next four rooms. In the center of the room is Canova's statue of *Venus,* sent to Florence by Napoleon as a replacement for the looted Uffizi *Venus de Medici.*

PAINTINGS/TITIAN: *The Concert* (★) is an early work (c.1510-13), which passed as a Giorgione for 250 years after its purchase in 1654 by Cardinal Leopold; *Portrait of Pietro Aretino* (1545) (★), a talented, roistering Venetian intellectual who thought so highly of this likeness that he presented it to Cosimo I; and *Portrait of a Lady, "La Bella"* (1536) (★), with perhaps the same model as the *Venus* in the UFFIZI. Of the two glowing landscapes by Rubens, *Peasants Returning from the Fields* (c.1637) (★) is the finer. The *Portrait of Julius II* is a contemporary copy of Raphael's original, now in the National Gallery in London.

SALA DI APOLLO: On the ceiling (1647-60): *The Young Prince Converses with Apollo,* protector of the Arts and Sciences. Paintings: Guido Reni's late masterpiece *Cleopatra; Sacred Family and Deposition* by Andrea del Sarto; Rosso Fiorentino's *Madonna Enthroned with Saints* (1522), enlarged to its present size when it was bought from the church of S. Spirito. Titian: the intensely romantic *Portrait of a Man* (c.1540) (★), called "The Englishman" because the subject was thought to be the Duke of Norfolk; and *The Magdalen* (c.1531) (★), more ripe than repentant.

SALA DI MARTE: Ceiling (1645-7): the Medici arms surmounted by the grand-ducal crown dominate the composition. Paintings: Tintoretto's finest work in the gallery, *Portrait of Luigi Cornaro;* Van Dyck's *Cardinal Bentivoglio* (c.1623), Papal Ambassador to Flanders and France; Titian's *Ippolito de' Medici* (1532), dressed as a grandee of Hungary and painted 3 years before he was poisoned at Gaeta; Rubens' *Consequences of War* (1638), an allegory of the Thirty Years' War. Mars, escaped from the arms of Venus, destroys Harmony, The Arts, and Family Life. Rubens himself explained "that grief-stricken woman in black" as "the unfortunate Europe, who, for so many years now, has suffered plunder, outrage, and misery." Also by Rubens, *The Four Philosophers,* a self-portrait with his brother and two scholars.

SALA DI GIOVE: This was formerly the grand-ducal throne room. The frescoes (1643-6) portray the eponymous god in the center and other gods in the lunettes. Paintings: Raphael's portrait of a woman, *La Velata* (c.1516) (★), whose virtuoso handling of the sleeve contrasts with the purity of outline that was to influence Ingres; Bronzino's very early *Portrait of Guidobaldo della Rovere;* Andrea del Sarto's graceful *St John the Baptist as a Boy* (1523) (★), which once belonged to Cosimo I and hung in the Uffizi Tribuna (the background has been damaged by early restoration); Fra Bartolommeo's monumental *St Mark* (1514-16), and *Deposition* (c.1516) (★), which was his last and greatest work, left partly unfinished; and Perugino's *Madonna Adoring the Christ Child,* known as the "Madonna del Sacco" after the bolster on which the child is seated.

SALA DI SATURNO: The last of Pietro da Cortona's fresco sequence (1663-5) was executed by Ciro Ferri. From c.1515, Raphael's *Madonna della Seggiola* (of the chair) (★) is now, as always, the most popular picture in the Palatine. In the 19thC, the waiting time for permission to copy her was 5 years. The legend is that the circular panel was taken from the end of a wine cask, but the more plausible explanation for the tondo is Raphael's wish to master a traditional Florentine compositional challenge. Also by Raphael are portraits of *Agnolo* (★) and of *Maddalena Doni* (c.1505-6) (★), which were painted a few years after their marriage (an occasion celebrated also by Michelangelo's *Doni Tondo* in the UFFIZI). Leonardo's *Mona Lisa* suggested Maddalena's pose. *Portrait of Tommaso Inghirami* (c.1515) (★), an important figure at the court of Leo X — Raphael reveals his character through the treatment of his hands as well as of the face; and the *Grand-ducal Madonna* (c.1504-5), so-called because the Grand Duke Ferdinand III, who bought it in 1799, took it with him wherever he traveled. The beauty of Perugino's *Deposition* (1495) (★) has been revealed by cleaning.

SALA DELL'ILIADE: Neoclassical decorations. Paintings: Justus Sustermans' *Portrait of Waldemar Christian, Prince of Denmark* (c.1662), the artist's best-known work; Andrea del Sarto's *Assumption of The Virgin* (c.1527), based on the similar, earlier composition on the opposite wall; Artemisia Gentileschi's dramatic *Judith;* Raphael's portrait of a pregnant woman, *La Gravida* (c.1504-8) (★); and Velázquez' *Philip IV on Horseback,* a studio work sent to Florence as a model for an equestrian statue. In the center of the room, *Charity* (1824) by L. Bartolini.

SALA DELL'EDUCAZIONE DI GIOVE: Paintings: Caravaggio's *Sleeping Cupid* (c.1608); and Cristofano Allori's *Judith* (★), one of the most universally admired 17thC Florentine paintings for its technical perfection and ravishing use of color.

SALA DELLA STUFA: This room was formerly a bathroom. The **frescoes** (1637-41) (★) represent the Four Ages of Man and are among Pietro da Cortona's minor masterpieces.

SALA DI BAGNO: An early 19thC bathroom.

SALA DI ULISSE: Paintings: Moroni's *Portrait of a Woman,* intensely human; Raphael's *Madonna of the Impannata* (1514), the *impannate* being the waxpaper-paned windows in the background; and Cigoli's expressive *Ecce Homo.*

SALA DI PROMETEO: Paintings: Filippo Lippi's *Madonna and Child* (c.1452), the quintessential Early Renaissance picture; Signorelli's *Holy Family;* D. Beccafumi's *Holy Family.* Off the Sala di Prometeo are four rooms decorated in the 1830s. Paintings include landscapes by C. von Poelenburg; Titian's portrait of *Tommaso Mosti* (1526); A. del Sarto's *Stories of Joseph* (1520-23); G. Schalken's *Girl with a Candle;* and fruit paintings by Rachele Ruysch.

SALA DEL POCCETTI: The room commemorates the artist whose frescoes glorifying the House of Medici decorate the ceiling. Paintings: Rubens' *Portrait of a Woman,* probably Catherine Manners, Duchess of Buckingham; D. Fetti's two genre-like parables; F. Furini's exuberant *Hylas and the Nymphs.*

VOLTERRANO WING: Pictures by 17th and 18thC artists, notably Furini, Giovanni da S. Giovanni, Cigoli, Bilivert and Salvator Rosa. First room: Volterrano's *A Trick of the Parish Priest Arlotto* (c.1650) illustrates an anecdote about Arlotto, a jokester priest who lived in the Mugello in the 1440s. Last room: the most complete collection in existence of fruit paintings by 17thC Neapolitan woman artist Giovanna Garzoni.

Argenti Museum ☆

Entrance from near left corner of courtyard ☎212557 ▧ *Open Tues-Sat 9am-2pm; Sun 9am-1pm. Closed Mon.*

Despite its name, this is not primarily a museum of silverware. The exquisite treasures bought or commissioned by the Medici and Lorraine dynasties contained here form one of the richest displays of luxury craftsmanship in the world. There is no better place to follow the changing taste of Florence's rulers, from the sublime collection of Lorenzo's antique vases to the ridiculous, ingenious opulence that appealed in later centuries. The exhilarating Baroque frescoes of the ground-floor apartments, used as reception rooms for important visitors by Ferdinand II, are rare in Florence for their sense of fun.

SALA DI GIOVANNI DI S. GIOVANNI: Frescoed by Giovanni (1634-36), Furini (1638-42) and others, for the marriage of Ferdinand II and Vittoria delle Rovere, this room is one of the final, most exuberant tributes the Medici were to pay to Lorenzo the Magnificent.

SALA BUIA: Lorenzo's collection of **antique vases (★)** is the glory of the museum. That a sensitive, discriminating poet-diplomat would have his initials carved on such objects shows the confidence of Renaissance man. **Grotticina**: Carved wooden relief by Grinling Gibbons given to Cosimo II by Charles II of England. The next rooms are frescoed with stupendous illusionist architecture by Agostino Mitelli and historical or allegorical subjects by A. M. Colonna (1638-44). The **Sale degli Avori** have Baroque ivory fantasies, some beautiful, some bizarre jokes.

FIRST FLOOR: The rooms left of the stairs contain the silver treasure of the Archbishop of Salzburg, brought to Florence in 1815 by Ferdinand III. In the following are examples of the not altogether healthy grand-ducal interest in anthropology. To the right of the stairs in the **Sala dei Cammei**: A wonderful collection of cameos, with a *pietradura* mosaic of the Piazza della Signoria (1598). **Sala dei Gioielli: Pietradura ex-voto** (1617-24) of Cosimo II, a portrait in precious stones, the ultimate in grand-ducal decadence; and a fine collection of Baroque pearls and engraved classical gems mounted on rings.

Gallery of Modern Art (Galleria d'Arte Moderna)

☎287096 ▨ Open Tues-Sat 9am-2pm; Sun 9am-1pm. Closed Mon.

In the 19thC when tourists, even more singlemindedly than today, came to Florence to study the work of artists long dead, this is what living Tuscan artists were producing: stuffy, academic paintings, orgasmic nudes and elaborate furniture. In the middle of the 19thC Italian painters reacted with their own Impressionist Movement. They are known as the Macchiaioli and their work is to be found in Rms XXIII-XXVI, which also afford rare views of the Oltrarno and the nave of SANTO SPIRITO. The gallery houses some 2,000 works in its 30 rooms.

APPARTAMENTI MONUMENTALI *(☎ 210323; open Mon-Sat 9am-2pm; Sun 9am-1pm; ticket also valid for the Palatine Gallery):* Occupying the right half of the first floor, this apartment, which includes the Savoy throne room, contains no major work of art but is notable for some very fine late Neoclassical decoration. Most elegant are the oval Queen Margherita's Dressing Room (late 18thC) and the Neoclassical Sala Bianca, where fashion shows now take place beneath superb stuccowork by G. Albertolli (1776-80).

MERIDIANA PALACE *(open Tues-Sat 9am-2pm, Sun 9am-1pm; closed Mon ▨):* Behind the right wing of the Pitti, this sub-palace was built in the late 18thC by Peter Leopold Lorraine, for the sake of a southwest prospect and direct access to the gardens. It was also the preferred residence of Victor Emmanuel. It houses a splendid **Costume Gallery**, recently enriched with a bequest by Umberto Tirelli, of stage and film costumes designed by the Florentine Piero Tosi. The remains of the **Contini-Bonacossi Collection** of Italian and Spanish paintings, much of which has now been sold abroad, are open only by appointment *(☎218341).*

PONTE VECCHIO ★

Map 3D3 ◁€

The Ponte Vecchio spans the Arno at its narrowest point and is very likely the site of the Roman bridge that carried the N-S traffic of the Via Cassia. The present structure dates from 1345, when an earlier bridge was rebuilt so solidly that it has withstood all subsequent floods. The jewelers of the Ponte Vecchio were among the first to be notified of the impending flood of 1966. Their stock was saved but their shops, and Vasari's corridor, which crosses the river above the E side of the bridge, were severely damaged. It has survived many other dangers. The oldest bridge in Florence was the only one spared in August 1944, but the retreating German army blocked access to it, mining Por S. Maria to the N and Borgo S. Jacopo to the S.

The Ponte Vecchio was the Sarajevo of medieval Italy. At its N end, where an equestrian statue of Mars then stood, Buondelmonte dei Buondelmonti was assassinated on the Easter morning of 1215, and what was a smoldering personal vendetta erupted into the Guelf-Ghibelline civil wars.

There have been shops on the Ponte Vecchio since the 13thC, occupied first by tanners, then butchers, linen merchants, greengrocers and blacksmiths. In 1593 Ferdinand I decided that these "vile arts" were inappropriate to a passage linking the two grand-ducal palaces. The shops were cleared and rented at twice the price to 41 goldsmiths and eight jewelers. The present jewelers may not be able to trace their occupancy back that far, but most have been here for many generations.

(See also SHOPPING.)

PORTA ROMANA
Map 1E2.
Porta Romana is the southernmost of the old city gates and one of the modern city's busiest exits. Erected in 1326, the tower has been cropped but the doors are original, as is the 14thC fresco of the Madonna. A stretch of preserved walls runs N along Viale Petrarca to Piazza T. Tasso. To the S is the old Siena road and the new road to Poggio Imperiale and IMPRUNETA. The Viale dei Colli Alti winds eastward from Porta Romana to Piazza F. Ferrucci, and it is now sometimes possible to walk along the city walls as far as the BELVEDERE. In the villa in Via Colombaia, Florence Nightingale was born in 1820.

RUCELLAI PALACE ▥ ★
Via della Vigna Nuova 18. Map 3C2. Only open to special group tours.
Probably the most beautiful and certainly the most carefully considered of all Florentine palaces, Alberti's Palazzo Rucellai was the first in Florence to conform to the Classical Orders.

It was built in the 1450s for Giovanni Rucellai who, after an early retirement from business, devoted himself to scholarship. Bernardo Rossellino supervised the construction of the palace, the cost of which in labor alone must have been exorbitant. Alberti's complex and subtle design is chiseled onto a flat stone surface. If you look carefully, you can see where the stone blocks meet across the drawn rustication.

Contemporary documents leave unanswered many crucial questions about the Rucellai. Even the attribution to Alberti, although generally accepted on stylistic grounds, is undocumented. But examination of the stone work during the most recent restoration confirms the theory that Alberti's plan suggested only the five bays on the left (as you face the palace); the left door would thus have been the central and only entrance. It was very likely Giovanni Rucellai himself that supervised the extension of the module to the right, until he was interrupted by a financial crisis caused by the loss at sea of two ships. Along the entablature, Fortune's Sail, the Rucellai heraldic device, alternates with the Medici Diamond Ring — a reminder of the political alliance of the two families.

The **Rucellai Loggia**, opposite the palace, was probably made for the wedding celebrations of Giovanni's son to a grand-daughter of Cosimo il Vecchio. It belongs to the 1460s, and if the design was suggested by Alberti, the execution was oddly clumsy, as you can see from the inside (the Loggia is often used for art exhibitions). This was the last of the Florentine family loggias, which became impracticable due to the rising cost of land, and therefore unfashionable. It could only have been built for a person as rich and as conservative as Giovanni Rucellai, who acquired more than half a dozen properties to create the site.

The ground floor of the palace is partly occupied by the **Alinari Museum of Photography** (☎ *213370* 🔊 *open 10am-7.30pm; closed Wed).*

Behind the palace is the **Marino Marini Museum** *(Piazza S. Pancrazio* ☎ *219432* 🔊 *open summer 10am-1pm and 4-7pm; winter 10am-6pm; closed Tues),* handsomely installed in the former church of S. Pancrazio.

The adjacent **Rucellai Chapel** (★ *Cappello del Santo Spirito, open Sat 5-7.30pm)* is entered from the Via della Spada. Alberti designed this chapel, the first barrel-vaulted building in the city, in 1467 to house Giovanni Rucellai's funerary monument, the **Aedicule of the Church of the Holy Sepulcher**. A likeness in miniature of the original antique church in Jerusalem, this aedicule is Alberti's most fascinating work, epitomizing everything he stood for as an artist. Inside the aedicule is a damaged fresco of the *Resurrection* by Baldovinetti. The wall opposite the entrance separating the chapel from the church was built in the 19thC.

SANTISSIMA ANNUNZIATA 🏛 ✝ ★
Map 2B4.

The **Via dei Servi**, which links SS. Annunziata to the Duomo, was built as a processional route between the two most important of the Florentine churches dedicated to the Virgin. It is named after the Servite Order, of which SS. Annunziata is the mother church. On the Feast of the Virgin's Nativity, the Via dei Servi is lined with candy stalls, and children carry paper lanterns from the Duomo to SS. Annunziata.

As you walk from the Duomo, notice among the 16thC palaces three on the left: the **Pucci palace** *(entrance in Via de' Pucci),* with an imposing but battered carved emblem of Leo X on the corner; the **Niccolini palace** *(#15)* built in 1550 to a design by Baccio d'Agnolo; and, on the corner of Piazza SS. Annunziata, the **Grifoni** (1557-63), one of the few brick palaces in Florence, built by Ammannati for one of Cosimo I's courtiers, now used as the regional government headquarters.

Although Piazza SS. Annunziata is architecturally the most harmonious open space in Florence, the apparently unified design was achieved over a period of nearly two centuries. The square had assumed its present size by the 14thC, but the first attempt to regularize it was Brunelleschi's loggia of the **Innocenti Hospital** (Spedale degli Innocenti) (1419-26). The central arch of the church portico was built in the mid-15thC, probably by Antonio da Sangallo the Elder. Next, chronologically, came the **loggia of the Servite Confraternity** (1516-25), by Antonio da Sangallo the Younger and Baccio d'Agnolo, deliberately mimicking the Innocenti across the square. Finally, in the early 17thC, the church portico was extended into a loggia.

The equestrian **statue of Ferdinand I** in the center of the square is Giambologna's last work, finished in 1608 by his pupil P. Tacca. It is the subject of Browning's poem *The Statue and the Bust*. Also by Tacca are the two small, fantastic, poison-green fountains (1629).

The Spedale degli Innocenti was the first foundling hospital in the world, and Brunelleschi's **loggia** (𝕀𝕀𝕀 ★) is the first building in Florence to apply Classical ideas to the Tuscan Romanesque style. The original loggia consists of the central nine bays. Ten of the ceramic tondos of swaddled babies (c.1487) are by Andrea della Robbia; the two at either end, however, are imitations.

Innocenti Gallery (Galleria dell'Instituto degli Innocenti)
Piazza SS. Annunziata 12 ☎ *243670. Map 4A5* ▨ *Open Mon, Tues, Thurs-Sat 9am-2pm; Sun and holidays 8am-1pm. Closed Wed.*
This gallery on the first floor contains works by, among others, Luca della Robbia, Piero di Cosimo and Domenico Ghirlandaio, including his *Adoration of the Magi* (1488).

The **Church** (★) of SS. Annunziata was founded in 1234 by seven aristocratic families. It became an important shrine, visited by pilgrims from all over Europe, after it was dedicated in the 14thC to a miraculous image of the Virgin Annunciate. Michelozzo, who was the brother of the Servite Prior, rebuilt the church between 1444-81.

The central door under the portico leads to Michelozzo's atrium, known as the **Chiostro dei Voti** after the life-sized wax effigies the pilgrims left of themselves. By the 17thC there were some 600 of these ex-votos in the church; all have disappeared. The **frescoes** (★) are important, but badly faded. Illumination is poor, so go in daylight or bring a flashlight. **Right portico wall:** the *Assumption* (1517) by Rosso Fiorentino; the *Visitation* (1516) by Pontormo. **Right wall, far corner:** the *Birth of the Virgin* (1514) by Andrea del Sarto. **Nave wall:** right of nave entrance, the *Arrival of the Magi* (1511) by Andrea del Sarto. **Left of nave entrance:** *The Nativity* (1460-2), which is Baldovinetti's masterpiece, badly eroded by time and damp, but still showing one of the loveliest landscapes in Tuscan art. **Left of the entrance from the portico, on the left wall:** *Miracles of S. Filippo Benizzi* (1509-10), five of Andrea del Sarto's earliest frescoes.

The extravagantly stuccoed and gilded **nave** and side chapels, decorated in the 16th-19thC when SS. Annunziata was, as indeed it still is, the fashionable church of Florence, are in striking contrast to the strict harmony of the square. Immediately to the left of the nave entrance is the **tempietto** designed by Michelozzo for Piero di Cosimo to house the

105

Miraculous Image of the Virgin, whose head is traditionally said to have been painted by an angel, but which has been repainted so often that it is now of no artistic importance. The *tempietto* bears an inscription, which will interest students of the Florentine character, that reads: "The marble alone cost 4,000 florins."

Many of the nave chapels contain splendid Baroque and Neoclassical decorations. One of the best is the first on the left, the **Feroni Chapel** (1692) by G. B. Foggini. Over the altar, in an ornate, twisting frame, is the *Vision of St Julian* (★) by Castagno (c.1455). The fresco was white-washed 100 years after the artist's death as the result of an untrue story told by Vasari that Castagno had murdered Domenico Veneziano. In the second chapel on the left is Castagno's powerful fresco (1454-5) depicting the *Trinity* (★), with St Jerome between the Madonna and St Mary Cleofe; and in the chapel to the right of the chancel, there is a marble *Pietà* by Bandinelli, who is buried here with his wife.

The **chancel**, known as the Tribune or Rotonda, was begun by Michelozzo in 1451, finished by Manetti in 1477 according to advice given by Alberti, but much altered by 18thC decorations. The chapel opposite the nave entrance was decorated by Giambologna for his own grave and those of other Flemish artists working in Florence; the frescoes are by Poccetti. In the next chapel to its left is Bronzino's *Resurrection* (c.1550).

The **Chiostro dei Morti** is entered from the left door under the facade portico. Over the door in the far right corner is one of Andrea del Sarto's most loved and famous works, the *Madonna del Sacco* (1525) (★).

SANT'APOLLONIA, CASTAGNO MUSEUM ▥ ★
Via XXVII Aprile 1 ☎ 287074. Map 2B4 ▣ Open Tues-Sat 9am-2pm; Sun 9am-1pm. Closed Mon.

Shortly after his return from Venice in 1444, Andrea del Castagno painted his *Last Supper* (★) for the nuns of S. Apollonia. The refectory of their former convent is now a museum centered round this fresco, which is probably the best known and most influential of all *Last Suppers,* apart from Leonardo's in Milan. The scene is set in a fantastic marbled niche. Christ has not yet revealed the mystery of the sacrament. The sculptured peasant faces of the disciples are calm. On this side of the table the brooding figure of Judas prepares us for the announcement, "One of you shall betray me." Vasari said Castagno looked and behaved like a Judas, and there is certainly something sinister about much of his work.

Above the *Last Supper,* and of at least the same powerful quality, are Castagno's three *Scenes from the Passion,* which have tragically deteriorated. Their sinopie, uncovered when the frescoes were detached for restoration, are displayed on the opposite wall. Castagno's *Famous Men and Women,* painted for the Villa Pandolfini at Legnaia and at one time hung in this museum, are now on view in the UFFIZI.

SANTI APOSTOLI ▥ †
Map 3D3.

Charlemagne did not found SS. Apostoli, despite the boast on the inscription on the otherwise modest facade; nevertheless, this beautiful little church in the center of medieval Florence is very old.

The portal is 16thC, probably by Benedetto da Rovezzano, but the **interior** (★), apart from the 15th-16thC side chapels, is the earliest on this side of the Arno except for the Baptistry of the DUOMO, with which it is roughly contemporary. Vasari confirms what will be obvious to anyone who knows the churches of SANTO SPIRITO and SAN LORENZO when he tells us that Brunelleschi was profoundly influenced by SS. Apostoli.

Looking at the nave and aisles from the altar end, one might almost believe that Brunelleschi designed this interior. In the right aisle, second altar, is Vasari's *Immaculate Conception* (1541), one of his best and most reproduced paintings, historically important as the most scholarly pictorial representation of a popular belief. At the top of the left aisle is a large terra-cotta tabernacle by Giovanni della Robbia, which is of better quality than many of his works. Next to it is Benedetto da Rovezzano's **tomb of Oddo Altoviti** (1507), whose palace, also by Benedetto, stands on the s side of the square.

The tiny Piazza del Limbo takes it name from the unbaptized babies who once buried here. To the left of the church is a relief of the *Madonna and Child* by Benedetto da Maiano on the flank of the Rosselli del Turco palace, the facade of which, by Baccio d'Agnolo (1517), is in Borgo SS. Apostoli.

SANTA CROCE ▥ † ★

☎ 244619. Map 2D5. Open Mon-Sat 7am-12.30pm, 3-6.30pm; Sun 3-5pm.

"Wait then for an entirely bright morning; rise with the sun, and go to Santa Croce, with a good opera-glass in your pocket."

If you are going to Santa Croce to study the numerous and instructive *trecento* frescoes, you should follow Ruskin's advice. But do leave plenty of time. Ruskin scorned the Renaissance, but no modern tourist would want to rush in and out of the Pazzi Chapel and miss some of the finest Renaissance sculptures in Florence.

Santa Croce is not a particularly cheerful quarter. Before the 1966 flood, which caused terrible damage in this low-lying area, it was densely populated with working-class families and craftsmen's workshops. Many of these people have now moved elsewhere and the craftsmen have been replaced by the so-called leather factories, which sell to tourists. But it is still a neighborhood that stretches one's sense of history. This was the center of the dyeing trade, one of the foundations of Florentine mercantile prosperity in the 14th-16thC. One of its main streets is still called Corse dei Tintori, and some of the palaces were built to accommodate the dyeing vats (see HORNE MUSEUM). The imagination is carried back much further by three streets that trace the semicircular outline of the Roman amphitheater immediately to the w of the Piazza S. Croce.

The great Franciscan preaching church was began in 1294, possibly by Arnolfo di Cambio, "with Giotto at his side and Dante looking on" — or so Ruskin liked to imagine. The Franciscans, as he says, wanted a church for "preaching, prayer, sacrifice, burial," not for "self-glorification or town-glorification." Be that as it may, consecration was delayed by a

107

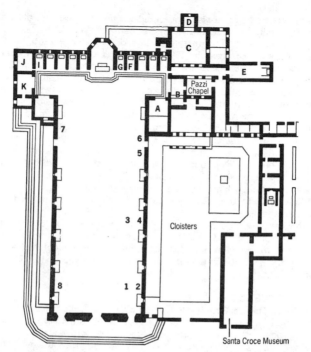

Santa Croce Museum

KEY **1** Madonna and Child (relief carving) **2** Tomb of Michelangelo **3** Pentagonal marble pulpit **4** Monument to Vittorio Alfieri **5** Donatello's Annunciation **6** Tomb of Leonardo Bruni **7** Tomb of Carlo Marsuppini **8** Monument to Galileo **A** Castellani Chapel **B** Baroncelli Chapel **C** Sacristy **D** Rinuccini Chapel **E** Novitiate Chapel **F** Peruzzi Chapel **G** Bardi Chapel **H** Chancel **I** Bardi di Vernio Chapel **J** Niccolini Chapel **K** Bardi Chapel

schism in the order. This lasted until the 15thC, when the Renaissance artists who worked here were evidently indifferent to Franciscan ideals of self-abnegation.

Because Michelangelo and Galileo, among other great Italians, are buried here, S. Croce can be regarded as a kind of pantheon of Italian genius. 19thC Romanticism found this idea irresistible and must take the blame for the hideous facade, which was paid for by an Englishman, as well as the unfortunate statue of Dante in the square, and the minaret-like Gothic bell tower.

Apart from these anachronisms, the square looks much as it did in the 16th and 17thC, when football matches and other spectacles were staged here by the grand dukes. A disc, dated February 10, 1565 on the ground floor of the frescoed Palazzo dell'Antella *(#21)* marks the center line. The palace (1619), by Giulio Parigi, was frescoed in 20 days by 12 assistants

108

of Giovanni da S. Giovanni. Less picturesque but architecturally more strenuous is the Serristori-Cocchi palace *(#1, opposite the church)* attributed to Baccio d'Agnolo.

During the period of puritanical hysteria induced by Savonarola, heretics were burned in this square, and book burnings continued until 1580. Earlier, in the prime years of the Medicean Republic, S. Croce was the setting for elaborate pageants in honor of Lorenzo the Magnificent's betrothal to Clarice Orsini and of Giuliano's love for Simonetta Vespucci.

The immense, barn-like **church interior** *(★ see plan opposite)* is T-shaped: a broad nave crossed at the bottom by a straight row of 12 chapels. The nave side chapels were added in 1560 by Vasari; the floor is paved with some 276 tombstones (14th-19thC).

The most outstanding monuments in the nave are as follows, starting with the right nave. **1.** Relief carving of the *Madonna and Child* (1478) by A. Rossellino. **2.** *Tomb of Michelangelo* (1570) by Vasari; there is a sad irony about this tomb made by the servant-artist to Cosimo I for the artist who always refused to work for the tyrannical duke. **3.** Pentagonal marble pulpit (1472-6) by B. da Maiano. **4.** *Monument to Vittorio Alfieri* (1810) by Canova. **5.** Donatello's *Annunciation* (c.1435) (★) in gilded *pietra serena;* the architectural surround was designed in collaboration with Michelozzo. **6.** *Tomb of Leonardo Bruni* (1444) by B. Rossellino, a prototype for Florentine funerary sculpture. Left nave: **7.** *Tomb of Carlo Marsuppini* (1453) by Desiderio da Settignano, directly influenced by the *Bruni* tomb. **8.** 18thC *Monument to Galileo* by Giulio Foggini.

Chapels: **A. Castellani Chapel** — frescoes of *Scenes from the Lives of Saints Anthony Abbot, Nicolas, John the Divine and John the Baptist* (c.1385) by A. Gaddi and pupils. **B. Baroncelli Chapel** — frescoed (1332-8) by T. Gaddi with *Scenes from the Life of Mary;* on the altar is the restored polyptych of *The Coronation of the Virgin,* painted in Giotto's studio, probably by T. Gaddi. **C. Sacristy** — 16thC intarsiaed and inlaid bench chest; the beautiful *Crucifixion* on the right wall is by T. Gaddi. **D. Rinuccini Chapel** — frescoes (c.1365) by Giovanni da Milano and the Master of the Rinuccini Chapel: right wall, *Scenes from the Life of Mary Magdalen;* left wall, *Scenes from the Life of the Virgin;* note also the Gothic wrought-iron gate (1373). **E. Novitiate Chapel** (1445) by Michelozzo, commissioned by Cosimo il Vecchio — on the altar, a terra-cotta tabernacle of the *Madonna and Child with Angels and Saints* (c.1480) by Andrea della Robbia or a close follower. Galileo is buried in this chapel.

The two chapels to the right of the chancel, the **Peruzzi (F.)** and the **Bardi (G.)**, were frescoed by Giotto and pupils at the height of his mature powers. An overwhelming influence on Masaccio and thus on the whole of *quattrocento* Florentine painting, they were covered with whitewash in the 18thC. Rediscovered in the 19thC, they were subjected to heavy overpainting. When these accretions were removed in this century the Bardi Chapel emerged in much better condition than the Peruzzi. Enough is left to help one solve the puzzle but not quite enough to give instant esthetic pleasure. **F. Peruzzi Chapel** (★) — frescoes (c.1326-30) on the right wall show *Scenes from the Life of St John the Divine;* on the left wall, *Scenes from the Life of St John the Baptist.* **G. Bardi Chapel** (★) — Ruskin

109

compared this chapel to "a large, beautiful, colored Etruscan vase inverted over your heads like a diving-bell." Frescoes (c.1315-20) of *Scenes from the Life of St Francis;* altarpiece on panel (c. 1250-60) by the Master of the Bardi Chapel. Above the arch outside the chapel, notice the moving *St Francis Receiving the Stigmata.*

H. Chancel — frescoes and stained glass (c.1380) of the *Legend of the True Cross* by A. Gaddi; the *Crucifix* over the altar is by the Master of the Fogg Pietà. **I. Bardi di Vernio Chapel** — frescoes (1335-8) show *Scenes from the Life of St Sylvester* by Maso di Banco; ask the sacristan to open the gates to the Niccolini and Bardi chapels. **J. Niccolini Chapel** — a remarkable anticipation of the 17thC Baroque style built in 1579-85 by Antonio Dosio. **K. Bardi Chapel** — the wooden **crucifix** by Donatello is supposed to be the one criticized by Brunelleschi for looking like a peasant on a cross. To the right of the church is the entrance to the **cloisters**, the **Pazzi Chapel** and the **Santa Croce Museum**.

Santa Croce Museum and Pazzi Chapel ★
Piazza Santa Croce 16 ☎ 244619. Map 2D5 ☒ Open summer 10am-12.30pm, 2.30-6.30pm; winter 10am-12.30pm, 3-5pm. Closed Wed.

Brunelleschi planned the Pazzi Chapel around 1430. Building began in 1443, and the upper part of the facade was completed after his death. The **interior** (★) was more successful even than the SAN LORENZO Old Sacristy, and probably sums up the modern ideal of the early Renaissance more completely than any other single monument in Florence; there is no other place that has such a calming and restorative effect on the spirits.

But it is not quite perfect. As one can see in the corners where fragmentary pilasters are awkwardly squeezed, Brunelleschi did not fully solve the structural problem he set himself here. The blue and white terra-cotta **tondos** of the *Apostles* in the chapel are by Luca della Robbia; the polychrome tondos of the *Evangelists* in the pendentives have been attributed to Brunelleschi.

MUSEUM: The most important works are in the refectory. Cimabue's *Crucifixion* (★) is one of the most tragic victims of the 1966 flood. Donatello's St Louis of Toulouse (★) was originally made in 1423 for ORSANMICHELE. The detached fresco of *The Last Supper* on the far wall is Taddeo Gaddi's best work.

On the long walls are fragments of frescoes by Orcagna, recovered from the church where they were found beneath Vasari's altars. Bronzino's *Christ in Limbo* (1552) in room 4, was painted as an altarpiece but was considered too hedonistic to place in the church.

The **second cloister** is entered from the far right-hand corner of the first cloister, past a very fine portal by Benedetto da Maiano. Finished in 1453 by a close follower of Brunelleschi, this is one of the most beautiful cloisters in Florence.

SAN FELICE ▥ †
Map 3E2.

This church, in its busy little triangular piazza a few steps from the Pitti, has an attractive Renaissance facade attributed to Michelozzo. The interior is calm, spacious and much restored; it has a large and fine crucifix, from the studio of Giotto, over the right side door.

I heard last night a little child go singing.
'Neath Casa Guidi windows, by the church,
O bella libertà, O bella!
(Elizabeth Barrett Browning, *Casa Guidi Windows*)

This may have been the first battered wives' center. In the Renaissance its Dominican nuns offered refuge to women who fled from their husbands. The Brownings lived at **Casa Guidi** *(Piazza S. Felice 8, open Mon-Fri afternoon)* for 15 years until Elizabeth's death in 1861. As she was a passionate supporter of the Risorgimento, Elizabeth's existence was marred by a loathing for her neighbor, Leopold II.

SANTA FELÌCITA 🏛 †

Map 3E3.

There has been a church on this site for nearly 2,000 years, the first being a hiding place and burial ground for early Christians. In the Renaissance the Benedictine nuns of S. Felìcita ran a successful quarry in their properties behind the church, but the building was much altered in the 16thC when it was used as a private chapel by the Medici dukes. In 1736 it was thoroughly remodeled by Ferdinand Ruggieri, who did not, however, disturb the facade portico built by Vasari in 1564 to support his aerial corridor, which passes through the church on its way from the Uffizi to the Pitti. Today the oldest monument in the square is the granite column erected in 1381.

INTERIOR: To the right of the entrance is the Brunelleschian **Capponi Chapel** decorated by Pontormo from 1525-8. The *Deposition* (★) over the altar is really a meditation on the beautiful, weightless body of the dead Christ. It is probably Pontormo's most intensely felt and emotionally affecting masterpiece — the figure in brown on the right may be a self-portrait. On the right wall is his *Annunciation*, revealed as another masterpiece by cleaning in the 1960s. In the pendentives of the cupola are four **tondos of the Evangelists** (the *St Mark* is by Bronzino). The grand-ducal tribunes are on either side of the nave W of the transepts. The charming choir (1610-20) is by Cigoli.

Around the corner from the square in Via Guicciardini is Palazzo Guicciardini *(#15)*, birthplace of the historian Francesco Guicciardini and still occupied by his descendants.

SAN FIRENZE 🏛 †

Map 4D5.

The facade of S. Firenze, which unites three separate earlier buildings, is the biggest and best 18thC Baroque spectacle in Florence. On the left is the **facade of the church of S. Filippo Neri** designed by Ferdinando Ruggieri in 1715. The central and right-hand sections (1772-75), formerly the church and convent of S. Apollinare, now the **Tribunal**, is by Zanobi del Rosso. Opposite is the elegant **Gondi palace** (1490-1501) by Giuliano da Sangallo, which has a splendid courtyard.

SAN FREDIANO
Map 1C2. Bus 13 to Piazza T. Tasso.

San Frediano is the artisans' quarter of the Oltrarno and the only neigh-borhood in central Florence that retains something of its old working-class atmosphere. The most prominent landmark is the dome of the 17thC church of **S. Frediano in Cestello**; the handsome building on the *lungarno* end of its piazza was built as a granary for Duke Cosimo III. Just to the w is the Porta S. Frediano (1324) in a well-preserved section of the last circle of communal walls built in 1284-1333.

SAN GAETANO ▥ †
Via Tornabuoni. Map 3C3. Rarely open except for services.

Undoubtedly the best Baroque church facade in Florence, built by Gherardo Silvani in 1648.

A plaque on the corner of Via de' Corsi and the Tornabuoni commem-orates the production in 1594 of the first opera, *La Dafne,* by Jacopo Peri and Jacopo Corsi, the owner of the original palace on this site.

SAN LORENZO ▥ † ★
Map 3B3.

To build their parish church, the Medici hired Brunelleschi for the first and only time. Begun in 1419 on the site of a much older church, S. Lorenzo was built, embellished and extended by some of the greatest artists and most skillful craftsmen of the 15th-17thC. Most of this work was initiated, supervised and paid for by the successive members of the Medici family who are buried here.

Seen from its busy market square, S. Lorenzo is an impressive if not harmonious complex. The taller of the two domes at the chancel end covers the Cappella dei Principi; the shallower cupola completes Miche-langelo's New Sacristy. The bell tower is 18thC and the unexciting statue of Giovanni delle Bande Nere (1540) is by Bandinelli. Michelangelo's model for a proposed facade, commissioned in 1516 but judged unac-ceptable by his Medici patrons, is on display in the MICHELANGELO MUSEUM.

The **interior** (★) is one of the most understatedly powerful in Italy, designed by Brunelleschi in 1420 but completed after his death by A. Manetti in 1460. The delay was caused by financial crises in the Medici banks, but it is evident that there were no constraints on expenditure during the final construction. Even the *pietra serena* capitals and the arches that define the space were carved by leading sculptors of the day, including Antonio Rossellino.

Highlights are as follows: **1.** The *Marriage of the Virgin* (1523), an elegant and vivid picture by Rosso Fiorentino. **2.** A fine and in its day influential **marble tabernacle** (c.1460) by Desiderio da Settignano. **3.** and **4. Bronze pulpits** by Donatello (c. 1460), his last works, finished by pupils; the **Deposition panel** and **Resurrection panel** are by Donatello's own hand. **5.** Bronzino's whirling, emotionally empty fresco of the *Martyrdom of St Lawrence* (1565-69). **6.** Martelli Chapel. *The Annunciation* (c.1440) by Filippo Lippi.

The **Old Sacristy** (Sagrestia Vecchia) (★) is entered from the left

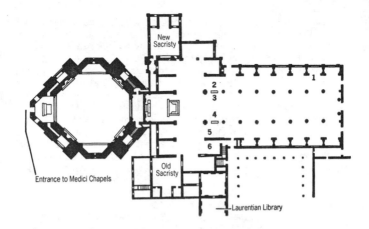

New Sacristy

1

2
3

4

5

6

Entrance to Medici Chapels

Old Sacristy

Laurentian Library

transept. Brunelleschi's early masterpiece (1422-8), the only structure he designed that was completed in his lifetime, was commissioned by Giovanni di Bicci de' Medici, founder of the Medici banking fortune. One of the first mathematically conceived architectural spaces of the Renaissance, its strict geometry, a perfect cube completed by a hemispherical umbrella dome, is emphasized by the placing of Giovanni di Bicci's tomb at the center of the sacristy, beneath a table on which the porphyry disc is exactly the same diameter as the base of the lantern above.

To the left of the entrance is Verrocchio's elegant Monument to Piero and Giovanni de' Medici. Giovanni di Bicci's son, Cosimo il Vecchio, commissioned Donatello's **sculptural decorations** some time in the 1430s (their exact date is unknown). They consist of: the four painted stucco medallions illustrating *Scenes from the Life of St John the Evangelist* (Giovanni di Bicci's patron saint) in the pendentives; the painted stucco **tondos of the four Evangelists** in the lunettes; and the **bronze doors** flanking the apse. Donatello was responsible for the architecture of the doors, as well as the wonderful bronze relief panels, which depict the Apostles, the Evangelists and Martyrs engaged in vivacious debate, using the sign language of monastic silent orders and the conventional gestures used in the pulpit. Brunelleschi disliked these doors because the "little facades" cluttered his carefully balanced space.

Cleaning in the late 1980s has revealed the expressive power of Donatello's stuccoes, which he modeled at great speed using only his hands and a few simple tools. The astrological fresco in the cupola over the altar chapel has also been cleaned. It was painted by an unknown artist in the second quarter of the 15thC. In the room to the left is a fine but unattributed lavabo bearing Piero de' Medici's motto *Semper*.

Laurentian Library (Biblioteca Medici-Laurenziana) ▥ ★
Piazza S. Lorenzo ☎*210760* ▣ ✘ *Open Mon-Sat 9am-1pm. Closed Sun.*
This library, entered via the 15thC cloister to the right of the church,

was designed by Michelangelo in 1524-34, to house the collection of Classical and humanist manuscripts founded by Cosimo il Vecchio, later removed to Rome by Leo X and finally returned to Florence by Clement VII, who commissioned the building.

VESTIBULE: An early, dramatic, sophisticated break with the rational, Classical principles of 15thC Florentine architecture, and one of the most original and unsettling rooms ever created, the vestibule was intended to amuse and challenge Michelangelo's Medici patrons. The staircase, which fills nearly the entire floor space, was left unfinished by Michelangelo and completed in the 1550s by Vasari and Ammannati.

LIBRARY: The comparatively simple rectangular space is a deliberately calming contrast to the vestibule. Michelangelo also designed the wooden ceiling and reading desks. The marble intarsia floor, designed by Tribolo, repeats the ceiling's Medici motifs of the ram's skull and the motto *Semper.* Among the codices is the Medici *Virgil.*

Medici Chapels (Cappelle Medicee) ★
☎ 213206 ■■ ✗ *Open Tues-Sat 9am-2pm; Sun and holidays 9am-1pm. Closed Mon. Entrance from Piazza di Madonna degli Aldobrandini. Extra ticket needed for the Michelangelo fresco drawings.*

On the way to the chapels, you pass through the lofty crypt that is paved with tombstones of the Medici and Lorraine grand dukes. The tomb of Cosimo il Vecchio is in a room below. Signs direct visitors to the right-hand staircase leading to the Cappella dei Principi, but it makes more sense historically to take the left staircase and start with the **New Sacristy** (Sagrestia Nuova) (★). This was Michelangelo's first realized architectural creation, begun in 1520 and left unfinished, after interruptions, in 1534. It is an answer, half respectful and half rebellious, to Brunelleschi's Old Sacristy. Imitating the Old Sacristy, it makes a totally different impression because, as Vasari tells us, Michelangelo would not conform to the ideas of "measure, order and rule" that were the essence of Brunelleschi's style.

Leo X and Clement VII, who paid for the New Sacristy, were less concerned to glorify the two Medici dukes entombed here than to strengthen the authority of these dukes' bastard heirs, and the statues of the dukes in niches over their respective tombs are, at the least, idealized portraits, if they are portraits at all. The melancholy mood of the sculptures made between 1524-1533 probably expresses Michelangelo's despair at the fall of the Florentine Republic. The catenary curve of the tomb volutes was later copied exactly by Ammannati (who did some restorative work on the New Sacristy) in the 1550s, for his bridge at SANTA TRÌNITA. Michelangelo's original design provided for a further pair of figures at the end of each tomb.

On the left, as you face the altar, is the **tomb of Lorenzo, Duke of Urbino** (grandson of Lorenzo the Magnificent); the reclining figures represent Dawn and Dusk. On the right is the **tomb of Giuliano, Duke of Nemours** (Lorenzo the Magnificent's youngest son), with allegorical figures of Day and Night.

Lorenzo the Magnificent and his brother Giuliano are buried in the simple tomb opposite the altar. To confuse matters further, the Giuliano and the Lorenzo "the Magnificent" (a common courtesy title in the 16thC), to whom Machiavelli successively dedicated *The Prince*, are the dukes whose remains lie in Michelangelo's tombs and not the more famous 15thC Medici buried here in near anonymity. On this tomb is Michelangelo's deeply moving *Madonna and Child* (1521), which is flanked by *S. Cosma* by Montorsoli, and by *S. Damiano* by Raffaele da Montelupo.

From the room to the right of the choir, a staircase leads down to a corridor, its walls covered with charcoal drawings made by Michelangelo during the siege of 1530. They include studies for the New Sacristy tomb figures.

The **Chapel of the Princes** (Cappella dei Principi) was designed by several architects including Vasari, Don Giovanni de' Medici and Buontalenti, and built by Matteo Nigetti from 1602. This portentous, claustrophobic grand-ducal shrine, clad entirely in *pietradura*, is really a monument to Ferdinand I, who ordered it. It was the most expensive of all Medici building projects and the one that posterity, until recently, was to judge as being in the worst taste. The ground plan is based on that of the Baptistry (see DUOMO). A room in the **Opificio delle Pietre dure** *(Via degli Alfani 78 ☎ 210102, temporarily closed during 1992)* is devoted to the design and construction of this chapel.

SAN MARCO, FRA ANGELICO MUSEUM (Museo dell' Angelico) ★

Piazza San Marco ☎210741. Map 2B4 ▨ Open Tues-Sat 9am-2pm; Sun and holidays 9am-1pm. Closed Mon.

The **convent and cloisters** of S. Marco were Cosimo il Vecchio's greatest gift to Florence. Cosimo acquired the convent for the Dominican friars of Fiesole. The architect Michelozzo's only work of genius was transmuted by the painter Fra Angelico into a supremely noble expression of balanced Christianity: sincere, compassionate, mystic, learned.

S. Marco witnessed one of the turning points in Florence's history. By the end of the 15thC, Florentines had been swung off-center into a hectic, puritanical religiosity incited by Savonarola, who became Prior of S. Marco in 1491. The Medici were expelled in 1494, and Jesus Christ was proclaimed King of Florence, with Savonarola acting as political leader. In 1498 the crowds who had fervently responded to his charisma turned against him. S. Marco was besieged, and Savonarola was captured, tried and burned at the stake in the Piazza della Signoria.

In 1869 the suppressed convent of S. Marco became a museum honoring Fra Angelico. Today it is a nearly complete one-man show of his *oeuvre*. Most of his greatest panel paintings have been assembled here, brought in from churches, guilds, and other galleries including the UFFIZI, which now retains only two Angelicos.

> The sources of Fra Angelico's feelings are in the Middle Ages, but he *enjoys* his feelings in a way which is almost modern; and almost modern also are his means of expression.
> (Bernard Berenson, *Italian Painters of the Renaissance*, 1930)

115

From the vestibule one enters Michelozzo's **Cloister of S. Antonino**. Most of the frescoes are 16thC, but some of the lunettes and the *Crucifixion with St Dominic* in the far left corner are by Angelico. To the right of the entrance is the **Ospizio dei Pellegrini** (★), which is the room where pilgrims were offered hospitality. It now houses 20 panel paintings by Angelico, which are well labeled as to date and provenance. The cult of Angelico as a naive painter stops here — if his spirit was still medieval, his technique was fully informed by the Early Renaissance. Some outstanding works in this room are the *Deposition* (c.1435) from S. Trìnita; the *San Marco Altarpiece* (1438-43) with the Medici patron saints Cosma and Damian; the *Virgin Enthroned* (c.1433), painted for the linen drapers guild, the Linaiuoli; and the 35 *Scenes from the Life of Christ,* completed by Baldovinetti.

Across the courtyard, in the **Sala Capitolare** (the Chapter House), is Angelico's grand, mystic vision of the *Crucifixion* (★) (c.1442). Nearby in the cloister is the bell of S. Marco, the *Piagnona,* which gave the signal for the siege of the convent that led to the imprisonment of Savonarola. In the refectory, to the left of the stairs, is Dom. Ghirlandaio's clear, descriptive *Last Supper,* a variation on the one in the OGNISSANTI refectory.

On the first floor, the 44 **dormitory cells** (★) were frescoed by Angelico and assistants from 1439-45. At the top of the stairs is Angelico's justly famous *Annunciation.* If time is short, visit at least: cell **1**. *Noli Me Tangere,* **3**. *Annunciation,* **6**. *Transfiguration,* **7**. the *Crowning with Thorns,* and **9**. the *Coronation of Mary.*

The **library**, between cells **42** and **43**, is Michelozzo's most inspired interior. This was the first public library in Europe, thanks to Cosimo il Vecchio, who donated the manuscripts. Cells **38** and **39** at the bottom of this corridor were reserved for Cosimo's retreats. Cell **11** was the prior's quarters, occupied by Savonarola, whose **portrait** by Fra Bartolommeo is in the vestibule, cell **12**.

The adjacent church of **S. Marco** (1437-52) was built by Michelozzo, but subsequently updated by Giambologna in 1585, by P.F. Silvani in 1678 and by various 18thC decorators. The uninspired facade dates from 1780. The early 18thC canvas of the *Madonna in Glory* in the center of the wooden ceiling is by G.A. Pucci. The second altarpiece on the right, the *Madonna Enthroned with Saints* (1509), is by Fra Bartolommeo; and over the third altar is an early 8thC mosaic, the *Madonna in Prayer.* On the left side of the nave are the tomb slabs of the 15thC humanists Pico della Mirandola and Poliziano.

The administrative offices of the University of Florence, the various faculties of which are scattered all over the city, are on the E side of the square *(#4),* in the building where Cosimo I kept lions and which was used in later years as the grand-ducal stables.

SANTA MARIA MADDALENA DEI PAZZI † ★
Borgo Pinti 58. Map 2C5.

Santa Maria Maddalena dei Pazzi was a Carmelite nun and member of the banking family who died in 1609 and was canonized in 1685. This church, originally built by Giuliano da Sangallo, was renamed and redesigned in her honor in 1628 by Luigi Arrigucci, who retained Giuliano's side chapels. The frescoes in the nave (1677) are by Jacopo Chiavistelli. The chancel was extended and richly decorated in the year of her canonization by P.F. Silvani, C. Ferri and P. Dandini, with two canvases by Luca Giordano. In the sacristy, off the bottom of the right aisle, is some good late Baroque stuccowork (1767).

The rest of the church complex is something of a box of surprises: frescoes by Poccetti in the Cappella del Giglio; an elegant **courtyard** (1492) by Giuliano da Sangallo, important as the first building project to carry out Alberti's instruction that arches must be supported on square pillars. But the compelling reason to visit S. Maria Maddalena dei Pazzi is in the old chapter room of the convent *(open 9am-noon, 5-7pm* 🔾*)*, where Perugino's **fresco of the Crucifixion** (1493-6) (★) covers one wall. This lovely composition, set in a severe illusionist architectural frame, echoes the peace of the landscape bathed in early morning light.

Nearby, in Borgo Pinti 68, is the large **Panciatichi Ximenes palace**, c.1499, built by Giuliano and Antonio da Sangallo as their own palace and enlarged by Gherardo Silvani in 1620. Napoleon stayed here in June 1796.

SANTA MARIA MAGGIORE 🏛 ✝

Via de' Cerretani. Map 3B3.
The interior is a pleasing mixture of 13thC Gothic as reinterpreted by an early 20thC restoration, with 17th-18thC Baroque decoration. The side altars are by Gherardo Silvani with frescoes and canvases by Giuseppe Pinzani, Pier Dandini, Volterrano, Onorio Marinari and Vincenzo Meucci.

The prize possession of the church is in the chapel left of the high altar. This 13thC polyptych of the *Madonna and Child* was attributed to Andrea di Cione by Berenson, but is now thought to be by Coppo di Marcovaldo.

SANTA MARIA NOVELLA 🏛 ✝ ★

☎ 210113. Map 3B2. Open Mon-Sat 7-11.30am, 3.30-6pm.
Next to the station and only 5 minutes from the Duomo, S.M. Novella nevertheless seems remote from the rest of Florence, as indeed it was

before the final ring of walls embraced the area and the Mugnone, which once flowed here through vineyards, was diverted N of the Fortezza da Basso. The feeling that one might almost be in a different city is emphasized by the only Florentine church facade completed in the 15thC and by the high proportion of comfortable but undistinguished 19thC buildings, which fill gaps left in the 16thC when the population of Florence

had not yet expanded as rapidly as expected. In the 19thC S.M. Novella was known as the "Mecca of Foreigners." Henry James, William Dean Howells, Emerson, Longfellow and Shelley were among the literary visitors who chose to stay just a little to one side of the inspiring but noisy city.

The church of S.M. Novella was built from 1246 by the Dominicans, successful protagonists at that time of a puritanical movement similar in its aims to the 16thC Reformation, and far stricter than the doctrine propounded by the Franciscans, whose rival preaching church was begun 48 years later at SANTA CROCE. The Dominicans had taken possession in 1221 of an old church that occupied the transept of the present building, and in 1245 the piazza was opened out to receive the crowds attracted by the Dominican preacher St Peter Martyr. The new church buildings, supervised by a succession of Dominican architects, were completed by 1360. A compromise between contemporary French and native Italian styles, S.M. Novella was the first Gothic church in Italy to break away from the imported Cistercian mold.

It was in S. Maria Novella that Boccaccio described the protagonists of the *Decameron*, talking of plague, and it was the fear and consequences of the plague of 1348 that occasioned the building of many of the chapels and cloisters. But there is no hint of these gloomy associations with dogmatism and death in Alberti's brilliant rationalization of the 14thC facade. Honoring the Gothic forms of the existing facade, and retaining the lower arcade and the round window, he raised it into a mathematically organized space containable within a perfect square. The volutes, an invention much copied by later architects, conceal the nave aisles. His **facade** (★) was begun in 1456. As one can see from the Rucellai device that sails across the center and from the inscription under the pediment, the patron was Giovanni Rucellai and the date of completion 1470. The two astronomical instruments were placed here in 1572.

The **interior** was updated in 1565-71 by Vasari, who deprived the nave of color and light by whitewashing frescoes and shortening the aisle windows to allow for his side chapels.

The **nave** appears longer than it is, thanks to a trick of perspective played by the Gothic architects, who placed the supporting pillars at diminishing intervals. There are several distinguished monuments in the nave, but the outstanding work, halfway down the left wall, is Masaccio's *Trinity* (c.1427) (★), with Mary and St John flanked by the donors, members of the Lenzi family. The central figures are set in an illusionist Holy Sepulcher, which may have been suggested by Brunelleschi, who designed the marble **pulpit** on the nearest pillar.

LEFT TRANSEPT: The **Strozzi Chapel** occupies the raised chancel of the original Romanesque church. The **altarpiece** (1354-7) shows *Christ Giving the Keys to Peter and the Book of Knowledge to St Thomas,* by Orcagna. The frescoes (c.1351-7), by Nardo di Cione, have deteriorated: left wall, *Paradise;* altar wall, the *Last Judgment,* with Dante among the blessed; right wall, the *Inferno.* In the Sacristy is the *Crucifix* from the interior facade by Giotto. The **Gondi Chapel**, with striking **decorations in marble** (c.1503), by Giuliano da Sangallo, contains Brunelle-

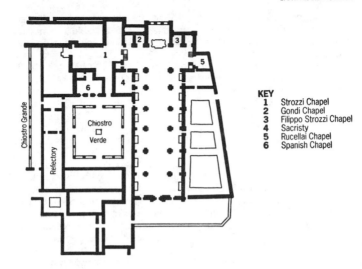

KEY
1 Strozzi Chapel
2 Gondi Chapel
3 Filippo Strozzi Chapel
4 Sacristy
5 Rucellai Chapel
6 Spanish Chapel

schi's famous *Crucifix,* his only surviving wooden sculpture, made, according to Vasari, in answer to Donatello's *Crucifix* in SANTA CROCE, which Brunelleschi judged too crudely realistic. In 1485-90 the chancel was decorated behind the high altar by Dom. Ghirlandaio with his most popular **frescoes** (★), commissioned by Giovanni Tornabuoni, Lorenzo de' Medici's uncle. Serious art historians used to dismiss this pretty narrative work as merely journalistic; Ruskin described them as not nice enough for nice people and not vulgar enough for vulgar people, and Henry James as "for the wicked, amusing world." But they are among the valuable pictorial documents we have of their period, and most modern visitors will be fascinated and charmed by them. Left wall: *Scenes from the Life of the Virgin.* Right wall: *Scenes from the Life of the Baptist.*

RIGHT TRANSEPT: The **Filippo Strozzi Chapel** is frescoed (c.1487-1502) by Filippino Lippi in a strange obsessive style steeped in Roman archeology and anticipating the Baroque: right wall, *Story of St Philip* (★) and left wall, *Story of St John the Divine* (★). Behind the altar is the **tomb of Filippo Strozzi** (1491-3) by Benedetto da Maiano. The **Rucellai Chapel** was raised in the 15thC. Duccio's Rucellai *Madonna,* now in the UFFIZI, has been replaced at the altar by Nino Pisano's marble *Madonna and Child* (after 1348). In the pavement is Ghiberti's bronze **tomb of Leonardo Dati** (1425).

Cloisters (Museo di Santa Maria Novella) ★

☎ 282187 ▧ *Open Mon-Thurs, Sat 9am-2pm; Sun 8am-1pm. Closed Fri. Entrance to left of church facade.*

The **Chiostro Verde** (c.1350) is so called because of the green tint of the **frescoes of the Old Testament**, executed in *terra verde* by Paolo Uccello and others between 1425 and c. 1450. They are tragically deteriorated. The two by Uccello are *The Creation of the Animals, Creation*

119

of Adam and Eve, and *The Original Sin* in the first bay; and the *Universal Deluge* (★) in the fourth bay, which is still recognizable as a masterpiece. The flood is depicted in the lunette, and the events following the subsiding of the waters below.

The **Spanish Chapel** (Cappellone degli Spagnoli) (★), built c.1350 as a chapter room of the convent, takes its name from Eleanor of Toledo's Spanish courtiers who used it for worship in the 16thC. The monumental didactic **fresco cycle** (1365-7) by Andrea da Firenze and assistants is a schematic depiction of the Catholic way of life, which is determined by the Life and Passion of Christ, as depicted in the vaults and on the altar wall. Ruskin called this "vaulted book the most noble piece of pictorial philosophy in Italy."

Left wall: theology, civilization and intellectual culture revealed by the Dominican saint and philosopher, Thomas Aquinas, who is surrounded by prophets, evangelists, fathers of the church and the seven virtues; the figures at the base of the fresco represent the seven theological and seven liberal arts. Right wall: Dominican teaching and the Dominican way of life as the road to redemption, with the church militant represented by an unrealized plan for the cathedral of Florence, the actual dome of which was not finished for another 80 years.

In the piazza, the large obelisks, resting on bronze tortoises, mark the limits of the chariot race established here by Cosimo I in 1563. At the far end is the graceful, post-Brunelleschian **Loggia di S. Paolo** (1489-96), with a terra-cotta lunette over the doorway by Andrea della Robbia. In the Via della Scala is a perfectly preserved 17thC pharmacy (see SHOPPING), and immediately to the NW of the piazza is the **central station** (1935), the first functionalist station building in Italy. Although admired by many, a joke made by a rival architect has stuck to the station: "I can see the box the station came in," he said, "but where is the station?"

SAN MINIATO AL MONTE 血 † ★

☎ *2342731. Map 2E5. Open winter 8am-noon, 2.30-6pm; summer 8am-noon, 2-7pm.*

The sight of S. Miniato invariably makes people smile. A small, venerable green and white jewel, it stands above the city on the highest of the hills immediately to the SE. Apart from the Baptistry (see DUOMO), it is the oldest and most loved church in Florence.

> The city unfolds in harmonious grey-brown tones, while the
> hills of Fiesole are already the colour of night. Only San Miniato
> still has a glow on its simple, lovable face.
> (Rainer Maria Rilke)

According to a medieval legend, S. Miniato, persecuted by the Emperor Decius and decapitated in the amphitheater, carried his head across the river and up the hill to this place. The commemorative church was built in the 11thC. It was here that the miraculous *Crucifix,* now in SANTA TRÌNITA, spoke to S. Giovanni Gualberto who went on to found the reforming Benedictine order of Vallombrosa. After the last expulsion of the Medici in 1527 the hill was fortified by Michelangelo and used during the siege as a key defense post against the army of Charles V (see Vasari's fresco in the PALAZZO DELLA SIGNORIA, Sala dei Cinquecento).

Thirty years later, the fortified church that had briefly been a symbol of Florentine love of freedom was occupied by the soldiers of the dictator Duke Cosimo I.

The facade dates from c.1090, except for the 13thC mosaic, which was restored in the 19thC when the Florentines loved S. Miniato perhaps a little too well; and the cop-

per eagle over the pediment, emblem of the Guild of Calimala, which administered the church, dates from 1288. The crenelated **Bishop's Palace** to the right was built in 1295 by Andrea dei Mozzi, Bishop of Florence, as a summer residence. During the 1529 siege, Baccio d'Agnolo's squat bell tower, then only just completed, was shielded by mattresses against the Spanish cannonballs. The lovely Romanesque **interior** (★) is marred only by the heavy hand of the 19thC restorer, who coated the stone column shafts with *scagliola* and brightened the polychrome ceiling. The smaller of the Corinthian capitals are Roman. The tapestry-like strip of **pavement**, inspired by Sicilian fabrics and one of the finest of its kind in Italy, is dated 1207 in the zodiac panel.

NAVE: The giant St Christopher frescoed on the right wall is by an unknown 14thC artist. At the bottom of the nave is Michelozzo's **Crucifix Chapel** (1448). The glazed terra-cotta vault is by Luca della Robbia. Off the left nave, the **Cardinal of Portugal's Chapel** (★), dating from 1461-6, is a model of collaborative Renaissance art *(ask the sacristan to open the gate)*. Commissioned by Alfonso V of Portugal to house the tomb of his nephew Cardinal James of Lusitania, who died in Florence in 1459, this exquisite chapel was built into the side of the basilica by A. Manetti. The **cardinal's tomb** on the right wall is by A. Rossellino. On the opposite wall, above the Bishop's throne, is Baldovinetti's *Annunciation,* on panel, carefully restored. The glazed terra-cotta **vault and tondos of the Holy Ghost and four Cardinal Virtues** are by Luca della Robbia. In the lunette facing the entrance are two *Angels in Flight,* frescoed by A. and P. del Pollaiuolo.

SACRISTY: This is to the right of the raised chancel. Frescoes by Spinello Aretino (1385-7) represent *Scenes from the Life of St Benedict.*

CHANCEL: The delightful marble **pulpit** (1209) is justly famous for its carving and intarsiaed fantasy animals. The 13thC mosaic in the apse was restored by Baldovinetti. Over the altar, left, is *S. Miniato* by Jacopo del Casentino.

CRYPT: The 36 columns are of various provenance. Frescoes in the vault show *Saints and Prophets* by Taddeo Gaddi.

Emerging from the church, one can wander for half an hour or so among the sweet, nostalgic 19thC and early 20thC tombs in the cemetery,

121

planned in 1839 by Niccolò Matas. The whole church complex retains examples from nearly a thousand years of funerary tradition.

SAN NICCOLÒ 🏛 ✝
Map 2D5.

The defense **tower of S. Niccolò** in Piazza Giuseppe Poggi was erected in 1324 and has been maintained at its original height by frequent restorations. The steps behind lead up to PIAZZALE MICHELANGELO. To the SW, Via Belvedere runs along the old walls and the 16thC bastion to Porta S. Giorgio and the BELVEDERE fortress. Or you could walk W along Via S. Niccolò and Via dei Bardi, two of the best-preserved (and noisiest) medieval streets in Florence, to the PONTE VECCHIO. The medieval road to SAN MINIATO from Porta S. Miniato is the way described by Dante in *Purgatorio XII.* See also WALK 4.

Opposite Porta S. Miniato is the church of **S. Niccolò Sopr' Arno**, with a 15thC interior made over in the 16thC. A modern restoration has emphasized the difference in taste between the two centuries by uncovering the 15thC frescoes but leaving the 16thC tabernacle frames. Sinopie of the restored frescoes are also displayed.

SAN SALVI ✝ ☆
Via S. Salvi 16 ☎*677570. Map 6D5* 📷 *Open Tues-Sat 9am-2pm; Sun 9am-1pm. Closed Mon.*

The work of Andrea del Sarto, Browning's "faultless painter," can sometimes seem boringly academic to modern eyes. But his masterpiece in fresco, the *Last Supper* (☆), which was commissioned in 1519 for the refectory of the S. Salvi monastery, is one of the most sumptuous visual treats in Florence. This is the perfect normative High Renaissance painting, in a near-perfect state of preservation. Its beauty saved it during the siege of Florence, when workmen, instructed to tear down any building near the city that might be used by the enemy, refused to destroy this picture.

Closed to the public after the 1966 flood, the refectory was reopened in October 1981. The monastery is now an asylum. A visit to S. Salvi could be combined with a day in SETTIGNANO and FIESOLE (see TUSCANY A TO Z). On the way from the center, notice Nervi's admirable **Stadium** (1932).

SANTO SPIRITO 🏛 ✝ ☆
Map 3E2.

When Florence was partitioned into four administrative sections in the 14thC, the city s of the Arno became the S. Spirito quarter. Piazza S. Spirito is still the heart of the OLTRARNO, and it is the square that connoisseurs of Florence often say they love most, the place where daily life seems least disturbed by tourists.

The most strikingly lovely of the palaces on the piazza is the **Guadagni** (1503-6) *(#10)*, attributed to Il Cronaca and with a fine courtyard in the manner of Giuliano da Sangallo. In the palace next door *(#9)* is an elegant staircase leading to the Pensione Bandini (see FLORENCE HOTELS).

The church of **Santo Spirito** was built on the site of an earlier

Augustinian monastery to a design by Brunelleschi. The foundation stone was laid in 1436 but the church was not completed until 1487, long after Brunelleschi's death. The delay was caused by financial difficulties, fire, and controversy over the interpretation of the master's design, which was fundamentally respected in the interior.

The modest voluted facade was applied in the 17thC. The slender bell tower (1503-17) is by Baccio d'Agnolo.

Brunelleschi's calm, rational **interior** (★) with its soaring forest of columns is spoiled only by the 17thC *baldacchino* in the chancel. The plan is a more subtle and complex variation on that of SAN LORENZO. Around the perimeter are 40 semicircular chapels. Those in the transepts and apse give the clearest impression one can find in modern Florence of how 15thC religious art looked in its original context; some of the chapels have inevitably been altered, but more than enough have been left as they were to help one imagine the paintings one sees in galleries back in their proper setting.

Don't miss: right transept, Filippino Lippi's **Nerli altarpiece** (c.1490) (★); and left transept, which is the most perfectly preserved part of the church, the **Corbinelli Chapel** (1492), with architecture and the sculptures by the young A. Sansovino. From the left nave, the door under the organ leads through a noble vaulted vestibule (1492-6), built by Cronaca to a design by Giuliano da Sangallo, into the octagonal **sacristy** (1489-92), also designed by Sangallo.

Refectory (Cenacolo di Santo Spirito)
Piazza S. Spirito 29 ☎ *287043* 🚾 *Open Tues-Sat 9am-2pm; Sun 8am-1pm. Closed Mon.*
This is the only part of the Gothic monastery to have survived the fire of 1471. The **frescoes**, badly damaged but of the greatest importance, were attributed by Ghiberti to Orcagna, an opinion not generally supported by modern scholarship.

SANTO STEFANO AL PONTE 🏛 †
Map 3D3.
The lower half of the facade and the attractive doorway are 13thC. The shoe of Buondelmonte dei Buondelmonti's horse is supposed to have been hung here after his assassination (SEE PONTE VECCHIO).

The remarkable **interior** (1649-55) by Ferdinando Tacca is unfortunately rarely open except for exhibitions. The raised chancel takes the form of an imaginary reconstruction of a Roman theater. Leading up to it is an extraordinary lasagna-like marble flight of stairs (1574) by Buontalenti, formerly in Santa Trìnita.

SANTA TRÌNITA 🏛 † ★
Map 3D2.
Piazza S. Trìnita is more a crossroads than a square. The central column, a gift from the Baths of Caracalla given by Pius IV to Cosimo I in commemoration of the victory of Montemurlo in 1537, doesn't really focus one's attention, which is pulled to the N along **Via Tornabuoni**, the fashionable shopping street and the widest in Florence, built on the

filled-in moat of the 12thC city walls and now lined with 13th-16thC palaces.

Spanning the Arno to the s is Ammannati's **Ponte S. Trìnita (★)** of 1567-70, which is the most graceful bridge in Europe. Michelangelo advised on the design, and the curve of the volutes is borrowed from his Medici tombs in SAN LORENZO. The bridge was destroyed by bombing in 1944 and rebuilt after the war exactly as it had been before. One-sixth of the original stone was retrieved from the Arno; the rest was supplied by the quarries in the Boboli Gardens, which were specially reopened. The head of the *Primavera* statue was recovered only in 1961.

On the NE corner of the square *(#1)* is the **Palazzo Bartolini Salimbeni**. The building was finished in 1521 just after Raphael's Pandolfini palace (see WALK 2 on page 70), which greatly influenced Baccio d'Agnolo's design for this, his most original palace. It was the first in central Florence to adopt the Roman tabernacle windows, and contemporary Florentines treated it as a huge joke, pinning notices on the facade saying that it looked more like a church. Baccio's reply is inscribed in Latin over the door: "It is easier to carp than to imitate." Michelangelo thought the cornice made the palace look comically like a man wearing a hat too big for his body. The palace is also known as the *Per Non Dormire* after the family motto inscribed over the windows. The courtyard is decorated with elegant *sgraffiti.*

The first church of S. Trìnita was built on this site by S. Giovanni Gualberto, founder of the Vallombrosan Order, in the late 11thC. The original Romanesque facade, depicted by Dom. Ghirlandaio in the Sassetti Chapel inside the church, was replaced by Buontalenti's uncharacteristically clumsy effort in 1594. The Gothic **interior** assumed its present appearance from c.1250 when Nicola Pisano is supposed to have begun the program of enlargement that continued through the 14thC.

RIGHT NAVE, FOURTH CHAPEL: Compare Lorenzo Monaco's pretty but heavily restored frescoes (c.1420-25) with his altarpiece panel of the *Annunciation.* The predella panels are especially fine. The gate is early 15thC.

RIGHT TRANSEPT: In the sacristy, the **tomb of Onofrio Strozzi** (1421), to the left of the altar, is an early example of Renaissance funerary sculpture. The second chapel to the right of the chancel is the **Sassetti Chapel (★)**, frescoed by Dom. Ghirlandaio (1482-6) with *Scenes from the Life of St Francis* against a Florentine background: the Piazza della Signoria, Piazza S. Trìnita, the old Ponte S. Trìnita. In the upper tier of the altar wall are portraits of, among other contemporary Florentines, Francesco Sassetti, who commissioned this chapel, Lorenzo the Magnificent, his adoring protégé Poliziano and his sons Piero, Giovanni and Giuliano. Over the altar is Ghirlandaio's *Adoration of the Shepherds* (1485), set in a Tuscan landscape. Francesco Sassetti and Nera Corsi, his wife, are portrayed on either side of the altar and are buried in the black marble **sarcophagi**, attributed to Giuliano da Sangallo, on the side walls.

LEFT TRANSEPT, SECOND CHAPEL: On the left wall, the **tomb of Bishop Benozzo Federighi (★)**, from 1455, is considered one of Luca della Robbia's masterworks for the intense humanity of the crucified

Christ in the central panel and the finely modeled face of the Bishop, a rare portrait by Luca. In the fifth chapel, the wooden statue of the *Magdalen* (c.1464), by Desiderio da Settignano and Benedetto da Maiano, invites comparison with Donatello's more tragic figure in the Cathedral Museum (see DUOMO). In the third chapel is an *Annunciation* by Neri di Bicci, with a sweet, inept Adam and Eve, borrowed from Masaccio's BRANCACCI CHAPEL.

LO SCALZO ▥ ★
Via Cavour 69 ☎ 472812. Map 2B4 ▣ Open Tues-Sat 9am-2pm; Sun 9am-1pm. Closed Mon. Ring bell for admission. Gratuity appreciated.

The Brotherhood of St John was known as *lo Scalzo* because its members went barefoot in obedience to the rule of poverty.

In 1511 Andrea del Sarto, then 25, began to decorate their cloister in *terra verde* with scenes in austere *grisaille*, from the life of John the Baptist. He worked here on and off for a period of 12 years, developing the fresco technique which can also be admired in color at SANTISSIMA ANNUNZIATA and SAN SALVI.

The earliest of the Scalzo frescoes is the *Baptism of Christ;* the last to be painted was the *Birth of St John the Baptist.* Notice also especially the *Visitation* (1524), *Charity* (1520) and *Justice* (1515).

The frescoes, badly damaged by damp, have been detached, restored, and replaced in their original positions.

SCIENCE MUSEUM (Museo di Storia della Scienza) ▥
Piazza dei Giudici 1 ☎ 293493. Map 4E4 ▦ ❋ Open Mon-Sat 9.30am-1pm; Mon, Wed, Fri 2-5pm. Closed Sun.

The medieval Castellani palace now houses the Science Museum. At one time it was the seat of the Civil Tribune or Giudici di Ruota, which gave its name to the piazza from which one enters the museum.

> I have discovered four planets, neither known nor observed by any one of the astronomers before my time, which have their orbits round a certain bright star, one of those previously known, like Venus and Mercury round the Sun, and are sometimes in front of it, sometimes behind it, though they never depart from it beyond certain limits. All which facts were discovered and observed a few days ago by the help of a telescope devised by me, through God's grace first enlightening my mind.
> (Galileo Galilei describing his discovery of the four satellites of Jupiter in *The Starry Messenger,* 1610.)

For nearly three centuries after Florence had lost its artistic supremacy the more intelligent members of the Medici and Lorraine grand-ducal families retained a passionate interest in all branches of science. In 1657 an Academy of Experiment, the Accademia del Cimento, was founded in the Pitti by Grand Duke Ferdinand II and his brother Cardinal Leopold, both pupils of Galileo. This is the historic nucleus of the museum, which is very large, carefully organized and clearly labeled. Printed guides are

125

loaned to visitors on each floor.

GROUND FLOOR: An alchemist's laboratory; early scales, music boxes, bicycles, fire extinguishers, and more.

FIRST FLOOR: Rm IV is hardly large enough for the giant **armillary sphere** made in 1593 for Ferdinand I by Antonio Santucci. The sphere demonstrates the theologically acceptable Ptolemaic theory in defiance of the sun-centered system evolved by Copernicus 50 years earlier. **Rm V:** in the case opposite the entrance is the **lens** with which Galileo discovered the four satellites of Jupiter, known as the Medici planets. Wonderfully delicate glass instruments from the Accademia del Cimento are displayed in the other two cases.

SECOND FLOOR: This floor, opened in 1975, was formerly the headquarters of the Accademia della Crusca, the scholarly body that sits in judgment on the purity of the Italian language. In **Rm II** is the **large burning lens** made for Cosimo III by Benedict Bregans of Dresden and later used by Sir Humphrey Davy and Michael Faraday to accomplish the combustion of a diamond. In **Rm IV** is the great lodestone (*Calamita*) given by Galileo to Ferdinand II. In **Rms V-VII** are anatomical wax models and 18thC surgical implements.

THIRD FLOOR: Minerals and crystals collected in the 18thC.

SIGNORIA, PIAZZA AND PALAZZO DELLA
*Piazza della Signoria. Map **4**D4.*

People who dislike Florence often object most to its main square, with its asymmetrical fortress palace, its rows of statues symbolizing conflicting ideologies, and its dull 19thC buildings. Lacking the gaiety and architectural unity of the central squares of Venice or Siena, the Piazza della Signoria will always tend to appeal more to the historical imagination than to the sense of pleasure.

The Piazza della Signoria is the political and commercial center of the city, as it has been for nearly seven centuries. The Palazzo Vecchio is still the city hall, and politicians still harangue the public from the *ringhiera*. Farmers still talk business outside the old commercial tribunal, now the agricultural center, on the corner of Via de' Gondi, and businessmen and bankers make deals over lunch at Cavallino. The only concessions to mass tourism are the postcard stalls, the high prices at the café Rivoire and the annual historic football game played here in costume.

Not long ago, the 18thC pavement of the piazza was removed to make way for extensive archeological excavations of the Roman and medieval remains below. Most of the hand-cut flagstones were, scandalously, lost or sold, and have been replaced — it is to be hoped temporarily — by ugly, machine-cut paving stones.

Savonarola was hanged and then burned here on May 23, 1498.

Palazzo della Signoria (Palazzo Vecchio) ⅲ ★
Piazza della Signoria ☎ *276465* ▧ *for State Apartments. Open Mon-Fri 9am-7pm; Sun and holidays 8am-1pm. Closed Sat.*

The foundation stone of the Palazzo della Signoria was laid in 1299. The design is traditionally attributed to Arnolfo di Cambio, but the building was not finished until at least a decade after his death. The

Signoria was the highest magistracy of the new guild-based regime established in 1293. Its members served for a period of only two months, during which they lived virtually as prisoners inside the palace. The palace, like the constitution, was designed to prevent the government from being overtaken by extremists — subversive activity in the streets of such a small city could be easily searched out from the tall watch tower, where the great bell, cast in 1322, tolled danger warnings and summoned the populace to "parliaments," or general assemblies.

The irregular shape of the palace and the off-center position of its tower were not, as is often thought, the result of Gothic whim. The trapezoidal plan derives from the reluctance of the then Guelf government to build on land previously owned by a Ghibelline family. The tower was thriftily erected on the foundations of an earlier family tower close to the church of S. Piero Scheraggio, incorporated into the UFFIZI in the 16thC. But the earliest entrance, on the N flank of the palace, was originally placed symmetrically. This side, facing Via de' Gondi, was extended in the late 15thC, when the Sala del Consiglio Maggiore was built over the customs hall.

The W side, facing the piazza, looks very much as it did in the 14thC, apart from the mezzanine windows enlarged by Michelozzo, and the absence of the 14thC *ringhiera,* or tribune, which was destroyed in the early 19thC. Almost nothing, however, remains of the original interior, which was remodeled from the mid-15thC to the late 16thC according to the needs of violently shifting styles of government, from the Medici-controlled republic to the revivals of true republicanism in 1494-1512 and 1527-30, to the hereditary duchy finally established in 1537.

A key date to remember when visiting the palace is 1540, when Cosimo I took the unprecedented step of moving his household from the ancestral MEDICI PALACE to the Palazzo della Signoria, which was converted into a ducal palace by his court architect Battista del Tasso. Ten years later, in 1550, Cosimo was persuaded by his wife Eleanor of Toledo to change the official residence to the PITTI.

> The Palazzo Vecchio — this stark, contrasting incarnation of the
> stern realities of medieval times set square amid the artistic
> glories of the past and the insignificant throng of modern
> *marchesini* — creates an impression of unparalleled grandeur
> and truth.
> (Stendhal, *Rome, Naples and Florence,* 1817)

The Signoria palace was henceforth known as the Palazzo Vecchio (the Old Palace). Vasari, who succeeded Battista as court architect in 1555, was instructed to decorate the courtyard and Sala del Consiglio in time for the wedding of Francesco de' Medici to Joanna of Austria in 1565. He labored on until his death in 1574, covering the walls of the old palace with carefully programed frescoes glorifying the achievements, ancestors, virtues and mythological counterparts of Cosimo I. Since few modern tourists share this single-minded adoration of Cosimo I, a tour of the palace can become a dispiriting experience.

Tour of the Palazzo

The two **gilded lions** and Christ's emblem were placed over the entrance in 1528, but an inscription on the same date, inspired by Savonarola's teachings, which originally read "Jesus Christ, King of Florence Elected by Popular Decree," was replaced with the present words *Rex regum et Dominus dominantium* (King of Kings and Lord of Lords) in 1851.

The **courtyard** was remodeled by Michelozzo in the middle of the 15thC. **Stuccowork** and **frescoes** of views of Austrian cities were added under Vasari for the wedding of Francesco de' Medici to Joanna of Austria in 1565. The **porphyry fountain** replaced the original well in c.1555; the original of Verrocchio's bronze **putto**, which was made in the previous century for the Medici villa at Careggi, is now located upstairs in the Cancelleria.

State Apartments (Quartieri Monumentali) ▉▉

Vasari's **staircase** (1560-3) leads to the **Salone dei Cinquecento** (1495-6), known also as the Sala del Consiglio Maggiore, originally built by Cronaca to house the enlarged representative government of the penultimate republic, but later modified and decorated under Vasari's direction. It is the largest room of its kind in existence and one of the most unpleasant, out of square and frescoed with Vasari's frantic wall paintings commemorating the Florentine victories over Pisa and Siena; the fresco program relates to Cosimo I, who is seen in glory on the ceiling.

Some of the statues, especially Vincenzo de' Rossi's *Hercules and Diomedes,* provide welcome comic relief. But the only beautiful thing in the room is Michelangelo's *Victory* (★), which was made for the tomb of Julius II some time between 1506-34 and presented to Cosimo I by the sculptor's nephew. Off this room is the windowless **Studiolo of Francesco I** (★), which is a treasure-trove of late Mannerist art, built as a retreat for Cosimo's solitary, gloomy son, who kept his most precious small possessions in the cabinets, decorated from 1569-73 by more than 30 artists according to an allegorical system dictated by Vincenzo Borghini to Vasari. Each wall represents one of the elements, Earth, Air, Fire and Water.

From the **Quartiere di Leone X** (1556-62), rebuilt and decorated by Vasari and others, a staircase leads to the Sala degli Elementi on the second floor. The Terrazza di Saturno, to the right of the stairs, commands a wonderful view to the SE and leads on to the **private apartments of Eleanor of Toledo**. The **chapel** (1540-5) (★) is frescoed by Bronzino.

At the end of the long Salotta di Eleanora, where the detached fresco of the *Expulsion of the Duke of Athens* (c.1343) shows the palace as it was in the 14thC, is the **Sala dei Gigli** (★), rebuilt between 1476-80 by Benedetto da Maiano. This is one of the few beautiful rooms in the palace and has **frescoes** (1481-5) by Dom. and Dav. Ghirlandaio. The intarsiate **doors**, with carved marble surround, and the figure of the *Baptist* (1476-81) above are by B. and G. da Maiano.

Off this room in the small **Cancelleria** is the original of Verrocchio's bronze **putto** (1476) from the courtyard fountain, and the famous 16thC

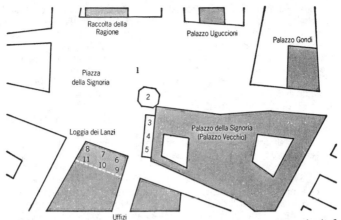

Uffizi

Portrait of Machiavelli, attributed to Santi di Tito; also the original relief carving of *St George and the Dragon* (c.1270) from the Porta S. Giorgio.

The **Sala dell'Udienza**, entered from the Sala dei Gigli through the intarsiate doors, was also rebuilt by B. da Maiano; the figure of *Justice* (1476-8) over the door is by the two Maiano. The **frescoes** (1550-60) are by Cecchino Salviati at his best. Donatello's *Judith and Holofernes* (★), probably made c.1456-60 for a fountain in the courtyard of the Medici Palace, was removed to the Piazza della Signoria after the expulsion of the Medici in 1494, when its subject acquired a new significance. It was brought inside from the piazza in 1980.

Returning through the Sala dei Gigli, the stairs lead up, past the euphemistically named **Alberghettino** where Cosimo il Vecchio and Savonarola were imprisoned, to the **tower** (★), which commands what is probably the best view of all. Down this flight of stairs is the **Mezzanine**, where pictures and sculptures left to the city in 1934 by the American Charles Loeser (**Collezione Loeser**) are displayed in three rooms. The treasures of the collection are Bronzino's *Portrait of Laura Battiferri* (★), who was Ammannati's poetess wife, and a marble *Angel* by Tino di Camaino.

Piazza

The row of statues, which runs from the northern part of the piazza in parallel with the facade of the palace, was deliberately aligned during the 16thC to point in perspective diminution toward the UFFIZI.

From N to S they are: **1.** Giambologna's equestrian statue of *Cosimo I* (1594). **2.** Ammannati's *Neptune Fountain* (1563-75), a reference to Cosimo's maritime victories — the embarrassed figure of Neptune, *Il Biancone*, the "White Giant," caused a 16thC critic to coin the rhyme, *"Ammannato, Ammannato, che bel marmo hai rovinato"* ("what beautiful marble you have ruined"). The nymphs and satyrs, which Ammannati came to regret as provocation of sinful thoughts when he fell under the influence of the Counter-Reformation, were made with the collabor-

129

ation of Giambologna and other younger artists. **3.** Copy of Donatello's *Marzocco* on an elegant 15thC base; the original is in the BARGELLO. **4.** Copy of Michelangelo's *David;* the original was moved to the ACCADEMIA in 1873. **5.** Bandinelli's infelicitous *Hercules and Cacus* (1553); Hercules was another of Cosimo's symbols. Flanking the entrance to the palace are two marble herms by Vincenzo de' Rossi and Bandinelli.

The **Loggia dei Lanzi** (★), as it has been called since the 16thC when German halberdiers *(landsknechte)* stood on guard here, was built in 1376-82 for important public ceremonies by Benci di Cione and Simone di Francesco Talenti, probably to a design by Orcagna. Michelangelo once advised that the arcaded module should be repeated all round the perimeter of the piazza, a plan that would have saved the square esthetically. The present arrangement of the statues dates from the 19thC.

At front, left to right: **6.** Cellini's *Perseus* (★), the casting of which (1545-54) is described in detail in his autobiography; the originals of the relief panels and small statues around the base are now in the BARGELLO. **7.** Two lions flanking the stairs; the one on the right-hand side is Classical, the other is a 16thC copy. **8.** Giambologna's *Rape of the Sabines* (1583).

Middle row, left to right: **9.** *Rape of Polyxena* (1866) by Pio Fedi. **10.** *Ajax (or Menelaus) Supporting the Body of Patroclus,* Roman copy of a 4thC BC Greek original. **11.** Giambologna's *Hercules Fighting the Centaur Nessus* (1599).

Against the back wall are six Roman statues of matrons or empresses. On the NE side of the square is the three-bay **Uguccioni** palace (c.1550); the design for the palace is generally thought to have been sent from Rome by Michelangelo. From the balcony a bust of Cosimo I looks out at the statue of himself mounted on horseback.

Raccolta d'Arte Moderna Alberto della Ragione
Piazza della Signoria 5 ☎ *283078* ▦ *Open Fri, Sat 9am-2pm. Closed Sun-Thurs.*
This collection of modern art, given to the city by the Genoese Alberto della Ragione, has been installed on two floors of the Casa di Risparmio, and provides a comprehensive overview of the mainstream figurative, landscape and still-life traditions in Italian painting from the 1930s to 1960s. Sculptures by Marini, Manzù and others; paintings by, among others, De Pisis, Mafai, Morandi. Of local interest are the views of and from Via S. Leonardo (see WALK 4 on page 73), which are by Ottone Rosai.

SPEDALE DEGLI INNOCENTI (Foundling hospital)   One of the inaugural
buildings of the Renaissance. (See SANTISSIMA ANNUNZIATA.)

STIBBERT (Museo Stibbert)
Via Stibbert 26 ☎ *475520. Map 6C4* ▦ 🚍 ✦ *compulsory, on the hour* ✿ *Open Mon-Wed, Fri, Sat 9am-1pm; Sun 9am-12.30pm. Closed Thurs.*
The Villa Stibbert is a house worthy of Citizen Kane. The private museum Frederick Stibbert created here in the late 19thC is not quite as large as Hearst's Californian monster mansion, but it is scarcely less amazing.

Of Italian-Scottish parentage, Stibbert was an obsessive collector of everything — from buttons to arms and armor. The **armor collection,** one of the most important in the world, is displayed on model pha-lanxes which one can imagine marching against one another through the innumerable, vast, gloomy rooms.

Nearby in the Via Bolognese is the **Villa La Pietra,** *(open to guided parties by arrangement).* It has one of the most beautiful Italian gardens in Tuscany, which was re-created by an Englishman at the turn of this century.

STROZZI PALACE ▥ ★
Map 3C3.

Of the hundred or so palaces built in 15thC Florence, the Strozzi was the largest. Filippo Strozzi acquired more than a dozen properties to create his site, and the building took 44 years to complete, from 1489 to 1536. Strozzi watched his palace being built from his small house, to the left (facing the palace from the piazza), which he built as tempor-ary accommodation.

The design of the Strozzi is based on G. da Sangallo's wooden model (see **Piccolo Museo,** below), but Cronaca, who supervised the building, made significant alterations; it was he who added the massive cornice, a reproduction of one from ancient Rome.

The palace is faced on three sides with huge blocks of *pietra forte,* supplied by four quarries including two in the BOBOLI. Apart from this sheer quantity of stone and the scrupulously Classical cornice, the exterior, which still conforms to the type of the MEDICI PALACE, was not architecturally innovatory. The fine **lamp brackets** by Niccolò Grosso on the corners, flanking the main entrance, are rare surviving examples of Renaissance ironwork.

The interior of the palace is the first of the Renaissance to be made completely symmetrical.

Piccolo Museo di Palazzo Strozzi
☎215990 ☒ *Open Mon, Wed, Fri 4-7pm.*

On the left side of Cronaca's splendid interior courtyard is the entrance to this small museum, which explains how the Strozzi was built. Here you can see the differences between G. da Sangallo's original model and the actual finished palace.

Vieusseux Library (Gabinetto Vieusseux)
Open Tues-Fri 9.15am-12.45pm, 3.15-6.45pm; Sat 9.15am-12.45pm. Closed Sun; Mon ☒

At the right of the courtyard, this lending library has always been a favorite meeting place for literary foreign residents, especially in pre-Risorgimento Florence when it was a center of liberal activity. Any member of the public can borrow for a nominal fee. About a third of the collection is in English.

The first-floor rooms of the palace are used to house temporary exhibitions.

TOPOGRAPHICAL MUSEUM   A pictorial history of the city's growth, generally known as FIRENZE COM'ERA.

UFFIZI ⅲ ★

Piazzale degli Uffizi 6 ☎*218341. Map 4D4* ▨▨ ⬛ *Open Tues-Sat 9am-7pm; Sun and holidays 9am-1pm. Closed Mon. Reserve well ahead for* ✗ *of the* CORRIDOIO*).*

The painters of 15thC Florence trained in one another's workshops and watched each other's progress with jealous eyes, each sparking off the other's genius and contributing to a chain of innovatory masterpieces which is one of the wonders of Western civilization. The largest and finest collection in the world of paintings from this period is to be found in Rms 7-15 of the Uffizi.

The building that parades in solemn double file from the Piazza della Signoria to the Arno was designed by Vasari in 1560 as a suite of offices for Cosimo I: hence the name Uffizi, which means offices, and the official mood of the handsome architecture. Buontalenti carried on the project after Vasari's death, continuing to make modifications and additions until 1586. In 1581 Francesco I had the upper loggias glazed and made into a museum, whence he could escape from state duties.

The remains of the Zecca, the Mint where the florin — a model for the value of other exchange currencies thanks to its reliable metallic quality — had been coined under the republic, were incorporated into the fabric of the building and explain the absence of colonnades at the base of the W wing where it joins the Loggia dei Lanzi. The former church of S. Piero Scheraggio was absorbed into the N end of the opposite wing; the gloomy statues in niches are 19thC.

In 1743 the Uffizi and its contents were bequeathed to the people of Florence by the Palatine Electress Anna Maria Lodovica, widow of the last Medici grand duke, Gian Gastone. The enlightened Lorraine dynasty continued to add to the extraordinary collection assembled by the Medici over the previous 300 years. In this century, the threat of vandalism, theft and damp has driven more and more masterpieces out of the churches and into this relatively soulless sanctuary.

But remember that this is not only a picture gallery. The superb Classical statues lining the stairs and corridors were regarded as the chief glories of the Uffizi until hardly more than 100 years ago (nobody looked at Botticelli with much interest until the 1880s). Shelley visited the Uffizi every day during his stay in Florence, but took notes only on the sculptures, and Gibbon toured the gallery 12 times before looking at a picture.

If you have not visited the Uffizi recently, you will notice changes. Following the removal of the State Archives from the ground floor rooms to Piazza Beccaria, the space available to the gallery has doubled. A modern system of air conditioning and lighting is gradually being installed, and the restoration of individual works of art is taking place.

The Uffizi attracts the highest attendance of any Italian gallery: more than 1½ million people a year, of whom at least half are foreigners. The lines for admission are often shorter late in the afternoon, when most of the coach parties have departed.

Beyond the ticket desk is a room containing the remains of S. Piero Scheraggio and Castagno's *frescoes* (★) of famous men and women (c.1450).

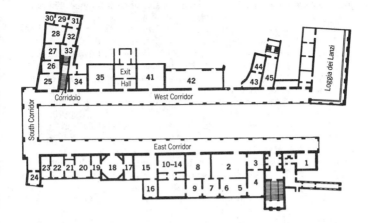

The elevator is for the picture galleries only. Opposite, at the end of the corridor, is a fresco of the *Annunciation* (1481) by Botticelli, damaged but still recognizable as one of his best works. Vasari's great staircase leads to the first floor. Exhibitions from the **prints and drawings collection** — otherwise closed to the general public — are frequently held in rooms to the left and are highly recommended. The staircase carries on to the picture galleries.

The collection is arranged chronologically through the gallery's two wings. The Florentine pictures are deliberately displayed in order to illustrate the impact made by one master upon another, from Giotto through to Michelangelo and the early Mannerists

East corridor
Usually closed, **Room 1** contains some antique carvings.

ROOM 2: Three huge **altarpieces of the Maestà (★)** offer a unique opportunity to examine the roots of Florentine and Sienese painting as they were to flower over the next 200 years. On the right, Cimabue's severe and massive image (c.1280) marks the epitome of the Byzantine Middle Ages. On the left, Duccio's composition (c.1285; beautifully restored in 1989) is similar, but notice the lighter construction of the throne, the more human relationship between Madonna and Child, and the treatment of the Madonna's hem, a virtuoso passage that anticipates the linear style of Simone Martini and Botticelli. In the center, Giotto's less cluttered altarpiece (c.1310; restored in 1991) achieves a new sense of realistic space by the use of *chiaroscuro* and the placing of the angels' heads at varying angles.

ROOM 3: In the second quarter of the *trecento*, Duccio's successors brought Sienese Gothic painting to a peak of sophistication. In Simone Martini's *Annunciation* (1333) (★) the exquisite, poetic vision and fluttering line are in marked contrast to Giotto's measured abstraction, but the psychological and spatial realism shows his influence. The saints are by Simone's brother-in-law Lippo Memmi.

Pietro Lorenzetti's altarpiece *Scenes from the Life of the Blessed Humility* (1341) is more interesting for the charming small panels than for the prosaic central figure. A. Lorenzetti's *Stories of St Nicholas of Bari* (c.1330) was painted in Florence, but the last panel, in which St Nicholas obtains miraculous supplies of grain for the starving population of Myra, is poetic and detailed in a way that Florentine painting rarely was.

ROOM 4: The painters of the Florentine *trecento* worked more successfully in fresco (see SANTA CROCE, SANTA MARIA NOVELLA) than on panel, and they are not especially well represented in the Uffizi. Here one can see the work of Bernardo Daddi, Taddeo Gaddi, Giottino and Orcagna.

ROOMS 5 AND 6: In the early *quattrocento,* nearly 100 years later than Siena and the rest of Europe, Florence produced its only great Gothic painter, Lorenzo Monaco, whose *Coronation of the Virgin* (1413) dominates the room. But his *Adoration of the Magi* (c.1420) is a far more contemplative, less elaborate picture than the visiting Gentile da Fabriano's contemporary treatment of the same subject on the far wall. Gentile's fairytale extravaganza *Adoration* (★) brings the International Gothic in this gallery to a resounding climax.

Credit for the delightful *Life of the Anchorites in the Thebaid,* now attributed to Gherardo Starnina and dated c.1400-10, has in the past been given to artists as disparate as Pietro Lorenzetti, Fra Angelico and Uccello. This is by no means the naive work it appears at first. The little figures are executed in the naturalistic manner of Giotto, and the sky, for the first time in this gallery and perhaps in the Renaissance, is blue, not gold.

ROOM 7: The earliest pictures in this important room are by artists whose full genius is better appreciated elsewhere in Florence. Masaccio and Masolino are represented here by a *Virgin and Child with St Anne* (1424). Fra Angelico's one-man show is in the Monastery of SAN MARCO, where one can compare this *Coronation of the Virgin* (1430) with a later fresco of the same subject. There are only two other pictures by Domenico Veneziano in Florence, neither currently on view (there are only 12 in the world). This *Sacra Conversazione* (1445-8) (★) is one of the supreme achievements of the Early Renaissance master of light. Its limpid colors and precisely described architecture give it the atmosphere of a perfect silence.

Domenico must have been deeply affected by the even greater genius of his pupil Piero della Francesca, whose diptych of *Federico da Montefeltro and Battista Sforza* (c.1460) (★) was painted in Urbino. The allegorical **triumphs** on the backs represent the cardinal virtues for Duke Frederico and the theological virtues for his duchess. The deep backgrounds evoke Piero's native landscape near Arezzo. Piero wrote a treatise about perspective, the new science that fascinated Paolo Uccello to the point of near insanity. This obsession is the real subject of the *Battle of San Romano* (★), painted 24 hours after the event in 1456 and hung in a room in the Medici palace. Two flanking panels were sold in the late 18thC and are now in the Louvre and the London National Gallery. The Uffizi piece is the least impressive of the three because of its inferior condition and relatively confusing composition.

ROOM 8: Filippo Lippi, a disciple of Masaccio, was much imitated in his own time. The latest and loveliest of the Uffizi Filippos is the *Madonna with Angels* (c.1465) (★), which scholars take as evidence of Botticelli's apprenticeship to the older master. For Filippo's major achievement in Tuscany, see PRATO (in TUSCANY A TO Z). Filippo's Sienese contemporary Vecchietta is represented by a *Madonna Enthroned* (1457). Notice also Baldovinetti's appealing works.

ROOM 9: The Pollaiuolo brothers, Antonio and Piero, were sculptors, engravers and goldsmiths as well as painters. Piero is usually judged to be the lesser talent, mainly on the evidence of these *Six Virtues* (1469), ordered by the Merchants' Tribunal. The seventh, *Strength,* was Botticelli's first public commission. The virtues do indeed seem crude and static when compared to Antonio's tiny but vividly dramatic panels of *The Feats of Hercules* in the case between the windows. Antonio's interest in anatomy drove him to undertake human dissections. He was, above all, one of the most gifted draftsmen of the Renaissance, an innovator in the use of line to convey muscular action. In the same case are two exhilarating scenes from the grisly *Story of Judith,* painted by the young Botticelli when he was still under the influence of Pollaiuolo.

ROOMS 10-14: The great Medici Botticellis hang in this room, converted into one large area. Botticelli was the greatest linear painter before Matisse, and the powerful melodic line and lyrical nostalgia of his art can touch the heart even of those who fail to grasp his meaning. The *Primavera* (★) (c.1480) was painted for an adolescent cousin of Lorenzo de' Medici. Until recently scholars disagreed about just what it depicts. Many now accept a revealing new gloss, which relates the subject matter to the conventions of early Renaissance Italian love poetry.

The central figure is the ideal woman; a man who sees her will be conquered and forever changed by Cupid's arrow. The picture "reads" from right to left, possibly because, like Petrarch's poetry, it conveys a memory. In comes the Wind God Zephyr. At his touch, flowers grow from the lips of Chloe, the happily married nymph, who becomes Flora, goddess of spring. On the other side of the woman are her "companion" qualities (beauty and generosity, represented by the three graces) and Mercury, god of eloquence, conciliation and reason, pointing upward to heaven.

The *Birth of Venus* (c.1485) (★) was commissioned after Botticelli's return from Rome and later hung next to the *Primavera. The Adoration of the Magi* (c.1475) (★) is one of a series of *Adorations* from the 1470s; others are in Washington and London. This one is of special interest because members of the Medici family appear among the adoring Magi. Lorenzo de' Medici is at the left foreground, Botticelli himself is in yellow on the extreme right. The *Man with a Medallion of Cosimo il Vecchio* (c.1475-80) may be another self-portrait. The *Madonna of the Magnificat* (c.1482) (★) is perhaps the loveliest of his religious paintings, and all the more so now that it has been cleaned; its elaborate curving design has been compared to a section cut through a rose. The *Calumny of Apelles* (c.1495-1500) is one of the few late Botticellis in the Uffizi. The frenzied, dazzlingly stylized execution reflects the political and moral earnestness that afflicted many sensitive Florentines at the end of the century under the influence of Savonarola.

The large *Adoration of the Shepherds* (c.1475) known as the *Portinari Altarpiece* (★) is by the Flemish master Hugo van der Goes.

It was commissioned in Bruges by a Medici bank agent, Tommaso Portinari. This marvelous feat of naturalistic painting had a profound effect on all artists who saw it after its arrival in Florence in 1488. The other Flemish work, Roger van der Weyden's *Entombment of Christ* (c.1450), was painted in Florence. Dom. Ghirlandaio, Filippino Lippi, Botticelli and Lorenzo di Credi, all influenced by the van der Goes, are represented in this section of the room. For Ghirlandaio and Filippino see SANTA MARIA NOVELLA and SANTA TRÌNITA.

ROOM 15: There is no complete or completely accepted Leonardo in the Uffizi, but no other gallery possesses such fascinating evidence of his early development. His earliest known piece of work, done when he was still in his teens working in Verrocchio's studio, is the profiled angel in the *Baptism of Christ* (begun c.1470). Vasari tells us that Verrocchio, recognizing that this angel was beyond his own very considerable capabilities, abandoned the painting. Vasari does not mention the *Annunciation* (c.1475) (★), and its attribution has been debated by opposing teams of distinguished art historians since it was brought into the gallery in 1867.

The unfinished *Adoration of the Magi* (1481) (★) is really a drawing rather than a painting, the preparatory scaffolding he left behind when Leonardo moved to Milan in 1482. To appreciate how startlingly in advance of its time this conception was one need only compare it with Lorenzo di Credi's small *Annunciation* (1485), a faultlessly graceful piece typical of its period. Piero di Cosimo's *Perseus Liberating Andromeda* (1515-20) and *Immaculate Conception* (c.1505-10) shows this idiosyncratic artist more at home with the mythological subject. Note also Signorelli's *Crucifixion with Mary Magdalen* and the Umbrian Perugino's *Pietà*.

ROOM 18: The Tribune (★) was designed in 1584 by Buontalenti as an inner temple of the arts, and was restored in 1970 to something like its original appearance. When Zoffany painted the Tribune in 1775 for Queen Charlotte of England, this windowless octagonal room was one of the high points of the Grand Tour. The best works of art in the gallery were displayed here, but nothing in Florence had such drawing power as the *Medici Venus* (★), which was a Roman copy of a Praxitelean figure of the 4thC BC, brought into this inner sanctum in the 17thC by Cosimo III, who is said to have feared that she might corrupt the morals of art students in Rome.

For nearly 200 years she remained a potent sex symbol for educated Europeans, inducing a cultural-erotic trance that men struggled to describe in prose and poetry. Engravings, drawings and reproductions of all sizes flooded across the Alps. Louis XIV had her copied in bronze. She was the only statue in Florence called to Paris by Napoleon. In the puritanical 19thC, a plaster cast in Philadelphia was kept under lock and key. Nathaniel Hawthorne found himself panting as he approached her along the Uffizi corridors. We cannot easily share such raptures today; but it is as well to be reminded of the vagaries of taste when in an art gallery.

Among the many fine 16thC portraits in the Tribune are Vasari's *Lorenzo de' Medici* and Pontormo's *Cosimo il Vecchio* (both posthumous); Bronzino's *Lucrezia* and *Bartolomeo Panciatichi;* and *Eleanor of Toledo with her Son Giovanni I.* Two famous charmers are Rosso Fiorentino's *Musical Angel* and Bronzino's *Don Giovanni de' Medici.*

ROOM 17: Entrance (from the Tribune only) is often barred. The room of the Hermaphrodite takes its name from a Hellenistic copy (2ndC BC) of an extraordinarily sensual bisexual figure.

ROOM 19: Signorelli's *Holy Family* (c.1491) anticipates Michelangelo's *Doni Tondo* in Rm 25. By Perugino are *Madonna and Child with Saints* (1493) and the fine portrait of *Francesco delle Opere* (1494), a Florentine craftsman.

ROOM 20: Dürer's *Portrait of the Artist's Father* (1490) and *Adoration of the Magi* (1504). Lucas Cranach's *Adam* and *Eve* (1528) face Dürer's *Adam* and *Eve.*

ROOM 21: Venetian paintings, notably Giovanni Bellini's hypnotic *Sacred Allegory* (c.1495) (★), the allegorical significance of which has never been satisfactorily explained. The attributions to Giorgione in this room are questionable.

ROOM 22: Holbein's almost tactlessly faithful *Portrait of Sir Richard Southwell* (1536); Altdorfer's *Martyrdom* and *Departure of St Florian* (c.1525).

ROOM 23: Two superb Mantagnas (★), the tiny *Madonna of the Rocks* and the *Adoration of the Magi* (both c.1489); and Correggio's *Rest on the Flight into Egypt.*

South corridor

Fine views and Classical sculptures.

West corridor

This section of the gallery originally housed workshops and laboratories. The 16thC conception of "art" embraced the crafts and sciences. Among the tapestries, note particularly the *Passion of Christ* series, woven in Florence, and the Flemish *Scenes from the Life of Jacob.*

ROOM 25: The *Holy Family* (1504), known as the *Doni Tondo* (★), brilliantly restored in 1985, is the only painting in Florence by Michelangelo, although there are drawings in the MICHELANGELO MUSEUM and at SAN LORENZO. It was commissioned by Angelo Doni on the occasion of his marriage to Maddalena Strozzi during the period when the artist was in Florence working on the *David.* In opposition to Leonardo, Michelangelo held that sculpture was the supreme art, and this tondo aspires to three dimensions. The Classical past, represented by a frieze of nudes in the upper half, is linked to the new Christian era by the figure of John the Baptist. With its emphasis on gesture and deliberately shocking colors, this was a key picture for the 16thC Mannerists. The inventors of Mannerism, Pontormo (see Rm 27) and Rosso Fiorentino, whose astonishing

137

Moses Defending the Daughters of Jethro (1523-4) (★) hangs next to the *Doni Tondo,* were both deeply neurotic — agoraphobic, morbid and asocial and, until 50 years ago, ignored or despised by critics. Today the gratuitous violence of Rosso's *Moses* (the text from *Exodus* says nothing about all this wrenching and pounding) and its jarring, acid colors may seem very modern. In fact it was painted for a patron known for his violent temper.

ROOM 26: For Andrea del Sarto see also PITTI, SAN SALVI and LO SCALZO. *Madonna of the Harpies* (1517) (★) is a masterpiece of his early maturity. Raphael's *Virgin of the Goldfinch* (1506) shows the influence of his first contact with Florentine artists; his penetrating, scholarly portrait of the first Medici Pope *Leo X with Cardinals Giulio de' Medici and Luigi de' Rossi* (c.1519) (★) is one of his finest late works.

ROOM 27: Pontormo began his career as one of Andrea del Sarto's many satellites, but by the time he painted the *Supper at Emmaus* (1525) he had discovered other models; in this case it was a woodcut by Dürer. His masterpieces are elsewhere in and near Florence. See SANTA FELÌCITA, and CARMIGNANO, GALLUZZO and POGGIO A CAIANO in TUSCANY A TO Z.

ROOM 28: Titian's euphemistically entitled *Venus of Urbino* (1538) (★) is not a Venus but a pin-up, one of the most intimate, alluring female nudes ever painted. Visitors to Florence have been falling in love with her since she arrived in 1631 as part of the inheritance of Vittoria delle Rovere. For Byron she was "*the* Venus," while for Mark Twain, writing in 1880, this image was "the foulest, the vilest, the obscenest picture the world possesses." Other fine Titians include *Flora* (c.1515), *A Knight of Malta* (c.1518), and portraits of *Eleanora* and *Francesco Maria della Rovere,* Duke and Duchess of Urbino (1537).

ROOM 29: Parmigianino was the leading central Italian Mannerist. The striking, intricate *Virgin of the Long Neck* (★), left unfinished at his death in 1540, is his best-known work.

ROOMS 32-34: Veronese, Moroni, Sebastiano del Piombo. Also some rare French 16thC paintings. Note the Clouet *Portrait of Francis I.*

Returning to the corridor via Rm 34, the entrance to Vasari's CORRIDOIO is on the right.

ROOM 35: The Umbrian master Federico Barocci's *Madonna of the People* (1575-9); Tintoretto's *Leda* (1570) and portrait of *Jacopo Sansovino* (1566), and *A Venetian Admiral.*

ROOM 41: Rubens and Van Dyck.

ROOM 42: The large collection of 20thC self-portraits is out of place in this fine Neoclassical room, which has housed the 4thC Roman sculptures of *Niobe and her Children* (★) since 1790.

ROOM 43: Caravaggio's *Sacrifice of Isaac* (c.1590), *Bacchus* (c.1589), and *Medusa* (after 1590). Also, Claude Lorraine's *Seascape* (1677).

ROOM 44: 17thC Dutch paintings including two self-portraits of Rembrandt as a young (1634) and old (1664) man.

ROOM 45: 18thC French, Venetian and Spanish paintings by Nattier, Chardin, G. B. Tiepolo, Canaletto, Guardi and Goya.

At the end of this corridor are the WCs, and a pleasant bar that opens onto a terrace that looks out over the Loggia dei Lanzi.

EXIT HALL (FORMERLY ROOMS 34-40): The famous *Wild Boar* is a Roman copy of a 3rdC BC Hellenistic original and was the model for Pietro Tacca's *Porcellino Fountain* in the Mercato Nuovo. The exit staircase is by Buontalenti.

ZOOLOGICAL MUSEUM (La Specola)

Via Romana 17 ☎ 222451. Map 3F2 🔲 🎨 ♣ *Zoological section open Mon, Thurs, Fri 9am-noon. Anatomical models rooms open Tues, Sat 9am-noon. Both sections open on second Sun of month 9.30am-12.30pm.*

The Torrigiani palace, which houses the Zoological Institute, is known as "La Specola" after the astrological observatory set up here in 1775 by Grand Duke Peter Leopold.

The museum, on the second floor, is divided into two sections. The Zoological Museum consists of a collection of specimens arranged in order of organic complexity from mollusks to mammals, including hunting trophies donated by Victor Emmanuel, and ending with a small selection of wax models of human and animal anatomy.

The full collection of some 600 **anatomical wax models (☆)** is displayed in the next rooms. They are among the most extraordinary objects in Florence, and remind one just how deep are the roots of the Florentine fascination with human anatomy. The Renaissance artist P. Pollaiuolo dissected corpses in order to improve his understanding of how the human body works. Here, from 1775-1814, an artist, Clemente Susini, and a physiologist, Felice Fontana, collaborated to make these tinted wax reproductions of every part of the human body. The famous *Embryonic Twins* and models of reproductive organs are in a room off Corridor 31. Next door are the macabre *Plague Victims* by the late 17thC Sicilian Gaetano Zumbo.

The zoological section will eventually be removed to a new science museum in Via Circondaria, which will hold all the major Florentine natural history collections.

The day before yesterday, as I descended upon Florence from the high ridges of the Apennine, my heart was leaping wildly within me. What utterly childish excitement! "Behold the home of Dante, of Michelangelo, of Leonardo da Vinci," I mused within my heart. "Behold then this noble city, the Queen of Medieval Europe! Here, within these walls, the civilization of mankind was born anew...."
(Stendhal, *Rome, Naples and Florence,* 1817)

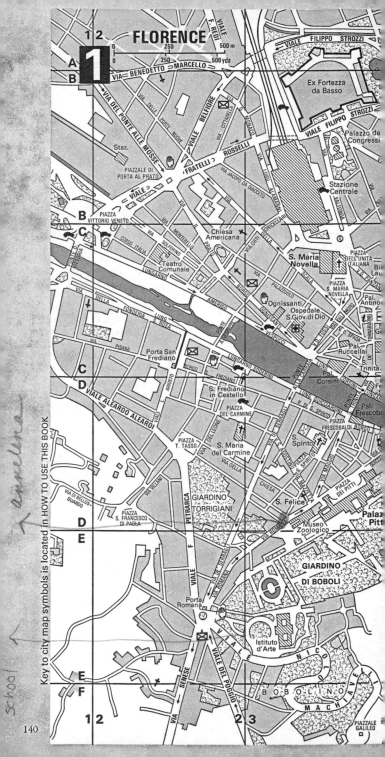

FLORENCE

A
B

1

500 m
500 yds

VIA BENEDETTO MARCELLO

VIALE F. REDI

VIALE FILIPPO STROZZI

Ex Fortezza
da Basso

VIALE FILIPPO STROZZI

Palazzo de
Congressi

VIA DEL PONTE ALLE MOSSE

VIA DELLE PORTE NUOVE

VIALE BELFIORE

VIA CITTADELLA

Staz.

PIAZZALE DI
PORTA AL PRATO

FRATELLI ROSSELLI

VIA JACOPO DA DIACCETO

Stazione
Centrale

VIALE

B

PIAZZA
VITTORIO VENETO

VIA MONTEBELLO

VIA CURTATONE

VIA DELLA SCALA

VIA DEGLI ORTI

C

PONTE DI VITTORIA

CORSO ITALIA

SOLFERINO

Chiesa
Americana

S. Maria
Novella

PIAZZA
DELL'UNITÀ
ITALIANA

Bi
Lau

Teatro
Comunale

LUNGARNO

VIA

BORGO

PALAZZUOLO

Ognissanti

PIAZZA
S. MARIA
NOVELLA

Pal.
Antino

Pal.

LUNG. FONDERIA

VIA DELLA
FONDERIA

VIA DELLA ROSA

VIA PISANA

Porta San
Frediano

BORGO

LUNGARNO SODERINI

Ospedale
S.Giov. di Dio

PONTE VESPUCCI

AMERIGO

LUNG.
CARLO

LUNGARNO

VESPUCCI

DE TORNABUONI

Pal.
Ruccellai

DE SPADA

VIA DEI FOSSI

Ga

Trinita

C

ARIOSTO

BORGO FREDIANO

S. Frediano
in Cestello

LUNG.
BUICCIARDINI

Pal.
Corsini

D

VIALE ALEARDO ALEARDI

PIAZZA
DEL CARMINE

V. DI S. SPIRITO

Pal.
Frescoba

VIA DEL LEONE

S. Maria
del Carmine

VIA DELLA
CHIESA

S. Spirito

PIAZZA
FRESCOBALDI

BORGO S.

PIAZZA
T. TASSO

PIAZZA
SANTO
SPIRITO

S. Felice

PIAZZA
DEI PITTI

VIA DI BELLOS-
GUARDO

PETRARCA

GIARDINO
TORRIGIANI

VIA ROMANA

Museo
Zoologico

Palaz
Pitti

PIAZZA
S. FRANCESCO
DI PAOLA

VIA VILLANI

D
E

VIALE

VIA DI SERRAGLIO

GIARDINO
DI BOBOLI

VIALE ALEARDO

Porta
Romana

VIA ROMANA

Istituto
d'Arte

E
F

VIALE SENESE

VIALE DEL POGGIO

B O B O L I N O

M A C H I A V E

PIAZZALE
GALILEO

Key to city map symbols is located in HOW TO USE THIS BOOK

1 2

2 3

← aurelina

← school

School

Cy

141

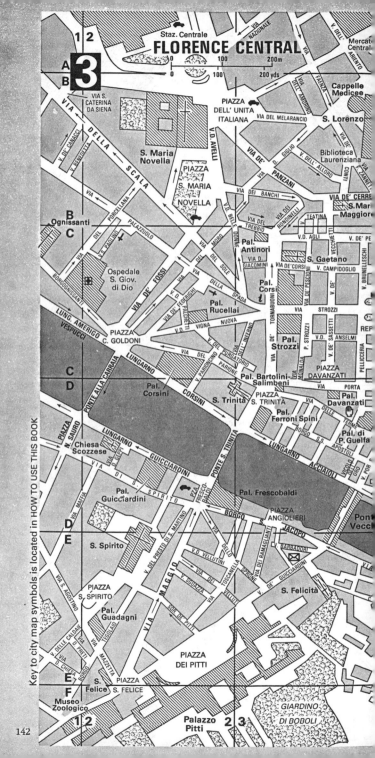

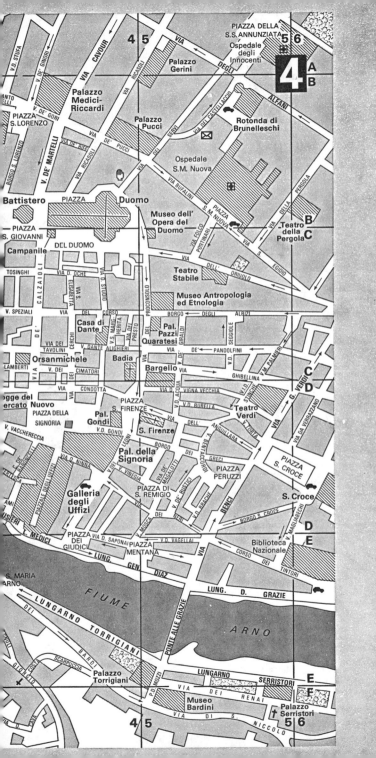

FLORENCE ENVIRONS

0 1 2 3 km
0 1 2 miles

Monte Acuto
609

Prato
Bologna

PRATO
CALENZANO

Autostrada del Sole

FIRENZE-
NORD

Autostrada Firenze-Mare

A1

SESTO FIORENTINO

Colonnata

Quinto Alto

VILLA DI
CASTELLO

Quinto
Basso

Castello

V. Reginal

B Maccione
C Fso. Reale

Via Pratese

Osmannoro

AEROPORTO
DI' PERÈTOLA

A11

Firenze Nova

Pistoia

Brozzi

Quaracchi

Perètola

Viale A. Guidoni
Novoli
Via D. Novoli

Ponte di
Mezzo

Via F. Baracca

S. Donnino

SS66

Via Pistoiese

C
D

F. ARNO

Ponte dell'
Indiano

le Cascine

V. Del Por

Ippodromo

Mantignano

Isolotto

Pza.
Vene
Ponte
D. Vittoria

Pisa,
Livorno

Autostrada del Sole

A1

Carraia

Viale Etruria

SS67

Legnaia

Monte
Uliveto

S. VITO

l'Olmo FIRENZE-SIGNA

Ponte
a Greve

S. Quirico
a Legnaia

Via Di Soffiano

Bellosguardo

Ro

Piscetto

Casellina

il Cantone

Via Di Scandicci

Soffiano

VILLA ANTINORI

SCANDICCI

le Bagnese

VILLA MONNA LISA

CASTELLO DI
MARIGNOLLE

F. Greve

Marignolle

SS2

Mosciano

A1

la Gora

Gall

CERTOSA

Giogoli

FIRENZE-
CERTOSA

Siena,
Roma

1 2   2 3

Where to stay in Florence

Making your choice

Florence is a thriving commercial city as well as a magnet for mass tourism; and although new hotels are opening all the time to meet the demand, it is still wise to reserve rooms well in advance.

RATINGS AND PRICES: Hotels are now at least as expensive as in any other busy European city. Prices and the quality of accommodations are strictly controlled, by the Regional Tourist Board, within each of five categories, and these are indicated by stars.

Symbols used in this chapter denote many categories of information, from ⌂ (quiet hotel) to ⚏ (conference facilities). The luxury hotel symbol (▥) is awarded in only a small number of cases. For a full explanation of symbols, see page 7.

Price categories given in the following listings are intended only as rough guides to average prices. There are five bands: cheap (▢), inexpensive (▤), moderate (▥), expensive (▦) and very expensive (▧). See HOW TO USE THIS BOOK on page 7 for their approximate corresponding prices. Note that other extras, such as breakfast, telephone calls, laundry and use of the frigobar can add up alarmingly.

LAST-MINUTE RESERVATIONS: If you need a hotel at the last minute, try the **Hotel Information and Booking Office** (Ufficio Informazionie Prenotazioni Alberghiere — ☎282893).

DISCOUNTED RATES: Most of the large commercial hotels offer preferential rates for groups of more than 20. Flight/hotel packages, especially off-season, are always excellent value.

BREAKFAST: Be sure to check in advance whether or not breakfast is included in the price of the room. It is always very expensive (you are paying for the service) and will rarely be as good as what is offered by the local bar. If breakfast is included and you choose not to take it, it will be deducted from the bill, but usually only on request.

HOTEL RESTAURANTS: Fewer and fewer hotels maintain their own restaurants. Those that do have improved their food, and half board, where available, can save money on restaurants.

NOISE: Despite controls on traffic in the center, Florence is a noisy city. If you are sensitive to noise, ask for a room on the garden or courtyard, or choose a hotel just outside the city (see BAGNO A RIPOLI, FIESOLE, CASTELLO, SESTO FIORENTINO and SETTIGNANO).

See also ACCOMMODATIONS on page 47, and WORDS AND PHRASES at the end of the book, for general vocabulary and sample reservation letter.

FEATURED HOTELS CLASSIFIED BY PRICE

INEXPENSIVE (▢)
Bandini Sorelle
Liana
Morandi alla Crocetta
Pendini
Rigatti
**INEXPENSIVE (▢) to
   MODERATE (▢▢)**
Balestri
Silla
Villa Azalee
MODERATE (▢▢)
Annalena
Augustus
Beacci Tornabuoni
David
Le Due Fontane
Il Guelfo Bianco
Hermitage
Jennings-Riccioli
Loggiato dei Serviti
Palazzo Ricasoli
Porta Rossa
Quisisana e Pontevecchio
Residenza
Royal
Villa Belvedere

**MODERATE (▢▢) to
   EXPENSIVE (▢▢▢)**
Continental
Lungarno
Monna Lisa
Principe
Roma
Villa Carlotta
EXPENSIVE (▢▢▢)
Baglioni
Berchielli
De la Ville
J & J
Kraft
Montebello Splendid
Plaza Lucchesi
Torre di Bellosguardo 🏨
**EXPENSIVE (▢▢▢) to VERY
   EXPENSIVE (▢▢▢▢)**
Regency 🏨
Savoy
VERY EXPENSIVE (▢▢▢▢)
Excelsior
Grand Hotel CIGA
Helvetia & Bristol 🏨
Villa Cora 🏨
Villa Medici

Florence hotels A to Z

ANNALENA
Via Romana 34, 50125 Firenze ☎ *222402*
🖷 *222403. Map 3F2* ▢▢ *20 rms, all with
bathrm* 🆎 ⓐ ⓑ 📺 ≪ 🔺 �🔺 ▢ 🔺 ♈
Location: Opposite the Boboli Gardens.
A comfortably furnished, spacious *pensione* on the first floor of a 15thC palace
and overlooking the largest private garden in Florence.

AUGUSTUS
Piazzetta dell'Oro 5, 50123 Firenze
☎ *283054* 🖷 *570110* 🖷 *268557. Map
3D3* ▢▢ *72 rms, all with bathrm* 🔺 🔺 🔺
🆎 ⓐ ⓑ 📺 🔺 ≵ & ▢ 🔺 ≪ ♈ 🔺 ⓞ
Location: Near Ponte Vecchio. A mod-

ern building sheltered by its own tiny
square in the heart of the city.

BAGLIONI
Piazza Unità Italiana 6, 50123 Firenze
☎ *218441* 🖷 *570225* 🖷 *215695. Map
3B2* ▢▢▢ *195 rms, all with bathrm* 🔺 🔺 🔺
🔺 🆎 ⓐ ⓑ 📺 ≵ & ▢ 🔺 ♨ *(on roof)*
🔺 ♈
Location: Opposite Central station. An
enormous, efficient, well-staffed hotel,
ideal for business people.

BALESTRI
Piazza Mentana 7, 50122 Firenze
☎ *214743* 🖷 *2398042. Map 4E4* ▢▢ *to*

147

▥ 50 rms, all with bathrm ▦ ▬ ▣ 📧
⊡ ⊡ ▥ ♨ ⌂ ⌂ ✻ ⟨⟨ ❄ ♨

Location: On the Arno, 5 minutes E of Ponte Vecchio. A decent and very central 19thC hotel that has been run by four successive generations of the same family since it opened in 1888. It has been modernized but retains a comfortable if not particularly stylish atmosphere.

BANDINI SORELLE ❀

Piazza Santo Spirito 9, 50125 Firenze
☎215308. Map *1D3* ▥ 13 rms, 5 with bathrm ⥥ ▣ 📧 ⌂ ♨ ৬ ▥ ♈

Location: In the heart of the Oltrarno. This unpretentious and extremely reasonable old *pensione* is a rare survival in Florence and it is usually booked up months ahead. The beds and bathrooms seem a bit like school, but the furniture and management are charming.

BEACCI TORNABUONI

Via Tornabuoni 3, 50123 Firenze
☎268377 ☒283594. Map *3C3* ▥ 30 rms, all with bathrm ▦ ▬ ▣ ⥥ 📧 ⊡
⊡ ▥ ⌂ ♨ ৬ ▢ ▣ ♨ ⟨⟨ ❄

Location: N end of Via Tornabuoni. Alinari prints, faded chintzes, and rubber plants in big pots give a dignified old-fashioned feel to this well-known *pensione* on the top three floors of the 14thC Palazzo Minerbetti. Regulars include writers, fashion buyers, actors and ministers of state, mostly from English-speaking countries, who are grateful for the homey but unintrusive atmosphere and comfortable rooms (the good reading lights are an unaccustomed luxury in Florence). There is a roof terrace for taking breakfast and drinks. Meals can also be served in your room.

BERCHIELLI

Lungarno Acciaioli 14, 50123 Firenze
☎264061 ☒575582 ☒218636. Map *3D3* ▥ 74rms, all with bathrm ▦ ▣ 📧
⊡ ⊡ ▥ ৬ ⌂ ♨ ▢ ▣ ⟨⟨ ❄ ♨

Location: On the Arno, near the Ponte Vecchio. A handsome old hotel that was modernized in the early 1980s.

CONTINENTAL

Lungarno Acciaioli 2, 50123 Firenze
☎282392 ☒580525 ☒283139. Map *3D3* ▥ to ▥ 48 rms, all with bathrm ▦
▣ 📧 ⊡ ⊡ ▥ ⌂ ♨ ♨ ▢ ▣ ✿ *(on roof)* ⟨⟨ ❄

Location: Near Ponte Vecchio. An efficient hotel in a modern building incorporating the 13thC Torre Guelfa dei Consorti. Bedrooms were enlarged, modernized and sound-proofed during 1992.

DAVID ❀

Viale Michelangelo 1, 50125 Firenze
☎681695 ☒574553 ☒680602 ▥ 26 rms, all with bathrm ▦ ▬ 📧 ⊡ ⊡ ▥
♨ ▢ ▣ ✻ ⟨⟨ ❄ ♈

Location: Near the Firenze-Sud autostrada junction. A pleasant private hotel in a shady garden; nicely decorated in an unfussy country style. Some rooms are noisy.

DE LA VILLE

Piazza Antinori 1, 50123 Firenze
☎2381805 ☒570518 ☒2381809. Map *3C3* ▥ 75 rms, all with bathrm ▦ ▬ ▣
📧 ⊡ ⊡ ▥ ⌂ ♨ ৬ ▢ ⤢ ▣ ⟨⟨ ❄ ♈

Location: N end of Via Tornabuoni. A modern (1961) hotel next to the Palazzo Antinori. The building is soundproofed, and the furnishings show comfortable good taste.

LE DUE FONTANE

Piazza SS. Annunziata 14, 50122 Firenze
☎210185 ☒575550. Map *4A5* ▥ 48 rms, all with bathrm ▦ ▬ ▣ 📧 ⊡ 📧
⌂ ৬ ♨ ▢ ▣ ⟨⟨ ❄

Location: 5 minutes' walk NE of Duomo. A comfortable, tastefully modernized but somewhat anonymous hotel facing the most architecturally harmonious square in Florence.

EXCELSIOR

Piazza Ognissanti 3, 50123 Firenze
☎264201 ☒570022 ☒210278. Map *1C3* ▥ 203 rms, all with bathrm ▦ ▬
▣ ⥥ 📧 ⊡ ⊡ ▥ ⌂ ♨ ৬ ▢ ▣ ⟨⟨ ❄ ♈

Location: 10 minutes W of Ponte Vecchio. The grand old hotel of Florence is owned by the CIGA chain and retains all the solid, spacious luxury of the 1920s — but not, alas, the stylish service. Red marbled pillars, wooden ceilings, polished furniture; every comfort, from thick pastel carpets to enormous bathrooms.

GRAND HOTEL CIGA

Piazza Ognissanti 1, 50123 Firenze
☎288781 ⌨570055 ⌨217400. Map 1C3 ▥ 107 rms, all with bathrm ▦ ⟶ ⥤ ▣ ᴀᴇ ⊙ ⊙ ᵛⁱˢᵃ ✥ ❧(winter garden) ☐ ☞ ⟨⟨ 🏋 ☡
Location: 10 minutes w of Ponte Vecchio, opposite the Excelsior. Before World War II the Grand was one of the famous Swiss-run hotels of Europe. In 1986 it reopened as part of the CIGA chain (which also owns the **Excelsior** across the piazza). Since then, it appears to have been searching for an individual style to match the high prices. The latest refurbishment, completed in 1990, has gone for "Florentine-Renaissance" rooms frescoed and hung with tapestries. Marble bathrooms.

IL GUELFO BIANCO ❧

Via Cavour 29, 50129 Firenze ☎288330 ⌨570596 ▥ 21 rms, all with shower ▣ ▦ ᴀᴇ ⊙ ᵛⁱˢᵃ ✥ ☐ ☞ ⟨⟨ ❧ ☡
Location: Between the Duomo and San Marco. A decent, no-frills private hotel of a kind that is nowadays all too rare in Florence, and is not as noisy as its location on a busy bus route might indicate. Front bedrooms are triple-glazed, and those at the back face a private garden or the hotel's own small courtyard. Furnishings are stronger on comfort than on style, but the reception is unusually courteous.

HELVETIA & BRISTOL ▥

Via dei Pescioni 2, 50123 Firenze ☎287814 ⌨572696 ⌨288353. Map 3C3 ▥ 52 rms and suites, all with bathrm ▦ ⟶ ▣ ⥤ ᴀ ᴀᴇ ⊙ ⊙ ᵛⁱˢᵃ ᴀ ✥ ☐ ☞ ❧(winter garden on roof) ⟨⟨ ☡ 🏋
Location: Just off n end of Via Tornabuoni. This venerable 19thC hotel, restored and reopened in 1989 by the Charming Hotel chain, aims to be the most exclusive, comfortable and elegantly intimate of the centrally located luxury hotels — a veritable home away from home for those who can afford it. Courteous and professional personal service matches the carefully re-created period decorations. Bedrooms are spacious; marble-tiled bathrooms are equipped with Jacuzzis. And the restaurant is succeeding in its aim to be one of the best hotel dining rooms in Florence.

HERMITAGE

Vicolo Marzio 1, Piazza del Pesce, 50122 Firenze ☎287216 ⌨212208. Map 3D3 ▥ 22 rms, all with bathrm ▦ ⊙ ᵛⁱˢᵃ ⥤ ⟨⟨ ✥ ☞ ☡❧ (on roof).
Location: Near Ponte Vecchio. A comfortable, modern *pensione.* The dining-room and roof garden look out over tiled roofs onto the historic center.

J & J

Via di Mezzo 20, 50121 Firenze ☎240951 ⌨570554 ⌨240282. Map 2C5 ▥ 20 rms, all with bathrm ▦ ⟶ ▣ ᴀᴇ ⊙ ⊙ ᵛⁱˢᵃ ⥤ ᴀ ☐ ☞ ✾ ⟨⟨ 🏋 ☡
Location: Near Santa Croce. A chic, pretty and blessedly peaceful new private hotel set in a 16thC monastery and popular with designers and fashion buyers. Every bedroom is different: some have frescoed ceilings or their own terraces or courtyards, or overlook unusual roofscape views.

JENNINGS-RICCIOLI

Corso Tintori 7, 50122 Firenze ☎244751 ⌨575849. Map 4E6 ▥ 55 rms, all with bathrm ᴀᴇ ⊙ ⊙ ᵛⁱˢᵃ ✥ ☞ ⟨⟨ Often closed mid-Nov to mid-Mar.*
Location: On the Arno, near S. Croce. This famous hotel was completely renovated in 1986 and has lost its formerly seedy reputation. About half the rooms overlook the Arno. #21 is E.M. Forster's Room with a View.

KRAFT

Via Solferino 2, 50123 Firenze ☎283054 ⌨571523 ⌨2398267. Map 1C2 ▥ 78 rms, all with bathrm ▦ ▣ ⥤ ⟶ ᴀᴇ ⊙

🔲 📼 📷 ♨ ☐ 🎞 《 ♒(on roof) 🍷 ♨

Location: Near Le Cascine. An extremely well-managed hotel situated in a relatively peaceful part of the city and owned by the son of the great Swiss hotelier. Efficient more than charming. Forgettable food.

LIANA ♣

Via Alfieri 18, 50121 Firenze ☎245303/4 📠2344596. Map *2C5* ▥ 24 rms, 18 with bathrm 🔌 AE 🔲 📼 🎞 ☐ ♿ 🎞 ❦ 🍷 《

Location: 15 minutes E of Duomo. A pleasant villa in a quiet street on the edge of the center. It housed the British Embassy from 1864-70 but these days is decorated in dubious taste. All the rooms face onto a large garden that is planted with mature trees.

LOGGIATO DEI SERVITI ♣

Piazza SS. Annunziata 3, 50122 Firenze ☎219165/289592 📠575808 📠289595. Map *4A5* ▥ 29 rms, all with bathrm 🔲 AE 🔲 🔲 📼 🎞 《 📷 ♨ ☐ ♨ 🍷

Location: 5 minutes' walk NE of Duomo. A new hotel installed with unfussy tact in the vaulted interiors of the early 16thC loggia of the Servite Confraternity, which mirrors Brunelleschi's Innocenti Loggia across the piazza.

LUNGARNO

Borgo S. Jacopo 14, 50125 Firenze ☎264211 📠570129 📠268437. Map *3D3* ▥ to ▥ 66 rms, all with bathrm 🔲 📷 AE 🔲 🔲 📼 🎞 《 📷 ♨ ☐

Location: Oltrarno, near Ponte Vecchio. A modern hotel (1968), which hangs over the Arno and, at the back, has been wrapped around the 13thC Torre Marsili. The most attractive rooms are the 14 overlooking the Arno and the 13 within the tower. The proprietor's collection of 20thC art is distributed throughout the hotel. Refurbishment of furnishings and bathrooms continues during 1993.

MONNA LISA

Borgo Pinti 27, 50121 Firenze ☎2479751 📠573300 📠2479755. Map *2C5* ▥ to

▥ 20 rms, all with bathrm 🔲 🔌 AE 🔲 🔲 📼 ☐ 🎞 ❦ 🍷 《

Location: 5 minutes E of Duomo. The Renaissance Neri Palace, part of which dates from the 14thC, retains the atmosphere of a proudly maintained private palace, with polished Tuscan brick floors and antique furniture, original vaulted wooden or frescoed ceilings, and an elegant *pietra serena* staircase. By contrast with the reception rooms, many of the bedrooms are disappointing, especially the singles, which are cramped and sometimes overheated. Most rooms overlook the pretty garden or courtyard; others are noisy. Service can be brusque.

MONTEBELLO SPLENDID

Via Montebello 60, 50123 Firenze ☎2398051 📠574009 📠211867. Map *1C2* ▥ 54 rms, all with bathrm 🔲 🚬 AE 🔲 🔲 📼 📷 ♨ ☐ 🎞 ❦ 🍷 ♨ 🍷

Location: Near the Teatro Comunale. A calm, solid hotel in two 19thC villas that have preserved something of their character and overlook a pleasant garden. Excellent conference facilities in a separate, Neoclassical house in the garden.

MORANDI ALLA CROCETTA ♣

Via Laura 50, 50121 Firenze ☎2344747 📠2480954. Map *2B5* ▥ 9 rms, all with bathrm 🔲 AE 🔲 🔲 📼 📷 ☐ 🎞 🍷

Location: Near SS Annunziata. A delightful, family-run hotel installed with charm and taste in part of the 16thC convent of the Crocetta. Much recommended to those who appreciate character as well as comfort and good value.

PALAZZO RICASOLI

Via delle Mantellate 2, 50129 Firenze ☎352151 📠574504 📠495001. Map *2A4* ▥ 100 apartments, all with bathrm 🔲 📷 AE 🔲 🔲 📼 📷 ♨ ♿ ☐ 🎞 ❦ ♨

Location: Near San Marco and the Palazzo dei Congressi. Efficiently equipped service apartments in a 16thC palace and its charmless modern annex. A sensible choice for families or business people. Secretarial services are available.

PENDINI

Via Strozzi 2, 50123 Firenze ☎*211170*
580278 210156. *Map* **3**C3 42
rms, 40 with bathrm ⊞ ➔ 📷 ‡ ✉ ⅌
Location: Piazza della Repubblica. A
busy, carefully managed *pensione* that
is dead central and has big, comfortably
furnished rooms.

PLAZA LUCCHESI

*Lungarno della Zecca Vecchia 38, 50122
Firenze* ☎*264141* 2480921. *Map* **2**D5
97 *rms, all with bath/shower* ⊞ ➔ 📷
➔ ⏢ ⊕ 🔟 🎟 ☎ ‡ ☐ ✉ ⅌ ⚏
Location: On the Arno, near S. Croce.
An efficient and friendly hotel specializ-
ing in high-class packaged groups.

PORTA ROSSA ✿

Via Porta Rossa 19, 50123 Firenze
☎*287551* 570007 282179. *Map*
3D3 *80 rms, 70 with bathrm* ⏢ ⊕ 🔟
🎟 ☎ ‡ ⚅ ☐ ✉ ⅌
Location: Off's end of Via Tornabuoni.
The Palazzo Torrigiani was a hotel as
early as the 14thC, but the present establishment dates from the 19thC and
retains a venerable charm that still appeals, especially to French and English
travelers. The bedrooms are huge and
can accommodate as many as six beds.
Groups are welcome.

PRINCIPE

*Lungarno Amerigo Vespucci 34, 50123
Firenze* ☎*284848* 571400 283458.
Map **1**C3 *to* 21 *rms, all with bathrm*
⊞ ➔ 📷 ⏢ ⊕ 🔟 🎟 ☎ ‡ ☐ ✉ ⚏
《 ⅌
*Location: On the Arno, near Ognis-
santi.* A loyal American clientele ap-
preciates the character of this elegantly
faded small hotel where some bedrooms retain old brocade wall-hang-
ings and marble bathrooms.

QUISISANA E PONTEVECCHIO

*Lungarno Archibusieri 4, 50122
Firenze* ☎*216692/215046* 268303.
Map **4**D4 *37 rms, 34 with bathrm* ⏢
⊕ 🔟 🎟 ‡ ✉ 《 ⅌
Location: Near the Ponte Vecchio. The
magnificent wrought-iron elevator sets
the tone, and the atmosphere of the

century-old *pensione* has been carefully preserved in all but two respects:
the plumbing and the prices. The film
of *A Room with a View* was set here.

REGENCY 🏨

Piazza M. d'Azeglio 3, 50121 Firenze
☎*245247* 571058 245247. *Map*
2C5 *to* 34 *rms, all with bathrm* ⊞
➔ 📷 ➔ ⏢ ⊕ 🔟 🎟 ☎ ‡ ☐ ✉ ⚏
《 ⚏ ⅌
Location: 15 minutes E of Duomo. This
small hotel in its tranquil tree-lined
square might have been imported direct
from Paris. The bedrooms are in dazzling but well-judged color combina-
tions, but some are small for the price.

RESIDENZA ✿

Via Tornabuoni 8, 50123 Firenze
☎*284197/218684* 570093. *Map* **3**C3
24 *rms, 20 with bathrm* ➔ ⏢ ⊕ 🔟
‡ ✉ ⚏ *(on roof)* 《 ⅌
Location: Centrally positioned. A
charming, reassuringly old-fashioned
and unfussy hotel, on the top floors of
a Renaissance palace. No frills, but the
staff pride themselves on their courtesy.
Family apartments are also available.

RIGATTI ✿

Lungarno Generale Diaz 2, 50122 Firenze
☎*213022. Map* **4**E4 *28 rms, 15 with
bathrm* ‡ 🎋 ⚏*(on roof)* 《
*Location: On the Arno, between the Uf-
fizi and S. Croce.* A superb position on
the top two floors of the Palazzo Alberti,
with spacious rooms, an elegant drawing room hung with old brocade, and
an outstanding view from the terrace.

ROMA

Piazza S. Maria Novella 8, 50123 Firenze
☎*210366* 575831 215306. *Map*
3B2 *to* 51 *rms, all with bathrm* ⊞
🔘 ⏢ ⊕ 🔟 🎟 ☎ ‡ ⚅ ☐ ✉ 《 ⅌
Location: Near the main rail station.
The Roma reopened several years ago
as an efficiently modernized hotel with
immaculate, comfortable, anony-
mously decorated bedrooms.

ROYAL

Via delle Ruote 52, 50129 Firenze

☎483287 🖷490976. Map *2B4* ▥ 39 *rms, all with bathrm* ▦ ➤ 🅰🅴 ⬤ 🆅🆂🅰 ⬗ 🝾 ◻ ⬤ 🎾 ✌ 《€

Location: Near S. Marco. A convenient base for touring to the N and W, or for any traveler requiring absolute peace and quiet. This handsome 19thC palace overlooks its own gardens, but the interior decor does less to lift the spirit.

SAVOY
Piazza della Repubblica 7, 50123 Firenze
☎283313 🖾570220 🖷284840. Map *4C4* ▥ to ▦ 101 *rms, all with bathrm* ▦ ➤ ▨ 🝾 ⇌ 🅰🅴 ⬤ 🆒 🆅🆂🅰 ⬗ 🛆 ◻ 🖃 🞈 ✌ 《€

Location: In the heart of the historic center. The most central of the grand old Florentine hotels is efficient but rather impersonal.

SILLA ♨
Via dei Renai 5, 50125 Firenze ☎2342888 🖷2341437. Map *4F5* ▥ to ▥ 32 *rms,* 30 *with bathrm* ▦ 🅰🅴 ⬤ 🆒 🆅🆂🅰 🝾 ⬗ ◻ ◻ 🖃 《€ ✌ *Closed Dec.*

Location: Oltrarno, near Ponte alle Grazie. An airy, spacious *pensione,* which is especially attractive in summer. There is a large terrace, and the view across the Arno is fringed by trees in the little park.

TORRE DI BELLOSGUARDO 🏛
Via Roti Michelozzi 2, 50124 Firenze
☎2298145/229529 🖷229008 ▥ 16 *rms, all with bathrm* ➤ ▨ 🅰🅴 ⬤ 🆒 🆅🆂🅰 🝾 ⬗ 🖃 🞈 《€ ⚶ ✌

Location: One minute by car or 7 minutes' walk by private footpath from Porta Romana. This beautiful and refined private hotel was opened in 1988 in a 16thC villa set in spacious gardens, olive groves and orchards (which supply the fruit for breakfast). It commands the most spectacular of all views of Florence. Each large bedroom is decorated in restrained good taste, with well-chosen antiques, and is adjoined by an efficient bathroom.

VILLA AZALEE
Viale Fratelli Rosselli 44, 50123 Firenze
☎214242/284331 🖷268264. Map *1B2*

▥ to ▥ 25 *rms, all with bathrm* ▦ ➤ 🝾 🅰🅴 ⬤ 🆒 ◻ 🖃 ✌ 《€

Location: On the beltway (ring road) NE of the center. A private hotel in a 19thC villa set in pleasant gardens. Bedrooms, some of which give directly onto the garden, are decorated with pretty chintzes. Conveniently situated for the rail station, Perètola airport and Firenze-Mare autostrada.

VILLA BELVEDERE
Via Benedetto Castelli 3, 50124 Firenze
☎222501 🖾575648 🖷223163 ▥ 27 *rms, all with bathrm* ▦ ➤ 🅰🅴 ⬤ 🆒 🝾 ⬗ 🖃 🞈 《€

Location: Poggio Imperiale, 3km (2 miles) S of Florence. Just the hotel for a peaceful family vacation, in a reconstructed Medici villa overlooking Florence.

VILLA CARLOTTA
Via Michele di Lando 3, 50125 Firenze
☎2336134 🖾573485 🖷2336147. Map *1E2* ▥ to ▥ 27 *rms, all with bathrm* ▦ ➤ 🝾 ⇌ 🅰🅴 ⬤ 🆒 🆅🆂🅰 🝾 ⬗ ◻ 🖃 🞈 ⚶ ✌ 《€

Location: Near Porta Romana and Boboli Gardens. On a quiet street lined with privately-owned 19thC villas, this *pensione* maintains a high standard of comfort.

VILLA CORA 🏛
Viale Machiavelli 18, 50125 Firenze
☎2298451 🖾570604 🖷229086. Map *1E3* ▥ 48 *rms, all with bathrm* ▦ 🖃 ➤ ⇌ 🝾 🅰🅴 ⬤ 🆒 🆅🆂🅰 ⬗ 🛆 ◻ 🖃 🞈 🝾 《€ ⚶ 🞈 🏌 🏊 ◐ ✌

Location: Near Boboli Gardens. This sumptuous Neoclassical villa in a large private park retains its extravagant mid-19thC Rococo features: elaborate fireplaces, gilded stucco, frescoed ceilings, Venetian-glass chandeliers. It would still suit the Princess Eugenia, who stayed in 1876. Today, although the hotel often caters to expensively packaged tourists and businessmen, the service is unusually sympathetic. Guests can be ferried into Florence by the hotel's car service — or take a 20-minute stroll through the Boboli Gardens into the Pitti. Its restaurant with piano bar, the **Taverna Machiavelli**, is next door.

VILLA MEDICI 🏨
Via Il Prato 42, 50123 Firenze ☎2381331 ☎570179 ℻2381336. Map **1C2** ▥ 108 rms, all with bathrm ▦ ▣ ═ 🅐🅔 🅓 🅒🅓 🏠 🛎 🕭 ▢ 🖼 🐾 《 ≈ 🐎

Location: Near Le Cascine. The frontage is that of an 18thC Corsini villa; the rest was built in 1960 in a style that would suit James Bond. In the immaculate apartments, all somber chintzes and dark wood, international businessmen and art dealers conclude deals in private. Most of the rooms have balconies and overlook the gardens.

Alternative accommodations

"RESIDENZE"
For a stay of more than a few days, and especially if you are traveling with small children or prefer not to depend on restaurants, you might choose a *residenza* (service apartment) instead of a hotel. One of the nicest is **La Fonte** *(Via s. Felice a Ema 29 ☎224421 ▥)*, in a handsome Renaissance villa $1\frac{1}{2}$ km (1 mile) s of the center. The most efficient of the inner-city residences is the **Palazzo Ricasoli**, see above.

"PENSIONI"
Although there is no longer an official classificiation for the rough, reliable residential *pensioni,* it is still possible to find cheerful, clean and often inexpensive accommodations, even in the heart of the city. There are still a number of small, old-fashioned private hotels in Florence that retain something of the atmosphere famously evoked by the film of *A Room with a View.* One of the best known in Florence is the **Beacci Tornabuoni**. Others include the **Annalena, Hermitage, Residenza Rigatti** and **Silla**.

Some recommended 1- and 2-star hotels: **Bandini Sorelle** *(Piazza Santo Spirito 9 ☎215308, see page 148);* **Alessandra** *(Borgo SS. Apostoli 17 ☎283438);* **Cestelli** *(Borgo SS. Apostoli 25 ☎214213);* **Costantini** *(Via de' Calzaiuoli 13 ☎215128);* **De Lanzi** *(Via dell'Oche 11 ☎288043);* **Donatello** *(Via V. Alfieri 9 ☎2477416).*

YOUTH HOSTELS
The Italian Youth Hostel Association (Associazione Italiana per la Gioventù) has its headquarters in Rome *(Via Cavour 44, 00184 Roma ☎(06) 462342 ℻ (06) 4741256).* In Florence, the youth hostel (Ostello della Gioventù) is at Viale Europa *(☎601451).* These hostels are available only to members of the Youth Hostels Association.

OTHER EFFICIENCY (SELF-CATERING) ACCOMMODATIONS
The Tuscan countryside also has many villas, castles and farmhouses to rent (see page 47), and there are even small villages converted into hotels or residences. If you would like to rent a Florence apartment or a Tuscan villa, try the English-speaking agency **Florence and Abroad** *(Via S. Zanobi 58, 50129 Firenze ☎490143).*

Eating and drinking

Dining out in Florence

Visitors to Florence, even natives of other parts of Italy, are often surprised by the stark simplicity of the restaurants in which some of the city's most delicious and honestly-priced food is served. The traditional Florentine trattoria has plain white walls, washed or tiled, red-tiled floors and wooden tables, which are sometimes communal. The one-room *buca* — literally "hole" — or basement restaurant is characteristic. Service can be brusque if not downright rude: the Florentines are said to like it that way and have named some of their favorite eating places after the rough tongues of their proprietors. The classic example is **Sostanza**. Such restaurants are not necessarily inexpensive; and some, for example **Coco Lezzone**, the *vinaria* of **Cibrèo**, and **Il Latini**, are locally very fashionable.

MENUS: The traditional Tuscan trattoria menu will include hearty, earthy dishes, such as *crostini, fettunta, ribollita, bistecca, fagioli* and *castagnaccio.* Pasta, which is not a Tuscan specialty, is often over-cooked and insipid, even in otherwise reliable trattorie. A wiser choice for a hot first course would be soup, or *fagioli* simply sauced with the delicious local olive oil.

Fish, now generally available (and always expensive), is particularly good at **La Capannina di Sante**, **Cibrèo**, **I Quattro Amici**, **Pierot** and **Vittoria**. Game is harder to find in Florence than in the country, but is well prepared at **La Maremma da Giuliano.**

Three **vegetarian restaurants** are **Almanacco** *(Via delle Ruote 30 ☎ 475030)*, **La Stazione di Zima** *(Via Ghibellina 70 ☎ 2345318)* and **Il Santommaso** *(Via Romana 80 ☎ 221166).*

The **Kosher restaurant** is **Il Cuscussù** *(Via Farini 2 ☎ 241890).* **Chinese restaurants**, which have multiplied in Florence lately, are disappointing, as there seem to be none with high standards.

FAST FOOD: For those tourists seeking fast, familiar food, there are now plenty of snack bars in the center serving pizzas, hamburgers, crepes, ice cream and so on. A list of recommendations is given at the end of this chapter.

Genuine Florentine fast food is available at *vinerie* or *fiaschetterie,* the best of which, at lunchtime, are often jammed full with hungry Florentines. ·Some, such as those in **Via dei Cimatori**, **Piazza dell'Olio** and under the **Volta di San Piero**, are just holes in the wall and serve nothing more than *crostini,* ham or salami sandwiches, and rough Chianti wine, which you gulp down while standing on the street. Others, those for example in **Via degli Alfani** and on the corner of **Via de' Benci** and **Via de' Neri**, also serve hot food and have a few tables.

EATING CLUBS: These are popular with Florentines and generally less expensive than restaurants. In most cases foreigners can become members, at no extra cost, merely by walking in and filling out a form. Two of the most interesting eating clubs are **Mirò** and the one next to **Alessi's** takeout, both listed below. Others include **Anzichè** *(Piazza del Carmine 29☎212532, open for lunch only)*, the family-run **Il Cavaliere** *(Via de' Pucci 4a ☎298879)* and **Il Guscio** *(Via dell'Orto 49 ☎223737, closed Sun-Mon)*.

AL FRESCO DINING: In Florence this is not normally a pleasure of summer life, as it is in some other Italian cities. A minority of restaurants in the center have gardens or put tables outside in fine weather. Some that do are **Barbano**, **Il Barone di Porta Romana**, **Cavallino**, **Carmine**, **La Capannina di Sante**, **Da Ganino** and the **Enoteca Pinchiorri**.

You can, however, dine outside, often on a terrace overlooking a spectacular view, in most of the many attractive country restaurants within easy driving distance of the city (see for example ARTIMINO, BAGNO A RIPOLI, CASTELLO, GREVE, IMPRUNETA, LASTRA A SIGNA, PRATOLINO, SAN CASCIANO IN VAL DI PESA and SETTIGNANO, in the TUSCANY A TO Z).

RESERVATIONS AND CLOSURES: Reservations are advisable for all restaurants, especially for Sunday lunch and in the spring and summer months. Many restaurants close on Sunday evening, and times are specified when restaurants are **closed**. During the summer, it is worth checking in advance, as management vacations often result in a period of closure for 3-4 weeks during July or August.

RESTAURANT PRICES: These have soared in recent years, and are not always justified by the poor quality of what is too often dished out to unsuspecting tourists. The good value symbol (♣) should help guide you to restaurants that really do aim to give value for money, and the particularly luxurious (⌂) are also marked. Other symbols show price categories, charge/credit cards and other noteworthy points. See page 7 for the full list of symbols.

For more essential reading around the subject, see also EATING IN TUSCANY on page 48, and TUSCAN WINES on pages 175-178.

One young man of fashion to the other, when asked if he liked Botticelli, had replied that he preferred Chianti. "Botticelli isn't a wine, you juggins, it's a cheese."
(Du Maurier cartoon, *Punch* magazine, 1880s)

FEATURED RESTAURANTS CLASSIFIED BY PRICE

INEXPENSIVE (▢)
Acquacotta ✿
Il Cavallino
La Maremma
Mossacce ✿
Le Quattro Stagioni
INEXPENSIVE (▢) to MODERATE (▢)
Del Fagioli ✿
Gauguin ✿
MODERATE (▢)
Antico Fattore
Buca dell'orafo
Cafaggi ✿
Cammillo
Al Campidoglio
Cantinetta Antinori
Celestino
Dino
Da Ganino
Il Latini ✿
Mirò ✿
Omero
Ottorino

Pierot
Il Profeta
Ruggero ✿
Sostanza
Torquato
MODERATE (▢) to EXPENSIVE (▢)
Cibrèo ✿
Le Fonticine
Garga
La Loggia
Mamma Gina
San Zanobi
EXPENSIVE (▢)
Bronzino
Capannina di Sante
Coco Lezzone
Harry's Bar
Otello
I Quattro Amici
VERY EXPENSIVE (▢)
Doney ⌂
Enoteca Pinchiorri ⌂
Sabatini ⌂

Florence restaurants A to Z

ACQUACOTTA ✿
Via dei Pilastri 51 (near Santa Croce)
☎242907. Map 2C5 ▢ Closed Wed.
Acquacotta, a vegetable soup served over toast and topped with a poached egg, is only one of the homey, well-prepared dishes served in this reliable, reasonably priced trattoria.

ANTICO FATTORE
Via Lambertesca 1-3 (near Uffizi)
☎2381215. Map 4D4 ▢ ▢ ▢ ▢ ▢
Closed Sun-Mon.
This was once *the* Florentine rendezvous of Italian writers and artists. The sustaining Tuscan peasant dishes are better than the pastas. Tables are communal and the service slipshod.

BRONZINO
Via delle Ruote 27 (near S. Marco and the Palazzo dei Congressi) ☎495220. Map

2B4 ▢ ▢ ▢ ▢ ▢ ▢ ▢ Closed Sun.
A spacious, well-managed restaurant popular for business lunches.

BUCA DELL'ORAFO
Volta de' Girolami 28 (near the Ponte Vecchio) ☎213619. Map 4D4 ▢ Closed Sun-Mon.
A cozy one-room "hole in the ground" that serves very decent Tuscan food as well as unusually good homemade pastas. Friendly and very Florentine, which is an unusual combination.

CAFAGGI ✿
Via Guelfa 35 (near San Lorenzo)
☎294989. Map 2B4 ▢ Closed Sun dinner, Mon.
A big, noisy, family-run trattoria, which serves excellent unlabeled wine and oil from the proprietors' farm in the Chianti.

CAMMILLO

Borgo S. Jacopo 57 (Oltrarno, near Ponte Vecchio) ☎212427. Map **3D3** ▥ ▤ ▭ ▨ ⊙ ⊙ ▨ *Closed Wed, Thurs.*

A pleasantly bright, family-run trattoria with a loyal American clientele who appreciate the *scampi al curry* and the unusually welcoming and expert service. The wine and oil from the proprietor's farms are always excellent, and in the white truffle season the *scaloppine di vitello tartufato* is sublime.

AL CAMPIDOGLIO

Via Campidoglio 8 (near Piazza Repubblica) ☎287770. Map **3C3** ▥ ▭ ▬ ▤ ▨ ⊙ ⊙ ▨ *Closed Tues.*

A large, immaculate, old-fashioned restaurant with a balanced regional and international menu. It is to be hoped that new management will maintain the high standard.

CANTINETTA ANTINORI

Piazza Antinori 3 (N end of Via Tornabuoni) ☎292234. Map **3C3** ▥ ▭ ⇒ ▤ ▨ ⊙ ⊙ ▨ *Closed Sat-Sun.*

In elegant rooms off the central courtyard of the 15thC Antinori palace, this chic, crowded restaurant serves products from the Antinori estates. You can take these as a quick snack at the bar or build them into a full dinner. Wines, oil, bread and cheeses are all excellent, as is the *galletto al Chianti.*

CAPANNINA DI SANTE

Piazza Ravenna ☎688345 *(at the s foot of Ponte da Verrazzano)* ▥ ▨ ▨ ⊙ ⊙ ▨ *Closed Sun; Mon lunch.*

Fresh fish and seafood are simply prepared and complemented by well-chosen white wines. The restaurant overlooks the Arno, and its interior rooms are romantic in the evening when candles are lit.

IL CAVALLINO

Via delle Farine 6 (Piazza della Signoria) ☎215818. Map **4D4** ▥ ▨ ▤ ≪ ▽ ▨ ⊙ ⊙ ▨ *Closed Tues dinner; Wed.*

Don't be suspicious of the star location — it might have turned Cavallino into a tourist trap, but hasn't. This is the sort of restaurant Florentines treat as a second home. Whether you dine alone with a book or with a party of friends, the service is quick and courteous and the food pleasant.

CELESTINO

Piazza S. Felicita (Oltrarno) ☎296574. Map **3E3** ▥ ▨ ▭ ▤ ▨ ⊙ ⊙ ▨ *Closed Sun.*

A small, immaculate and sometimes noisy trattoria run with highly polished professionalism.

CIBRÈO ♣

Via de' Macci 118 (near S. Croce) ☎2341100. Map **2D5** ▥ or ▥ ▭ ⇒ ▨ ▨ ⊙ ⊙ ▨ *Closed Sun-Mon.*

Possibly the most congenial and interesting restaurant in Florence serves refined and beautifully prepared Tuscan specialties that are not easily found elsewhere in the city. Don't pass up any of the four courses. Everything is delicious, and the seasonal *passati di verdura* and *sformati* offered in lieu of pastas are outstanding, as are the home-made desserts. (The *cibrèo*, a Tuscan chicken stew made from parts of the bird that are normally discarded, must be ordered in advance.) You can enjoy the same food for less than half the price, in the simpler surroundings of the *vinaria* on the other side of the kitchen. A café serving light meals all day and late into the night has opened across the street. Around the corner, **Cibrèo Alimentari** *(Via del Verrocchio 4 ☎677298)* sells local delicacies to take out.

COCO LEZZONE

Via Parioncino 26 (near Via Tornabuoni) ☎287178. Map **3C2** ▥ ▭ No cards. *Closed Sun; Tues dinner.*

A white-tiled trattoria that looks like a public lavatory (it was originally a dairy) and is nowadays always crammed with chic Florentines packed elbow-to-elbow at communal tables. The attraction is the high quality of the uncompromisingly Tuscan food, especially the thick peasant soups and simple meat dishes.

DINO

Via Ghibellina 51 (near Michelangelo Museum) ☎241452. Map 4C5 ▥ ▭ ▮ ▬ ▤ 𝗔𝗘 ⊙ ▦ *Closed Sun dinner; Mon.*

The menu of this coolly handsome *eno-gastronomico* is designed to accompany the Italian wines from the well-stocked cellar. The cheese board is excellent. Specialties include *risotto alla Renza, stracotto del Granduca* and *filetto di maiale al cartoccio.*

DONEY △

Piazza Strozzi 18 (just off Via Tornabuoni) ☎298206/218556. Map 3C3 ▥ 𝗔𝗘 ⊙ ⓒ ▦ *Closed Sun; Mon lunch.*

The new Doney, attractively installed in the vaulted rooms of the 15thC palace next to Palazzo Strozzi, is owned by Giorgio Armani and presumably intended for the sort of people who can afford to wear his clothes (available from his boutique next door). Florentines call it "Armani's restaurant" to distinguish it from the original Doney in Via Tornabuoni, which was one of the most distinguished rendezvous of early 20thC Europe.

ENOTECA PINCHIORRI △

Via Ghibellina 87 (near S. Croce) ☎242777. Map 4C5 ▥ ▭ ▮ ▬ ▤ ▤ 𝗔𝗘 ▦ *Closed Sun; Mon lunch.*

This establishment, on the ground floor of the 15thC Ciofi-Iacometti Palace, demands to be judged by the highest European standards. The proprietor, Giorgio Pinchiorri, has built up a cellar (there are enophiles who would call it the finest in the world) of international wines. His French wife is responsible for the elegant and subtle cuisine. If you choose the *menu de degustazione* and allow the waiter to fill your glass with the appropriate wine for each course, you will be able to sample the glories of the cellar without committing yourself to full bottles. A pilgrimage restaurant, but mainly, alas, for the super-rich and those on expense accounts.

DEL FAGIOLI ✿

Corso dei Tintori 47 (near S. Croce) ☎244285. Map 4E5 ▥ to ▥ ▭ *No cards. Closed Sat-Sun.*

This straightforward Tuscan trattoria is owned by relatives of the proprietors of **Coco Lezzone**. The atmosphere is less studiously pure, but the oil and wine are just as good and the *ribollita* sometimes better.

LE FONTICINE

Via Nazionale 79 (near the Station) ☎282106. Map 3A3 ▥ to ▥ ▭ ▼ ▬ 𝗔𝗘 ⊙ ⓒ ▦ *Closed Mon.*

The excellence of the cuisine, and especially the pasta, must be partly explained by the Emilian origins of the proprietress. Popular with visiting business executives.

DA GANINO

Piazza dei Cimatori 4 (near Piazza della Signoria) ☎214125. Map 4C4 ▥ ▭ ≪ ▬ ▤ 𝗔𝗘 ⊙ *Closed Sun.*

A tiny, welcoming trattoria that is tucked away in a miniature piazza. It offers first-class Tuscan cooking, especially the homemade pastas and the *torta di formaggio.*

GARGA

Via del Moro 48 (between Piazza Goldoni and S. Maria Novella) ☎2398898. Map 3C2 ▥ to ▥ 𝗔𝗘 ⊙ ⓒ ▦ *Closed Sun-Mon.*

This pretty restaurant, decorated with a touch of fantasy that makes a welcome change in Florence, is owned by a Canadian-Florentine couple who really understand food. Pasta is fresh, meat dishes exceptionally well prepared, and the *torta di formaggio* justly famous.

GAUGUIN ✿

Via degli Alfani 24 (near SS. Annunziata) ☎2340616. Map 4B6 ▥ to ▥ 𝗔𝗘 ▦ *Closed Sun; Mon lunch.*

A welcome new addition to the Florentine culinary repertory, this cheerful, small restaurant serves light, wholesome and interesting food with an emphasis on vegetables and inventive salads, as well as unusual and well-prepared pastas, crepes, and foreign dishes such as couscous, moussaka and chili con carne.

HARRY'S BAR
Lungarno A. Vespucci 22 (near Ognissanti)
☎*2396700. Map 1C3* 🎟 ⊡ 📖 ♇ *AE*
⊙ *VISA Closed Sun.*

Modeled on the original in Venice, but with no business connection, this is a haven for English-speaking visitors. Attentive bilingual service, a good selection of all-American cocktails, an adequate, short menu that hardly ever changes, and the best burgers in town.

IL LATINI ♣
Via Palchetti 6 (behind Palazzo Rucellai)
☎*210916. Map 3C2* 🎟 ⊡ *No cards. Closed Mon; Tues lunch.*

Love it or hate it — and you do have to be in the mood and very hungry — this noisy, crowded restaurant with its open kitchen, communal tables and hanging hams is one of the best places in Florence to enjoy robust Tuscan country cooking.

LA LOGGIA
Piazzale Michelangelo 1 ☎*2342832. Map 2E5* 🎟 *to* 🎟 ⊡ ♇ ⇇ 🖴 ♇ 📖 ➹
AE ⊙ ⊙ *VISA Closed Wed.*

The spectacular views over the city from the spacious 19thC *palazzina del caffè* make this an ideal venue for a first or last meal in Florence. The food is excellent, especially the honestly-prepared Tuscan specialties. Also a café.

MAMMA GINA
Borgo S. Jacopo 37 (Oltrarno, near Ponte Vecchio) ☎*2396009. Map 3D3* 🎟 *to* 🎟
⊡ 📖 🖪 *AE* ⊙ *VISA Closed Sun.*

Now under the same management as **La Loggia**, this famous old trattoria has an inviting atmosphere, high prices and a long menu, all designed to attract passing tourists.

LA MAREMMA
Via Verdi 16 (near S. Croce) ☎*244615. Map 4D5* 🎟 📖 ⊡ 🖪 *AE* ⊙ *VISA Closed Wed.*

A justly popular, family-run trattoria offering game in season as well as other delicious specialties. Don't miss the *prosciutto di cinghiale,* hard to find almost anywhere else.

MIRO ♣
Via San Gallo 57-59 (between San Marco and Piazza Libertà) ☎*481030. Map 2B4* 🎟 *No cards. Closed Sun.*

A recently opened and very popular neighborhood eating club (see page 155) is set in a spacious room, once a private theater, which has now been decorated using gently surreal touches. The short menu changes twice daily and offers some of the most delicious and sensibly inventive food in Florence.

MOSSACCE ♣
Via del Proconsolo 55 (between Duomo and Bargello) ☎*294361. Map 4C5* 🎟 ⊡ 🖪
📖 *AE* ⊙ *VISA Closed Sat-Sun.*

Although *mossacce* means "discourteous," Mossacce is really a very cheerful place and always full because the meat is so excellent and such good value.

OMERO
Via Pian dei Giullari 11 (Arcetri) ☎*220053. Map 6E4* 🎟 ⊡ ⇇ 🖴 ♇ *AE* ⊙ ⊙ *VISA Closed Tues.*

This classic Tuscan country restaurant overlooking the city and only half an hour's walk, or 5 minutes' taxi ride from the center, is ideal for a leisurely Sunday lunch. But stick to the specialties, which include a perfect *fettunta*, excellent *salumi, crostini, ribollita, pasta e ceci, panzanella* and *bistecca . Pollo schiacciato* (flattened over the wood fire) is generally over-cooked, and the deep-fried *carciofi* taste better *senza pastella* (without batter). Service can be lackluster. Good *salumi, pecorino,* oil and other delicacies on sale at the small grocery store at the front.

OTELLO
Via degli Orti Oricellari 36 (near the station)
☎*215819. Map 1C3* 🎟 ⊡ 🖪 📖 *AE* ⊙
⊙ *VISA Closed Tues.*

A large, comfortable, dignified restaurant more appreciated by foreigners than by Florentines. The salad trolley is welcome on hot days.

OTTORINO
Via delle Oche 12-16 (near Duomo)
☎218747. Map 4C4 ▥ ☐ ▦ AE ◉ ◉
▨ *Closed Sun.*
One of the city's oldest restaurants, but
now moved into spacious new
premises where the tastefully modernized Tuscan style of the decor is restful
on a hot day. The long menu is well
balanced.

PIEROT ✿
*Piazza Taddeo Gaddi 25 (across the Arno
from the Cascine)* ☎702100. Map 1C1 ▥
☐ AE ◉ ◉ ▨ *Closed Sun.*
Homey, honest and very popular restaurant serving classic Tuscan fish and
meat dishes.

IL PROFETA
Via Borgognissanti 93 (Ognissanti)
☎212265. Map 3C1 ▥ ☐ ▦ AE ◉ ▨
Closed Sun-Mon.
A soothingly understated one-room restaurant where the quality of the food
never seems to fall short of excellence.

I QUATTRO AMICI
*Via degli Orti Oricellari 29 (near the rail
station)* ☎215413/212992. Map 1B3 ▥
☐ ■ ▦ AE ◉ ◉ ▨ *Closed Wed.*
The newest fish-only restaurant, which
has a Michelin star, is spacious, cool and
elegantly appointed, if somewhat
charmless. The proprietors, four
friends, all have long years of experience in the restaurant and food business. All their fish is imported directly
from Porto Santo Stefano twice weekly.

LE QUATTRO STAGIONI
Via Maggio 61 (near the Pitti) ☎218906.
Map 1D3 ▥ ☐ ▦ AE ◉ ◉ ▨ *Closed
Sun.*
Two small rooms, usually crowded
with antique dealers and fashion
people from the Pitti Moda. The gener-
alized Italian food lacks real character,
but the multilingual service is refresh-
ingly graceful.

RUGGERO ✿
Via Senese 89 (near Porta Romana)
☎220542. Map 1E2 ▥ ☐ *Closed*

Tues-Wed.
This no-nonsense everyday trattoria
opposite the old horse-watering stop
on the road to Rome is owned by a
former cook at **Coco Lezzone**. The
hearty country food served there makes
an ideal Sunday lunch after a long walk.
They do a good fish soup on Fridays.

SABATINI ⌂
Via Panzani 9a (near the station)
☎211559. Map 3B3 ▥ ☐ ▦ ■ AE ◉
◉ ▨ *Closed Mon.*
Sabatini no longer has the reputation of
being the most famous and fashionable
restaurant in Florence. But it has a
pleasant environment and often one
eats better here than some critics suggest.

SAN ZANOBI
Via S. Zanobi 33a (near S. Marco)
☎475286. Map 2B4 ▥ to ▥ ☐ ▦ AE
◉ ◉ ▨ *Closed Sun.*
A calm, refined restaurant run by two
women who cater primarily to the
Florentine professional classes. They
serve inventive food, lovingly prepared.

SOSTANZA
Via del Porcellana 25 (near Ognissanti)
☎212691. Map 3C2 ▥ ☐ *No cards.*
Closed Sat-Sun.
Known as *il Troia,* which is Tuscan
slang for "pigsty," this is one of the
oldest working men's trattorie in
Florence. The prices have gone up, but
the *bistecca* is still very good and the
service still very rude.

TORQUATO
*Via Boccaccio 35 (on the way to Fiesole,
below San Domenico and near the Cure
market)* ☎575744 ▥ *Closed Mon dinner;
Tues.*
This restaurant, which backs onto the
Mugnone River, is popular with members of the San Domenico European
University and it is often very busy at
lunchtime. Here you can get an excellent variety of antipasti, as well as good
pasta, and simply cooked fresh fish
dishes.

Other recommendations

Giuseppe Alessi ♣ Via di Mezzo 26 ☎241821, map **2**C5 ▥ An outstandingly simple wine bar and takeout, owned by a skillful cook and culinary scholar who also runs the dining club next door.

Angiolino ♣ Via S. Spirito 36 ☎2398976, map **3**D2 ▥ Closed Sun dinner; Mon. A modest, traditional trattoria that never seems to alter.

Baldini Via il Prato 96 ☎287663, map **1**B2 ▥ Closed Sat.

La Baraonda Via Ghibellina 67 ☎2341171, map **4**C5 ▥ to ▥ ▤ ▣ Closed Sun.

Barbano Piazza Indipendenza 3 ☎486752, map **2**B4 ▥ ▤ ▣ ▨ ▨ Closed Wed and in winter. Attractive mainly for its large garden.

Il Barone di Porta Romana Via Romana 123 ☎220585, map **1**E2 ▥ to ▥ Closed Sun. Has a pleasant rustic atmosphere and romantic garden.

Belle Donne ♣ Via delle Belle Donne 16 ☎262609, map **3**B2 ▥ Closed Sat-Sun. A Florentine favorite for a quick, light lunch. Good mixed green salad.

Birreria Centrale Piazza Cimatori 1 ☎211915, map **4**C4 ▥ Closed Sat lunch; Sun. Open noon-midnight. Pleasant snacks and good Friuli wines.

Buca Lapi Via del Trebbio 1 ☎213768 ▥ ▤ ▣ ▨ ▨ map **3**B3. Closed Sun dinner; Mon. Does very good *bistecca*.

Buca Mario Piazza Ottaviani 16 ☎214179, map **3**C2 ▥ Closed Wed.

Da Burde ♣ Via Pistoiese 154 ☎317206 ▥ Closed evenings; Sun ▤ ▨ ▨ A big, traditional trattoria near Perètola airport.

Cambi ♣ Via Sant'Onofrio 1 ☎217134, map **1**C2 ▥ ▨ Closed Sun.

Da Carlino Diladdarno Via dei Serragli 108 ☎225001, map **1**D3 ▥ Closed Mon. Serves decent food until midnight to a mainly youthful clientele at communal tables.

Carmine Piazza del Carmine 18 ☎218601, map **1**D2 ▥ to ▥ Closed Sun in winter; Sat-Sun in summer. A rough and reliable old favorite now under a new, more ambitious management.

Frosali ♣ Via Guelfa 24 ☎219201, map **2**B4 ▥ ▤ ▨ ▨ Closed Tues. Popular neighborhood trattoria.

Leo in Santa Croce Via Torta 7 ☎210829, map **4**D5 ▥ Closed Mon.

La Macelleria ♣ Via S. Zanobi 97 ☎486244, map **2**B4 ▥ Closed Sun.

Mario ♣ Via Rosina *(no ☎)*, map **2**B4 ▥ Closed Sun. Popular with students. On the corner of the San Lorenzo Mercato Centrale.

L'Orologio ♣ Piazza Ferrucci 5 ☎6811729, map **2**D6 ▥ Closed Sun.

Palle d'Oro ♣ Via Sant'Antonino 43 ☎288383, map **3**B3 ▥ Closed Sun. A wonderful selection of filled rolls at the front, with a simple trattoria behind.

Paoli Via dei Tavolini 12 ☎216215, map **4**C4 ▥ ▤ ▣ ▨ ▨ Closed Tues. Inoffensive food in a spectacular environment.

Pennello   "La Casa di Dante," Via Dante Alighieri 4 ☎94848, map **4**C4 ▥ Closed Sun dinner; Mon. The vast array of serve-yourself anti-pasti makes a meal that you can tailor to the size of your appetite and pocket.

Pepolino   Via C.F. Ferrucci 16 ☎608905 ▥ ▣ ▣ ▣ ▣ Closed Sun. Near San Salvi and Campo di Marte.

Da Sergio ♣   Piazza San Lorenzo (*no* ☎), map **2**C4 ▢ to ▥ Closed Sun. An open secret hidden behind the market stalls along the N flank of San Lorenzo.

I' Toscano   Via Guelfa 70 ☎215475, map **2**B4 ▥ ▣ ▣ ▣ ▣ Closed Tues.

La Vecchia Cucina   Viale De' Amicis 1-2 ☎660143 ▥ ▣ ▣ ▣ ▣ Closed Sun. On the way to Fiesole, near San Salvi and Campo di Marte.

Vittoria   Via della Fonderia 52 ☎225657, map **1**C2 ▥ Closed Tues. Serves fish only.

Zàzà ♣   Piazza Mercato Centrale 26 (near San Lorenzo) ☎215411, map **2**B4 ▥ ▣ ▣ ▣ Closed Sun.

Zi Rosa   Via dei Fossi 12 ☎287062, map **3**C2 ▥ to ▥ ▣ ▣ ▣ ▣ Closed Thurs; Fri lunch. Has a pleasant atmosphere, serves reliable Antinori wines, and stays open late at night.

USEFUL TOURISTS' SNACK BARS AND PIZZERIE
La Bussola   Via Porta Rossa 58 ☎293376. Closed Mon. A useful pizzeria open until 2.30am.

Nuti   Via Borgo San Lorenzo 22 ☎210145. Closed Mon.

Old Bridge   Via de' Bardi 64, Oltramo ☎212915. Closed Mon. Serve-yourself restaurant with a terrace overlooking the Arno.

Queen Victoria   Por S. Maria, Ponte Vecchio. Large *tavola calda*, with garden.

Il Rifrullo   Via San Niccolò 57.

Refreshments

BARS
The bar is the nerve center of Italian daily life. If you need a telephone, a bus ticket, a rest room or simply want to ask directions, look for the nearest bar, which will never be far away.

In an Italian bar, anyone can drink anything at any time of day. Ordinary coffee *(caffè normale)* is a short, potent espresso; if you like it weaker, ask for *caffè lungo. Macchiato* is with a dash of milk; *corretto* is laced with brandy. The coffee is almost unfailingly excellent, and a *cappuccino* with a sweet roll makes a better and cheaper breakfast than you will find in any hotel. Many larger bars also sell pastries, sandwiches, ice cream, groceries, even light meals. Be aware that if you sit down the price doubles.

SNACKS

Inevitably, there are the ubiquitous pizzerias, as well as restaurants serving pizzas in addition to their other fare. Some bars serve one or two simple hot dishes, as well as sandwiches and pastries. But the local snack food — salamis, *crostini,* and the delicious peasant-style vegetable soups — can be eaten, standing up or at communal tables, in *fiaschetterie.*

Refer also to EATING IN TUSCANY on page 48.

CAFÉS

Although open-air cafés are not characteristic of Florence, there are four in the unlovely but central Piazza della Repubblica. The **Excelsior** hotel (see FLORENCE HOTELS A TO Z) serves a typical English tea in the afternoons.

ICE CREAM SHOPS

These have proliferated in the center. Those favored by connoisseurs include **Frilli** *(Via S. Niccolò 57 ☎23617, map 2D5, closed Wed),* which makes the best *semifreddo,* **Frullati** *(Via de'Renai 2, map 4F5, open afternoons and evenings only, closed winter),* which specializes in fresh seasonal fruit ice creams, and **Vivoli** *(Via Isola delle Stinche 7 ☎ 292334, map 4D5),* which is always adding new flavors to its large range of sometimes over-sweet ice creams. Ice cream addicts claim that perfect bliss is to be found only at the more remote **Badiani** *(Viale dei Mille 20 ☎ 501149, map 6D4, closed Tues),* celebrated for its *Buontalenti* enriched with egg-yolk.

The following offers a small selection of bars, cafés and ice cream shops.

DONNINI
Piazza della Repubblica 15 ☎211862. Map 3C3. Closed Mon.
The smallest bar in the piazza serves the most unusual hot sandwiches.

GIACOSA
Via Tornabuoni 83 ☎296226. Map 3C3. Closed Mon.
This is where the young elite meet for coffee and to buy pastries, *marrons glacés* and handmade chocolates. There are also sandwiches and hot snacks. The *Negroni* was invented here in the 1920s by Count Camillo Negroni.

GILLI
Piazza della Repubblica ☎296310. Map 3C3. Closed Tues.
This *belle-époque* café, where an orchestra plays old favorites in summer, is the most attractive and comfortable

ice cream shop (with good WCs) in Piazza della Repubblica.

LA LOGGIA
Piazzale Michelangelo 1 ☎287032. Map 2E5. Closed Wed.
From the 19thC *palazzina del caffè* you can look out past the "Not-the-Real-David" over the most famous introductory view of the city.

MANARESI
Via de'Lamberti 16 ☎87335. Map 4C4. Closed Sun.
The best and largest selection of freshly ground coffees, including decaffeinated.

MARINO
Piazza N. Sauro 19 ☎212657. Map 3D1. Closed Mon.
Some of the best fresh-baked croissants

163

in the Oltrarno. A good choice for a continental breakfast or late-afternoon snack.

PASZKOWSKI
Piazza della Repubblica 6 ☎ *210236. Map* **3***C3. Closed Mon.*
One of the few bars in Florence where you can eat a hearty American breakfast, Paszkowski is also fun when live bands play on summer evenings.

PROCACCI
Via Tornabuoni 64 ☎ *211656. Map* **3***C3. Closed Mon.*
As a treat, pamper your taste buds with a plate of Procacci's exquisite truffle rolls. Cold drinks only.

IL RIFRULLO
Via San Niccolò 55 ☎ *2342621. Map* **4***F6. Open until 1am. Closed Wed.*
Favorite rendezvous for young Florentines. Also a brasserie and creperie.

RIVOIRE
Piazza della Signoria 5 ☎ *214412. Map* **4***D4. Closed Mon.*
Not the exclusive tea room it once was, but the hot chocolate is superb, the *marrons glacés* famous, and the view of the Palazzo Vecchio probably justifies the high prices.

ROBIGLIO
Via dei Servi 112 ☎ *212784. Map* **4***B5. Also Via dei Tosinghi 11* ☎ *215013. Map* **4***C4. Open 8am-midnight. Closed Mon.*
A large and luscious selection of pastries. Specialties include *Saint-Honorés, millefeuilles,* meringues and *torta rustica.*

SCUDIERI
19 Piazza di San Giovanni 19. Map **4***B4. Closed Wed.*
Excellent coffee and pastries; conveniently located just opposite the Baptistry.

Nightlife and entertainment

Florence by night

Florence enjoys a livelier nightlife than many small Italian cities, thanks partly to its large student population.

CINEMA
The **Cinema Astro** *(Piazza San Simone* ☎ *222388, map 4D5, open eves, closed Mon)* shows English-language movies.

DISCOS AND PIANO BARS
The largest and most popular discos are **Space Electronic** *(Via Palazzuolo 37* ☎ *295082, map 3C2)* and the curiously named **Yab Yum** *(Via de Sassetti 5* ☎ *282018, map 3C3).*

Smaller discos and piano bars include **Full Up** *(Via della Vigna Vecchia 21* ☎ *293006, map 4D5)* and **Jackie O'** *(Via Erta Canina 24* ☎ *2342442, map 2E4).* The nightclub is **The River Club** *(Lungarno Corsini 8* ☎ *282465, map 3D2).*

MUSIC AND THEATER
The **Maggio Musicale**, a festival of concerts, recitals, opera and ballet, is held in various venues throughout the city during the period May to July. It is wise to reserve tickets well in advance through your travel agent.

In Florence, tickets are theoretically available from the rather inefficient box offices of the **Teatro Comunale** and **Teatro della Pergola**. However, it is usually less complicated to make reservations through hotel porters or local travel agents.

The principal venues in Florence for performances of music, opera, ballet and plays are:

Affratellamento   Via Giampaolo Orsini 73 ☎6812191, map **6**D5
Rondò di Bacco   Piazza Pitti 1 ☎2381664, map **3**E2
Teatro della Compagnia   Via Cavour 50 ☎217428, map **4**A4
Teatro Comunale   Corso Italia 16 ☎2779236, map **1**C2
Teatro Niccolini   Via Ricasoli 5 ☎213282, map **4**B4
Teatro dell'Oriuolo   Via dell'Oriuolo 31 ☎2340507, map **4**C5
Teatro della Pergola   Via della Pergola 10-32 ☎2479651/ 242361, map **4**B6
Teatro Variety   Via del Madonnone 47 ☎676942, map **6**D5
Teatro Verdi   Via Ghibellina 99 ☎2396242, map **4**D5

Shopping

What to look for

When shopping in Florence, bear in mind the Florentine character, which is unique in Italy and is as remarkable a legacy of the Renaissance as any church or monument.

At all social and economic levels, Florentines share a profound respect for two skills — craftsmanship and business — the activities that made Florence the richest city in 15thC Europe and which account for its modern prosperity. Even today, the Florentine shopkeepers are probably the most powerful political lobby in the city.

SHOPPING HOURS
Normally 9am-1pm, 3.30-7pm, with slight variations, but some in the center now stay open in the lunch hours as well. Most shops close on Monday mornings but open all day Saturday, except for food stores, which close on Wednesday. In summer some of the bigger stores close all day Saturday but open on Monday.

Many large stores will send your purchases abroad if you wish. A reliable independent packer and shipper is **Fracassi** *(Via Santo Spirito 11* ☎ *298340, map 3 D2)*.

WHERE TO SHOP
The **Via Tornabuoni** is the Madison Avenue of Florence. Most of the grandest shops are in or near it, around the Duomo, Piazza della Repubblica, Ognissanti, along the Lungarno, and across the Arno in and behind Borgo San Jacopo.

HOW TO SHOP
The businesslike Florentines understand comparative shopping and bargaining. An aggressive manner will get you nowhere, but even in big, established stores you can try asking for a discount *(sconto* or *gentilezza)* if you buy more than one item.

WHAT TO BUY
Locally-worked leather, silk and straw items (bags, hats and novelties) are usually good buys. Bookbinding, picture framing and reproduction antiques are traditional Florentine specialties, but some of the simpler work that was once done by local craftsmen is now carried out by Chinese immigrants.

ANTIQUES

Many of the established antique stores are in Via dei Fossi and Via Maggio, but look also in Borgognissanti, Borgo San Jacopo and Via Santo Spirito. Auctions are held in spring and fall at the **Casa d'Aste Pitti** *(Via Maggio 15* ☎ *287138, map 3 E2)*. An important antiques fair is held in alternate (odd) years in the Strozzi palace.

There are, however, two caveats. Florence is an active center of fabrication. Furniture made of old wood qualifies as "antique" under Italian law, but if you are importing to another country you may be charged full duty on items that are not genuinely antique. Important genuine pieces are in any case usually "notified" and may not be legally exported.

ARTISANS, RESTORATION AND REPRODUCTIONS

The narrow back streets of the Oltrarno, where the artisans' workshops are concentrated, are alive with the sounds of hammers and saws, and the odors of wood, glue and tanning leather. Florentine craftsmen are highly skilled in every branch of restoration, with many a Florentine-made reproduction innocently passed by experts and honest dealers.

BANCO BIANCHI & FIGLI

Viale Europa 117 ☎ *686118. Map 6D5.*
Bianco Bianchi is a master of the translucent stonework known as *scagliola* that is used to decorate floors and table tops. He will restore or reproduce old pieces or create new designs. Beautiful examples, including table tops inspired by 17thC patterns, are on display.

BARTOLOZZI & MAIOLI

Via Vellutini 5 and Via Maggio 13. Map 3E2.
Wood-carvers who will make anything from picture frames to life-sized lions to table legs. They were entrusted with the restoration of Monte Cassino after its destruction during World War II.

PONZIANI

Via Santo Spirito 27 ☎ *287958. Map 3D2.*
The Ponziani family have been restoring antique furniture since the late 19thC. They also make superb, hand-crafted reproductions of Italian, French and English styles.

RAFFAELLO ROMANELLI

Lungarno Acciaioli 72-78 ☎ *296047. Map 3D3* [AE] [◎] [◎] [VISA]
The firm has been making life-sized copies of the most famous sculptures as far back as 1860 and it will also make period fireplaces, tabletops and chess sets.

ZECCHI

Via dello Studio 19 ☎ *211470. Map 4C4* [AE] [VISA]
Zecchi stocks a full range of restorers' and artists' materials, many not available elsewhere in Europe. You can buy *lapis lazuli* from Afghanistan, pure gold leaf, powdered pigments for frescoes, natural gums and resins.

BOOKS, PRINTS AND ENDPAPERS

Italy was the home of printing and all the crafts of book production; and Florence has been catering to the needs of bookish foreigners for hundreds of years. Foreign-language books are now widespread and there are a number of internationally renowned specialist bookstores.

ALINARI
Via della Vigna Nuova 48 ☎*218975. Map 3C2* ⓐⓔ
The famous sepia photos of 19thC Florence; and one of the most complete archives of black-and-white photos of Italian art. The archive, and a museum of photography that mounts interesting temporary exhibitions, are in the ground floor of the RUCELLAI PALACE.

BM
Borgognissanti 4 ☎*294575. Map 3C1.*
This is an extremely useful shop that sells not only books in English, as well as Italian, on Florentine culture and history, but also maps, guidebooks, fiction and books for children.

CENTRO DI
Piazza dei Mozzi 1 ☎*2342666/7. Map 4E5* ⓒ
One of the most important serious art bookstores and publishers in Italy, hidden away in a basement. Their fine catalogs, produced for major European exhibitions, are on sale.

GIANNINI E FIGLIO
Piazza Pitti 37 ☎*212621. Map 3E2.*
This delectable little shop opposite the Pitti, founded in 1856, is the grandfather of all the paper stores.

LIBRERIA CONDOTTA
Via Condotta 29 ☎*213421. Open 9am-7.30pm. Map 4D4* ⓐⓔ ⓒ ⓥⓢ
A good selection of foreign-language books, guides, classics and books on art.

PAPERBACK EXCHANGE
Via Fiesolana 31 ☎*2478154. Map 2C5.*
More than 10,000 English-language titles in stock, mostly popular fiction. A recycling system gives you 25-40 percent of the original price of your old paperbacks toward any you buy at 75 percent of the cover price.

IL PAPIRO
Via Cavour 55 ☎*215262. Map 4B4* ⓐⓔ ⓒ ⓥⓢ *Branches at Piazza Duomo 24 and Lungarno degli Acciaioli 42.*
Specializes in marbled papers.

PITTI ARTE E LIBRI
Piazza Pitti 16 ☎*212704. Map 3E2* ⓐⓔ ⓒ ⓥⓢ
An elegant new shop with a good selection of specialist books on, for example, the decorative arts and cooking.

PORCELLINO
Piazza del Mercato Nuovo 6-8 ☎*212535. Map 4D4* ⓐⓔ ⓒ ⓥⓢ
The first self-service bookstore in Florence. The place to look for the catalogs and guides that are maddeningly not sold in museums and galleries.

SALIMBENI
Via M. Palmieri 14-16 ☎*2340904. Map 4C5.*
One of the most reputable specialist art and antiquarian bookstores in Europe.

SEEBER
Via Tornabuoni 70 ☎*215697. Map 3C3* ⓐⓔ ⓒ ⓒ ⓥⓢ
Founded in 1865 to serve the foreign community and now one of the largest and best known general bookstores.

IL TORCHIO
Via dei Bardi 17 ☎*2342862. Map 4E4.*
An exceptionally attractive range of printed papers at very reasonable prices. The artisans, who work immediately behind the shop, will make up orders in the paper and leather combination of your choice.

IL VIAGGIO
Via Ghibellina 117 ☎*218153. Map 2D5* ⓐⓔ ⓒ ⓒ ⓥⓢ
Specialists in tourist guides and maps, including nautical and aeronautical maps.

CLOTHES
Some of the best-known non-Florentine designers have outlets in and off the **Via Tornabuoni**, and it is here that you will find such names as

Armani, **Yves St-Laurent** and **Valentino**. Other fashion streets are **Via de' Calzaiuoli**, **Via de' Cerretani**, **Via Roma** and **Via Calimala**; and, across the Arno, **Via Guicciardini** and **Borgo San Jacopo**.

LUISA
Via Roma 19-21 ☎*217826-8 and Via del Corso* ☎*294374. Both map* **4C4** AE ⊙ ⊙ VISA *Open 9.30am-7.30pm.*
The most fashionable boutique in town and the first to stock Japanese labels. Also accessories and men's clothing.

NEUBER
Via Strozzi 32 ☎*215763. Map* **3C3** AE ⊙ ⊙ VISA
Clothing for men, women and children, all of very good quality and mostly bearing the labels of foreign houses.

PRINCIPE
Via Strozzi 21-29 ☎*216821. Map* **3C3** AE ⊙ ⊙ VISA
One of a Tuscan chain selling restrained clothes for men, women, children and babies, at all prices.

PUCCI
Via dei Pucci 6 ☎*283061. Map* **4B4** AE
The Marquese Emilio Pucci's famous designs can be bought from the atelier on the first floor of his ancestral palace. Entrance through the boutique at Via Ricasoli 59.

VALDITEVERE
Lungarno Soderini 1 ☎*282707. Map* **1C2** AE ⊙ ⊙ VISA
An exclusive boutique selling reticently classical clothes made from its own beautiful materials. The clothes are also on sale at **Gems** *(Via de' Bardi 76* ☎*210810, map 4 E4).*

DESIGN AND GIFTS

EDIZIONE &C
Via della Vigna Nuova 82 & 91 ☎*287839/ 215165. Map* **3C2**. *Also Via dei Pucci 22* ☎*295061. Map* **4B4**. *Both* AE ⊙ ⊙ VISA
Hand-woven writing paper, filofaxes, original diaries.

VICEVERSA
Via Ricasoli 53 ☎*298281. Map* **4B4**.
A reminder that Italians lead the world in imaginative modern design: gadgets, lighting, watches, clocks, executive toys.

FOOD
The local produce — dried mushrooms, new-season's dried beans, wild-boar hams, and especially the wonderful green-gold Tuscan olive oil — is so appetizing that you might well be tempted to bring home some edible gifts or souvenirs. Florentines who like to eat well do their grocery shopping at the huge, covered food-markets of **Sant'Ambrogio** and **San Lorenzo** (see STREET MARKETS) where the selection is enormous and the prices lower than in shops. Two high-class grocery and wine stores in the center are **Alessi** *(Via delle Oche 27-29, map 4 C4)* and **Vera** *(Piazza dei Frescobaldi 3* ☎*215465, map 3 D2).*

Take care when buying bottled olive oil. Genuine Tuscan *extra vergine* is scarce, labor-intensive and expensive. If the label does not bear the word *prodotto* (produced) as well as *imbottigliato* (bottled), the oil may come from anywhere in the world. Many wineries produce their

169

own oil. **Antinori** *(Piazza degli Antinori 3 ☎ 298298, map 3 C3)* is one of several that have outlets in Florence. The designer-oil of the moment is **Laudemio**, which is available at most good grocers and is very expensive. Just as delicious and much better value is the local oil you can often buy by the ladleful from big terra-cotta pots. One particularly friendly and helpful neighborhood store that sells its own oil in this way is **Vino e Olio** *(Via de'Serragli 29 ☎ 298708, map 1 D3)*.

If you have a discriminating sweet tooth, you will find the three most seriously excellent take-out pastry shops all located on the outer edges of the historic center. They are well worth the detour. **Dolce & Dolcezze** *(Piazza Beccaria 8 ☎ 2345458, map 2 C6)* claims with some justice to make the best chocolate cake in the world, but it would be hard to choose between it and the delectable cheese cake with pears *(torta di formaggio e pere)*. The specialty of **Gualtieri** *(Via Senese 18 ☎ 221771, map 1 E2)* is *torta iris* (an iced loaf cake made with iris corms, leaves, and, sometimes, flowers). **Sarti** *(Via Senese 147 ☎ 20164, map 1 F2)* is the place to buy the various kinds of *schiacciata alla fiorentina* (unleavened Lenten cake). Refer also to REFRESHMENTS on pages 162-163.

HEALTH AND BEAUTY

Florentines take their health and their looks seriously. **Pharmacies**, which are nearly as ubiquitous in Florence as bars, often retain their beautiful original fittings, make their own soaps, creams and specifics and are happy to give advice about minor ailments and beauty problems. The top **hairdressers** are **Luana Beni** *(Lungarno Guicciardini 7 ☎ 215240/284885, map 3 D2)*, a hushed, discreet salon patronized by the aristocracy; **Mario di Via Della Vigna** *(Via della Vigna Nuova 22 ☎ 294813/298953, map 3 C2)*, hairdressers to the Pitti fashion show models; and **Valentino** *(Via Tornabuoni 105 ☎ 212323, map 3 C3)*, the favorite of English and American visitors. For information about gyms and other sports facilities see pages 50-51.

ANTICA FARMACIA DI SAN MARCO
Via Cavour 146 ☎ 210604. Map 4B4.
This beautiful pharmacy, with its vaulted frescoed ceilings and rows of majolica jars, was founded in the 15thC by the Dominican monks of San Marco. Their specifics include an anti-hysteric, which might come in handy if you are visiting Florence in August. Excellent rose water and eau de cologne.

BIZZARRI
Via Condotta 32 ☎ 211580. Map 4D4.
This serious, unusual — and, you may think, well-named — shop is at least worth a look. Founded in 1842, it sells pure natural chemicals, essences and herbs, and will mix your own perfume if you know the formula.

OFFICINA PROFUMO-FARMACEUTICA DI SANTA MARIA NOVELLA
Via della Scala 16 ☎ 216276. Map 3B2.
A perfectly preserved grand-ducal pharmacy: superb hand-made soaps, creams, lotions for every skin type, plus a delectable potpourri, all made to original 17thC formulae. Service is notoriously grudging.

PROFUMERIA ALINE
Via Calzaiuoli 53 ☎ 215269. Map 4C4.
The largest selection of cosmetics and perfumes in town, with ranges such as Clinique and Lauder.

PROFUMERIA INGLESE
Via Tornabuoni 97 ☎ *263748. Map 3C3.*
Founded by an Englishman in 1843. The mahogany shelves are well stocked with cosmetics, soaps and perfumes, but the medicines have now been moved down the Via to the Farmacia Inglese.

JEWELRY AND SILVER

Brunelleschi, Verrocchio, the Pollaiuolo brothers, Cellini, Ghiberti: some of the greatest Florentine artists trained as goldsmiths. The shops on the Ponte Vecchio have been occupied by jewelers and goldsmiths since 1593.

At the **Casa dell'Orafo** *(Vicolo Marzio 2),* in a deconsecrated church near the Ponte Vecchio, there are to be found some 30 jewelers, each one a specialist in repairing, resetting or making pieces to clients' specifications.

BUCCELLATI
Via Tornabuoni 71 ☎ *296579. Map 3C3* [AE]
[◉] [◉] [VISA]
The Florentine branch of the famous Milanese family of jewelers makes handsome, Renaissance-inspired heavy pieces, often in chased gold.

GHERARDI
Ponte Vecchio 8 ☎ *287211. Map 3D3* [AE]
[◉] [◉] [VISA]
Known in Florence as the "official coral keeper," Gherardi's prices are about twice what you would pay in Naples, the source of most Italian coral, but the quality and design are superb. He also specializes in cultured pearls, jade, turquoise, tortoise-shell and cameos.

IL LEONE
Via S. Giovanni 13 ☎ *27848. Map 1D2.*
This silversmith makes, reproduces and repairs tableware at very low prices.

MANELLI
Ponte Vecchio 14 ☎ *213759. Map 3D3* [AE]
[◉] [◉] [VISA]
The Manelli family have been dealing in semiprecious and hard stones for four generations. These can be bought loose or can be strung into a necklace in half an hour. Earrings take a week.

MELLI
Ponte Vecchio 44-46 ☎ *211413. Map 3D3*
[AE] [◉] [VISA]
A rarified collection of antique jewelry, antique porcelains, silver and small *objets d'art.*

PAMPELONI
Borgo SS Apostoli 47 ☎ *289094. Map 3D3*
Vendors of exquisite silver tableware by Florentine craftsmen who also make for **Tiffany's**.

PICCINI
Ponte Vecchio 23 ☎ *294768. Map 3D3* [AE]
[◉] [◉] [VISA]
Jewelers to the jet set, although the Concorde set may find the designs slightly dated and the prices too high-flown. They also sell antique jewelry and silver, and will reset heirlooms. This is a long-established family firm founded in 1895.

RAJOLA
Ponte Vecchio 24 ☎ *215335. Map 3D3* [AE]
[◉] [◉] [VISA]
Here you can get very chic enamel work as well as pieces set with colored stones.

SETTEPASSI
Via Tornabuoni 25 ☎ *215506. Map 3C3* [AE]
[◉] [VISA]
The oldest and one of the grandest Italian jewelers, specializing in precious stones and Oriental pearls set to match the incomes and tastes of the wealthiest Italian families, and to adorn crowned heads of Europe. They also sell antique and modern silver.

171

TOZZI
Ponte Vecchio 19 ☎ *283507. Map* **3D3** 🗛🖻
🖲 🖭 🖭

A most beguiling stock of delicate objects — coral charms, gold-mesh purses, Baroque pearls — some old, some modern, and some real bargains to be found, if you know your own taste.

UGO PICCINI
Via Por S. Maria 9-11 ☎ *214511. Map* **3D3**
🗛🖻 🖲 🖭 🖭

More approachable — and affordable — than the grand jewelers of the Ponte Vecchio and Tornabuoni. Prices are fair and service pleasant. Attractive gold chains, priced by weight, make excellent presents for special occasions.

LEATHER
Leather is to Florence what glass is to Venice; that is to say there is altogether too much of it, and very little of what is most prominently on display bears the slightest relation to the unrivaled workmanship of the great artisans who are still active, and whose creations are found in the shops below.

Locally produced leather goods can be slightly cheaper than abroad. If you want to see how it's done, visit the **Peruzzi** leather factory and shop *(Borgo dei Greci 8* ☎ *263039, map 4 D5)*, which is open all day; or there is the one in the monastery of **S. Croce** *(Piazza S. Croce 16* ☎ *244533, map 4 D6)*.

ALESSANDRINI
Via Vaccherreccia 17 ☎ *216088. Map* **4D4**
🗛🖻 🖲 🖭 🖭

This is the Florence outlet for the leather handbags manufactured by the Tuscan firms Enny and The Bridge.

BELTRAMI
Via Calzaiuoli 31 and 44 ☎ *214030 and 212418. Map* **4C4** 🗛🖻 🖲 🖭 🖭 *Other branches at Via dei Pecori 16* ☎ *213290, map* **3C3**; *Via Calimala 9* ☎ *212288, map* **4C4** *and Via Tornabuoni 48* ☎ *287779, map* **3C3**.

Successful Florentine chain selling top quality men's and women's shoes, accessories and clothes.

BISONTE
Via del Parione 35 ☎ *215722. Map* **3C2** 🗛🖻
🖲 🖭 🖭

Home outlet for fashionably sporty and youthful canvas and leather bags made in Florence.

CELLERINI
Via del Sole 37 ☎ *282533. Map* **3C2** 🗛🖻
🖲 🖭

The Cellerini family are the most skilled

and stylish independent artisans to be found in the city. They make leather, lizard and crocodile handbags.

FERRAGAMO
Via Tornabuoni 2 ☎ *292123. Map* **3C3** 🗛🖻
🖲 🖭 🖭

Salvatore Ferragamo was the first of the internationally renowned Italian shoemakers. He started his career in Hollywood in 1914, and bought this palace in the Via Tornabuoni in 1937. The business now has branches all over the world and makes clothes, ties and scarves too — all in the master's stylish mould.

GUCCI
Via Tornabuoni 73 ☎ *264011. Map* **3C3** 🗛🖻
🖲 🖭 🖭

Home base for the durable and expensive leather status symbols.

MANNINA
Via de' Guicciardini 16 ☎ *282895 and Via de' Barbadori 23* ☎ *211060. Both map* **3E3**.
Extremely attractive and wearable hand-made shoes and handbags at reasonable prices.

PAPINI
Lungarno Archibusieri 10-14 ☎*287879.*
Map 4D4 [AE] [◎] [◎] [VISA]
The Papini family have made well-crafted bags, briefcases, suitcases and solid leather boxes for 100 years. They are also agents for Borbonese, Redwall and Basile.

RASPINI
Via Roma 25-29 ☎*213077. Map* 4C4 [AE] [◎] [◎] [VISA] Branches at Via Martelli 5-7, map 4B4 and Via Por S. Maria 72, map 3D3.

Raspini is one of the most glamorous names in Florentine leatherware, but unlike **Ferragamo** and **Gucci** it has no outlets abroad — only licensed imitators.

TADDEI
Piazza Pitti 6 ☎*219139. Map* 3E2.
Leather boxes, frames, desk sets and jewelry cases hand-made on the premises by a family whose members have been working with leather for a century.

LINENS AND LINGERIE
You will find a nice selection of embroidered linens in Via Por S. Maria.

LORETTA CAPONI
Borgognissanti 12 ☎*213668. Map* 3C1 [AE] [◎] [◎] [VISA]
The dreamily girlish nightdresses hand-embroidered exclusively for Loretta Caponi are among the prettiest, and the most expensive, things you will see in Florence.

IL PARNASO
☎*2298182/210909/261862. Map* 3E1.
Lace and linens are finely hand-embroidered to antique designs in Giorgio Calligaris' atelier on the first floor. Ring for an appointment.

PORCELAIN, CERAMICS AND HOUSEWARES
Locally made ceramics range from refined to rustic, antique to skilled repro.

RICHARD GINORI
Via Rondinelli 17 ☎*10041. Map* 3B3 [AE] [◎] [◎] [VISA]
Porcelains from the famous Ginori factory at Sesto Fiorentino.

MANETTI E MASINI
Via Bronzino 125 ☎*700445. Map* 5D3.
Began as restorers of antique majolica, and soon found they could produce exact copies. They sell charming fabrications of 18thC plates, tureens, vases and ceramic stoves, and also carry out repairs to china.

LA MÉNAGÈRE
Via dei Ginori 8 ☎*213875. Map* 4A4 [AE] [◎] [◎] [VISA]
An astounding selection of quality housewares in a comfortingly old-fashioned environment.

SBIGOLI
Via S. Egidio 4 ☎*2479713. Map* 4C5.
Sbigoli offers a vast array of terra-cotta pottery for the garden, table or oven. You can either choose from traditional designs or commission your own. If you supply measurements and photographs of breakages, the items can then be reproduced.

173

STREET MARKETS

Street markets can be more fun, and much cheaper, than shops.

MERCATO DELLE CASCINE
Map 5D3. Open Tues 7am-1pm.
This weekly market in the Cascine park is like a huge department store laid out under the poplars along the Arno.

MERCATO CENTRALE
Maps 3A3-4A4. Open Mon-Sat 7am-1pm, 4-7.30pm.
Immediately N of Piazza S. Lorenzo, this impressive 19thC cast-iron food market is the central outlet, wholesale and retail, for fresh meat, fish and vegetables, and also for cheeses, oils and countless other foods.

MERCATO NUOVO
Map 3D3. Open daily 9am-5pm.
The famous straw market, also known as the Porcellino. As well as straw, there are leather goods, ceramics, linens and other handmade goods.

MERCATO DELLE PIANTE
Piazza della Repubblica. Map 3C3. Open Thurs 7am-1pm.
A weekly flower market is held here under the central post office loggia.

MERCATO DELLE PULCI
Piazza dei Ciompi. Map 2C5. Open Tues-Sat 8am-1pm, 3.30-7pm; first Sun of each month 9am-7pm.
The flea market of Florence sells picturesque junk at irritatingly jumped-up prices, but is good for ex-votos and old postcards.

MERCATO DI SANT'AMBROGIO
Piazza Lorenzo Ghiberti. Map 2C5. Open weekday mornings.
A comprehensive food market with a more intimate atmosphere than the vast Mercato Centrale. There is a useful lunch counter and a coffee bar inside.

MERCATO DI SAN LORENZO
Maps 3B3-4B4. Open Mon-Fri 7am-2pm; Sat, holiday eves 4-8pm.
The biggest and most popular of the street markets sprawls all around the church of S. Lorenzo and into the adjacent streets. The best shoe bargains in Florence are to be found on the Borgo S. Lorenzo side, where sandals and espadrilles are half the price you might pay in the shops.

TEXTILES AND TRIM

Florence still manufactures some of the most gorgeous furnishing fabrics in the world. It is an industry that dates back to the Middle Ages.

ANTICO SETIFICIO FIORENTINO
Via della Vigna Nuova 97 ☎282700. Map 3C2.
Silk furnishing fabrics — taffetas, damasks, brocades, velvets, satins, borders, fringes and *passementerie* — will be made to order (minimum 30 meters) in any color or style. The factory across the Arno *(Via Bartolini 4 ☎282700, map 1 C2)* may be visited by appointment, but call ahead.

LISIO TESSUTI D'ARTE
Via dei Fossi 45 ☎212430. Map 3C2.
This astonishing firm was founded in 1906 by a master weaver who was inspired to reproduce the finest antique woven silk fabrics. Of the many designs taken from Old Master paintings, the Primavera brocade is the most popular. Lisio has made hangings for the Sistine Chapel as well as costumes for the Palio and for historic films, and his creations are exhibited in textile museums throughout the world. The most elaborate designs are produced at the rate of only a few centimeters a day. Prices, not surprisingly, are high, but you could follow the example of Florentine women, who buy just enough for an evening skirt or dress.

Tuscan wines

by Burton Anderson

Wine has been an element of Tuscan life for ages. We know that the Etruscans made wine three millennia ago. The Romans followed suit, and although vine cultivation lapsed during the Dark Ages, wine was back in prominence through the Renaissance, flourishing as nutrient of body and soul and as a source of inspiration for who knows how many works of art or grandiose ideas.

Tuscans in their time have contributed notably to the development of winemaking as art and science, to techniques of bottling and shipping wine and establishing the rituals that have grown around its service and consumption. Over the last two decades, Tuscany's vineyards and cellars have been transformed from generally rustic to prevalently high-tech, as the region has seized the lead in the styling of modern red wines. But since the hills have a broad range of microclimates, and winemakers insist on expressing individuality, wines often show variations in type from one place to another. This diversity makes Tuscan wine lists especially fascinating.

Tuscany's 26 wines of controlled name and origin or DOC *(denominazione di origine controllata)* include four of the nine with Italy's highest classification, the government-guaranteed DOCG. These are Brunello di Montalcino, Vino Nobile di Montepulciano, Chianti and the red wine of Carmignano.

Chianti is Italy's most prodigious classified wine, with seven zones covering the heart of the region from N of Florence to S of Chiusi, and from Pisa's coastal hills to the Apennines near Arezzo. Chianti first became famous in its rounded straw flask, but today most wine, including the *riserva,* which must be aged for at least three years, comes in straight, Bordeaux-type bottles.

Chianti's historical core is the Classico zone between Florence and Siena, although the territory expands to take in the wine towns of Montalcino, Montepulciano, San Gimignano, Carmignano and Pomino.

All Tuscan DOC red wines are based on the versatile Sangiovese grape, sometimes used alone (as in Brunello and Morellino di Scansano), sometimes mixed with other varieties (as in Chianti, Vino Nobile and the reds of Carmignano, Pomino, Elba and the Colline Lucchesi). Not all the fine reds are DOC, however: Tignanello, Le Pergole Torte, Flaccianello, Coltassala and Rosso di Cercatoia are but a few of the prized Sangiovese-based wines sold under proprietary names. These so-called "Super Tuscan" table wines may also be based on other varieties, notably Cabernet, which dominates in Sassicaia, Sammarco, Solaia and Tavernelle.

175

Modern winemaking techniques have improved the quality of Tuscan white wines, as outside varieties such as Chardonnay, Sauvignon and the Pinots have added fruitiness and fragrance to the rather bland native Trebbiano and Malvasia. Among DOC whites, Vernaccia di San Gimignano and Pomino have gained in stature. Montecarlo, Bianco di Pitigliano and Bianco Vergine Valdichiana also reach markets beyond the region.

Among the many unclassified whites, the modern light Galestro, made by several large houses, is popular. But by now every Tuscan estate or winery, large or small, makes a special white, although type and quality vary markedly.

Among sweet dessert or aperitif wines, Vin Santo, made from semi-dried grapes and well aged in small sealed barrels, is beloved by Tuscans, but, alas, production is painstaking and there is little of this true "holy wine" to be found. Lately, though, there have been signs of a comeback, as even large producers concentrate efforts on limited stocks of prestigious Vin Santo. There are, as well, a great many curiosities, experiments, and esoteric wines to be discovered. Although most such wine is unclassified, moves are afoot to create new official categories for modern red and white wines by a consortium of producers who use the term *Predicato*.

Everywhere, local wine of a recent vintage is served as the natural accompaniment to the local food. Many towns in Tuscany have an *enoteca,* a shop where local or regional wines can be bought. In Florence, the Palazzo dei Vini *(Piazza Pitti 15 ☎ (055) 213440)* displays Tuscan wines and hosts tastings, which are open to the public for a small charge on Thursday evenings.

Few regions combine the enjoyment of art and history with the pleasure of food and wine as excitingly as Tuscany. Most wine zones are within easy reach of Florence.

CHIANTI CLASSICO

For all the violent history that transpired in this hilly buffer zone between Florence and Siena, Chianti Classico is today one of the most idyllically handsome of all places where wine is made. Follow the Via Chiantigiana (SS222) s from Florence through Strada, Greve, Panzano and Castellina to Siena, through wooded hills where vines and olive groves, cypresses and pines surround medieval castles, villas and stone farmhouses.

The complete Chiantigiana route includes a detour through the domain of the original Chianti League, founded in the 13thC by the feudal barons of Castellina, Gaiole and Radda. This can be extended to take in the Castello di Brolio — where, in the 19th century, modern Chianti was invented by Baron Bettino Ricasoli — and the historic abbey of Badia a Coltibuono, as well as the villages of Volpaia, Vertine, Ama, Lecchi, Castagnoli, Villa a Sesta, Monti, San Felice, San Gusmé, Villa d'Arceno, Castelnuovo Berardenga and Vagliagli. Wandering is equally rewarding in the western part of the zone, through San Casciano, Sant'Andrea in Percussina, Mercatale, Montefiridolfi, Badia a Passignano and San Donato in Poggio.

Most Chianti Classico estates welcome visitors, although it is wise to make appointments through the Gallo Nero consortium's headquarters near San Casciano *(Via degli Scopeti 155-158 Sant'Andrea in Percussina* ☎ *(055) 8228245)*. Three historically important houses, Castello di Brolio-Barone Ricasoli *(*☎*(0577) 749710)*, Marchesi Antinori *(*☎*(055) 282202)* and Ruffino *(*☎*(055) 8368307)* are not in the *consorzio*. Ricasoli and Antinori will accept group visits if arranged ahead of time. Ruffino conducts regular tours through its cellars at Pontassieve or, by arrangement, to its properties in Chianti Classico. Antinori's wines are served at the Cantinetta Antinori in the center of Florence (see FLORENCE RESTAURANTS).

A complete selection of Chianti Classico is sold at the Enoteca del Gallo Nero in Greve, the hub of Chianti and the setting of an annual wine fair in early September. Many shops with selections of Chianti's wine and food products can be found in the zone. Some estates have a trattoria on the premises, among them Montagliari near Panzano (see GREVE), Badia a Coltibuono (see GAIOLE) and the Tavernetta Machiavelli "Albergaccio" on the Conti Serristori property at Sant'Andrea in Percussina (where Niccolò Machiavelli spent much of his exile from Florence). Borgo San Felice is a comfortable hotel-restaurant on the San Felice estate. Some 70 estates offer *agriturismo*, with houses or rooms to let, sometimes with full board. The consortium can provide information.

SIENA/MONTALCINO/MONTEPULCIANO/SAN GIMIGNANO

Siena is sometimes called the capital of Italian wine, partly because it is the center of Tuscany's most important production zones and also because the **Enoteca Italiana**, the public national wine library, is located in its Medici fortress. Although the displays may be seen only by appointment *(*☎*(0577) 288497)*, select wines can be tasted at a bar that is open daily.

The city makes a convenient headquarters for traveling oenophiles — in Siena's province are the original sector of Chianti Classico, the Chianti Colli Senesi zone, the vineyards of the exceptional Brunello di Montalcino and Vino Nobile di Montepulciano, and the white Vernaccia di San Gimignano.

Montalcino, a hill town 40km (25 miles) s of Siena, is the home of the fabled red Brunello and the even older but currently less renowned Moscadello di Montalcino. The Medici fortress in the center of town houses an *enoteca* and tasting bar of Brunello.

Outside Montalcino is one of Italy's most famous wine estates, Il Greppo of Biondi-Santi, which may be visited by appointment *(*☎*(0577) 848087)*. Nearby is Fattoria dei Barbi, which has a *taverna* offering the estate's wines and food products (see MONTALCINO). Poggio Antico *(*☎*(0577) 849200)* also has a good restaurant on the premises. Villa Banfi *(*☎*(0577) 864111)* welcomes visitors to its ultramodern cellars and vineyards. A wine museum and restaurant are being prepared in its Castello Banfi.

The lovely Renaissance town of Montepulciano, 37km (23 miles) farther E, is surrounded by the vineyards of Vino Nobile *(*☎*(0578)*

757844), whose *consorzio* will arrange tours to the various cellars. And in San Gimignano, whose towers jut over a landscape of vines and olives, many producers of the vigorous white Vernaccia sell bottles in individual shops.

FLORENCE/RUFINA/CARMIGNANO
Florence is itself a wine town, center of the Colli Fiorentini Chianti zone and headquarters of many important Tuscan wineries. Italy's outstanding collection of wines (including French and Californian) may be viewed in the cellar of the restaurant Enoteca Pinchiorri (see FLORENCE RESTAURANTS).

Rufina, a zone 20km (13 miles) E of Florence, makes some of the finest Chianti. Within its limits is the well-known wine house of Ruffino (see under Chianti Classico) and the Marchesi de' Frescobaldi (☎ *(055) 2381400)* properties of Nipozzano, Remole and Pomino. The latter is the lone producer of Pomino DOC, from a tiny zone adjacent to Rufina.

Carmignano, a zone some 25km (16 miles) W of Florence, produces a scarce red wine that was recently promoted to DOCG. There are only about a dozen producers whose wine can be sold as Carmignano, and only if approved by experts in a rigorous annual blind-tasting. The wines are displayed at a small *enoteca* in the center of town. The Fattoria di Artimino, in the Medici villa of the "Hundred Chimneys," is open to visitors.

OTHER ITINERARIES
The Consorzio Vino Chianti DOCG *(Lungarno Corsini 4, Florence* ☎ *(055) 212333),* which supervises production outside the Classico zone, can help arrange visits to estates in Colli Fiorentini, Rufina, Montalbano, Colli Aretini, Colli Senesi and Colline Pisane.

Nearly every center of interest to tourists has a wine area nearby. Pisa has Bianco di San Torpè to the SE. Lucca has two DOC zones, Rosso delle Colline Lucchesi, to the N, and Montecarlo, a white wine produced around the village of that name.

From farther E, near Montecatini Terme, comes Bianco della Valdinievole. In Arezzo province, the broad Chiana valley between Cortona and Montepulciano is the home of Bianco Vergine Valdichiana.

Tuscany's coast also produces good wines. The island of Elba is noted for red and white DOC wines, as well as a sweet red Aleatico di Portoferraio, which Napoleon reputedly liked.

In the Maremma hills of Grosseto province there are three DOCs: Morellino di Scansano, Bianco di Pitigliano and, adjacent to the Argentario peninsula, Parrina. Livorno province has the DOCs of Montescudaio, Val di Cornia and Bolgheri, although the most prestigious wines belonging to this last zone are the unclassified reds of Sassicaia, Ornellaia and Grattamacco.

> I believe that there is much happiness in people
> who are born where good wines are found.
> (Leonardo da Vinci)

KEY TO MAP PAGES

MAPS 7-15 : TUSCANY

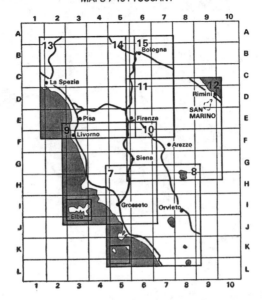

KEY TO AREA MAP SYMBOLS

- ⊂O⊃ Autostrada (with access point)
- Main Road / 4-Lane Highway
- Other Main Road
- Secondary Road
- Minor Road
- SS73 Road Number
- - - - Ferry
- Railway
- ✈ Airport
- - · - International Boundary
- - - Provincial Boundary
- ⩗ Good Beach
- Castle
- Abbey, Monastery
- Ancient Site, Ruin
- 12 Adjoining Page No.

```
0      5     10    15    20km
0            5         10miles
```

Key to area map symbols is located on first page of this area map section

7

T 4 5 Le Cornate
1060

G
H

*561

Montieri

Massa
Marittima

9

Tirli
Vetulonia

Gavorrano

Ribolla

O S C A N A

Chiusdino

10 S. GALGANO

Monticiano

SS223

5 6

Murlo

11 AB. DI
M. OLIVE
MAGGIOR

Buoncon

M. Quoio
647

F. Merse

SS441

SS73

M. Labbro
1193

Casale
di Pari

Montalcino

S. Quiri
d' Orci

Ba
Vig

Roccastrada

Civitella
Marittima

S. ANTIMO

Campagnatico

Batignano

Cinigiano

Castel
del Piano

Arcidosso

Pia

NECROPOLI
ETRUSCA

F. Bruna

ROVINE DI
ROSELLE
Roselle

Istia d' Ombrone

M. Labbro
1193

GROSSETO

SS322

M

Roccalbegna

SS323

SS323

Marina di
Grosseto

Principina
a Mare

F. Ombrone

Alberese

M. Bottigli
319

Scansano

Semproniano

ROVINE
ETRUSCHE

Saturnia

I
J
9

S. RABANO

Monti dell'Uccellina

M. Cornuto
246

Magliano
in Toscana

Montemerano

Pitig

Fonteblanda

SS323

S. BRUZIO

F. Albegna

Manciano

Talamone

SS1

SS74

M. Cavallo
234

M. Bellino
516

L. Acquato
378
M. Maggiore

LA ROCCA
DI MONT

Porto
S. Stefano

Orbetello

Capalbio

PONTE DELLA
ABBADIA

DEL GIGLIO

Monte
Argentario

COSA RUDERI
Ansedonia
TAGLIATA ETRUSCA
L. di Burano

VULC

K

Port' Ercole

GIANNUTRI

Montalto
di Castro

Campese

Giglio Castello
Giglio Porto

I. del Giglio

4 5

J

K

MARE

TIRRENO

(TYRHHENIAN SEA)

I. di Giannutri
Villa
Romana

4 5

6

SARDIN

CLE

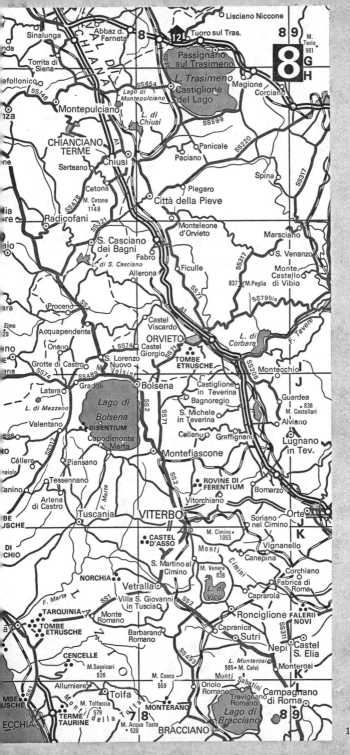

9

E
F

LIVORNO

Marina di Pisa
S. Piero a Grado
Tirrenia
Cascina
F. Arno Pontedera
S. Minia
SS67bis
13
3 4
SS67
Ponsacco
Palaia
SS555
SS555
Collesalvetti
Crespina
Capannoli
I. GORGONA
CORSICA
SARDINIA
Ardenza
Fauglia
Lari
SS439
Peccioli
Antignano
Montenero
Lorenzana
Terricciola
SS206
Casciana Terme
Orciano Pisano
S. Luce
Quercianella
Rosignano Marittimo
Castellina Marittima
SS1
Castiglioncello
Montecatini Val di Cecina
F. Era
SS439d
SS439
F
G
Vada
SS68
Riparbella
Montescudaio
F. Cecina
Marina di Cecina
Cecina
Bibbona
MARE
LIGURE
(LIGURIAN SEA)
Bolgheri
Larderello
Marina di Castagneto
(Donoratico Mare)
Castagneto Carducci
SS329
Monteverdi Marittimo
Monterotondo
SS398
Sassetta
G *I. Capraia* 1
H
Capraia
S. Vincenzo
M. Calvi 646
Suvereto
M.
58
1
Campiglia Marittima
Venturina
SS398
F. Cornia
SS1
Riotorto
SS439
Populonia
TOMBE ETRUSCHE
H
I
Piombino
Follonica
Gavorrano
Scarlino
M. d' Alma 559
SS322
Canale di Piombino
Golfo di Follonica
ELBA
Punta Ala
Tirli

Isola d'Elba 2 3 PIOMBINO
H
I
I. CAPRAIA
H
Marciana Marina
Biodola
Portoferraio
Rio Marina
Le Rocchette
Riva del Sole
Castiglione della Pescaia
Poggio
S. Martino
Marciana
Procchio
M. Capanne 1018
Laconia
Porto Azzurro
Fetovaia
Cávoli
Marina di Campo
Capoliveri
M. Calamita
413
I. Pianosa
I. PIANOSA
2 3

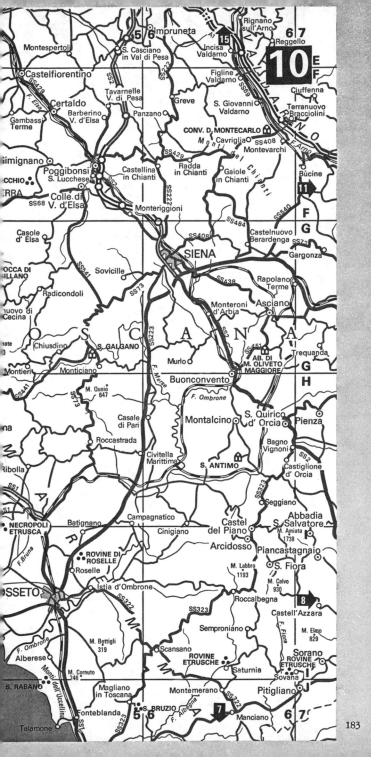

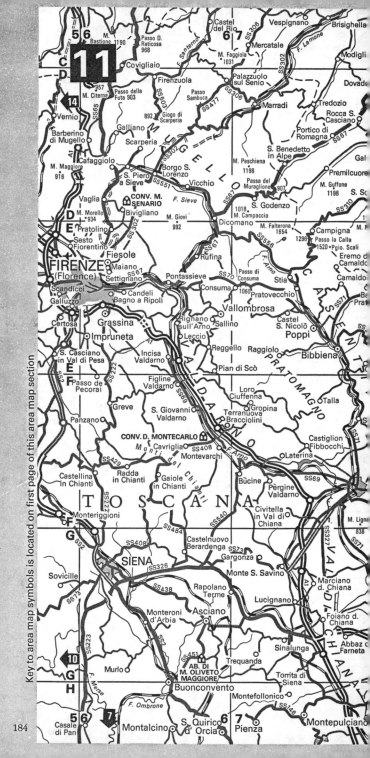

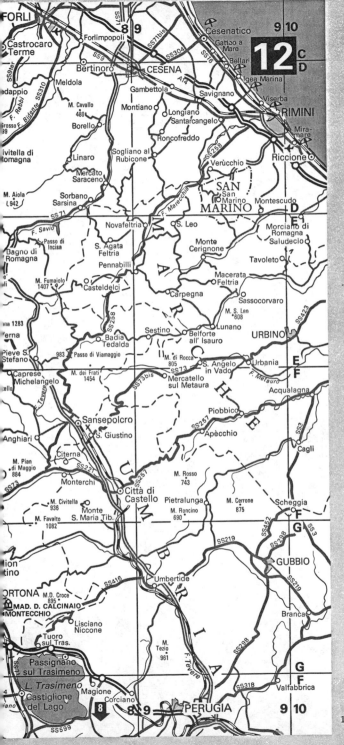

Key to area map symbols is located on first page of this area map section

1 2 M. Barigazzo • 1284

A
B **13**
Valmozzola

2 3
Calestano
Langhirano

SS62

F. Taro

A15

M. Montagnana 1312

SS523
Borgo
Passo del Bratello 953
Berceto
Passo della Cisa 1039
Comiglio
Tizzano V. Parma
Vetto
SS513

M. Grezzano 1245
M. Orsaro 1830
L. Santo
Pontremoli
M. Sillara • 1861
Monchio
Ramiseto
Castelnovo ne' Monti

F. Secchi

Filattiera
Passo di Lagastrello 1200
M. Alto 1904
Busana

B
C
Mulazzo
Bagnone
Villafranca in Lunigiana
Comano
SS63
L. Cerreto
Passo del Cerreto 1261
Passo di Pradarena 1579
Ligonchio
M. Cusna 2120

Tresana
Licciana Nardi
N

Pódenzana
Aulla
SS63
Fivizzano
Sillano
Giuncugnano
M. Prato 2053
Passo

S. Stefano di Magra
SS445
Casola in Lunig.
S. Romano
Villa Colle
SS324

Vezzano Lig.
SS62
Fosdinovo
Minucciano
M. Pisanino 1945
Castigl
Pieve

C
D
LA SPEZIA
Sarzana
SS446
Campo Cecina
L. di Vaglit
Vagli Sotto
Careggine
Castelnuovo di Garfagna

Portovenere
Golfo della Spezia
Lerici
SS1
LUNI
CARRARA
Gallicano

I. Palmaria
Fiaschettino
Avenza
MASSA

Montemarcello
Marina di Carrara
Montignoso
A P U A N E

Marinella di Sarzana
Marina di Massa
Seravezza
Pescaglia
Bo
Mo

Vittoria Apuana
Forte dei Marmi
Pietrasanta
Camaiore
Diecin

RIVIERA DELLA VERSILIA
Marina di Pietrasanta
M. Meto 370
Pon
Mor

Lido di Camaiore
SS439

D
E
MARE
VIAREGGIO
Massarosa
LUC

LIGURE
Torre del Lago Puccini
L. di Massaciuccoli
SS439

(LIGURIAN SEA)
SS1
A11
S. M
di G

Migliarino
SS12
S. Giu
Terme
Calc

Gombo
PISA
SS67
Vico

SS224
Marina di Pisa
S. Piero a Grado
SS1
SS67bis

E
F
I. Gorgona
Tirrenia
SS555

1 2
Collesalvetti
Fauglia

1 2
I. GORGONA
CORSICA
SARDINIA
2 3
LIVORNO
Ardenza
9

186

Key to area map symbols is located on first page of this area map section

15

A
B

BOLOGNA

IMOLA

FAENZA

FIRENZE (Florence)

Portomaggiore
S. Giorgio di Piano
Minerbio
Molinella
Argenta
Granaralo dell'Emilia
Budrio
S. Antonio
Anzola d'Emilia
Zola Predosa
Casalecchio di Reno
Castenaso
Conselice
Medicina
Massa Lombarda
Sasso Marconi
Ozzano d'Emilia
Mercatale
Castel S. Pietro Terme
Castel Guelfo
Bagnara di Romagna
Marzabotto
NECROPOLI ETRUSCA
Castel Bolognese
Casalfiumanese
Borgo Tossignano
Riolo Terme
Loiano
Sassoleone
Casola Valsenio
Brisighella
Monghidoro
Castel del Rio
Mercatale
Modigliana
M. Bastione 1190
Passo D. Raticosa 968
M. Faggiola 1031
Castiglione dei Pepoli
Covigliaio
F. Santerno
Palazzuolo sul Senio
Dovadola
M. Citerna 957
Firenzuola
Passo Sambuca
Marradi
Tredozio
Rocca S. Casciano
Sasseta
Vernio
Passo della Futa 903
Giogo di Scarperia 892
Portico di Romagna
Barberino di Mugello
Galliano
MUGELLO
S. Benedetto in Alpe
Premilcuore
Scarperia
M. Peschiena 1198
M. Guffone 1198
S. Sofia
Cafaggiolo
M. Maggiore 916
S. Piero a Sieve
Borgo S. Lorenzo
Vicchio
Passo del Muraglione 907
Vaglia
M. Senario 815
Bivigliano
F. Sieve
S. Godenzo
M. Campaccio 1018
M. Marino 1066
Campigna
M. Morello 934
M. Giovi 992
Dicomano
M. Falterona 1654
Passo la Calla 1296
Pgio. Scali T520
Pratolino
Sesto Fiorentino
Fiesole
Maiano
Settignano
Rufina
Passo di Consuma
Eremo di Camaldoli
Scandicci
Galluzzo
Certosa
Candeli
Bagno a Ripoli
Pontassieve
Consuma
Camaldoli
Grassina
Imprunet
Rignano sull'Arno
Saltino
Stia
Pratovecchio
Vallombrosa
Castel S. Nicolò
Poppi
Badia Prataglia
S. Casciano in Val di Pesa
Incisa Valdarno
Leccio
Reggello
Raggiolo
Bibbiena
Chitignano
Passo de Pecorai
Figline Valdarno
Loro Ciuffenna
Talla
PRATOMAGNO
Greve
Panzano
S. Giovanni Valdarno
Gropina
Terranuova Bracciolini
Subbiano

Tuscany A to Z

> I know that as the train emerges from its tunnel
> into the Val d'Arno, and I see once more
> the grey olive trees of Tuscany,
> I think of the grey-eyed Goddess of Wisdom
> and I feel that I have come home.
> (Kenneth Clark, *The Other Half,* 1977)

The joy of Tuscany is that almost any corner of its beautiful and varied landscape is likely to harbor some natural or man-made treasure. Within this A to Z section, text and symbols describe highlight attractions. The ★ denotes a recommended sight, the ☆ symbol means "worth a detour," and ⅲ identifies a building of special architectural interest. Hotels (✍) and restaurants (═) are suggested throughout, and more cursory listings note additional sights and reliable but less remarkable hotels and restaurants.

ABBADIA SAN SALVATORE
Map 8l7. 143km (89 miles) s of Florence, 75km (47 miles) s of Siena. 53021. Siena. Population: 8,232 i Via Mentana 97 ☎*(0577) 778608.*
This dour little industrial town near the summit of MONTE AMIATA has grown up around the medieval abbey of San Salvatore. Skiing and climbing are available nearby. The medieval center is near Piazza XX Settembre.

SIGHTS AND PLACES OF INTEREST

ABBAZIA DI SAN SALVATORE †
The abbey, founded in 743, became the richest and most powerful center of Benedictine feudalism in central Italy. All that remains is the 11thC church, adapted in the late 16thC and, below, the 8thC crypt, supported by 36 columns with wonderful capitals.
BORGO MEDIOEVAL (Old Town)
A rare and fascinating example of a Gothic-Renaissance mountain village that has remained almost completely intact.

═ **Sala Carli** *(Via Pinelli 46* ☎*(0577) 779444)* ▯ to ▯ 🔲 🔲 🔲 🔲 *closed Mon).*

✍ ═ Near the summit of MONTE AMIATA, 14km (9 miles) w, is **La Capannina**, a quiet skiers' hotel, with restaurant *(*☎*(0577) 789713* 🔲*789777* ▯ *open July-Sept, Christmas, Easter, and on special request).*

ABETONE

Map 14C4. 90km (56 miles) NW of Florence. 51021. Pistoia. Population: 859
i Piazza delle Piramidi, Abetone ☎(0573) 60383.

In the mountains above PISTOIA near the Tuscan-Emilian border,
Abetone is one of the oldest-established ski resorts in the Apennines,
with the most difficult and best-equipped runs in Tuscany. There is
also a short summer season for walkers and climbers.

Fir trees grow in the protected **forest of Abetone**. Nearby resorts
include **Cutigliano** and **San Marcello**.

☜ There are some 35 hotels, and they maintain an adequate but not luxurious
standard. One with a pleasant garden is **Bellavista** (☎ *(0573) 60028* ☐ *open
mid-Dec to mid-Apr, mid-June to mid-Sept).*

≡ **La Capannina** *(Via Brennero 256* ☎ *(0573) 60562* ▥ ▣ ◉ ◉ *closed
Tues dinner, Wed),* which has rooms; and the enoteca **Val Buia** *(Via Brennero
251* ☎ *(0573) 60134* ▥ *closed Tues).*

At Cutigliano, 12km (7½ miles) to the SE, is **Da Fagiolino** *(Via Carega 1*
☎ *(0573) 68014* ▥ *to* ▥ ▣ ◉ ◉ ▨ *closed Tues dinner, Wed, Nov).*

ANGHIARI

*Map 12F8. 105km (65 miles) SE of Florence, 28km (17 miles) NE of Arezzo.
52031. Pistoia. Population: 6,052.*

There are spectacular views of the upper Tiber valley as far as SANSE-
POLCRO from this attractive walled hill village. The battle of Anghiari
(subject of Leonardo's famous cartoon for an unrealized painting) was
fought in 1440 between Florence and Milan.

SIGHTS AND PLACES OF INTEREST

In the 18thC church of **Santa Maria delle Grazie** is a *Last Supper* (1531) by G. A.
Sogliani. The Renaissance **Palazzo Taglieschi** *(Piazza Mameli 16; ring for
admission)* houses a museum of local art and custom.

≡ **Alighiero** ♦ (☎ *(0575) 788040* ▥ *closed Thurs);* at Monterbone, 4km
(2½ miles) on the Arezzo road, is **Castello di Sorci** ♦ (☎ *(0575) 789066* ▥ ▣
▨ *closed Mon),* where you get five hearty, wholesome courses and as much wine
as you can drink, at a low fixed price.

See also SANSEPOLCRO.

SHOPPING **Busatti Tessitura** *(Via Mazzini 12* ☎ *(0575) 788424).* Specializes in linen, cotton, wool and hemp. Established 1892.

ANSEDONIA

*Map 7J5. 186km (115 miles) SW of Florence, 45km (28 miles) S of Grosseto.
58016. Grosseto.*

The rocky promontory on the S coast of Tuscany was the site of the
Roman city of Cosa, which was founded in 273BC and became the
center of a large and flourishing commercial and agricultural colony
that is now partly developed with holiday villas.

SIGHTS AND PLACES OF INTEREST

RUINS OF COSA
Entrance through Porta Romana.
After passing through the best preserved of the gates, the Roman main street leads to the Forum. Nearby, a recently excavated private house and garden have been partially reconstructed; the domestic objects and decorations can be seen in the small **museum/restoration center** built by the American Academy.

Above is the walled Acropolis and, at the highest point, the Capitolium (✦). Below, on the beach beyond the Roman port, long since silted up, is the so-called **Tagliata Etrusca**, a canal cut by the Romans between their port and the Lake of Burano.

Nearby at **Settefinestre** are the remains of an important 1stC BC Roman villa and its attendant farm buildings, which were rediscovered in 1980. The villa was known in the 15thC, and aspects of its plan bear a resemblance to Renaissance villas, particularly POGGIO A CAIANO.

The lake of Burano at Capalbio Scalo is a designated bird sanctuary.

🍴 **Il Pescatore** *(Via della Tagliata 13* ☎*(0564) 881201* ▥ *closed Tues, mid-Jan, Sept, Oct),* near the Tagliata. See also CAPALBIO, ORBETELLO, PORT'ERCOLE and PORTO SANTO STEFANO.

AREZZO ★
Map 11F7. 81km (50 miles) SE of Florence. 52100. Arezzo. Population: 92,087
i Piazza Risorgimento 116 ☎*(0575) 20839.*
Arezzo today is a busy, prosperous, provincial town at the center of the rich farming country of the Valdichiana and Valdarno. Its factories manufacture agricultural equipment, women's fashions, leather goods and costume jewelry; and its streets buzz with new, imported motor-bikes driven by stylish young Aretines with good jobs and a long, proud ancestry.

Etruscan Arezzo was one of the most powerful and sophisticated cities of the federation. Later, under the Romans, it became a key stronghold, thanks to its strategic location commanding all the passes of the central Apennines. Aretine craftsmen were famous throughout the Roman world for their metalwork and ceramics.

As an independent republic from the late Middle Ages its sympathies were predominantly Ghibelline, and it was in the Guelf-Ghibelline Battle of Campaldino in 1289 that Arezzo suffered its first defeat by the Guelf Florentines.

The republic recovered in the early 14thC under the leadership of Bishop Guido Tarlati, when the Duomo, Palazzo del Comune, the Pieve and the church of San Domenico were built, but finally surrendered to Florence in 1384. Petrarch, Spinello Aretino, Pietro Aretino and Vasari were all born in Arezzo. And it was a leading Aretine family, the Bacci, that was responsible for what is surely one of the most inspired com-missions in the history of Renaissance patronage — Piero della France-sca's frescoes in the church of San Francesco.

Events ‡ An antique market is held in the Piazza Grande, the main square, on the first Sunday of every month; the stalls do business from noon on the previous day. ‡ The annual historic spectacle is the Joust

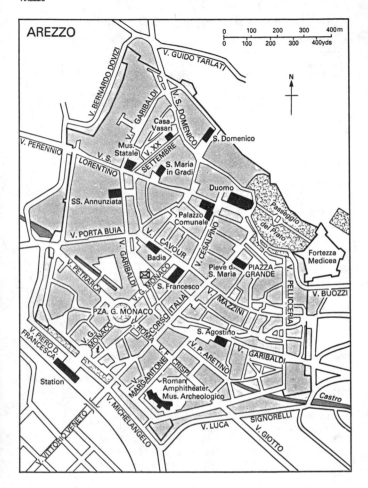

of the Saracen *(Giostra del Saracino)*, which takes place in the Piazza Grande on the first Sunday of September. ‡ An international choral festival in June attracts competitors from all over the world.

SIGHTS AND PLACES OF INTEREST

CASA DI GIORGIO VASARI 🏛 ★
Via XX Settembre 55.
Vasari lovingly supervised the building of his own house (1540-48), a delightful example of Mannerist domestic architecture. He also executed the frescoes, which are the most ingenuous and charming of all his creations.

DUOMO †
The imposing 13th-14thC cathedral of Arezzo has an early 20thC facade, a 19thC campanile and, on the right flank, an attractive 14thC portico. The interior is illuminated by high stained-glass windows by Guillaume de Marcillat of which the finest is the *Expulsion from the Temple* at the bottom of the right aisle. The 14thC tomb of *S. Donato* in the apse is a collaborative work by Sienese, Florentine and local artists. At the bottom of the left aisle is Piero della Francesca's oddly stiff *Magdalen* (after 1466), his only surviving work in Arezzo apart from the frescoes in San Francesco (see below). To its left is the magnificent *tomb of Bishop Guido Tarlati* (1330) by Agostino di Giovanni and Agnolo di Ventura, possibly to a design by Giotto. In the sacristy, entered from the left aisle, is a striking and strongly personal detached fresco of *St Jerome* by Bartolomeo della Gatta. The late 18thC Chapel of the Madonna of Comfort contains fine terra cottas by the Della Robbias.

MUSEO ARCHEOLOGICO MECENATE
Via Margaritone 10.
The loggia of the 16thC monastery, which now houses the **Archeological Museum**, is built round a curve of the 1stC BC Roman amphitheater. The famous **coralline vases** (✩), glazed according to a technique invented by Aretine craftsmen in the 1stC BC and later much copied, are in Rm. VII.

MUSEO STATALE D'ARTE MEDIOEVALE E MODERNA ▥
Via S. Lorentino 8.
Attractively arranged on three floors of the 15thC **Bruni-Ciocchi Palace**, which has a fine courtyard possibly designed by B. Rossellino. There are important paintings by local artists, notably Margaritone d'Arezzo, Parri di Spinello, Spinello Aretino, Bartolomeo della Gatta and Vasari; and, in Rms. VI to VIII, a fine **collection of majolicas** (13th-18thC).

PIAZZA GRANDE ✩ ▥
The main square of Arezzo is one of the liveliest and most architecturally heterogeneous in Tuscany. The NE side is closed by Vasari's handsome **loggia** (1573); its shop-fronts retain their original stone counters. On the w is the apse of the Pieve (see below) and the extraordinary layered facade of the **Palazzetto della Fraternità dei Laici**; its ground floor is Gothic (1377), the Renaissance first floor was begun after 1434 by B. Rossellino who made the sculptures, and the upper loggia was completed in 1460 by Giuliano and Algozzo da Settignano, who added the balustrade.

PIEVE DI SANTA MARIA ▥ † ✩
Corso Italia, Piazza Grande.
The rigorously ornate **facade** of this parish church is the outstanding example of Pisan-Lucchese Romanesque architecture in eastern Tuscany. The church was erected between the mid-12thC and early 14thC. Notice the fine relief carvings (1216) over the central portal. The tall campanile (1330) is the emblem of Arezzo; pierced by 40 bifore windows, it is known locally as "the tower of 100 holes."

The nave is divided by clustered columns supporting early Gothic arches. The oldest part of the church is the raised presbytery. Here is Pietro Lorenzetti's restored polyptych of the *Madonna and Saints* (1320), the artist's earliest known work.

SAN DOMENICO †
Piazza Fossombroni.
Built between 1275 and the early 1300s, San Domenico has a Romanesque portal and a Gothic campanile that retains two of its original bells. The interior is like a giant scrapbook of fragmented frescoes (15th-16thC). Over the high altar is a moving painted *Crucifix* (1260-65) by the young Cimabue.

SAN FRANCESCO ▥ †
The Franciscan basilica in the center of Arezzo was built in the 13th to 14thC in the simple Umbrian-Tuscan style; the campanile is 15thC. In the choir is one of the

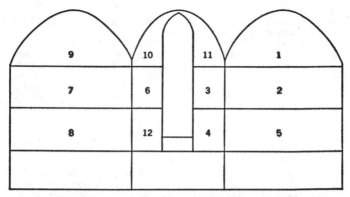

THE LEGEND OF THE TRUE CROSS: KEY **1** The Death of Adam **2** The Queen of Sheba Adoring the Holy Wood (left); The Queen of Sheba's Visit to Solomon (right) **3** The Burying of the Wood **4** The Dream of Constantine **5** Constantine's Victory over Maxentius **6** The Torture of Judas **7** The Discovery and Proof of the True Cross **8** The Victory of Heraclius over Chosroes **9** Heraclius Restores the Cross to Jerusalem **10 & 11** Prophets **12** The Annunciation

major artistic masterpieces of Europe: Piero della Francesca's noble, compelling **frescoes** (★), painted in the middle of his career; the subject is the *Legend of the True Cross*. The legend links man's original sin to his redemption by tracing a series of events whereby the tree from which Adam ate the forbidden fruit becomes the Cross on which Christ is crucified.

Earlier painted interpretations of the story can be seen in SANTA CROCE (see FLORENCE A TO Z) by Agnolo Gaddi and in San Francesco at VOLTERRA by Cenni di Francesco.

Piero's frescoes, painted in the 1450s, are badly decayed, especially on the w wall, and it takes time to adjust one's eyes to the complex dimensions of the scheme and the bare patches of plaster left by the latest restoration. To complicate matters further, the story is taken from different versions of the legend and is not related in chronological order. The two great battle scenes that face one another from the side walls are placed out of narrative sequence for the sake of artistic balance. The explanation that follows is keyed to the plan.

The tonality of the right wall is cooler, and the quality of the painting is higher than that on the left wall, which seems to have been executed with assistance. Scholars disagree about which wall was painted first and whether Piero continued to work on these frescoes after his return from his visit to Rome in 1459. The narrative unfolds as follows.

Right wall, apex (1): In the right section of the frame Adam announces his impending death; in the left section, the dead Adam is surrounded by his children and Seth plants a branch of the tree in his father's mouth. **Central band (2), left section:** The tree, grown so large that even Solomon cannot use it for his palace, has been made into a bridge over the River Siloam; the Queen of Sheba instinctively recognizes its sacred origins and kneels at the bridge. **Right section:** The Queen of Sheba is received by Solomon and predicts to him that a man will be nailed to the tree and the Jews will thereby be disgraced.

Right window wall, center (3): The beam is buried by Solomon's order; the scene deliberately prefigures the Carrying of the Cross. **Bottom (4):** Constantine is asleep in his tent on the eve of battle; an angel points to him announcing that he will be victorious if he looks for and defends the sign of the Cross.

Right wall, lowest band (5): The victory of Constantine over Maxentius.

Left window, middle section (6): Judas is tortured and reveals the whereabouts of the Cross.

Left wall, central band (7), left section: The Empress Helena discovers the Cross; in the background a view of Arezzo represents Jerusalem. **Right section:** Judas proves the Cross by raising a man from the dead; the church in the background recalls the architectural style of Piero's friend and fellow mathematician, Alberti. **Lowest band (8)**: 30 years after the discovery of the Cross, the Persian King Chosroes has stolen it from Jerusalem; he is defeated in battle by Heraclius, Emperor of the East. **Apex (9)**: Heraclius returns the Cross to Jerusalem.

> Piero had the power of creating forms which immediately
> satisfy us by their completeness; forms which reconcile the mathematical
> laws of proportion with the stress and tension of growth,
> forms which combine the resilience of a tree trunk
> with the precision of a pre-dynastic jar.
> (Kenneth Clark, *Piero della Francesca*, 1951)

The other frescoes in the chapel are outside the main narrative. The most important is the **Annunciation (12)**, on the lowest section of the left window wall, probably painted in 1466 after Piero's visit to Urbino. The **prophet** to the right of the window's apex **(11)** is by Piero, the one on the left **(10)** is by an assistant.

Returning to the nave, notice in the third chapel on the left the superb late 13thC **Crucifix of St Francis**, and in the second chapel the Pieroesque frescoes of the *Miracles of St Anthony of Padua* by Lorentino d'Arezzo. The glass of the rose window (1524) of the interior facade is by Guillaume de Marcillat.

Binoculars can be rented in the church shop.

OTHER SIGHTS

Other points of interest in Arezzo include the **Palazzo Comunale**; the **Fortezza Medicea**, which commands splendid views; the churches of **S. Maria in Gradi**, **SS. Annunziata**, **S. Agostino**, and the **Badia**; and, 1.5km (1 mile) to the s of the Piazza della Repubblica, the church of **S. Maria delle Grazie**, with a graceful portico by B. da Maiano. In summer it is pleasant to picnic in the **Passeggio del Prato**, the public gardens behind the Duomo.

☞ ═ CONTINENTALE

Piazza Guido Monaco 7, 52100 Arezzo ☎(0575) 20251 ▣(0575) 350485 ▥ 74 rms, all with bathrm ☲ ৬ ❤ ▤ ▣ ◉ ◉ ▥ ৬ ▢ ▱ ▰ *Restaurant closed Sun dinner, Mon.* Modern, comfortable and central hotel. The somewhat gloomy restaurant is a favorite with local businessmen.

═ Arezzo is one of the wealthiest cities in Italy. It is also the official birthplace of the now ubiquitous *pappardelle a la lepre*. Nevertheless, there is no outstanding restaurant in town. The obvious choice, for its location next to the Church of San Francesco and for its ambience, is the **Buca di San Francesco** (*Via San Francesco 1* ☎ *(0575) 23271* ▥ ▣ ◉ ◉ ▥ *closed Mon dinner, Tues, July*).

An alternative in the center is **Le Tastevin** (*Via de' Cenci 9* ☎*(0575) 28304* ▥ ▣ ◉ ◉ ▥ *closed Mon, Aug*).

La Fattoria ❖ 4km (2½ miles) sw at Olmo (☎ *(0575) 998770, closed Wed*) serves produce from a wine-making estate.

And **Del Pescatore** ❖ (*Via Sette Ponte 19B* ☎*(0575) 364096* ▥ *closed Wed*) is a decent trattoria located in a tiny hamlet on the Arno 10km (6 miles) to the northwest.

ARTIMINO

Map 14E5. 22km (14 miles) w of Florence. 50042. Firenze. Population 260.
An old, walled village in a wine-producing zone.

SIGHTS AND PLACES OF INTEREST

VILLA MEDICEA DI ARTIMINO ☆
✗ by appointment ☎*(055) 8718072/8718081.*
The smiling Medici villa near Artimino is built on a plateau of Monte Albano that
commands extensive views over the surrounding hills. Known as the "Villa of the
Hundred Chimneys," it was designed by Buontalenti in 1594 as a hunting lodge for
Ferdinand I.

The interior is decorated with good *pietra serena* fireplaces and frescoes
attributed to Poccetti and Passignano.

There is also an **Etruscan Museum** in the villa *(open 9am-1pm, closed Wed,
Sun)*, and the estate has a shop and small restaurant where its own wines are
offered for sale (see TUSCAN WINES on page 178).

SAN LEONARDO ▥ †
This well-preserved Romanesque church was allegedly founded by Countess
Matilda in 1107. It was constructed with Etruscan fragments from the nearby
necropolis of Pian di Rosello.

NEARBY SIGHTS

There are two Etruscan tombs near Comeana, 3km (2 miles) N, where signs point
to the **Tomba dei Boschetti** (7thC BC) and the monumental **Tomba di Monte-
fortini** *(*☎*(055) 8719420, open Tues-Sun 9am-1pm, closed Mon).*

❧ ➾ PAGGERIA MEDICEA ▥
Viale Papa Giovanni XIII 3 ☎*(055) 8718081* ✉*571502* ℻*(055) 8718080* ▥ *to* ▥ *37
rms, all with bath* ▤ ➘ ➚ AE ◉ ⦿ VISA ⌂ ⌂ ⛴ ⟨⟨ ↝ ⟲ ➼ ⛄ □ ⟁
A peaceful hotel in a 16thC villa. It has a restaurant, the **Biagio Pignatta** *(*☎*(055)
8718086* ▥ ➘ AE ◉ ⦿ VISA *closed Wed, Thurs lunch)*

➾   Try **Da Delfina** *(Via della Chiesa* ☎*(055) 8718074* ▥ *no cards, closed
Mon dinner, Tues* ➘*)*, a pleasant restaurant, specializing in game. Reservations
essential. See also LASTRA A SIGNA.

ASCIANO

*Map 11G6. 91km (57 miles) SE of Florence, 20km (12½ miles) SE of Siena.
53042. Siena. Population: 5,897.*
A walled medieval hill village in the upper Ombrone valley. The Corso
Matteotti is lined with interesting old houses.

SIGHTS AND PLACES OF INTEREST

MUSEO DI ARTE SACRA
Piazza Sant'Agata.
Left of the Travertine Collegiata di Sant'Agata (11thC but much restored) is this
notable collection of 14th-15thC Sienese School painting and sculpture. Of special
interest are the **polyptych** by the young Matteo di Giovanni; *St Michael and the
Dragon* by A. Lorenzetti; *Birth of the Virgin* by the Master of the Osservanza;
Madonna by Barna; and two graceful wooden statues of the *Annunciation* by
Francesco di Valdambrino.

MUSEO ETRUSCO
Corso Matteotti.
In the former church of S. Bernardino, this museum houses material from the Etruscan necropolis of Poggiopinci, 5km (3 miles) E of Asciano.

BAGNI DI LUCCA
Map 14D4. 101km (63 miles) NW of Florence, 27km (16 miles) N of Lucca. 55021/2. Lucca. Population: 7,991 i Via Umbertol 101 ☎(0583) 87946 (May-Oct).

The healing properties of the sulfur and saline waters at the Baths of Lucca were recognized from the 13thC, but it was a foreigner, Napoleon's sister Elisa Baciocchi, who gave Bagni di Lucca its Empire tone. Mrs Trollope was scarcely exaggerating when she wrote, "Bagni di Lucca belongs, like so much else in Italy, exclusively to foreigners."

The list of distinguished foreign literary visitors includes Montaigne, Heine, Lamartine, Shelley, Byron, Landor, the Brownings and Ouida.

A little seedy now, Bagni di Lucca is nevertheless an inexpensive place to take the waters or merely to savor the somewhat claustrophobic atmosphere created by the mild, humid climate, the mature plane trees, and the weight of nostalgia for the vanished Victorian presence. Those who enjoy hill-climbing will share the pleasure Shelley took here.

In the Piazza del Bagno is a charming early 19thC **bath house**, although it is now abandoned and crumbling. Just above is the **Palazzo Bonvisi**, where Shelley and Byron stayed and which Montaigne described. The **English Cemetery**, reached by a bridge over the River Lima behind the Circolo dei Forestieri, is sadly neglected.

Bridge, at Ponte a Serraglia, 3km (2 miles) w (☎(0583) 87147 ▯); or **Svizzera** *(Via Contessa Casalini 30 ☎(0583) 87114 ▯ to ▯ no cards, open May-Sept).*

Circolo dei Forestieri *(Piazza Varraud 10 ☎(0583) 86038 ▯ closed Mon, Jan).*

BAGNO A RIPOLI
Map 11E6. 7km (4 miles) SE of Florence. 50012. Firenze. Bus no. 33. Population: 25,139.

This suburb of Florence is named after the remains of a Roman bath. There is pretty hill country above, and, towards Florence, the impressive 14thC church of **S. Pietro a Ripoli** and **Abbey of Ripoli**.

VILLA LA MASSA
Via La Massa, 50010 Candeli, Firenze ☎(055) 666141 ▮573555 ▮(055) 632579 ▯ to ▯ 40 rms, all with bathrm ▯ ▯ ▯ ▯ ▯ ▯ ▯ ▯ ▯ ▯ ▯ ▯ ▯ ▯ ▯ ▯ ▯ ▯ ▯

A 16thC villa on the Arno, now a beautifully run and furnished hotel set in a romantic park. The restaurant, **Il Verrocchio** (▯ ▯) is outstanding.

CENTANNI
Via Centanni 7 ☎(055) 630122 ▯ ▯ ▯ ▯ ▯ ▯ Closed Sat lunch, Sun, Aug.
In an entrancing location, especially on a hot summer evening.

BARGA
Map 13D3. 111km (70 miles) NW of Florence, 37km (23 miles) N of Lucca. 55051. Lucca. Population: 10,952 i Piazza Angelio ☎(0583) 73499.
The prettiest hill town in the Garfagnana stands above an active, industrial new town.
Event　‡ An opera festival takes place in summer.

DUOMO (San Cristofano) ✝
The rectangular, buttermilk-colored Duomo, dating from the 9thC, contains an extraordinarily well-preserved late 12thC **pulpit**, sculpted with all the serious charm of the period with scenes from the *Lives of Christ and Mary*.

In the **apse** is a huge wooden statue of *St Christopher*. In the chapel to the right are attractive unglazed Robbianesque terra cottas. The **loggetta of the Podestà**, to the left of the Duomo, preserves a rare set of 15thC official measures.

☎ ☴　**La Pergola** (☎ *(0583) 711239* ⊞ *closed Fri in winter, Dec).*

BIBBIENA
Map 11E7. 59km (37 miles) SE of Florence, 32km (20 miles) N of Arezzo. 52011. Arezzo. Population: 10,716 i Via Cappucci ☎(0575) 93098.
This is the chief town of the Casentino, the remote upper valley of the Arno, enclosed by wooded mountains. The great monasteries of CAMAL-DOLI and LA VERNA are reached by road from Bibbiena. The 16thC **Dovizi Palace** — which once belonged to Benedetto Dovizi, influential playwright, secretary of Pope Leo X and patron of Raphael — stands opposite the 15thC church of **San Lorenzo**.

The main street leads uphill to the delightful Piazza Tarlati, which commands a view of the Casentino toward POPPI and where there is a clock tower in the remains of the medieval Tarlati fortress. The church of **SS. Ippolito e Donato**, rebuilt in the 14th and 15thC and later given a Baroque facelift, contains a *Madonna and Child* (1435) by Bicci di Lorenzo and a panel of the same subject (c.1420) by a rare artist, Arcangaelo di Cola da Camerino.

The attractive Renaissance church of **Santa Maria del Sasso**, off the La Verna road, has very fine inlaid 16thC choir stalls in its convent chapel.

☎ ☴ AMOROSI BEL ♣
Via Dovizi 18, 52011 Bibbiena, Arezzo ☎(0575) 593046 ⊞ 20 rms, 12 with bathrm▣
Restaurant closed Wed; last orders 7.30pm.
This old inn has a solemn turn-of-the-century atmosphere.

BIVIGLIANO
Map 11D6. 18km (11 miles) N of Florence. 50030. Firenze. Population: 620 i Via delle Scuole 4.
A summer resort on the w slope of Monte Senario.

High above the town is the **Convent of Monte Senario**, the mother house of the Servite Order, which was founded in the 13thC. The buildings date mostly from the late 16thC. There are stupendous views of the Arno and Sieve valleys.

NEARBY SIGHT
9km (5¾ miles) s is the 15thC Servite **Convent of La Maddalena**, with frescoes by Fra Bartolommeo.

🏊 🍽 **Giotto Park** *(Via Roma 9-11, 50030 Bivigliano* ☎*(055) 406608* [Fx]*(055) 406730* [ℐ] [AE] [◆] [CB] [VISA] *35 rms, all with bathrm. Restaurant closed Tues* 🍴*).*

🏊 🍽 See FIESOLE.

BORGO SAN LORENZO
Map 11D6. 29km (18 miles) NE of Florence. 50032. Firenze. Population: 14,724.
The principal center of the Mugello (see ROUTE 6 on page 65), the old town was destroyed by an earthquake in 1919 and is now heavily industrialized.

NEARBY SIGHTS
3km (2 miles) N, approached by a fine avenue of cypresses, is the church of **S. Giovanni Maggiore**, with an 11thC campanile and, inside, a rare Romanesque intarsiaed ambo.

Just 0.5km (3½ miles) w is **S. Piero a Sieve**, where the parish church contains a terra-cotta font in the style of Luca della Robbia; above is Buontalenti's **S. Martino fortress**.

To the NE of S. Piero a Sieve, a country road leads to the **Convento del Bosco ai Frati** *(visits by request* ☎*(055) 848111)* one of the original Franciscan communities, rebuilt (1420-38) by Michelozzo. In the sacristy is a wooden *Crucifix* attributed to Donatello. Two villas, **Cafaggiolo** and **Trebbio**, both built by Michelozzo for the Medici, are to the w of S. Piero a Sieve beyond Novoli.

7km (4 miles) SE is **Vespignano**, birthplace of Giotto. The house designated as Giotto's is N of the road. Farther along is **Vicchio**, where Fra Angelico was born and where Benvenuto Cellini took refuge from 1559-71 in the house next to the Oratory in Corso del Popolo.

3.5km (2 miles) NE of **Scarperia**, an industrial and crafts center with a fine Palazzo Pretorio of 1306, is the village of **Sant'Agata**, with a strikingly unusual Romanesque Pieve. The road to the N climbs through the mountain pass of Scarperia at 882m (2,894ft), the "little Switzerland" of the Mugello, which is known locally as *il Giogo*.

🏊 🍽 The **Villa Ebe** *(Via Ferracciano 11* ☎*(055) 8457507* [ℐ] [AE] [CB] [VISA] *restaurant closed Mon)* is in an 18thC villa surrounded by a large park. **La Felicina** *(Piazza Colonna, San Piero a Sieve (* ☎*(055) 848016* [ℐ] [AE] *closed Sat; Sept)* also has rooms.

🍽 Two useful restaurants at Barberino di Mugello are **Le Capannine** *(Viale Don Minzoni 88, Cavallino Mugello (near the autostrada exit)* ☎*(055) 8420078* [ℐ] 🍴 *no cards, closed Mon)* and **Il Cavallo** *(Viale della Repubblica 7* ☎*(055) 841363, closed Wed)*, which does good cheeses and fresh fish as well as meat.

CAMALDOLI
Map 11E7. 71km (44 miles) SE of Florence, 46km (28 miles) N of Arezzo. 52010. Arezzo. Population: 50.
Camaldoli, mother house of a reforming order of the Benedictines

founded in the early 11thC by St Romauld, stands isolated high in the Apennines above the Casentino. Its buildings are mostly of the 17th-18thC, and of little interest apart from the 16thC **pharmacy**.

NEARBY SIGHT

2.5km (1½ miles) above the monastery, at 1,104m (3,622 feet), is the **eremo** (hermitage) where the medieval monks lived in absolute isolation in the midst of their magnificent forest. The delightful Baroque church of **Il Salvatore**, and the 20 monastic cells, including the one occupied by St Romauld, may be visited.

≈ IL CEDRO
Via di Camaldoli 20, Moggiona, 5km (3 miles) s on the Poppi road ☎(0575) 556080 ▢ ▭
▦ *No cards. Closed Mon.*
A serious and popular small restaurant overlooking the mountains. Specialties are *tortelli di patate, capriolo, cinghiale, fritti di verdure.*

CAPALBIO
*Map 7J6. 182km (113 miles) sw of Florence, 18km (11 miles) NE of Ansedonia.
58011. Grosseto. Population: 3,950.*
This walled medieval village retains its 14thC ramparts and steep medieval streets. It is a center of horse-breeding and is near the large **Maremma hunting reserve**, which is open to the public in season *(inquiries to Riserva Turistica di Caccia dell'Ente Provinciale per il Turismo, Castello Collacchioni* ☎*(0564) 896024).*

≈   Capalbio is well endowed with attractive, aromatic restaurants, which serve hunters' food, especially wild boar (try the wild boar sausage) and roebuck cooked in unusually appetizing ways. Most light open fires in the winter and spread onto terraces in summer.
    Trattoria Da Maria *(Via Comunale 3* ☎ *(0564) 896014)* ▥ ▣ ▥ *closed Tues, Feb);* or **Trattoria Toscana** *(Via Vittorio Emanuele 2* ☎*(0564) 896028* ▢ ▥ *closed Wed).*

CAPRESE MICHELANGELO
*Map 12F8. 123km (76 miles) sE of Florence, 45km (28 miles) NE of Arezzo.
52033. Arezzo. Population: 1,799.*
An agricultural hill village where Michelangelo was born on March 6, 1475, while his father was the Florentine magistrate *(podestà).* The magistrate's house, the **Casa del Podestà**, is opposite the entrance to the restored 14thC **Castello**.

❧ ≈   **Fonte della Galletta** ♣ 6km (4 miles) to w at Alpe Faggeto *(* ☎ *(0575) 793925* ▢ *to* ▥ ▣ *closed Oct-Apr, restaurant closed Wed)* for game and mushrooms, and views over the Tiber valley.

CARMIGNANO
Map 14E5. 22km (14 miles) w of Florence. 50042. Firenze. Population: 7,691.
This little town is surrounded by vineyards that produce the venerable Carmignano wines (see TUSCAN WINES on page 178).

SAN MICHELE †
In this Gothic parish church, over the second altar on the right, hangs Pontormo's *Visitation* (c.1530) (★), one of his greatest and best-known masterpieces.

⇒ See ARTIMINO and LASTRA A SIGNA.

CARRARA

Map 13D2. 126km (80 miles) NW of Florence, 55km (34 miles) N of Pisa. 54033. Massa-Carrara. Population: 70,213 i Piazza 2 Giugno 14 ☎(0585) 70894.

To reach the cathedral in what remains of the old center of Carrara, one must penetrate a vast, modern boom town that still thrives on the quarries that have yielded their famous marble for more than 2,000 years.

Today this is one of the major world sources of marble, producing 500,000 tons each year.

SIGHTS AND PLACES OF INTEREST

Piazza Alberica boasts some fine **Baroque palaces** including Pietro Tacca's birth place. In Piazza C. Battisti is the Neoclassical **Teatro degli Animosi** (1840), admired by Dickens and other 19thC travelers.

DUOMO ⋔ † ☆
An ornate version of the Pisan-Lucchese style. The lower facade and portal date from the 12thC, and the elaborately carved Gothic upper story, with its rose window, was added in the 14thC. The simple, elegant interior contains a 14thC *Virgin Annunciate* and Gothic-style *Angel.*

MOSTRA NAZIONALE MARMI E MACCHINE
Viale XX Settembre ♣
A permanent exhibition demonstrating techniques of marble quarrying, cutting and carving. The **quarries** themselves are spectacular; those 7km (4 miles) to the E, at Colonnata, and 5km (3 miles) to the NE at Fantiscritti, will admit visitors.

◐ **Michelangelo** *(Via Carlo Rosselli 10 ☎(0585) 777161-3* ▥ ▦ ▣ ▦ ▦ *).*

⇒ **Soldaini** *(Via Mazzini 11 ☎(0585) 71459* ▥ *closed Sun dinner, Mon)* is cool and pleasant.

CASCINA

Map 14E4. 75km (47 miles) SW of Florence, 17km (10 miles) SE of Pisa. 56021. Pisa. Population: 34,701.

In this center of furniture manufacture is the 12thC **Pieve di Santa Maria**, a remarkably well-preserved example of the Pisan Romanesque style. The 14thC **Oratory of San Giovanni** has interior frescoes dating from 1398, by Martino di Bartolomeo.

NEARBY SIGHTS

Vicopisano, 6km (3½ miles) to the NE, retains picturesque 14thC fortifications restored by Brunelleschi. 9km (5½ miles) to the NW is Calci, with a fine 11thC Pisan-Romanesque **Pieve**.

Nearby on the Montemagno road is the **Certosa di Pisa**, a splendid complex of 17th-18thC Baroque buildings.

CASTELLINA IN CHIANTI

Map 11F6. 50km (31 miles) s of Florence, 21km (13 miles) N of Siena. 53011. Siena. Population: 2,843.

This small town was the first seat of the medieval Chianti League and one of the original centers of the Chianti Classico wine-growing zone. The medieval **Rocca** was extended by the Florentines in 1400; Etruscan remains include the 4thC BC tomb of Montecalvario, and a well.

❖ SALIVOLPI
Via Fiorentina, 53011 Castellina in Chianti, Siena ☎(0577) 740484 ☒(0577) 741034 ▥ *19 rms* ▨ ▨ ▨ ▨ ▨ ▨
A charming family-run hotel.

❖ ≡ TENUTA DI RICAVO
53011 Castellina in Chianti, Siena ☎(0577) 740221 ☒(0577) 741014 ▥ *25 rms, all with bathrm* ▨ ▨ ▨ ▨ ▨ ▨ ▨ ▨ ▨ ▨ ▨ ▨ ▨ *Closed Dec-Mar. Restaurant closed Mon, Tues lunch.*
4km (2½ miles) s, on San Donato road. An isolated medieval farming village transformed into an excellent Swiss-managed hotel.

❖ ≡ VILLA CASALECCHI
53011 Castellina in Chianti, Siena ☎(0577) 740240 ☒741111 ▥ *19 rms, all with bathrm* ▨ ▨ ▨ ▨ ▨ ▨ ▨ ▨ ▨ *Closed Nov-Mar.*
1km (½ mile) s, on Siena road. Enfolded in a pine wood in the hills.

❖ At San Leonino, 9km (5½ miles) s off the Siena road, is the unpretentious, rustic **Belvedere di San Leonino** *(* ☎*(0577) 740887* ☒*(0577) 741034* ▥ *to* ▥ ▨ ▨ *).*

≡ **Albergaccio** *(Via Fiorentina 35 (* ☎ *(0577) 741042)* ▥ *to* ▥ ▨ ▨ ≡ ▨ *Closed Sun; Mon lunch)* is an elegant new restaurant where the cooking and presentation are so far perfect in every detail.

La Torre *(Piazza del Comune (* ☎*(0577) 740236* ▥ ▨ ▨ ▨ ▨ *closed Fri)* offers a generous choice of traditional rustic dishes.

❖ ≡ See also suggestions under GAIOLE , GREVE and RADDA IN CHIANTI.

CASTELLO

Map 5B3. 6km (3½ miles) NW of Florence. 50019. Firenze. Bus #14 to Careggi from Florence Duomo or station.

The name Castello derives from an ancient Roman *castellum* or reservoir from which the Romans transported water to Florence by way of an aqueduct. Here, at the base of Monte Morello, are three important Medici villas within pleasant walking distance of one another. The two earliest Medici villas, **Trebbio** and **Cafaggiolo**, are a short drive up the Via Bolognese (see ROUTE 6 on page 65), and ARTIMINO and POGGIO A CAIANO are to the w.

SIGHTS AND PLACES OF INTEREST

VILLA MEDICEA DI CAREGGI ▥
Viale G. Pieraccini 17 ☎*(055) 4277501. Visits by appointment.*
The villa of San Piero at Careggi was acquired by the Medici in 1417 and extensively remodeled from the 1430s by Michelozzo. The loggiaed wing to the left of the

facade may have been added later in the 15th century, possibly by Lorenzo de' Medici. The house was surrounded by working farms; but the Medici used it primarily for rest, recuperation from illness and study. "I came to the villa at Careggi not to cultivate my field but my soul," wrote Cosimo il Vecchio in a letter to the philosopher Marsilio Ficino. Cosimo died at Careggi, as did his son Piero and his grandson Lorenzo.

The villa was burned and looted after the expulsion of the Medici, and restored in the 16thC by Pontormo and Bronzino.

VILLA MEDICEA DI CASTELLO 🏛 ☆

Via Castello 47 ☎(055) 454791. Garden open 9am-sunset, closed Mon.

Cosimo de' Medici was brought up at Castello. After his election as head of the Florentine government in 1537, he commissioned Niccolò Tribolo to design a lavish and novel garden in celebration of the abundance brought to the region by the waters of Florence and Tuscany under the virtuous rule of Cosimo.

The project was carried forward by Vasari after 1554, and at the end of the century the garden was expanded by Cosimo's son Ferdinando. The original plan, which represented a miniature Tuscany, was greatly altered in the late 18thC, but some of its outstanding features survive.

The great **fountain**, designed and modeled by Tribolo in the 1550s, was the most ambitious ever seen by that time; its culminating sculpture of *Hercules and Anteus* was executed by Ammannati in 1559. The **grotto** (★), probably designed by Vasari and completed c.1572, is one of the most delightful and original creations of the Italian Renaissance. The animals were carved from variegated marbles by Antonio di Gino Lorenzo. The bronze birds by Giambologna, which originally decorated the vault, are now in the BARGELLO in Florence.

On the top terrace above the formal gardens, is the crouching bronze half-figure known as *January*. It represents the Apennine mountains in winter and was cast by Ammannati in 1565.

VILLA MEDICEA DELLA PETRAIA 🏛

Via della Petraia 40 ☎(055) 451208 ⚲ Open 9am-sunset; closed Mon. The villa closes one hour earlier than the gardens.

The garden of Petraia climbs the hillside above Castello, to which it is connected by a magnificent English-style park. The old castle at the summit of the hill, of which the adapted central tower remains, was rebuilt from 1591-97 by Buontalenti for Ferdinando de' Medici, who had become grand duke of Tuscany in 1587 and must have enjoyed the extensive view over his domain from the piano nobile.

In the courtyard, which was glazed over in the 19thC by Victor Emmanuel II, who used it as a ballroom, is a pleasing fresco cycle glorifying the Medici, by Volterrano.

The garden was much modified in the 19th and early 20thC. Tribolo's marble **fountain** (c.1545) was moved in the 18thC, to the upper terrace, from its original site at Castello. The culminating nude female figure wringing her hair represents the city of Florence personified by Venus. It was executed by Giambologna in 1572.

❦ ☰ VILLA LE RONDINI

Via Bolognese Vecchia 224, 50139 Castello, Firenze ☎(055) 400081 ✉575679 🖾(055) 268212 ▥ to ▥ 44 rms, 40 with bathrm � 🏨 AE ⓢ ⓞ ▥ 🖾 🖾 ✿ 《 ☰ ♨ 🛇 ♠ ☕

A peaceful hotel in a 16thC villa on the hill of Monterinaldi.

☰ LO STRETTOIO

Serpiolle ☎(055) 4250044 ▥ ▭ 🏨 ☰ ➤ 《 Open dinner only 8pm-midnight. Closed Sun, Mon, Aug.

Refined Tuscan cooking in an old mill overlooking Florence. Reservations are essential.

CASTELNUOVO BERARDENGA

Map 10G6. 20km (12½ miles) E *of Siena. 53010 Siena. Population: 6,276.*
This is the market town of the productive wine- and olive-growing area where the SE margins of the Chianti meet the barren clay hills of the Crete. It is reached from Siena by a fine road that runs through land-scape reminiscent of the backgrounds of Sienese paintings.

The town itself is pleasant but unremarkable, apart from the tower and other remains of a **castle** built by the Sienese in 1366, and the park of the **Villa Chigi**, which is owned by the Monte dei Paschi bank. At **Pacina**, 2.5km (1½ miles) sw, there is a striking baroque church, S. Maria Maddalena, with a cylindrical 9thC campanile and an altarpiece of the Madonna and Child by Andrea di Niccolò.

❧ ☰ RELAIS SAN FELICE

Castelnuovo Berardenga, Siena 53019 ☎*(0577) 359260* Ⓕ*(0577) 359089* 🛏 *54 rms in 7 houses* ▥ ⬛ ☎ 🗔 📷 🔌 ≪ ⚲ ≋ ⚹ Ⓐ🅴 🔲 🔵 🖼 *Closed mid-Nov to Feb.*
This reconstituted hill-village just to the N opened in 1991 as a hotel, with rooms and suites in the restored houses. It has several restaurants and a conference center.

❧ ☰ VILLA ARCENO ⬛ 🏛

San Gusmè, Siena 53010 ☎*(0577) 359066* Ⓣ*574047 ARCENO* Ⓕ*(0577) 359030. 16 rms, all with bath* 🛏 *to* 🛏 ⬛ Ⓐ🅴 🔌 🔵 🖼 ✥ 🗔 ዿ ≋ ♨ ✓ ⚹ *Closed Feb.*
This supremely elegant hotel opened in the summer of 1991 in a handsome Neoclassical villa set in a 2,500-acre estate of vineyards, olive groves and oak woods. The bedrooms and reception rooms are impeccably furnished, in a quiet taste that is in keeping with the style of the villa; service is reassuringly practiced; and the restaurant serves a refined Tuscan cuisine complemented by wines and olive oil from the estate. There is a romantic early 19thC park with hidden lake and follies, an 18-hole golf course under construction, and a hunting reserve (wild boar and pheasant) accessible to guests in the season.

☰ OSTERIA DEL TRENTA

At Villa a Sesta, 12km (7½ miles) SE *on SS484* ☎*(0577) 359226* 🛏 ■ *Closed Tues, Wed.*
One of the most interesting restaurants in the area; but be aware that you will be expected to sample everything on the set menu — which is sometimes explained by a singing waiter. The French proprietress prefers Tuscan food, and understands how to bring out the flavors of local ingredients. The soft ewe's-milk cheese, *raveggiolo,* for example, which is hard to find even in its native region, is served simply on a bed of fresh salad greens.

☰ Also: **Pappus** *(Via del Chianti 30-34* ☎ *(0577) 355282* 🛏 *to* 🛏 Ⓐ🅴 🔵 🖼 *closed Mon; late Jan; Feb).*

CASTIGLION FIORENTINO

Map 11G7. 100km (62 miles) SE *of Florence, 17km (10½ miles)* S *of Arezzo. 52043. Arezzo. Population: 11,164* 𝒊 *Corso Italia 111.*
This walled market town, a major center in the Valdichiana, slopes down a hill above the Arezzo-Cortona road.

SIGHTS AND PLACES OF INTEREST

The graceful 16thC **Loggia del Vasari** in the central Piazza del Municipio frames a fine view, and from the castle keep above it one can see over the Valdichiana as far as MONTE AMIATA.

PALAZZO COMUNALE/PINACOTECA

Piazza del Municipio.
The most notable works in the gallery include a cheering 15thC reliquary bust of *St Ursula* as a shy, happy girl, made in the Rhineland; a 13thC Umbrian painted crucifix; and paintings by Bartolomeo della Gatta. There are also paintings by Bartolomeo della Gatta in the **Collegiata** and, in the adjoining **Pieve**, a *Deposition* (1438) by Signorelli. The late 13thC church of **S. Francesco** has a *St Francis* (1280-90) by Margaritone d'Arezzo.

NEARBY SIGHTS

On a hilltop 4km (2½ miles) to the s, is the imposing 13thC **Castello di Montecchio Vesponi** *(not open to the public),* given by the Florentines to the English *condottiere* Sir John Hawkwood.

CASTIGLIONE DELLA PESCAIA

Map 9I4. 162km (101 miles) s of Florence, 22km (14 miles) w of Grosseto. 58043. Grosseto. Population: 8,376.
The main coastal resort of the Maremma is also a busy fishing village, and private and professional craft moor in the lively harbor at the mouth of the River Bruna. Above is the 14th-15thC **Rocca Aragonese** defending the original medieval village, which is now over-gentrified. To the s stretch sandy beaches.

DAVID

At Poggiodoro, 2km (1¼ miles) N ☎(0564) 939030 ☒939031 ▭ 26 rms, all with bathrm ▤ ☰ ▱ AE ◉ ◍ ▥ ▱ ✿ ◀ ≈ ℘ ♨ ➡ ☒ *Closed mid-Oct to Easter.*
A quiet modern hotel with the benefit of superb views.

RIVA DEL SOLE

58043 Castiglione della Pescaia, Grosseto ☎(0564) 933625 ☒500034 ☒(0564) 935607 ▭ 175 rms, all with shower ▤ ◆ AE ◉ ◍ ▥ ▱ ◀ ⅙ ☒ ☐ ✿ ≈ ➡ ℘ ➡ ☰ ♨ ☒
A large, modern hotel in a new resort 3km (1¾ miles) up the coast.

☰ **Da Romolo** *(Via della Libertà 10 ☎(0564) 933533* ▭ AE ◍ ▥ *closed Tues, Nov)* is the best of the fish restaurants.

Tana del Cinghiale *(☎(0564) 945810)* at Tirli, 17 km (11 miles) N is a hunting lodge that specializes in wild boar. It has 7 rooms.

CERTALDO

Map 10F5. 40km (25 miles) sw of Florence, 40km (25 miles) Nw of Siena. 50052. Firenze. Population: 15,899.
Certaldo Alto, the fortified red-brick village where Boccaccio spent much of his life and died in 1375, stands above a modern suburb in the valley of the Elsa. The village was rebuilt in the 15thC and restored, a little too crisply, in the 19thC and again after World War II.

SIGHTS AND PLACES OF INTEREST

CASA DEL BOCCACCIO

Via Boccaccio 18. Open Mon, Thurs 4.30-7.30pm; Wed 9am-noon.
A postwar reconstruction of a house that possibly belonged to Boccaccio's family.

PALAZZO PRETORIO
Piazza del Comune. Open Tues-Sun, summer 9am-noon, 4-7pm; winter 10am-noon, 3-7pm.
Rebuilt in the 15thC, this palace has a pretty courtyard with quattrocento frescoes by P.F. Fiorentino and, in the adjacent chapel, fresco fragments by Gozzoli and Giusto d'Andrea.

SS. MICHELE E JACOPO †
Boccaccio's tomb was removed in 1783 by those who disapproved of his work. The modern tomb carries his own epitaph and his portrait bust (1503) by G.F. Rustici.

EXCURSION
The Franciscan convent of **San Vivaldo** is 20km (12½ miles) sw along a twisting road. The present buildings, from the early 16thC, are enfolded in the forest of Boscolazzeroni. The pilgrim chapels, each with a painted terra-cotta scene from the Passion, are unique in Tuscany.

There are fine Romanesque churches at **Pieve a Chianni**, **San Pancrazio** and **San Lazzaro a Lucardo**.

≡   See SAN GIMIGNANO.

CHIANCIANO TERME
Map 8H7. 120km (75 miles) SE of Florence, 85km (53 miles) SE of Siena. 53042. Siena. Population: 7,294 **i** *Piazza Italia 67* ☎*(0578) 63167 and Piazza Gramsci* ☎*(0578) 31292. Parco Stabilmento Acqua Santa* ☎*(0578) 64054.*
If you are driving from Chiusi, you will see two Chiancianos: the old hill town and, below it, the modern spa, which is one of the most important in Italy. The curative powers of the waters have been valued since the Roman age, and there are various types of water, for internal consumption or bathing.

A lovely rural road 7.5km (5 miles) to the s leads to **Sarteano**, a well-preserved medieval village of Etruscan origin, whose Neoclassical church of **S. Martino** contains Beccafumi's beautiful late *Annunciation* (1546); then, after 14km (9 miles), it brings you to the Etruscan village of **Cetona.**

♋   There are some 200 hotels and boarding houses of all categories open during the period from Easter to October.

≡   See CHIUSI.

CHIUSI
Map 8H7. 126km (79 miles) SE of Florence, 67km (42 miles) s of Arezzo. 53043. Siena. Population: 9,108 **i** *Via Petrarca 4* ☎*(0578) 20003.*
The Etruscan city of Camars, one of the greatest of the lucomonies, is best known to classical scholars and readers of Macaulay's epic poem *Horatius*, for its king, Lars Porsena, who carried out an attack on Rome in 508BC.

Today Camars lies buried around and under the little town of Chiusi, whose street plan is that of Clusium, the Roman military colony it became in 296BC.

SIGHTS AND PLACES OF INTEREST

DUOMO †
Beneath the campanile of the Romanesque cathedral, which is constructed from building fragments of the two earlier civilizations, is a large **cistern**, possibly 1stC BC. To visit, apply to the Museo Etrusco.

MUSEO NAZIONALE ETRUSCO ★
One of the outstanding Etruscan museums in Italy. The material, excavated from the vast necropolis surrounding the city, notably demonstrates the influence of Greece, Mesopotamia, Egypt and Rome on this sophisticated and receptive culture. There is a superb and varied collection of cinerary urns and sarcophagi, of which the most famous is the sarcophagus depicting the battle of the Gauls with a **portrait of Lars Sentinates** on the cover.

Also noteworthy are specimens of the heavy black *bucchero* ware, imitating metal, which was made only in Chiusi, and an unusually fine collection of Attic vases.

NECROPOLI ETRUSCA
✗ compulsory. Visits only permitted with guides from the Museo Etrusco.

The most notable Etruscan tombs are: to the N, along the Via delle Tombe Etrusche; the c.3rd-4thC BC **Tomba della Pellegrina**, with fine sarcophagi; the 5thC BC **Tomba della Scimmia** (Monkey Tomb), which retains rare wall paintings; and the **Tomba del Granduca**, with cinerary urns. To the E: the 5thC BC **Tomba Bonci Casuccini**, with its original door and frescoes of games; and the 1stC BC **Tomba delle Tassinaie**.

☞ **Il Patriarca**, located at the Querce al Pino autostrada exit (☎ *(0578) 274007* ▥ *)*, is set in a park that is scented in summer with the blossom of lime trees.

⇛ LA FRATERIA DI PADRE ELIGIO
10km (6 miles) s at Cetona in the Convent of San Francesco ☎*(0578) 238015/238261* ☞ ▥ ⇛ *Closed Tues, Jan.*
A first-class restaurant, with good local wines, in the refectory of a converted Franciscan convent. Five rooms.

⇛ 2.5km (1½ miles) to the N, on shore of Lake Chiusi, **La Fattoria** (☎ *(0578) 21407* ▥ 📧 🔲 🔳 ▥ *closed Feb; Mon except July-Sept* 🔁 *)*, where tiled floors and beamed ceilings give a farmhouse atmosphere. Also has rooms.

Zaira *(Via Arunte 12* ☎ *(0578) 20260* ▥ 📧 🔲 🔳 ▥ *closed Mon in winter)* is a delightful restaurant in the center. It has an extensive cellar of Italian wines and an inventive menu.

COLLE DI VAL D'ELSA
Map 10F5. 49km (30 miles) s of Florence, 25km (15 miles) NW of Siena. 53034. Siena. Population: 15,618.
There is an impressive view of this two-tiered town from the MONTERIG-GIONI road. The upper town has conserved its medieval street plan and some fine architecture.

Colle di Val d'Elsa has been a manufacturing center of fine crystal glass from the mid-14thC. The town was fiercely contested between Siena and Florence in the 13thC, and became part of the Florentine dominion in 1333.

The architect and sculptor Arnolfo di Cambio was born here in 1232.

SIGHTS AND PLACES OF INTEREST

COLLE ALTA ☆

The upper town, and the remains of its 12th-13thC fortifications, are strung along the ridge of the hill. Notice the frescoed palace facades in Via XX Settembre and other streets. The **Porta Nuova**, leading to the Volterra road at the end of Via Gracco del Secco, is a fine piece of late 15thC military architecture, probably by Giuliano da Sangallo. The medieval village is reached by a bridge from which there are fine views; straddling the ravine is the splendid unfinished Mannerist **Palazzo Campana** (1539) by Giuliano di Baccio d'Agnolo.

The **Via del Castello** opens into Piazza del Duomo, where the 14thC Palazzo Pretorio houses the **Antiquarium Etrusco** displaying material excavated from a necropolis near Monteriggioni. Inside the Baroque **Duomo** (1619) is a bronze *Crucifix* over the high altar attributed to Giambologna, and a bronze lectern by P. Tacca.

The **Palazzo Vescovile** *(Via Castello 27)* houses a little **Museo d'Arte Sacra**, where ecclesiastic vestments and objects and a late 14thC Sienese school triptych are displayed in one frescoed room.

In the old Palazzo dei Priori is the **Museo Civico**, with pictures by R. Manetti, P. F. Fiorentino and others; under a loggetta are frescoes by S. Ferri of *David and Goliath* and *Judith and Holofernes*. Toward the bottom of Via Castello *(#63)* is the early 13thC **tower-house** of Arnolfo di Cambio.

COLLE BASSA

The lower town is also known as il Piano, and its hub is the lively Piazza Arnolfo di Cambio. Nearby in Via dei Fossi is the church of **S. Agostino**, which has an unfinished 13thC facade. Its beautiful 16thC interior was designed by Antonio da Sangallo the Elder.

❧ VILLA BELVEDERE

Colle di Val D'Elsa, 53034 Belvedere ☎*(0577) 920966* ᴱˣ*(0577) 271370* ▥ *to* ▥ *15 rms, all with bathrm* ➤ ⌂ ▣ 回 ⊙ 回 ➾ ❦ ⏿ ⏚ ♞ ➾ 🐟 ♟

This hotel in an 18thC villa, a former residence of Tuscan grand dukes, is set in a park planted with magnificent old trees. Under the same management as the Palazzo Ravizza in Siena.

≕ ARNOLFO

Piazza Santa Caterina 1 ☎*(0577) 920549* ▥ ≕ ♞ ᴬᴱ ⊙ 回 ᵛᴵˢᴬ *Closed Tues.*

The atmosphere, of a hushed temple of food, verges on the pretentious. But the professionally prepared seasonal specialties justify the Michelin star. The wines, served with ceremonious solemnity, are fabulous. Reservations essential.

❧ ≕ **La Vecchia Cartiera** *(Via Oberdan 5-9* ☎*(0577) 921107* ᴱˣ*(0577) 923688* ▥ *to* ▥ ᴬᴱ ⊙ 回 ᵛᴵˢᴬ ▤ *restaurant closed Sun dinner, Mon* ♞*)*.

≕ **L'Antica Trattoria** *(Piazza Arnolfo di Cambio 23* ☎*(0577) 923747* ▥ ᴬᴱ ⊙ 回 ᵛᴵˢᴬ ♞ *closed Mon dinner, Tues)* is an elegant restaurant that serves an outstanding herb risotto.

8km (5 miles) N, at Poggibonsi, is **Alcide**, a reliable fish restaurant *(Viale Marconi 67a* ☎*(0577) 937501* ᴱˣ*(0577) 981729* ▥ *to* ▥ ᴬᴱ ⊙ 回 ᵛᴵˢᴬ *closed Wed, July)*.

EXCURSION

A minor road runs S off the Volterra road from S. Maria delle Grazie, through beautiful countryside to the old hill towns of **Casole d'Elsa** (14km/9 miles) and **Radicóndoli** (32km/20 miles), both on map **10**G5.

COLLODI
Map **14**D4. *63km (39 miles)* NW *of Florence, 17km (10 miles)* NE *of Lucca.*
51014. Pistoia. Population: 2,233.
Just to the W of PESCIA is the village where Carlo Lorenzini, author of
Pinocchio, spent his youth and gained his pen name, Carlo Collodi.

SIGHTS AND PLACES OF INTEREST

PARCO DI PINOCCHIO
✿ *Open daily until sunset.*
Games, statues and pavilions on the theme of Pinocchio and his creator.
VILLA GARZONI GARDENS ✫
▥ *Open daily.*
The most famous of Tuscan Baroque gardens was laid out in the 17thC and further
embellished with waterworks, statuary and French *parterres* in the late 18thC by
Ottaviano Diodati.

≡ **Gambero Rosso** *(Via S. Gennaro 2* ☎ *(0572) 429364* ▥ ▣ ▨ *closed
Mon dinner, Tues, Nov),* is convenient, but there are better restaurants at PESCIA
and in and near LUCCA.

CORTONA ✫
Map **12**G8. *102km (63 miles)* SE *of Florence, 32km (20 miles)* SE *of Arezzo.*
52044. Arezzo. Population: 22,561 ℹ *Via Nazionale 72* ☎ *(0575) 630352.*
The mythical founder of Cortona was Corythus, father of Dardanus,
which suggests that Cortona was older than Troy; and certainly the
town was already long established when it was occupied by the Etruscans in the 8th-7thC BC. The Romans took over in the 4thC BC; and in
217BC the main Roman army was destroyed nearby at Lake Trasimeno
by the Carthaginian general Hannibal. The commune that emerged
from the Dark Ages in the 12thC was brutally sacked by Arezzo in
1258, recovered in the 14thC under the steadying rule of the Casali
lords, and was eventually sold to Florence in 1411.
    The new association with Florence and the arrival of Fra Angelico,
who spent some 10 years in the monastery then attached to San Domenico, freed the art of Cortona from the archaizing domination of Siena.
In the second half of the 15thC, Cortona produced its own great native
painter, Luca Signorelli, whose work can be seen in the Diocesan
Museum and the church of San Niccolò. The painters Pietro da Cortona
and the Futurist Gino Severini were also natives of Cortona.
    Modern Cortona, the principal town of the Valdichiana, is a serious
place inhabited by farmers and bookish foreigners.
    The brown sandstone buildings of the old town are scattered down
the steep upper slope of Monte Sant'Egidio and wrapped in medieval
walls, which incorporate large sections built by the Etruscans. The main
street, Via Nazionale, known locally as Ruga Piana because it is the only
level street, leads from Piazza Garibaldi to the medieval nucleus, Piazza
Repubblica.
Events ‡ Market day is Saturday. ‡ There is an annual antique fair
from August 25 to September 25.

SIGHTS AND PLACES OF INTEREST

Leave time to explore some of the atmospheric old streets: Vie Benedetti, Maffei, Guelfa, Roma, Dardano and Berretini.

MUSEO DELL'ACCADEMIA ETRUSCA ▥

Palazzo Pretorio, Piazza Signorelli.

The Palazzo Pretorio, which houses the Etruscan Academy, was built in the 13thC and was later the residence of the Casali rulers; it was extended in the 17thC. In the main hall is the centerpiece, the famous but repulsive 5thC BC **Etruscan Lamp** (★), the largest and most elaborate Etruscan object of its kind. Small Etruscan objects are displayed in the glass cases, and among the pictures are the entrancing Greco-Roman painting on slate of the *Muse Polyhymnia,* and a very fine Pietro da Cortona *Madonna and Saints.*

The following rooms are filled with an intriguing, badly-labeled miscellany of Egyptian objects, porcelains, a good coin collection and, at the end, a small room devoted to Gino Severini.

MUSEO DIOCESANO ▥

Piazza Trento Trieste.

This important museum is opposite the Duomo in a former church, which was modified and partly frescoed by Vasari. Its rather gloomy atmosphere is lit up with the glowing spirituality of Fra Angelico's *Annunciation* (1433) (★); the predella is unusually fine, especially the episode of the *Meeting at the Golden Gate.* The other Angelico, a triptych of the *Madonna and Child with Saints,* also has a superb predella depicting *Scenes from the Life of St Dominic.*

Most notable among a number of Signorellis are his *Deposition* and *Communion of the Apostles.* Other highlights are the Sassetta *Madonna and Saints;* P. Lorenzetti's *Crucifix* and *Madonna and Angels;* and the Roman **sarcophagus** decorated with Amazons and Centaurs, which was greatly admired by Brunelleschi and Donatello.

At the far end of Via Dardano is the **Porta Colonia**, the best-preserved section of Etruscan wall, which commands a wonderful view.

OTHER SIGHTS

The most charming of the churches is **San Domenico**, which contains frescoes by Fra Angelico and Signorelli, and an altarpiece of the *Assumption* (c.1485) by Bartolomeo della Gatta. Behind it are public gardens where one may walk and enjoy fine views of the plain below. The **Sanctuary of St Margaret**, farther along Via S. Margherita, is an ugly 19thC church, which conserves the beautiful Gothic **tomb of St Margaret** by Angelo and Francesco di Pietro. From there it is a short climb to the **Fortezza Medicea**, which commands another magnificent view.

NEARBY SIGHTS

MADONNA DEL CALCINAIO ▥ ✝ ★

3km (2 miles) s, off Camucia road. For entry ask custodian, who lives in adjacent farmhouse.

A masterpiece of church architecture, designed (1485-1513) by the military engineer Francesco di Giorgio, the interior is notable for the springing energy of the space, which is organized so that the crossing is lit at all times of day by the round windows above. Vasari's answer, the church of **Santa Maria Nuova** (1554), is above the town.

There are four **Etruscan tombs** in the vicinity. Those at Sodo, to the NW toward Arezzo, and at Camucia, to the s toward Lake Trasimeno, are under huge mounds of earth known as *meloni,* and date from the 7th-6thC BC. The two near the Madonna del Calcinaio, the Grotta di Tanella and the Tanella Angora, may date from the 4thC BC.

3.5km (2 miles) to the NE, in a lovely situation, is the **Convent Le Celle**, founded by St Francis between 1211-21; one may visit St Francis' cell and the little 16thC church.

✤ OASI G. NEUMANN
Via Contesse 1, 52044 Cortona ☎ *and* ⊠(0575) 630354 ▥ *36 rms, all with bathrm* ▄ ▣ ▭ ▨ ≪ ✿ ☙ ▦ *Closed Oct-Mar.*
Just outside the walls to the S, in a former convent surrounded by a park.

✤ SAN MICHELE
Via Guelfa 15 ☎(0575) 604348 ⊠(0575) 630147 ▥ *32 rms, all with bathrm* ▣ ▣ ▣ ▨ ✦ ▢ ▱ *Closed Jan-Feb.*
All mod cons, in a medieval street in the center.

▬ **Tonino** *(Piazza Garibaldi 1* ☎ *(0575) 630500* ▥ ▣ ▣ ▣ ▨ ▰ *closed Mon dinner, Tues)* is a noisy restaurant known for its antipasti.

Outside the town center is **Il Falconiere** at San Martino (☎ *(0575) 612679* ▥ *closed Wed, Feb)*, which does *nouvelle cuisine*.

Also **Fonte dei Frati** on the Camucia road *(Case Sparse 294* ☎ *(0575) 601370* ▥*)*, noted especially for its vegetable antipasti and memorable *tagliolini al limone*.

ELBA (Isola d'Elba) ★
Map 9I2-3. Province: Livorno. By ferry: from Piombino to Portoferraio, Rio Marina and Cavo, 1hr by car ferry, 30mins by hovercraft (ferries run frequently through the day, reservation advisable July-Aug); from Livorno, daily boat takes 3hrs direct to Portoferraio or 5hrs with stops at islands of Gorgona and Capraia. By air: summer flights from Pisa. Population: 28,429.

Elba is the largest of the Tuscan islands, at 27km (17 miles) long and 18km (11 miles) across at its widest, E end, with an extremely irregular coastal perimeter measuring nearly 150km (93 miles). The highest point is the summit of the granite Monte Capanne (1,018m/3,340ft.), which dominates the wild western lobe of the island. Around the rest of the coast, majestic cliffs alternate with inviting sandy bays backed by evergreens.

The iron ore of Elba has been mined for at least 3,000 years. The Greek name for the island was Aethalia (Soot Island). The Etruscans transported the iron ore in great quantities to the mainland for smelting at Piombino; the main port was named PORTOFERRAIO (Port Iron) in the 8thC.

The more recent history of Elba was affected by two of the great modern imperialists, Duke Cosimo I of Florence and Napoleon. In 1548 Cosimo built and fortified Portoferraio and called it Cosmopolis. His ostensible purpose was to police the pirate-infested Tyrrhenian Sea; his more compelling motive was to gain a stronghold against the forces of Spain and France.

In the end, he was obliged to share control of the island with the Spanish, who built their own fortress at PORTO AZZURRO.

In 1814, the Congress of Vienna ceded Elba to Napoleon as his dominion in exile. He spent nine restless months here, reforming the administration of the island, furnishing his two villas, and plotting his escape, which took place on February 26, 1815.

The island can now offer to vacationers many facilities for sailing, waterskiing, underwater fishing, tennis, golf and riding.

The standard of the hotels on Elba is extremely variable. Many hotels insist on half-board, which is a pity, because their kitchens are rarely able to cope with the fresh fish that is the great gastronomic treat of Elba. Nearly every species of Mediterranean fish is caught in its clear waters — and which one you order will determine the price of your meal.

All the local wines are excellent, with a distinctive flavor from the minerals in the soil.

CAPOLIVERI

Map 9l3. 5km (3½ miles) sw of Porto Azzurro. Population: 2,397.

An isolated mining, fishing and wine-producing village on the SE of the island below the iron mountain of Monte Calamita. Stunning views.

Antares, 8km (5 miles) N at Lido (☎ *(0565) 940131* Fx *(0565) 940084* ☐ *to* ☐ AE ⊙ CD VISA *closed Nov-Mar)* is a quiet hotel with good views.

Il Chiasso (☎ *(0565) 968709* ☐ *all cards, closed Tues, Nov-Easter).*

CAVOLI

Map 9l2. 18km (11 miles) w of Portoferraio.

The loveliest small bays on the s coast and near the golf course of Acquabona.

Bahia at Seccheto, *(57034 Campo nell'Elba* ☎ *(0565) 987065* Tx 590220 Fx *(0565) 987020* ☐ *58 rms, all with bath* AE ⊙ CD VISA ➡ *closed late-Oct to Easter)* is a charming sea-side hotel all on one floor, hidden away in a delicious park planted with olives, lemons, oranges, and hibiscus.

At Fetovaia, 4km (2½ miles) to the w, are two quiet little *pensioni:* **Lo Scirocco** (☎ *(0565) 987060* Fx *(0565) 987244* ☐ *to* ☐ CD VISA *open Apr-late Oct)* is a handsomely decorated private hotel overlooking a relatively isolated beach; and **Galli** (☎ *(0565) 987065* Fx *(0565) 987011* ☐ *open Apr-Oct).*

LACONA

Map 9l3. 14km (9 miles) s of Portoferraio. Population: 200.

A quiet bathing resort on the s coast at the head of the long promontory that Napoleon made into his hunting estate.

Capo Sud

Lacona, 57037 Portoferraio, Isola d'Elba ☎*(0565) 964021* Fx*(0565) 964263* ☐ *to* ☐ *39 rms, all with bathrm* ➡ ➡ ⊙ ⌂ ⌂ ⌄ ⟨⟨ ⤴ ⌘ ⌘ ♈ *Pool opens 1993. Closed Oct-Apr.*

A quiet and comfortable group of cottages.

MARCIANA

Map 9l2. 27km (17 miles) w of Portoferraio. Population: 2,272.

This wine-producing village on the slope of Monte Capanne is dominated by the ruined castle of the Appiano lords, the hereditary rulers of Elba in the Middle Ages. The **Antiquarium** displays prehistoric, Etruscan and Roman material.

The **summit of Monte Capanne** (☆) is reached by funicular (🚡) in 30 minutes, or by mule in about $2\frac{1}{2}$ hours.

A 40-minute drive to the NW is the sanctuary of the **Madonna del Monte**, where Napoleon stayed in 1814.

🏨 At Sant'Andrea, 6km (4 miles) NW is **Cernia** *(57030 Marciana* ☎ *(0565) 908194* Ⓕ*x(0565) 908253* ▥ *AE* *VISA* *)*. There is also the **Piccolo Hotel Barsalini** *(*☎*(0565) 908013* Ⓕ*x(0565) 906364* ▥ *AE* ◐ *VISA* *)*. Both are peaceful hotels with gardens, and are closed Nov-Mar.

🍴 **Publius** at Poggio *(*☎*(0565) 99208* ▥ *to* ▥ *AE* ◐ ◐ *VISA* *closed Mon, Dec to mid-Mar)*, has good Tuscan cooking and one of the loveliest views on Elba.

MARCIANA MARINA
Map 9I2. 20km (13 miles) w of Portoferraio. Population: 1,907.
A relatively unspoiled fishing village in a lovely open position.

🏨 **Gabbiano Azzurro** *(*☎ *(0565) 99226* Ⓕ*x(0565) 99497* ▥ *to* ▥ *AE* ◐ *VISA* *)* is modern and straightforward.
  Also, **Marinella** *(*☎ *and* Ⓕ*x(0565) 99018* ▥ *to* ▥ *AE* ◐ ◐ *VISA* *)*.

🍴 Popular fish restaurants on the harbor: **Rendez-Vous da Marcello** *(Piazza della Vittoria 1* ☎*(0565) 99251* ▥ ▤ *AE* ◐ ◐ *VISA* 🍴 *closed Wed; mid-Nov to mid-Dec; mid-Jan to mid-Feb)* and **La Fiaccola** *(*☎ *(0565) 99094* *AE* ◐ *VISA* *closed Thurs)*.

MARINA DI CAMPO
Map 9I2. 17km (11 miles) sw of Portoferraio. Population: 1,732.
This fishing village and bathing resort commands a wide arc of sandy beach on the Gulf of Campo on the S coast.

🏨 **Dei Coralli** *(*☎ *(0565) 976336* Ⓕ*x(0565) 977748* ▥ ◐ *VISA* *open mid-Apr to mid-Oct)* is a peaceful pensione. See also CAVOLI.

🍴 **Bologna** *(Via Firenze 27* ☎*(0565) 976105* ▥ *AE* ◐ ◐ *VISA* *Closed Tues in winter)* is a big, cheerful fish restaurant in an old boat house.
  Also **Da Gianni** *(at La Pila Airport* ☎*(0565) 976965* ▥ *to* ▥ *closed Nov-Feb)*.

PORTO AZZURRO
Map 9I3. 15km (9 miles) se of Portoferraio. Population: 2,960.
The center of the Spanish protectorate in the 16th to 17thC, Porto Azzurro is still a charming sight from the Narengo side of the Gulf of Mola, although the harbor front has been spoiled by timid development.

To the N is the massive **Fortezza di Portolongone**, built by the Spanish in 1603; soon afterward, they built the sanctuary of the **Madonna di Monserrato**, which still stands 1.5km (1 mile) N of the town.

PORTOFERRAIO
Map 9I3. Population: 11,135.
The busy main town of Elba is magnificently situated on a promontory that gives shelter to its fine harbor. The old port is guarded by two fortresses that were built by Cosimo I in 1548, the large **Forte del Falcone** and the picturesque **Forte della Stella**.

SIGHTS AND PLACES OF INTEREST

Palazzina Napoleonica dei Mulini ☆
Napoleon created his residence in exile from two old windmills above the city near Forte della Stella. The furnishings for this delightful little palace were commandeered from his sister Elisa's house at Piombino; the plate and library were brought from Fontainebleau.

Villa Napoleonica di San Martino ☆
6km (4 miles) to w, on Marciana road.
Even in exile, an emperor must have a country estate; Napoleon filled this modest villa with personal symbols.

The long Neoclassical **Pinacoteca Foresiana** (1851), nearby, houses a large collection of 16th-19thC art.

➱ Residence le Picchiae
57037 Portoferraio ☎*(0565) 933072* 🔠 *933186* ▥ *to* ▥ *49 rms and 15 apartments, all with bathrm* ▦ 🍴 🏠 ≈ 🐟 🐟 ═ 📷 📺 ≪ ⟆ 🏌 ♟ ♗ *Closed Nov.*
8km (5 miles) s of Portoferraio, off Porto Azzurro road. A modern, peaceful hotel offering marvelous views.

➱   Also **Fabricia,** which is 8km (5 miles) SE at Magazzini *(Loc. Magazzini 57037 Portoferraio* ☎*(0565) 933181* 📠*590033* 🔠*(0565) 933185* ▥ *76 rms, all with bathrm* ═ ♗ *AE* 💳 *closed Oct-Apr).*

Villa Ottone, at Ottone 11km (7 miles) SE *(* ☎*(0565) 933042* 🔠*(0565) 933257* ▥ *to* ▥ *AE* 💳 *VISA open mid May-Sept).*

Two less expensive *pensioni:* **Acquaviva Park,** at Acquaviva 4km (2½ miles) w *(* ☎*(0565) 915392* 🔠*(0565) 916903* ▥ *to* ▥ *open Apr-Oct).*

Paradiso *(* ☎*(0565) 939034* 🔠*(0565) 939041* ▥ *open Apr-Sept).*

➱ ═ Hermitage
Loc. Biodola, 57037 Portoferraio ☎*(0565) 936911* 📠*500219* 🔠*(0565) 969984* ▥ *to* ▥ *120 rms, all with bathrm or shower* 🍴 ▦ ═ *AE* 📷 *VISA* ≋ ≈ ≪ 🐟 ⟆ ≀ ⚓ ♗ ♟
Its restaurant is also called **The Hermitage** *(* ☎*969932)* ▥ *AE* 📷 *VISA* 🍴 *Both closed Oct-Apr.*
Discreetly set into a hillside over a beautiful bay, 10km (6 miles) sw at La Biodola.

Another hotel, **La Biodola** *(* ☎*(0565) 936811* 🔠*969984* ▥ *AE* 📷 *VISA closed end Oct to mid-Mar)* is under the same management.

═   In the town, with pleasant outdoor tables, is **La Ferrigna** *(Piazza Repubblica 22* ☎*(0565) 9141129* ▥ *to* ▥ *AE* 📷 *VISA* 🍴 *closed Tues; winter).*

Also **Da Elbano** *(* ☎*(0565) 914628* ▥ *closed Mon, Oct-Nov)* at Casaccia on the road to La Biodola.

PROCCHIO
Map 9l2. 10km (6 miles) sw of Portoferraio. Population: 532.
One of the chief sandy-beach resorts on the N coast.

➱ Désirée
Lido di Spartaia. 57030 Procchio ☎*(0565) 907311* 📠*590649* 🔠*(0565) 907884* ▥ *80 rms, all with bathrm* ▦ ═ 🍴 *AE* 💳 📷 *VISA* 🛁 ≈ 🐟 ♗ 🎞 🎬 🏖 ≈ ≀ ⟆ ⚓
🏌 *Closed mid-Oct to Easter.*
A modern and anonymous but efficiently managed hotel with good access to a range of leisure facilities.

➱   Also at Spartaia is **Valle Verde** ☎*(0565) 907545* 🔠*(0565) 907965* ▥ *to* ▥ *AE* 💳 📷 *VISA closed mid-Oct to end Apr),* with a pretty garden.

A very simple hotel at Procchio is **Delfino** *(* ☎*(0565) 907455* ▥*).*

RIO MARINA
Map 9I3. 20km (12 miles) E of Portoferraio. Population: 2,420.
This is the principal mining town of Elba, and on the third floor of the Palazzo Comunale is an interesting little **mineral museum**.

The **iron mines** may be visited on Saturday in summer by appointment (☎ *(0565) 962001).*

➡ **La Canocchia** *(Via Palestro 3* ☎ *(0565) 962432* ▥ ▤ ▣ ▨ *closed Mon).*

EXCURSIONS

ISLAND OF CAPRAIA
Boats depart from Portoferraio daily in summer, Monday and Wednesday in winter; the journey takes 2-3 hours each way. Map 9G1-H1.

⚓ ➡ **Il Saracino** *(* ☎ *(0565) 905018* ▣ *(0565) 905062* ▥ ▨ *closed Oct-Mar).*

ISLAND OF MONTECRISTO
Hotels and travel agents will arrange group visits to the deserted island, which is now designated as a nature reserve.

EMPOLI
Map 14E5. 33km (20 miles) W of Florence. 50053. Firenze. Population: 45,802.
The vast and unlovely sprawl around Empoli, an important center of glass manufacture, disguises exceptional works of art. The painters Jacopo Chimenti, called Empoli, and Pontormo, were born here. The modern composer Ferruccio Busoni was also a native. There is a festival of his work in fall.

SIGHTS AND PLACES OF INTEREST

COLLEGIATA ▥ ✝
At the historic center of Empoli is the church that marks the western limit of the influence of the Florentine Romanesque; the lower section of its facade dates from 1093. The upper part is a post-World War II reconstruction of F. Ruggieri's late 18thC "rationalization."

PINACOTECA DI SANT'ANDREA ★
Piazza della Propositura ☎*(0571)72220. Open Tues-Sun 9am-12pm, also 4pm-7pm on Thurs, Fri, Sat. Closed Mon.*
The museum, which incorporates the Baptistry of the Collegiata, houses an important collection of painting and sculpture dating from the Tuscan Renaissance, and artists whose works are on display include Bicci di Lorenzo, Pontormo, Antonio and Bernardo Rossellino, Tino di Camaino, Mino da Fiesole, Masolino, and Gherardo Starnina.

In the 14thC church of **Santo Stefano** in Via S. Stefano there is a *Madonna and Child* (1424) and other frescoes by Masolino.

➡ At Bacchereto there is **Fontemorana** *(20 Via Fontemorana* ☎*(055) 8717086)* ▥ ▣ ▨ *closed Tues.)*

For other restaurants see also ARTIMINO and LASTRA A SIGNA.

FIESOLE ☆

Map 11E6. 8km (5 miles) NE of Florence. 50014, Firenze. Population: 14,788. The #7 bus from Florence (Piazza della Stazione) takes 35mins.

When Florence was a mere cluster of buildings on the Arno, Fiesole, on its conical hill overlooking the valleys of the Arno and the Mugnone, was one of the chief cities of Etruria. Some scholars place the Etruscan settlement as early as the 8thC BC, although the town is not recorded until 225BC. Faesulae was an important Roman military colony from 80BC and was later the capital city of Roman Etruria. In 1125 Florence sacked and superseded its mother city.

Pietra serena, the cool gray stone that was employed so effectively by Florentine architects, originated from the nearby quarries of Monte Ceceri.

Fiesole is slightly cooler than Florence in summer, although the difference is often wishfully exaggerated.

Event　‡ The Estate Fiesolana, a festival of concerts and films, takes place in the Roman Theater in July-August.

SIGHTS AND PLACES OF INTEREST

The main square, on the site of the Roman Forum, is the **Piazza Mino da Fiesole**. The Romanesque Cathedral of San Romolo in the NW corner was enlarged in the 13th and 14thC. The exterior was made dreary by a well-intentioned 19thC face-lift. The **Cappella Salutati**, to the right of the choir, contains two fine works by Mino da Fiesole: the tomb of Bishop Salutati, and a tabernacle of the *Madonna and Saints*.

Immediately behind the north flank of the Duomo are the **Archeological Zone**, **Municipal Museum** and **Bandini Museum**.

The **Archeological Zone** *(open winter 10am-4pm, summer 9am-7pm)* is worth visiting for its atmosphere and views as well as for the Roman Theater (c.80BC), which had a capacity of 3,000. It was rediscovered in 1809 and excavated in 1873. To the right are the baths, discovered in 1891, and to the left the Roman-Etruscan temple, first fully revealed in 1918. The Municipal Museum has nicely displayed exhibits of archeological material, mainly excavated in Fiesole.

The **Bandini Museum** *(open winter 10am-1pm, 3pm-6pm; summer 9.30am-1pm, 3pm-7pm, closed Tues)* houses a miscellany of furniture, majolica, early Renaissance pictures and Etruscan fragments.

The church of **S. Francesco** is a stiff 5-minute climb from the w end of Piazza Mino; the path gives onto magnificent views of Florence and the Arno valley. This 14thC church was enlarged in the 15thC but was nearly ruined by ill-considered restoration in the early 20thC. The cloisters are charming, and there is a little museum of Etruscan remains and materials collected by Franciscan missionaries in the Orient.

Below S. Francesco are the public gardens and the ancient **basilica of S. Alessandro**, on the site of the Roman temple of Bacchus. The wonderful marble columns dividing the interior space are Roman.

Two other museums are the **Antiquarium Costantini** *(Via Portigiani 9, open winter 10am-4pm; summer 9am-7pm)*, which has a collection of Greek, Etruscan and Italian ceramics; and the **Primo Conti**

Museum *(Via Dupré 18, open 10am-1pm; closed Sun, Mon)*. But no sight in Fiesole is as moving as the stretch of **Etruscan wall** that runs along Via delle Mura Etrusche at the bottom of the archeological zone.

NEARBY SIGHTS

BADIA FIESOLANA 血 † ★
Ask at porter's lodge for entry.
300m NW of San Domenico, this was the cathedral of Fiesole until the 11thC, and is now part of the European University. Cosimo il Vecchio commissioned an unknown architect to rebuild the church in the mid-15thC.

The unfinished **facade** (1464) incorporates the little green and white Romanesque facade of the earlier church. The superb cruciform **interior** is one of the glories of Renaissance architecture.

SAN DOMENICO 血 † ★
In this hamlet, 1.5km (1 mile) SW of Fiesole, is the monastery of S. Domenico, built for Dominican monks in the early 15thC. Fra Angelico took religious orders here and was Prior from 1449-52. The church portico and campanile were added in the 17thC by Matteo Nigetti. The **interior** was remodeled in the late 15th-early 16thC, when the elegant stone arches to the nave chapels, some by Giuliano da Sangallo, were added. Over the first altar on the left is the fascinating **altarpiece** by Fra Angelico (c.1428), with its background repainted by Lorenzo di Credi (c.1501); it was recently cleaned.

In the convent, to the right of the church portico *(ring for admission)*, the Chapter House has a fresco of the *Crucifixion* by Fra Angelico. His fresco of the *Madonna and Child*, now damaged, was in the church.

VILLA MEDICI
Via Vecchia Fiesolana. Open on request. Apply to Signora Anna Mazzini.
"Michelozzo's simple arcaded cube was the first modern villa designed without thought or possibility of material gain," writes James Ackerman, who identifies this villa as the source of a sequence of later pleasure villas, from POGGIO A CAIANO to Le Corbusier's Villa Savoye. Cosimo de' Medici chose the site for its panoramic view and commissioned Michelozzo in the early 1450s to build the villa for his son Giovanni.

The appearance of the original villa, which was substantially altered in the 16thC, is recorded in the background of Ghirlandaio's fresco of the *Assumption of the Virgin* in the church of SANTA MARIA NOVELLA in Florence.

VILLA PALMIERI
Via Boccaccio 128. Can be visited with Agriturist (see page 52) or on request. Apply to Signora Bellandi.
This may have been the site of the garden of Boccaccio's *Decameron*. But the existing house was built in 1697, and the garden much altered in the 19thC. Queen Victoria, who stayed here twice, planted one of the cypresses in 1888.

❧ ⇌ VILLA SAN MICHELE 🏨
Via Doccia 4, 50014 Fiesole ☎*(055) 59451* 📠*570643* 📠*(055) 598734* 🛏 *28 rms, all with bathrm* ➡ 🖩 🏠 🗚 ◉ ◍ 🖵 △ ◻ ◱ 🛥 ⟪ ⇌ 🚣 *Closed Nov-Mar.*
In a 14thC villa enlarged in the 15thC by Santi di Tito, the hotel, now under the same management as the Cipriani in Venice, is almost too luxurious for comfort. But some of the smaller bedrooms are really too cramped to justify the stupendous price (even though it includes one *à la carte* meal in the excellent restaurant).

❧ ⇌ **Villa Aurora** *(Piazza Mino da Fiesole 39* ☎*(055) 59100* 📠*(055) 59587* 🛏 *to* 🛏 🗚 ◉ ◍ 🖩 *closed Sun dinner, Mon, Nov)*, is in a pleasant vine-clad villa facing the central square. It has views of the Arno valley from the back.

⚓ ➥   9km (6 miles) NE at the Olmo intersection near the Convent of La Maddalena (see BIVIGLIANO) is **Dino** *(Via Faentina 329* ☎*(055) 548932* Fx*(055)548934* ⬛ AE ◉ ◙ ▦ *restaurant closed Wed)*, a cheerful country inn and pizzeria.

⚓   There are three less expensive hotels:
Bencistà at San Domenico *(Via B. da Maiano 4* ☎ *and* Fx*(055) 59163* ⬛ *no cards)*, a peaceful old-fashioned pensione with an attractive garden.
Villa Bonelli *(Via Francesco Poeti 1* ☎*(055) 59513* ⬛ *)*, an efficiently managed modern hotel in a quiet street near the center.
Villa San Girolamo *(Via Vecchia Fiesolana 12* ☎*(055) 59141* ⬛ *)* in an old convent.

RESTAURANT-PIZZERIAS   Piazza Mino is lined with bars and restaurant-pizzerias, which stay open late in summer. The local favorite is **Mario**. Below the center, on the San Domenico Road is **Le Lance** *(Via Mantellini 2/b* ☎*(055) 599000), closed Mon, Tues lunch)*, which has a terrace.

➥   See also PRATOLINO and SETTIGNANO.

FORTE DEI MARMI
Map **13***D2. 104km (65 miles)* w *of Florence, 34km (21 miles)* NW *of Lucca. 55042. Lucca. Population: 10,193.*
Although not quite as exclusive as it was in the decades before and after World War II, Forte dei Marmi is still the quiet, discreet upper-class resort of the Versilia, laid out in neat rows among the pine woods and visited mainly by Italian bankers and industrialists from Milan and Turin. The **fort** (1788) stands in the central piazza.
    If you have not booked a hotel, you will find a good selection of all categories in Viale Morin.

⚓ AUGUSTUS ▦
Viale Morin 169,55042 Forte dei Marmi, Lucca ☎*(0584) 80202* ▦*590673* Fx*(0584) 89875* ▥ *70 rms, all with bathrm* ▦ ➤ ➦ ➢ AE ◉ ◙ ▦ *Closed mid-Oct to Apr.*
One of the famous luxury hotels of the Versilia in a group of villas and rustic cottages scattered throughout a green park on the edge of the sea. Its annexe, the **Augustus-Lido** *(Viale Morin 72* ☎*(0584) 81422)* occupies an old villa that once belonged to the Agnelli family.

⚓ BYRON ▦
Viale Morin 46, 55042 Forte dei Marmi, Lucca ☎*(0584) 86052* ▦*501131* Fx*(0584) 82352* ▥ *30 rms, all with bathrm* ➤ AE ◉ ◙ ▦ ➥ ▱ ⌂ ♞ ♨ ⬛ ✿ ⛲
Three period-furnished art nouveau villas, which have been joined together.

⚓ HERMITAGE
Via Cesare Battisti ☎*(0584) 80022* ▦*590673* Fx*(0584) 81442* ▥ *70 rms, all with bathrm* ▦ ➤ ➦ ➥ AE ◉ ◙ ▦ ⌂ ♨ ⚒ ⬛ ▱ ✿ ♞ ✦ ⚲ ♞ ➤ ☀ ◎ *Closed Oct-May.*
This peaceful modern-rustic hotel in the residential quarter is surrounded by a large park with an extra-big swimming pool.

⚓ TIRRENO
Viale Morin 7,55042 Forte dei Marmi, Lucca ☎*(0584) 83333* Fx*(0584) 83335* ▥ *59 rms, all with bathrm* ➦ ➥ AE ◉ ◙ ▦ ▱ ✿ ✦ ♞ ⚲ ⚒ *Closed Oct-Easter.*
An attractive second-category hotel in an old villa.

⚲ Also: **Goya** *(Via Carducci 69* ☎*(0584) 81741* 🅵🅡*(0584) 81744* 🎬 🅰🅴 🔼 🆑 🆅🅸🆂🅰 *Closed 3 weeks in Jan).*

Kyrton *(Via Raffaelli 16* ☎*(0584) 81341* 🅵🅡*(0584) 81342* 🎬 🅰🅴 🆅🅸🆂🅰 *closed Nov to Apr).*

Raffaelli Park *(Via Mazzini 37* ☎*(0584) 81494* 🆃🆇*590239* 🅵🅡*(0584) 81498* 🎬 *to* 🎬 🅰🅴 🔼 🆑 🆅🅸🆂🅰*).*

Raffaelli-Villa Angela *(Via Mazzini 64* ☎*(0584) 80652* 🆃🆇*590239* 🅵🅡*81498* 🎬 *to* 🎬 🅰🅴 🔼 🆑 🆅🅸🆂🅰 *closed Oct to Mar).*

Villa Roma Imperiale *(Via Corsica 9* ☎*(0584) 80841* 🅵🅡*(0584) 82839* 🎬 🅰🅴 🔼 🆅🅸🆂🅰 *).*

══ LORENZO
Via Carducci 61 ☎*(0584) 84030* 🎬 ═ ☷ 🅰🅴 🔼 🆑 🆅🅸🆂🅰 *Closed Mon in winter.*

The fashionable restaurant of Forte dei Marmi specializes in the freshest fish available on the day. Luxurious pastas, e.g., *fettuccine con aragosta, farfalline al ragù di pesche, ravioli ai funghi.*

══ Also: **La Barca** *(Viale Italico 3* ☎*(0584) 89323* 🎬 🅰🅴 🔼 🆑 🆅🅸🆂🅰 *closed Tues, mid-Nov to early Dec).*

Madeo, 3km (2 miles) SE *(Via Giambattista Vico 75* ☎*(0584) 84068* 🎬 *closed Wed, Nov),* cooks fish and meat in a wood-burning oven and has a pretty garden.

Lo Squalo Charlie *(Viale Morin 57* ☎*(0584) 86276* 🎬 🅰🅴 🔼 🆑 🆅🅸🆂🅰 ⇦ *closed Tues, Wed lunch; open dinner only in July, Aug).*

GAIOLE IN CHIANTI
Map **11**F6. *69km (43 miles)* SE *of Florence, 28km (17 miles)* NE *of Siena. 53013. Siena. Population: 2,627.*

The medieval lord of this market town in the Chianti Classico zone was one of the founders of the original Chianti league. On a hill to the E, which can be climbed in 15 minutes on foot, is the medieval village of **Barbischio**.

The fortified **Fattoria Meleto** stands in the midst of its vineyards 2.5km (1½ miles) to the S. The ramparts of the castle of **Vertine** rise above the road to RADDA IN CHIANTI. To the S is the **Castello di Brolio-Ricasoli** (see TUSCAN WINES on pages 175-178).

⚲ ══ CASTELLO DI SPALTENNA 🏛
Via Spaltenna, 53013 Gaiole in Chianti. Just above Gaiole to the w ☎*(0577) 749483* 🅵🅡*(0577) 749269* 🎬 *17 rms, all with bathrm* 🅰🅴 🔼 🆑 🆅🅸🆂🅰 ⇦ 🍸 🏊 🍷 ⋙ ♨ ⛳ 🚪 🖼 ☷ *Closed Jan-Mar. Restaurant* 🎬 ☐ ═ ⇦ 🍸 *Closed Mon, Tues half day.*

The restaurant, in the monastery of the 13thC Pieve di Spaltenna, is all the rage with members of the Chiantishire set, who welcome such novelties as *coulibac, soufflé, "prego"*steak, and the chef's paté. The courtyard is especially pretty when candle-lit on a summer's evening.

══ BADIA A COLTIBUONO 🏛
Coltibuono, 5km (3 miles) to NE ☎*(0577) 749424* 🎬 ☐ ═ ⇦ ━ ⇦ 🅰🅴 🔼 🆑 🆅🅸🆂🅰 *Closed Mon, early Nov to mid-Dec.*

The 11thC ex-monastery buildings (which include a Romanesque church) are now part of an active wine estate, where wine and oil are on sale. The proprietor's wife, the magnificently named Lorenza de' Medici, runs a luxurious cookery course in the Badia.

≡≡ The rough and ready restaurant on the Brolio estate is usually full of local families and farm-workers in overalls, all enjoying the excellent fish and fried potatoes.

GALLUZZO (CERTOSA DEL) ⅢⅡ ✝ ☆

Map 5E3. 6km (4 miles) s of Florence ☎(055) 2049226. Bus #36 or 37 from Florence ⊡ ✗ compulsory. Open Tues-Sun summer 9am-noon, 3-7pm; winter 9am-noon, 3-6pm. Closed Mon.

The **monastery**, which stands impressively above the Via Cassia, was founded by the Florentine Niccolò Acciaiuoli in 1342. The **Pinacoteca** is housed in the Gothic **Palazzo degli Studi**; the dominating works are Pontormo's damaged **lunettes** of the Passion cycle (1522-25), detached from the *chiostro grande*. They were painted while he was living in the monastery during a plague in Florence and, although deeply influenced by Dürer, are striking examples of the Mannerist style Pontormo helped to invent. There are also paintings by Mariotto di Nardo, Dürer and Ridolfo Ghirlandaio.

The church of **S. Lorenzo**, in its large 16thC courtyard, has a high *pietra serena* facade (1556). The interior is divided into two sections: the **Monks' Choir** (with good 16thC stalls) and the **Lay Brethren's Choir**.

A staircase leads to the subterranean chapels where members of the Acciaiuoli family are buried. The superb **tomb-slab of Cardinal Agnolo II Acciaiuoli** was attributed to Donatello by Ruskin and others, but is now thought to be 16thC. Notice also especially the late 14thC Gothic **monument to Niccolò Acciaiuoli**.

The monastic complex includes the *parlatorio*, with 16thC stained glass; the *sala capitolo*, with a frescoed *Crucifixion* by Mariotti Albertinelli; and the *chiostro grande*, embellished with 66 terra-cotta medallions of *Saints and Prophets* by Andrea and Giovanni della Robbia. Off the *chiostro grande* are the cells.

The pharmacy sells liqueurs distilled in the monastery.

❧ ≡≡ The **Relais Certosa** *(Via Colle Ramole 2 ☎(055) 2047171 ▥ to ▥* ▤ ▣ ▣ ▥ *) has a large park with tennis courts.*

≡≡ **Bibe** *(Via delle Bagnese 1 ☎(055) 2049085 ▥ to ▥ closed Wed, Thurs lunch).* A typical Tuscan trattoria, entered through a charming country store, run by the fifth generation of the same family and known for its fried frogs' legs.

GARGONZA ⅢⅡ

Map 11G7. 80km (50 miles) SE of Florence, 28km (17 miles) SW of Arezzo. 52048. Arezzo.

The 13thC houses in this tiny fortified village, where Dante took refuge after learning of his exile from Florence, can be rented by the week or, out of season, by the night. Gargonza is freely open to visitors, and is complete and unspoiled within its walls.

❧ ≡≡ CASTELLO DI GARGONZA

Info and reservations: Count Roberto Guicciardini, Castello di Gargonza, 52048 Monte San

Savino, Arezzo ☎(0575) 847021 📠(0575) 847054 ▥ to ▥ 35 rms in 20 houses, all with bathrm ⬥ AE ● ▥ ⌂ 🛇 ❄ ⛏ 🐎 ⛉ ▼ Closed Jan.
The interiors have been attractively modernized, and the high position, surrounded by woodland, is open to cooling breezes and extensive views of the Valdichiana.

The restaurant, **La Torre di Gargonza** (☎ *(0575) 847065* ▥ *to* ▥ ⛴ *closed Tues; Jan),* just outside the walls, offers traditional Tuscan country cooking.

GIGLIO
*Map **7**K4. 14km (9 miles) SE of Monte Argentario. By boat: 1hr from Porto Santo Stefano. 58013. Grosseto. Population: 1,706 **i** Via Umberto I 44 ☎(0564) 809265.*
The second largest island in the Tuscan archipelago, Giglio is wilder, poorer and much smaller than ELBA, being only 8.5km (5 miles) long and 5km (3 miles) across at its widest.

The three centers — **Giglio Porto**, **Giglio Castello**, a hilltop town, whose maze of steep traffic-free streets is surrounded by walls built to deter pirates, and **Campese** — are linked by a hair-raising bus service. Campese is the main sand-beach resort, and there are other sand beaches at Cala dell' Arenella and Cala delle Cannelle. The island is rich in rare species of wildlife. Boats depart for Giannutri (see PORT'ERCOLE).

�   **Arenella**, in Giglio Porto (☎ *and* 📠*(0564) 809340* ▥ *),* is quiet and adequately comfortable, with sea views.

🍴   **La Vecchia Pergola** (☎ *(0564) 809080* ▥ *closed Tues, Feb)* has a terrace overlooking the harbor.

GREVE
*Map **11**F6. 27km (17 miles) S of Florence, 40km (25 miles) N of Siena. 50022. Firenze. Population: 10,232.*
The main market town of the Chianti is graced with a delightful asymmetrical central square, Piazza Matteotti, lined with porticoed 17thC buildings. It is a good place to shop for wine, and the **Macelleria Falorni** *(Piazza Matteotti 69 ☎(055) 853029 closed Mon, Wed and Thurs afternoon)* sells outstanding hand-butchered *salumi*.
Events   ‡ Market day is Saturday. ‡ Wine fair in September.

🌿 VILLA LE BARONE
Via San Leolino 19,50020 Panzano in Chianti, Firenze ☎(055) 852215 📠(055) 852277 ▥ 27 rms, all with bathrm ⬥ 🍴 🛏 AE ▥ ⌂ 🐴 🛇 ⋙ ❄ ▼ Closed Nov-Mar.
An exceptionally attractive country villa in an isolated position.

🌿 🍴 VILLA SANGIOVESE
Piazza Bucciarelli 4, 50020 Panzano in Chianti, Firenze ☎(055) 8544577 📠(055) 852463 ▥ 19rms, all with bath ● ▥ ❄ ⋙ 🐴 Closed Jan, Feb. Restaurant closed Wed.
A recently restored 19thC villa, with three apartments in the farmhouse next door. The restaurant has a nice terrace with splendid views.

🍴   The calm, pleasant **Giovanni da Verrazzano** *(Piazza Matteotti ☎(055) 853189* ▥ *to* ▥ AE ● ● ▥ ⛴ *closed Sun dinner, Mon, Jan and Feb)* also has some rooms.

▅▅ TRATTORIA DEL MONTAGLIARI
Via di Montagliari 28 (on the SS222), Panzano in Chianti ☎*(055) 852184* ▥▥ *to* ▥▥ ▅▅ 🚗
🚗 《 🆎 🅾 *Closed Mon.*
Giovanni Cappelli's trattoria on the Montagliari wine estate is as attractive in winter, when fires are lit, as in summer, when you can eat outside overlooking the Chianti hills, although there have recently been negative comments about the quality of the service. Specialties include homemade *pappardelle* with game sauces according to the season, and excellent *chianina* beef.

▅▅ CASPRINI ♣
Passo dei Pecorai, 5km (3 miles) to N ☎*(055) 850716* ▢▢ ▢▢ ▄▄ ▅▅ 🚗 🚗 《 🆎
Closed Wed, Aug.
A classic family restaurant. Specialties are homemade pastas and desserts.

GROSSETO
Map 7I5. 141km (87 miles) S *of Florence, 73km (45 miles)* S *of Siena. 58100. Grosseto. Population: 69,301* **i** *Viale Monterosa 206* ☎*(0564) 22534.*
Grosseto is the principal city of the Tuscan Maremma, the coastal plain where the natives regard themselves as a special and separate breed of Tuscans, toughened by centuries of hardship and proud of their land's recently restored fertility.

In the period of the great Etruscan cities that flourished here, the area to the NE of Grosseto was a navigable gulf. By the Middle Ages it was a freshwater lake, and eventually subsided into malaria-infested swampland.

The history of the Maremma after the fall of the Roman Empire was that of a battlefield contested by Florence, Siena, the Papal States and pirates from the Barbary Coast. When it became part of the Sienese territories in the late Middle Ages it was scantily populated; and in the mid-18thC, two centuries after the Florentine conquest of Siena, the area was nearly deserted.

The first effective efforts to reclaim the land and rid the Maremma of malaria were initiated by the Lorraine grand duke Leopold II in 1828; but it was not until the early years of this century that significant progress was made. In 1943-44, Grosseto was the victim of severe bombing raids. The early 1950s saw a systematic program of agricultural incentives and repopulation, and the population of Grosseto has expanded to more than five times its postwar size.

It is against this violent background that Grosseto today must be read. Its spirit is that of a modern city that has not quite discovered its own character.

SIGHTS AND PLACES OF INTEREST
The main square is Piazza Rosselli, just to the N of Porta Nuova. What remains of the original urban nucleus is contained within an impressive hexagon of bastioned **brick walls** built by the 16thC Medici. Traffic is prohibited in the center.
DUOMO †
Originally built in 1294-1302, but the imitation Romanesque facade dates from 1845; inside is a 15thC font and, in the left transept, an *Assumption* by Matteo di Giovanni.

MUSEO ARCHEOLOGICO E D'ARTE DELLA MAREMMA ☆
Via Mazzini.
The collection is displayed chronologically, beginning with prehistory and ending with 13th-17thC paintings on the second floor.

The **ground floor** is largely devoted to material excavated from ROSELLE. On the **first floor** is a topographical explanation of the Etruscan Maremma and material from the sites. On the **second floor** are 13th-17thC Sienese pictures, of which the most noteworthy are Sassetta's *Madonna of the Cherries* and Pietro di Domenico's *Pietà.*

SAN FRANCESCO †
Piazza della Independenza.
A 13thC Gothic church. Over the high altar is an early Duccio *Crucifixion.*

▆ **La Maremma** *(Via Fulceri P. dei Calboli 5* ☎*(0564) 21177* ▢ ▣ ▣ ▣ ▣ *closed Sun dinner, Mon, Aug),* near the museum, offers a huge menu.

The **Enoteca Ombrone** *(Viale G. Matteotti 69-71* ☎*(0564) 22585* ▢ ▣ ▣ ▣ ▣ *closed Sun dinner, Mon, Jan, late June-late July)* has an extensive cellar and the most ambitious kitchen.

Buca San Lorenzo *(Via Manetti 1* ☎*(0564) 25142* ▢ ▣ ▣ ▣ ▣ *closed Mon).*

At Istia d'Ombrone, 7km (4½ miles) E, **Terzo Cerchio** *(Piazza del Castello 1* ☎*(0564) 409235* ▢ *closed Mon, Nov)* is a good place to sample the traditional country cooking of the Maremma.

IMPRUNETA
Map 11E6. 14km (9 miles) s of Florence. 50023. Firenze. Population: 14,884.
This large agricultural village is located on a plateau overlooking the Greve and Ema valleys.
Event   ‡ The lively agricultural fair of St Luke is held in mid-October.

SIGHTS AND PLACES OF INTEREST

SANTA MARIA DELL' IMPRUNETA ▥ †
The fine porticoed facade that overlooks the main square was added in 1634; the tall bell tower is 13thC. The design of the handsome **aedicules** (1456) flanking the entrance to the polygonal presbytery is attributed to Michelozzo, and they are embellished with terra-cotta decorations by Luca della Robbia. To the right of the church are two pretty cloisters.

▆ Two popular restaurants with pleasant terraces are **I Cavallacci** *(Viale A. Moro 3* ☎*(055) 2313863* ▢ *to* ▢ ▣ ▣ ▣ ▣ *closed Mon, Tues lunch, Aug)* and, 12km (7¼ miles) E at S. Polo in Chianti, is **Il Merendero** *(Viale Lavagnini* ☎*(055 855019, open summer only),* which specializes in *antipasti.*

LASTRA A SIGNA
Map 14E5. 13km (8 miles) w of Florence. 50055. Firenze. Population: 17,000.
Although unpromisingly set in an industrial zone and badly damaged during World War II, the historic center retains its 14thC walls. The **Loggia di S. Antonio** (1411) could be an early work by Brunelleschi, and the exterior of the **Palazzo Pretorio** has terra-cotta coats of arms and a handsome window of 1570.

223

ANTICA TRATTORIA SANESI
Via Arione 33 ☎*(055) 8720234* ▭ ▨ ▣ ▢ ▦ *Closed Sun dinner, Mon, Aug.*
A classic Tuscan restaurant with the welcoming, genuine atmosphere of an old coaching stop. The steaming platters of pasta are irresistible, especially when sauced with truffles or asparagus. *Finocchiona, bistecca fiorentina* and game in season are all exactly as they should be.
   Reservations are essential.

   And across the Arno at S. Donnino is **Angiolino** *(Via Trento 739* ☎*(055) 8739438 Closed Sun dinner, Mon* ▭ ▨ ▣ ▦ *)*, which specializes in sheep meat: roasted, grilled and even served, instead of the more familiar *lepre*, with *pappardelle*. See also ARTIMINO.

LA VERNA
Map 12E8. 75km (47 miles) SE of Florence, 58km (36 miles) N of Arezzo. 52010. Arezzo.

MONASTERY †
This monastery, reached by a beautiful twisting road, is 26km (16 miles) from BIBBIENA. It was founded in 1214 by St Francis, who received the stigmata here on September 14, 1224. The chief artistic attractions are the Andrea della Robbia terra cottas in the churches, of which the loveliest are the *Annunciation* and *Adoration of the Child* in the Chiesa Maggiore.
   Above the monastery is a magnificent **forest** of old beeches and firs.

LIVORNO
Map 9F3. 116km (72 miles) w of Florence, 19km (12 miles) s of Pisa. 57100. Livorno. Population: 177,101 ℹ *Piazza Cavour* ☎*(0586) 33111; at the port, Palazzo Dogana* ☎*(0586) 25320.*
The major commercial port of Tuscany and still one of the greatest in the Mediterranean, Livorno was the creation of the Medici grand dukes: their most ambitious and successful project. The transformation of the medieval fishing village into a port that would more than compensate for the silted-up port of Pisa was initiated by Cosimo I in 1571. Six years later, the new "ideal city" of Livorno designed by Buontalenti was founded.
   In 1593, Ferdinand I declared Livorno an open city, guaranteeing tax exemptions, free trade with all international ports, and freedom of worship for all religions; and in 1621 that remarkable Englishman, Robert Dudley, the marine engineer in the service of the grand dukes, completed the extension of the harbor with his great Medicean mole (harbor wall).
   By 1600 Livorno had a population of 5,000, activated, then as now, by a substantial Jewish community. 18thC foreign visitors found it a charming as well as prosperous city, with many fine contemporary palaces. These disappeared along with the charm and the historic center during the bombardments of 1943.
   The old English name Leghorn, from the early Italian Legorno, is rarely used today except, of course, to describe the type of straw hat first made here in the 19thC.

SIGHTS AND PLACES OF INTEREST

The old pentagonal center envisaged by Buontalenti is bisected by its· main street, Via Grande, which links the huge harbor complex with the Piazza Repubblica. The city is guarded by two fortresses: the **Fortezza Nuova** (1590) above Piazza Repubblica, and the **Fortezza Vecchia** (1534), in the harbor, which was designed by Antonio da Sangallo the Younger.

MONUMENT TO FERDINAND I ("Quattro Mori" or "Four Moors")
Piazza Micheli.
Facing the old harbor, this esthetically controversial monument consists of Giovanni Bandini's statue (1595) of *Ferdinand I wearing the order of St Stephen*, and the *four bronze Moors* added by Pietro Tacca in 1626. Some admire these straining Michelangeloesque figures; others say they combine ineptitude with unfeeling virtuosity.

The diarist John Evelyn, who was of the first opinion, described the scene he witnessed in this piazza in 1644 when Livorno was the chief slave port of the northern Mediterranean: "Here... is such a concourse of slaves, Turcs, Moors and other nations, that the number and confusion is prodigious; some buying, others selling, others drinking, others playing, some working, others sleeping, fighting, singing, weeping, all nearly naked, and miserably chained."

The **English Cemetery** *(Via Verdi 63)* was the first Protestant cemetery in Italy. The 18thC Scottish novelist Tobias Smollett lies here.

MUSEO CIVICO G. FATTORI
Villa Fabbricotti.
Contains a collection of paintings by the Macchiaioli, and several Modiglianis.

🗨 🍴 **Gran Duca** *(Piazza Micheli 16* ☎*(0586) 891024* ▫ *)* faces the harbor.

🍴 **Antico Moro** *(Via Bartelloni 59* ☎*(0586) 884659* ▫ AE *closed Wed, Aug);* **La Barcarola** *(Viale Carducci 63* ☎*(0586) 402367* ▫ *to* ▫ AE ◆ ◉ VISA *closed Sun)* is a fish restaurant with a lively atmosphere.

Alla Chetichella *(Via E. Rossi 18* ☎*(0586) 899029* ▫ *closed Mon,* **Il Fanale** *(Scali Novi Lena 15-17* ☎*(0586) 881346* ▫ *closed Tues; early Jan),* or **Da Rosina** *(Via Roma 251* ☎*(0586) 800200* ▫ AE ◆ ◉ VISA 🍴 *closed Thurs).*

Wine bars in the center include the **Cantina Nardi** *(Via Cambini 6* ☎*(0586) 808006* ▫ *closed Sun; Aug-Sept);* **Cantina Senese** *(Borgo Cappuccini 95* ☎*(0586) 890239* ▫ *closed Sun);* also **Enoteca DOC** *(Via Goldoni 42* ☎*(0586) 887583* ▫ AE ◆ ◉ VISA *closed Mon).*

LUCCA ★
*Map **13**D3. 74km (46 miles)* w *of Florence, 22km (14 miles)* NE *of Pisa. 55100. Lucca. Population: 88,437* ℹ *Via Vittorio Veneto 40* ☎*(0583) 493639.*
Alone of all the Tuscan city states, Lucca resisted the thrust of Florentine imperialism and remained independent of united Tuscany until as late as the 19thC.

The town is still a separate and special place, its narrow medieval streets, red-brick palaces and tower houses and elaborate Romanesque churches encircled by the best-preserved 16th-17thC walls to be found anywhere in Italy.

A Roman colony from 180BC, capital city of Tuscany under the medieval Lombard and Frankish emperors, and a free commune from 1119, Lucca emerged in the early 14thC as the second richest city in Tuscany. Under the forceful leadership of the merchant-soldier Castruccio Castracani, Lucca became a serious threat to Florence; but Castracani's death in 1328 left the government divided and open for short periods to subjection by its enemies.

In 1369 Lucca was granted a charter of independence by the Emperor Charles IV. Representative governments alternated with periods of signorial rule. Several palaces built by the powerful Guinigi *signori* are still standing. Paolo Guinigi, leader of the government from 1400-1430, gave the city its greatest single work of art — the effigy of his second wife, Ilaria del Carretto, which can be found in the Duomo.

In the mid-16thC, the oligarchy closed ranks against the populace. Thus protected from internal opposition, the Republic built a new ring of walls as a fortification against the threat of Cosimo I's pan-Tuscan policies, and retained its autonomy until 1799.

In 1805, Napoleon gave Lucca to his sister Elisa Baciocchi, a tireless social reformer and patroness of the arts, who laid out Piazza Napoleone. In 1817 the city passed as a duchy to Maria Louisa de Bourbon; and in 1847, Lucca was finally absorbed into the Tuscan grand-duchy.

> Anna Pavlovna Scherer to Prince Vassily, in July 1805:
> "Well, prince, Genoa and Lucca are now no more
> than private estates of the Bonaparte family."
> (First sentence of *War and Peace,* Leo Tolstoy, 1868)

Even in the 19thC, a depressed period for most Italian cities, John Ruskin found "the streets clean — cheerfully inhabited, yet quiet; nor desolate, even now." It remains one of the most quietly civilized small cities in Europe: conservative and prosperous but thrifty, friendly to foreigners yet resistant to mass tourism, its beautiful monuments well-kept but not over-restored.

The Romanesque churches of the Tuscan silk town are in the Pisan style, richly embroidered with polychrome marble insets and relief carvings executed for the most part by visiting Lombard and Pisan sculptors. Another, later visitor, Jacopo della Quercia, carved a number of works for Lucca including his early masterpiece, the tomb of Ilaria del Carretto.

The most talented local sculptor, hardly represented outside his native city, was Matteo Civitali.

In the 16th-18thC, the Lucchese nobility built grand summer retreats in the cool hills to the NE. These villas are among the most exhilarating examples of Mannerist and Baroque architecture in Tuscany. The anglicized gardens of many of the villas testify to the long-standing special relationship with Britain.

Events   ‡ The birthplace of Luigi Boccherini and Giacomo Puccini is still musically active. Concerts and organ recitals of sacred music are often performed in the churches, in the Villa Bottini *(Via Elisa)* and other venues.   ‡ The feast of the Sacro Volto (the Holy Visage), on

September 14, is celebrated on the previous evening with a candle-lit procession. ‡ An itinerant antique market comes to Piazza San Martino on the third Saturday and Sunday of each month.

SIGHTS AND PLACES OF INTEREST

Lucca is a tiny city, enclosed by a 4-km (3-mile) ring of walls. It is less than a 20-minute walk from end to end. The tree-shaded Piazza Napoleone, laid out in French style in 1806, is the main square of the modern city. The Neoclassical monument (1843) to Maria Louisa de Bourbon in the center of the square is by Lorenzo Bartolini. The Palazzo della Provincia (begun 1578) on the w side was based on designs by Ammannati, but has been frequently remodeled.

Piazza San Michele, on the site of the Roman Forum, is the center of the old part of the city, which preserves its Roman grid plan and streets lined with medieval and Renaissance palaces.

The shaded path on the ramparts (★) offers a pleasant walk.

> Lucca is Tuscany still living and enjoying,
> desiring and intending. The town is a charming mixture
> of antique "character" and modern inconsequence;
> and not only the town, but the country —
> the blooming, romantic country which you admire
> from the famous promenade on the city-wall.
> (Henry James, *Tuscan Cities,* an essay from *Italian Hours,* 1894)

AMPHITHEATER (Anfiteatro Romano)
Piazza Anfiteatro (off the n end of Via Fillungo)
The oval outline of the Roman amphitheater, traced by stuccoed medieval houses, forms one of Lucca's most picturesque piazzas.

BOTANICAL GARDEN (Orto Botanico)
Via del Giardino Botanico 14 ☎491311. Open summer, Tues-Sun, 9am-noon, 3.30-6.30pm; winter Tues-Sat 9.30am-1.30pm 🔲 *𝒓 by appointment.*
The Botanical Garden contains plants, herbs and trees native to the province of Lucca or naturalized since the garden was founded in 1820. The collection is serious and well labeled, and is charmingly landscaped for strolling as well as for study.

DUOMO (San Martino) † ★ 🏛
The Cathedral, which is dedicated to St Martin, was begun in 1070 and modified over the next 400 years. The tiered upper part of its asymmetrical **facade** (1204) was largely the work of Guidetto da Como. The right-hand arch of the **portico** was made narrower than the other two, to accommodate the earlier base of the **campanile**, whose upper part was completed in the late 13thC. The statue of St Martin is a copy of the 13thC original, which is now on the inner facade. Under the portico are fine relief carvings (begun 1233). The charming **apse** dates from 1308.

The **interior**, with its high and airy clerestory, was rebuilt in Gothic style in the 14th-15thC. The inlaid **pavement** was designed by Civitali and assistants, and the marble intarsia at the center, illustrating the *Judgment of Solomon,* was executed by Antonio Federighi. Four of Puccini's ancestors served in this church as organists and choir-masters; the 17thC organ is still in use.

In the left transept is Jacopo della Quercia's **tomb of Ilaria del Carretto** (★), who was the second wife of Paolo Guinigi. This is Jacopo's earliest surviving masterpiece (c.1406) and the first sculptural creation of the Renaissance to use as decorative motifs putti and garlands derived from Roman examples. Ruskin, who was more than half in love with the serenely beautiful effigy of Ilaria, described it as "the loveliest Christian tomb in Italy." A recent restoration has caused an uproar in the art world, with some experts claiming that the patina has been crudely scrubbed.

The expressive statue of *St John the Evangelist* (★) is also by Jacopo. In the adjoining chapel is a glowing altarpiece of the *Madonna with Sts Stephen and John the Baptist* (★) (1509), one of Fra Bartolommeo's masterpieces.

In the left nave is the *tempietto* (1484) by Matteo Civitali. It houses the *Volto Santo,* the effigy of Christ which is carried through the city in procession on Holy Cross eve. It was supposedly begun by Nicodemus, the Pharisee who helped to swathe the crucified body, and later miraculously completed.

In the right transept, the tomb of Pietro da Noceto (1472) is by Civitali, as are the two angels flanking the tabernacle in the Chapel of the Holy Sacrament and the monumental S. Regalo altarpiece (1484). Also by Civitali is the pulpit (1498) in the right nave. In the sacristy, off the right nave, is a *Madonna with Sts Peter, Clement, Paul and Sebastian* by Domenico Ghirlandaio.

A **Cathedral Museum** (Opera dell'Duomo) will soon be installed at 5 Piazza Antelminelli. There is talk of moving the Ilaria into this museum.

GUINIGI TOWER (Torre Guinigi)
Via Sant'Andrea. Open summer 9am-7pm, winter 10am-4pm 🚋

The mid-14thC tower of one of the Guinigi palaces may be ascended by way of an iron staircase. The top, which is planted with a surprising little grove of ilex trees, gives a magnificent panorama of the pantiled roofs and churches of Lucca and the mountains beyond.

Via Sant'Andrea runs between Lucca's two best-preserved medieval streets: **Via Fillungo** (which is the favored venue for the evening *passeggiata*) to the w; and to the E, **Via Guinigi**, where the two Case dei Guinigi, which were built in the 14thC and remodeled in the 16thC, face each other.

MUSEO NAZIONALE DI VILLA GUINIGI 🏛
Via della Quarquonia. Open Sun-Tues 9am-2pm; closed Mon 🚋

The large red-brick Villa Guinigi was built (outside the medieval walls, which are traced by the nearby Via del Fosso) in 1418 for Paolo Guinigi. It houses a very interesting collection of sculpture and paintings brought in from churches and palaces in the city and province.

Ground floor: Contains Etruscan and Roman pieces excavated locally, as well as relief panels and sculptures by Lucchese sculptors of the 8th-15thC. There is also a room of carvings by Civitali, notably a bas relief *Ecce Homo*. The charming lions in the garden are from the city walls.

First floor: 13th-19thC paintings, intarsia work, furniture and textiles. One of the painted crosses is signed by (?) Berlinghiero Berlinghieri. Other notable works include the triptych of the *Madonna and Child* attributed to Martin Heemskerk, and Fra Bartolommeo's early *God the Father* (1509) and *Madonna della Misericordia* (1515). There are also works by Vasari, Jacopo Ligozzi and Pompeo Batoni, who was born in Lucca but worked mainly in Rome.

PINACOTECA NAZIONALE E MUSEO DI PALAZZO MANSI 🏛
Via Galli Tassi 43. Open Tues-Sat 9am-7pm; Sun, hols 9am-2pm. Closed Mon 🚋

The 17thC Mansi palace, recently restored, retains much of its original furniture, hangings and decorations. On the first floor, the **Salone da Ballo** is decorated with inept but amusing *trompe l'oeil* frescoes. The **Pinacoteca**, left off the ballroom, is hung with throw-outs from the main Medici collection given to Lucca by Leopold II. It is worth the visit for Luca Giordano's *St Sebastian* and Beccafumi's *Continence of Scipio*.

Off the ballroom to the right is an impressive enfilade of small rooms hung with 17thC Flemish tapestries, leading to a bedroom which has a suite of gilded furniture and 18thC silk hangings made in Lucca.

SAN FREDIANO 🏛 ✝ ★

The church was built from 1112-47 on the site of a 6thC basilica. The mosaic of the *Ascension* on the facade, possibly by Berlinghiero, was heavily restored in the 19thC. The pleasing, unspoiled Romanesque **interior** (★) contains good works of art. The columns of the nave have handsome Classical capitals. In a bay to the right of the entrance is a strange and impressive 12thC **font** (★) carved with reliefs of the story of *Moses*, the *Good Shepherd*, and the *Apostles*. There is also a lunette of *The Annunciation* by Andrea della Robbia and a charming polychrome *Virgin Annunciate* by Civitali.

Left aisle: In the second chapel there are delightful frescoes (c1509) by Amico Aspertini of *Stories of San Frediano and St Augustine*. In the fourth chapel is a beautiful carved altarpiece of the *Madonna and Child with Saints* (1422) by Jacopo della Quercia (with assistance) in which the elaborate Gothic drapery contrasts with the Renaissance faces; it has a superb low-relief predella.

Via Cesare Battisti, which runs sw from the church, is lined with fine 17th and 18thC palaces, and leads to **Palazzo Controni-Pfanner** (1667) *(Via degli Asili 33 open summer 10am-5pm, closed Mon; open winter by appointment* ☎491449). The palace, which houses a museum of local 18th and 19thC costume, has an attractive external staircase and an 18thC garden.

SANTA MARIA FORISPORTAM 🏛 ✝
Via Santa Croce

So called because it was built outside the Roman walls, S. Maria Forisportam has a fine and typical 13thC Pisan-style facade, which was enlarged in the 16thC when the interior was also re-arranged. The fourth altar on the right has a painting of *St Lucy* by Guercino.

SAN MICHELE IN FORO 🏛 ✝ ★

A few steps to the N of Piazza Napoleone, Piazza San Michele occupies the site of the Roman Forum and is still used as a market place and rendezvous. On the corner of Via Vittorio Veneto is the Renaissance **Palazzo Pretorio**, designed by Civitali and altered in the 16thC.

The tall, richly decorated marble facade of the church of **S. Michele** is one of the most beautiful examples of Pisan-Lucchese Romanesque architecture, a typical representation of what Ruskin, who often sketched it, called "the perfectest phase of round-arched building in Europe."

Begun in the 12thC, the upper part belongs to a 14thC project, abandoned for lack of funds, to raise the height of the nave. The apse is in the Pisan style, possibly by Diotisalvi.

The only outstanding work of art inside is a panel painting of *SS. Helena, Jerome, Sebastian and Roch* by Filippino Lippi, in the right transept.

The house where Puccini was born, now a **museum of Puccini memorabilia**, is off Via Poggio *(Corte San Lorenzo 9, open summer 10am-6pm, winter 10am-4pm* 📷 *)*.

HOTELS IN THE CENTER

🛏 UNIVERSO
Piazza del Giglio 1 (next to Piazza Napoleone) ☎*(0583) 493678* 📠*501840* 🛏 *72 rms, all with bathrm* ☲ 🛎 📺 🗖 ⚡ ⚭ 🍸 ⫽

A pleasant, slightly shabby 19thC hotel in the center, often frequented by Ruskin. The hotel has, of course, been modernized since then, but the atmosphere probably hasn't changed much. Some of the bedrooms have much more character than others, and some have splendid views of the Duomo. Parking can sometimes be arranged.

🏕   There is also: **Diana** *(Via del Molinetto 11* ☎ *490368* ▯▯ *no cards)*, which is a small hotel in a pretty street near the Duomo; or **La Luna** *(Via Fillungo, Corte Compagni 12* ☎ *493634* ▯▯ *to* ▯▯ 🆎 ⧫ ◎ 🆅*)*, which is near the Roman amphitheater. The best room, which has a painted ceiling and a marble fireplace, will accommodate a family.

HOTELS NEARBY

🏕 HAMBROS PARCO HOTEL
6km (3½ miles) ε on the Pescia road, 55010 Lunata ☎ *and* 🅵🆇*(0583) 935355* ▯▯ *57 rms, all with bathrm* 🆎 ⧫ ◎ 🆅 🗀 ▯ 🛏 ♨ ⚲ ☂ 🏋
A 19thC villa in a small park, cheerlessly modernized and recently opened as a reasonably efficient hotel where the service can, at times, be brusque.

🏕 VILLA CASANOVA
At Balbano, 10km (6 miles) w, 55050 Nozzano ☎ *and* 🅵🆇*(0583) 548429* ▯▯ *to* ▯▯ *40 rms* 🍽 🏚 🚗 🏡 ⛷ 🎣 ⚲ ⚡ 🎿 *Open summer only.*
A country hotel in an 18thC villa.

🏕 VILLA DI CORLIANO �🏛
10km (6 miles) sw toward Pisa at Rigoli, 56010 San Giuliano Terme ☎*(050) 818193* ▯▯ *18 rms* 🚗 🆅
A frescoed villa in a fine park, managed by descendants of its original patrician owners.

🏕 ⧉ VILLA PRINCIPESSA
5km (3 miles) outside on the SS12R, 55050 Massa Pisana ☎*(0583) 370037* 🅵🆇*590068* 🅵🆇*(0583) 379019* ▯▯▯ *44 rms, all with bathrm* ▦ 🚗 🆎 ⧫ ◎ 🆅 🏡 ⚲ ⚲ 🏋 ♨ ▯ 🚗 ☂
A luxuriously converted 18thC villa in a noble park, now a popular venue for Italian business conferences.

RESTAURANTS WITHIN THE WALLS

The Lucchesi enjoy a robust, healthy and distinctive traditional cuisine. One of its glories, famous since Roman times, is the mild, full-flavored local olive oil. Specialties that are not always found outside the province include *gran farro* (emmer soup), *garmugia lucchese* (vegetable soup made in early summer), *torta coi biscari* (a tart made with swiss chard, pine nuts and candied quince).

⧉ BUCA DI SANT'ANTONIO
Via della Cervia 3 (near Piazza San Michele) ☎ *and* 🅵🆇*55881* ▯▯ *to* ▯▯▯ ▦ 🆎 ⧫ ◎ 🆅 ☂ *Closed Sun dinner, Mon.*
The modest exterior conceals the only Michelin star in the center: a dignified, traditional restaurant with pleasant but sometimes haphazard service and a menu featuring specialties from the Garfagnana such as *capretto garfagnino allo spiedo.*

⧉ GIULIO IN PELLERIA ♧
Via delle Conce 45 ☎*55948* ▯▯ *to* ▯▯ *Closed Sun, Mon. No cards.*
This big, bright and very popular restaurant in the old tanners' neighborhood is the

place to sample hearty local peasant dishes at reasonable prices. The long menu is recited verbally and not much English is spoken.

Del Teatro *(Piazza Napoleone 25* ☎*493740* ▥ AE ⬛ ⬛ ▥ *closed Thurs)* is the restaurant of the hotel **Universo**, but is now under separate management. Service is professional and attentive, the food understated, fresh and well-prepared.

The **Gelateria Veneta** *(Via Vittorio Veneto 74, near Piazza Napoleone, closed winter)* serves wonderful homemade ice cream.

RESTAURANTS NEARBY

If you wish to dine beyond the city walls in the countryside near Lucca, you are spoiled for choice.

⫣ LA MORA

9km (5½ miles) N *near Ponte a Moriano, Via Sesto di Moriano 1748* ☎*(0583) 57109* ▥ ⫧ ⫸ AE ⬛ ⬛ ▥ *Closed Wed dinner, Thurs, Oct.*

A century-old tavern that has long been one of the famous grand Tuscan country restaurants. The wine list is outstanding, as is the *gran farro* and the fish from the Serchio River. The adjoining enoteca sells wines and local olive oil.

⫣ VIPORE

9km (5½ miles) NW *off the Camaiore road at Pieve S. Stefano* ☎*(0583) 59245/395107* ▥ *to* ▥ ⫸ ▦ ⫧ AE ⬛ ⬛ ▥ *Closed Mon, Tues lunch.*

This charming hill-top restaurant has one of the most spectacular positions in the province. The young proprietor, Cesare Casella, is a culinary philosopher-artist who uses the 40-odd herbs from his garden, the local olive oils, seasonal vegetables and game — and the experience of regular trips abroad — to create a delicate and original cuisine. Take his advice and allow plenty of time for your meal. The grocery store sells local and foreign quality produce.

Ciapino is on the strada panoramica off the old road to Pisa above Molina di Quosa *(* ☎*(050) 850059* ▥ ⫧ *summer: open Mon-Tues, Thurs-Sat dinner only; Sun lunch and dinner; closed Wed; winter: open Sat dinner, Sun lunch and dinner, closed Mon-Fri),* a cozy, homey restaurant that serves simple, country fare, including grills cooked over an open oak-wood fire. It has a terrace for summer dining.

There is also the ambitious **Solferino** *(San Macario in Piano* ☎*(0583) 59118* ▥ *to* ▥ ⫸ ⫧ AE ⬛ ⬛ ▥ *closed Wed, Thurs lunch).*

SHOPPING

Locally made shoes can often be bought at bargain prices. The delicious honey and the extra virgin olive oil from the country around Lucca are sometimes sold from market stalls; but when buying oil, look for the numbered sticker that ensures that it is real, estate-grown oil and not a blend.

Via del Battistero is lined with antique stores.

VILLAS AND GARDENS NEAR LUCCA ★

The three great villas regularly open to the public are in the hills NE of Lucca, off the old Pistoia road, and are very close to one another.

VILLA MANSI 🏛

Segromigno in Monte ☎*(0583) 928114* 🚽 *Open summer 9am-1pm, 3.30-8pm; winter 10am-12.30pm, 3.30-5pm. Closed Mon.*

The villa, first built in the 1500s, owes its present appearance to an 18thC reconstruction, when part of the garden was laid by the Sicilian architect Filippo Juvara. His Lago di Diana survives; but the rest of the park was relandscaped as an English park in the 19thC.

The villa preserves late 18thC decorations.

VILLA REALE 🏛

Marlia ☎*(0583) 30108. Garden only open 🏃 (obligatory) on the hour; summer Tues-Thurs, Sun, 10-11am, 4-6pm; winter Tues-Sun 10-11am, 3-6pm, or by appointment* 🚽

The most famous and imposing of the villas near Lucca was built in the 17thC for the Orsetti family. It became the Royal Villa when Elisa Baciocchi made it her favorite summer residence and adapted and redecorated the villa in First Empire style.

Fortunately much of the original Baroque park survives — with its "rooms" enclosed by hedges, fountains and grottoes. The greatest of many delights is the green **theater** (1652), which is complete with wings, backdrops and terra-cotta actors on the stage.

VILLA TORRIGIANI 🏛

Camigliano ☎*(0583) 928889. Open summer 9.30-11.30am, 3-7.30pm; winter Sun only or by appointment* 🚽

The villa was built in the 1500s and, in the 17thC, was given its spectacular Mannerist facade facing the valley.

Survivals from the Baroque garden include the delicious secret garden, nympheum and ingenious surprise water jets. Other parts of the park are in the Romantic English style.

OTHER SIGHTS NEAR LUCCA

Romanesque churches near Lucca include the **Pieve di Brancoli** on the Abetone road; and, in the direction of Pisa, **San Giovanni Battista** and **Santa Maria Assunta**.

The dramatically impressive **aqueduct** that runs straight across the countryside for 12km ($7\frac{1}{2}$ miles) is not, as you might think, Roman. It was built in 1820-30 in the reign of Marie Louise de Bourbon, to carry water to Lucca from a spring near Capannori.

MAGLIANO

Map 7J5. 27km (17 miles) SE of Grosseto. 59051. Grosseto. Population: 4,219.
A magnificently situated hilltop town of Etruscan origin surrounded by well-preserved Renaissance walls. The church of **San Giovanni Battista** is an attractive blend of Romanesque, Gothic and Renaissance; and the church of the **Annunziata** contains a *Madonna and Child* by Neroccio.

Just a $\frac{1}{2}$-hour walk to the SE can be found the romantic ruin of the Romanesque church of **San Bruzio** and the remains of the Etruscan necropolis.

🍴 **Aurora** *(Via Chiasso Lavagnini 12* ☎*(0564) 592030* ▥ 💳 💳 *closed Wed, Nov)*; **Da Wilma**, 8km (5 miles) N at Pereta *(Via Roma* ☎*(0564) 505079* ▥ *to* ▥ *closed Thurs, Nov).*

MASSA

Map 13D2. 115km (71 miles) NW of Florence, 45km (28 miles) NW of Pisa.
54100. Massa-Carrara. Population: 65,814.

A booming, untidy frontier town at the mouth of the Frigido valley below the foothills of the Apuan Alps, Massa did not become part of Tuscany until 1859, and it is still the least "Tuscan" of Tuscan provincial capitals.

Piazza Aranci, the old center, is dominated by the startling 17thC **Palazzo Cybo Malaspina**, which encloses an attractive loggiaed court-yard (1665) by G.F. Bergamini. The **Duomo** has a modern facade and a Baroque interior.

Above the town is the medieval **Rocca** and a Renaissance palace which was the residence of the 16thC Malaspina Dukes.

⌘ ≡ IL BOTTACCIO

5km (3 miles) SW at Montignoso, Via Bottaccio 1 ☎*(0585) 340031* ℻*(0585) 340103* ▥
to ▥ ▤ ▣ AE ⊙ ⊙⊙ ▨ ⇗ ⁀ ≡ ⇔ *Closed Mon.*

Located in an otherwise not especially distinguished area, this restaurant, which occupies a beautifully converted old olive mill, is one of the greatest gastronomic surprises and treats in all Tuscany. Although the menu changes frequently, nothing seems ever to be less than perfect. Also a relais, with 8 superbly furnished suites.

MASSA MARITTIMA

Map 9H4. 132km (79 miles) SW of Florence, 64km (40 miles) SW of Siena.
58024. Grosseto. Population: 10,297.

The mineral-rich territory of Massa Marittima was mined by the Etrus-cans and Romans; the copper and silver mines were the economic base of the independent republic that was constitutionally established in 1225 and flourished proudly until it was conquered by Siena in 1335.

The Duomo, one of the most beautiful and richly decorated churches in Tuscany, was erected during the period of communal independence; and the first miners' code in Europe was drawn up in the city in 1310.

Event ‡ The Balestra del Girofalco, a crossbow competition with a mechanical falcon as target, takes place in medieval costume on May 20 and the second Sunday in August.

SIGHTS AND PLACES OF INTEREST

The town is in two distinct parts: the Romanesque lower town (Città Vecchia) is linked by Via Moncini to the Gothic upper town (Città Nuova), which was built after the Sienese conquest.

The center of the old town is Piazza Garibaldi.

DUOMO (San Cerbone) ▥ ✝ ★

This lovely cathedral in the Pisan Romanesque-Gothic style was completed be-tween 1287-1304. The **relief carvings** over the portal depict five episodes in the life of Saint Cerbonius, patron saint of the cathedral, with the beguiling beasts who helped him. The campanile rising from the arcaded left flank was largely recon-structed in the 1920s.

At the top of the right aisle is the font where St Bernardino was baptized in 1380, with relief carvings (1267) by Giraldo da Como, and a 15thC tabernacle rising from

233

its center. In the chapel to the left of the high altar is a panel painting of the *Madonna della Grazie* (c.1316), closely influenced by Duccio's *Maestà* in SIENA.

Ask the sacristan to unlock the access door to the subterranean chapels. In the polygonal undercroft is the exquisite **Arca di San Cerbone** (1324), Saint Cerbonius' tomb, created by the Sienese sculptor Coro da Gregorio in a painterly style influenced by illuminated manuscripts.

Opposite the Duomo is the **Palazzo Comunale** (town hall), created from a complex of 14th-15thC tower houses.

MUSEO/PALAZZO DEL PODESTÀ ▥

The magistrate's palace, c.1230, now houses a small archeological collection as well as some Sienese pictures; outstanding is Ambrogio Lorenzetti's *Maestà*.

UPPER TOWN (Città Nuova)

The upper town is guarded by the huge **Fortezza dei Senesi**, built by the Sienese after their conquest of Massa Marittima in 1334 and joined, by a long flying arch, to the earlier **Torre del Candeliere** *(which may be climbed Tues-Sun 10.30am-12.30pm, 3.30-6.30pm).*

Its center is Piazza Matteotti, from where the Corso Diaz leads to the Gothic church of **San Agostino** (1299-1313), which possesses interesting 16th-17thC pictures by Empoli, Pacchiarotti, Lorenzo Lippi and others.

The **Museum of Mining** (Museo della Miniera) *(open Tues-Sun ✗ compulsory)* is in the s of the town, near Via Corridoni.

➤ **Taverna del Vecchio Borgo** at Via Parenti 12 *(☎ (0566) 903950 ▯ ◧ ▨ closed Mon; Sun dinner in winter; mid-Jan to mid-Feb).*

MONTALCINO
Map 7H6. 109km (67 miles) s of Florence, 41km (25 miles) s of Siena. 53024. Siena. Population: 5,702.

Montalcino stands on an olive-clad hill above the Ombrone and Asso valleys. The site was inhabited by the Etruscans and Romans, and in the early Middle Ages was in the possession of the Benedictine Abbey of **Sant'Antimo** (see below).

A period of communal independence came to an end in 1260 when the town was subjected to Sienese rule after the battle of Montaperti. Montalcino provided sanctuary for Sienese aristocrat Republicans who fled their besieged city in 1555. Sienese gratitude is still expressed twice a year when the standard bearers representing Montalcino occupy the place of honor in the procession that precedes the Palio.

Brunello di Montalcino is one of the great Italian wines. See TUSCAN WINES on pages 175-178 for advice about where to taste this and other local wines.

SIGHTS AND PLACES OF INTEREST

Piazza del Popolo is the main square. The **Palazzo Comunale** with its high tower dates from the 13th-14thC; the imposing loggia was added in the 14th-15thC. Above, in Piazza Garibaldi, can be found the church of **Sant'Egidio**, which was built by the Sienese in 1325. Over the first altar on the left, notice the wooden Crucifixion (15thC) framed by 16thC inlaid wooden doors.

There are sweeping views from the Neoclassical **Duomo** (1818-32) and from the church of the **Madonna del Soccorso**.

The **Rocca**, which dominates the town, was built by the Sienese in 1361 and was one of the most crucial defense posts of the Republic. The bastion was added by the Medici after the conquest of Siena. Inside is an *enoteca* of local wines, where you can also sample the local cheeses, oil, hams and other good things that might make up a picnic.

MUSEO CIVICO E DIOCESANO

Via di Ricasoli 29.

Located below the Rocca, this museum houses 14th-15thC Sienese pictures, ecclesiastic objects including a 12thC illuminated Bible, and some 15thC polychrome wooden statues. There is also a separate archeological collection.

In Piazza Cavour is the former pharmacy of the Hospital of Santa Maria, frescoed by V. Tamagni.

NEARBY SIGHT

SANT'ANTIMO ▥ † ★

Near Castelnuovo Abate, 8km (5 miles) to s. Apply for entry to custodian in Castelnuovo Abate.

This radiantly lovely Romanesque church, set in a gentle golden valley, is built of travertine with architectonic decorations in the alabaster and translucent onyx that was quarried locally. It dates mostly from the early 12thC. The monastery was founded, according to tradition, by Charlemagne early in the 9thC. The doorway on the left flank, adorned with geometric carvings in the Lombard style, and the crypt, survive from the earlier building. The beautiful interior is embellished with fine capitals. There are frescoed apartments off the clerestory.

⊗⌁ ⊑ **Il Giglio** ♣ *(Via Soccorso Saloni 5 ☎ (0577) 848167 ▯ to ▥ closed Mon; early Jan to mid-Feb)* is a small, simple hotel in the center.

⊑ TAVERNA AND FATTORIA DEI BARBI

2km (1¼ miles) s of Montalcino, off the Sant'Antimo road ☎(0577) 849357 ▯ to ▥ No cards ⬧ ▯ ⊑ ⋒ Closed Tues dinner, Wed.

Superb Brunello wines complement traditional local dishes made from produce grown on this well-known wine-making estate.

⊑ LA CUCINA DI EDGARDO ♣

Via Saloni 9 ☎(0577) 848232 ▥ 🆎 ◉ ◐ 🔤 Closed Wed, Jan.

A tiny and very interesting restaurant where you must follow the advice of the proprietor. Reservation is essential.

MONTE AMIATA

*Map **7**H6.*

The isolated conical peak of this extinct volcano, 1,738m (5,702ft) high, is visible from Siena and features in much of its art.

"Surely here, if anywhere in the world," wrote the Sienese Pope Pius II in his *Commentaries,* "sweet shade and silvery springs and green grass and smiling meadows allure poets." The upper slopes are equipped for skiing and climbing.

The summit is most easily reached from ABBADIA SAN SALVATORE, the most populous center. Other, more charming villages, are Arcidosso, Bagnone, Castel del Piano, Piancastagnaio and Santa Fiora.

MONTECATINI TERME

Map **14***D4. 49km (30 miles)* NW *of Florence, 49km (30 miles)* NE *of Pisa. 51016. Pistoia. Population: 21,764* **i** *Viale Verdi 66a* ☎*772244.*

One of the most famous and fashionable spas in Europe, Montecatini Terme was laid out in the early 20thC around a stately park. The warm saline waters are recommended for liver ailments and skin problems. The **Stabilimento Tettuccio** is the smartest place to take the waters, and its café is the main rendezvous. The season extends from April to November.

From Viale A. Diaz, a funicular railway ascends to the beautifully situated old town, **Montecatini Alto**. To the N there is lovely walking country in the Valdinievole.

Montecatini has some 500 hotels, mainly clustered around the **Parco delle Terme**; most open only during the season.

🐾 ➡ The best known luxury hotel is the **Grand Hotel e la Pace** *(Via della Torretta 1* ☎*(0572) 75801* [Fx]*(0572) 78451* ▥ *)* [AE] [◈] [CD] [VISA] *closed Nov-Mar)*, which has a good restaurant.

🐾 If you find the atmosphere of Montecatini a little oppressive, try a hotel just outside the town: **Grotta Giusti**, 5km (3 miles) SE at Monsummano Terme *(Via Grotta Giusti 171* ☎*(0572) 51165* [Fx]*(0572) 51269* ▯ [AE] [CD] *closed mid-Nov to Mar)*, has spa and sports facilities and is set in a peaceful park.

Park Hotel Sorgenti, 2km (1¼ miles) outside at Pieve a Nievole *(*☎*(0572) 951116* [Tx]*575487* [Fx]*(0572) 95231* ▯ [AE] [CD] [VISA]*)*, is in a pleasant country house furnished with antiques and surrounded by a large park.

➡ **Pier Angelo** is at Via IV Novembre 99 *(*☎*(0572) 771552* ▯ *to* ▥ ▦ [AE] [◈] [CD] [VISA] *closed Sun, Mon lunch, Aug)*: skillfully prepared and dramatically presented seasonal dishes in a restored Art Nouveau villa.

➡ A classy wine bar in the center and popular with the gilded youth is the **Enoteca da Giovanni** *(Via Garibaldi 27* ☎*(0572) 71695* ▥ [◈] [CD] [VISA] 🍴 ▦ *closed Mon)*. At Borgo a Buggiano, there is **Da Angiolo** *(Piazza del Popolo 2* ☎*(0572) 32014* ▯ [AE] *closed Mon, Tues, Aug)*, which specializes in absolutely fresh and very simply prepared fish, sea food and meat all of the highest quality. And above the town at Pietre Cavate is **Pietre Cavate** *(*☎*(0572) 73664* ▯ *to* ▥ [AE] [VISA] *closed for lunch except Sun, all day Wed and mid-Aug)*, which is in a large farmhouse commanding wonderful views, and does excellent Tuscan cooking, including outstanding peasant soups.

NEARBY SIGHT

8km (5 miles) S at Ponte Buggianese is the church frescoed by the modern painter Pietro Annigoni.

MONTEFOLLONICO

Map **8***H7. 112km (70 miles)* SE *of Florence, 60km (37 miles)* SE *of Siena. 53040. Siena. Population: 820.*

A walled hill village overlooking the Orcia and Chiana valleys. An unpaved road from MONTEPULCIANO can be walked in about 45 minutes.

➡ **LA CHIUSA**
Via della Madonnina 88 ☎*(0577) 669668* ▥ *with rooms* ▭ ➡ 🐾 ⟨⟨ 🍸 [AE] [◈] [CD] [VISA]
Closed Tues, Jan-Mar, Nov.

Like so many of the greatest Italian restaurants, La Chiusa specializes in local produce prepared according to the most refined culinary traditions of the area. Before embarking on the feast you would be wise to discuss the menu and ceiling price with the enthusiastic young proprietors. Specialties include *collo d'oca farcito, pappardelle Dania* and *anatra al finocchio*.

MONTE OLIVETO MAGGIORE
Map 11G6. 104km (65 miles) SE of Florence, 36km (22 miles) SE of Siena. 53020. Siena.

THE ABBEY ✝
The red-brick buildings of this abbey, which date from the 14th-18thC, are magnificently situated above the barren clay hills near SIENA. Their institutional appearance is the result of a 19thC restoration.

The **chiostro grande** is decorated with important but heavily-restored and over-painted frescoes of *Scenes from the Life of St Benedict*. Nine are by Signorelli (1497-98), the rest by Sodoma (from 1505). In the church, the intarsiaed **choir stalls** (1503-05) by G. da Verona are highly sophisticated exercises in perspective.

≈ **La Torre** *(☎ (0577) 707022 ▢ ▣ ▦ closed Tues, Christmas)* offers a warm welcome and serves good country fare.

MONTEPULCIANO ☆
Map 8H7. 119km (74 miles) SE of Florence, 65km (40 miles) SE of Siena. 53045. Siena. Population: 14,297 i Via Ricci 9 ☎(0578) 757442.
Like PIENZA, 14km (9 miles) to the W, Montepulciano is neither town nor village, but a miniature Renaissance city. See these two little hill cities one after another and you will have captured the essence of the 15thC urban ideal as realized by some of the most distinguished Italian architects of the period. From the 12thC, Montepulciano modeled itself on Florence and Siena, its political masters. Its fortifications were rebuilt when Montepulciano fell to the Sienese in 1495-1511.

Agnolo Ambrogini, the leading humanist poet and scholar of the 15thC and tutor to Lorenzo de' Medici's children, was born in Montepulciano and called himself Poliziano after the medieval Latin name of his birthplace, Mons Politianus. The Jesuit Cardinal Robert Bellarmine was largely responsible for the flourish of Baroque architecture that followed.

Vino Nobile di Montepulciano is a redoubtable Tuscan wine (see page 177).
Event ‡ An annual music festival, the Cantiere Internazionale d'Arte, takes place here in July to early August. Founded in 1975 and run by a distinguished international committee, it emphasizes community involvement in performances of 20thC music.

SIGHTS AND PLACES OF INTEREST

THE CORSO
Follow the Corso from Porta al Prato to the far end of the town and loop back along its western edge.

The Corso can be divided into three parts. **Via Gracciano nel Corso** is lined

237

with good Renaissance palaces. **Palazzo Avignonesi** *(#99)* is attributed to Vignola; the **Cocconi** *(#72)* is attributed to da Sangallo the Elder. The lower story of the **Palazzo Bucelli** *(#81)* is faced with a mosaic of Etruscan and Roman tombs and cinerary urns. On the right is Michelozzo's delightful, Gothic-Renaissance church of **Sant'Agostino**; the lovely terra-cotta relief over the portal of the *Madonna and Child with Sts John the Baptist and Augustine* is also by Michelozzo.

In the **Via di Voltaia nel Corso**, the palace on the left, the **Cervini** *(#21)*, with graduated rustication and a breaking-wave frieze, was designed by Antonio da Sangallo the Elder but not completed.

Farther along on the left is the church of **Gesù**, which has a charming curved Baroque interior.

The last stretch of the Corso, **Via dell'Opio**, leads to the Via del Poliziano past #5, the house where Poliziano was born in 1454, to the Gothic church of **S. Maria dei Servi**, which has a Baroque interior.

DUOMO †

The highest point of Montepulciano is its civic and religious center, the wide and splendidly varied **Piazza Grande**, with the Duomo closing its s side. Designed by Ippolito Scalza and built on the site of the earlier parish church from 1592-1630, the Duomo contains a superb altarpiece of the *Assumption* (1401), which is possibly Taddeo di Bartolo's best work. Michelozzo's **Tomb of Bartolomeo Aragazzi** was dismantled in the 17thC and is now displayed in fragments placed to the left of the entrance, on the first two pillars of the nave, on either side of the altar and elsewhere.

Notice also, across in the right nave, the 15thC Sienese School polychrome *Annunciation.*

The **Palazzo Comunale**, next to the Duomo, was begun in the late 14thC, but its facade is later, possibly designed by Michelozzo. From the top of its tower you can see a panorama of southern Tuscany and into Umbria. Opposite are the **Tarugi** *(#3)* and **Contucci** *(#6)* palaces by Antonio da Sangallo the Elder.

MUSEO CIVICO ▥

Via Ricci 11. Open summer only Tues-Sun 10.30am-12.30pm, 4.30-7.30pm. Closed Mon.
The Gothic **Neri-Orselli Palace** houses 13th-17thC paintings, terra cottas and 15thC illuminated choir-books.

NEARBY SIGHT

SAN BIAGIO ▥ † ★

Situated just outside the town to the sw, this church (1518-45) is the masterpiece of Antonio da Sangallo the Elder. The densely classicizing interior, all in the same pale honey travertine, is weighted with loyalty to the architectural principles of Bramante. The **Canon's House** and **well head** were also designed by Sangallo but completed posthumously.

☜ ⇌ IL MARZOCCO ❧

Piazza Savonarola 18 ☎*(0578) 757262* ▯ *18 rms, 13 with bathrm* ▣ ▣ ▣ ▥ ▱ ▱
Conveniently located inside the walls, this very appealing small hotel-restaurant offers clean, cozy rooms and good, simply prepared food.

☜ A peaceful and friendly, if somewhat faded, alternative would be **Panoramic**, 3km (2 miles) to the SE *(* ☎ *and* ▣*(0578) 798398* ▯ ▣ ▣ *).*

⇌ **La Grotta** *(* ☎ *(0578) 757607)* is a pleasant restaurant immediately opposite San Biagio.

⇌ See also MONTEFOLLONICO.

MONTERIGGIONI

Map 10F5. 55km (34 miles) s of Florence, 15km (9 miles) NW of Siena. 53035. Siena. Population: 6,573.

A complete medieval village encircled by 13thC walls that were built by the Sienese against the Florentines: Dante likened the 14 towers to giants in the *Inferno XXXI*.

The **Museo del Seminario Arcivescovile** has Vecchietta's moving and remarkable detached fresco of the *Lamentation* (c.1445).

NEARBY SIGHT
ABBADIA ISOLA †

Less than 3km (1¾ miles) SW, this tiny village conserves a Romanesque church in the Lombard style from the 11thC Cistercian abbey of S. Salvatore. The church possesses an altarpiece (1471) by Sano di Pietro, a fresco of the *Madonna and Child with Saints* by Taddeo di Bartolo, an early 15thC font and an Etruscan-Roman cinerary urn. In the priest's house is a *Madonna and Child*, possibly by Duccio.

⊨█ IL POZZO

Piazza Roma 2 ☎(0577) 304127 ▥ ▣ ▣ ▣ ▨ ▭ *Closed Sun dinner, Mon.*
A pleasant and popular country restaurant serving routine Tuscan food.

⋙⊨   At Strove, 4km (2½ miles) to the SW are **Casalta** *(☎(0577) 301002* ▥ *closed mid-Nov to mid-Mar, restaurant closed Wed)* and the **San Luigi Residence** *(☎(0577) 301055* ▣x*(0577) 301167* ▥ to ▥ ▣ ▣ ▣ ▨)*, which is in a converted farmhouse surrounded by olive groves.

MONTE SAN SAVINO

Map 11G7. 86km (53 miles) SE of Florence, 22km (14 miles) SW of Arezzo. 52048. Arezzo. Population: 7,565.

An agricultural hill village, birthplace of the sculptor Andrea Sansovino. The main street is the **Corso Sangallo**, which is lined with fine palaces and churches.

The little church of **Santa Chiara** (1652) contains terra cottas by Sansovino and other sculptors, and includes his earliest important work, an altarpiece of *Sts. Laurence, Roch and Sebastian* and the exquisite tabernacle to the left of the high altar, which he carried out in collaboration with Andrea della Robbia.

Sansovino is also thought to have designed the handsome Corinthian **Loggia dei Mercanti** farther along the Corso.

The **Palazzo Comunale** opposite is by Antonio da Sangallo the Elder. In Piazza di Monte is the church of **S. Agostino**, with a handsome Gothic portal. Inside, there are early 15thC frescoes and, over the high altar, an *Assumption* (1539) by Vasari.

Lucignano, a short drive to the s, is an exceptionally attractive hill town. It has retained its elliptical medieval plan and commands a panorama of the Valdichiana. The Museo Comunale has a fine collection of mainly Sienese pictures.

    You could overnight at **Sangallo** *(Piazza Vittorio Veneto 16* ☎*(0575) 810049* ⬜ 🆔 💠 🅾 💳 *)*.

    Le Terrazze *(* ☎*844111, closed Mon);* or **Da Toto** *(Piazza Tribunale* ☎*(0575) 836988* ⬜ *closed Tues),* at Lucignano, 6km (4 miles) to the s.

    See also GARGONZA.

MONTI DELL'UCCELLINA, PARCO NATURALE DELLA MAREMMA ☆
Map 10I5-J5. 157km (98 miles) s of Florence, 17km (10 miles) s of Grosseto. Entrance at Alberese ☎*(0564) 407098* 📠 ✗ *compulsory, on foot in summer* ❀ *Open Wed, Sat, Sun, hols.*

The extremely varied ecological balance of the coastal terrain is protected in the Maremma Nature Reserve, which is at its loveliest in early June when the broom is in flower.

    Demonstrations of cattle roping are sometimes given by the local *butteri* (cowboys).

    Pizza Alberese *(* ☎*(0564) 407134* ⬜ *)* serves fish as well as pizza and has tables outside. Or try **Da Remo** *(* ☎*(0564) 405014* ⬜ *)* at Rispescia Stazione.

    See also TALAMONE.

ORBETELLO
Map 7J5. 183km (113 miles) s of Florence, 43km (27 miles) s of Grosseto. 58015. Grosseto. Population: 13,500.

Ortobello was the capital of the Spanish Garrison States, the *Presidii,* from 1557; and it retains something of the atmosphere (and the faces) of a Spanish colonial town. The fortifications on the mainland side were initiated by the Sienese and extended by the Spanish. The Spanish powder works has recently been restored.

The **Duomo** retains a pretty Gothic facade (1376) decorated in the Sienese style. In the first chapel on the right is a rare pre-Romanesque marble altar-front. The **Museo Civico** has archaic sculpture and the pediment of an extraordinary 2ndC BC Etruscan temple.

    Presidi *(Via Mura di Levante 34* ☎ 📠*(0564) 867601* ⬜ 🅾 💳 *)* is a sensible, friendly hotel on the lagoon.

    Da Egisto *(Corso Italia 190* ☎*(0564) 867469* ⬜ *to* ⬜ 🆔 💠 🅾 💳 *closed Mon, Nov)* ; **Il Nocchino** *(Via dei Mille 64* ☎*(0564) 860329* ⬜ *closed Mon);* **Osteria del Lupacante** *(Corso Italia 103* ☎*(0564) 867618* ⬜ 🆔 💠 🅾 💳 *closed Wed, Nov).* **Laguna Blu** does good ice creams.

    Two restaurants 7km (4½ miles) NE on the Via Aurelia near Orbetello Scalo, both with rooms, are **Il Cacciatore** *(* ☎*(0564) 862020* 📠*863038* ⬜ *closed Wed* 🆔 🅾 💳 *)* and **La Ruota** *(* ☎*(0564) 862137* 📠*864123* ⬜ 🆔 💠 🅾 💳 *closed Thurs, Feb).* See also ANSEDONIA, PORT'ERCOLE and PORTO SANTO STEFANO.

PESCIA

Map **14***D4. 61km (38 miles)* NW *of Florence, 19km (12 miles)* NE *of Lucca.*
51017. Pistoia. Population: 18,979.

This horticultural and paper-making center in the Valdinievole is re-nowned for its carnations and asparagus. The town has been divided into five districts or *quinti* since the 13thC. The civic center, Piazza Mazzini, is on the right bank of the River Pescia; the religious center, Piazza del Duomo, on the left bank.

SIGHTS AND PLACES OF INTEREST

PIAZZA MAZZINI

The long, narrow square is a lively architectural farrago of 14th-19thC houses, closed at the s end by the 15thC **Oratory of the Madonna di Piè di Piazza**, possibly designed by Brunelleschi's adopted son Buggiano, and at the N end by the 13th-14thC **Palazzo dei Viacri**.

In the nearby Piazza S. Stefano is the **Museo Civico**, with Tuscan paintings dating from the 14th-16thC.

DUOMO †

The Baroque Duomo (1693) has a late 19thC facade and a sturdy Romanesque-Gothic campanile. Inside are the Renaissance **Turini Chapel** by G. di Baccio d'Agnolo, and the remains of a 13thC ambo.

SAN FRANCESCO †

Via Battisti.

The restored interior of this Gothic church contains a rare Romanesque painting by Bonaventura Berlinghieri of *St Francis* (1235), which was executed only 9 years after the death of the saint. The Brunelleschian **Orlandi-Cardini Chapel** (1451) may have been designed by Buggiano.

Also in Via Battisti is the 11th-14thC **Oratory of Sant' Antonio**, which contains a moving wooden group of the *Deposition.*

The huge steel and glass flower market, the **Nuovo Mercato dei Fiori**, occupies a site of 40,000sq.m (431,000 square feet) on the road to Chiesina Uzzanese.

NEARBY SIGHTS

3km (1¾ miles) to the E of Pescia is the beautifully situated village of **Uzzano**. There are good Romanesque churches in and around the villages of Castelvecchio, Montecarlo, Villa Basilica and S. Gennaro.

⇛ CECCO ✿

Via Francesco Forti 96 ☎*(0572) 477955* ▥ ▭ ⇛ 🏧 AE ⓒ VISA *Closed Mon.*

Pleasant service and exceptional food. In April and May the local *asparagi giganti* should be tried. Specialties include pastas and *pollastrino al mattone*.

✆ ⇛   **Villa delle Rose** at Via del Castellare 46, 51012 Castellare di Pescia (☎ *(0572) 451301* ℻ *444003* ▥ ▤ AE ⓒ ⓒⓓ VISA *closed Mon, Tues lunch)* is a peaceful hotel with a swimming pool and a cool park.

Also, restaurant **La Fortuna** *(Via Colli per Uzzano 18* ☎ *(0572) 477121* ▥ *closed lunch, Sun, Aug).*

PETRIOLO

Map **10***H6. 30km (19 miles)* SW *of Siena, 43km (27 miles)* NE *of Grosseto.*
Grosseto.

"This place is... in a deep valley made by the Farma River. It is famous for its trout. All around it rise lofty mountains, rocky but wooded and grassy too.... Here for twenty days the Pope had the warm waters poured through a pipe onto the crown of his head; for the physicians said this would be beneficial, since his brain was too moist," wrote Pius II, who took the waters here in 1460.

The little spa town is still surrounded by serenely lovely countryside and encircled by 15thC walls, built, according to the Pope, "that brigands might not lie in wait for the bathers" as had sometimes happened in the past.

❧ ☰ GRAND HOTEL TERME DI PETRIOLO
58045 Civitella Paganico, Pari, Grosseto ☎*(0564) 908871* ☒*501281* ☒*(0564) 908712*
▥ *58 rms, all with bathrm* ▤ ☖ AE ⊙ ⊙ ▥ ☖ ⚱ ☐ ⌂ ⚓ ⚘ ⚲ ⛳ ☥ ⛲ ⊙
A well-managed and fully-equipped health spa. The service is unusually pleasant, and the restaurant, **Le Ginestre** (▥ ▤ ⚑ AE ⊙ ⊙ ▥), serves fresh, carefully prepared local produce.

PIENZA ★
Map 8H7. 120km (75 miles) s of Florence, 52km (33 miles) s of Siena. 53026. Siena. Population: 2,622.
Few men have left such a vivid and complete picture of their period as did Enea Silvio Piccolomini in his candid autobiography, the *Commentaries*. Born in 1405 of an impoverished branch of a noble Sienese family, he rose to become Pope as Pius II from 1458-64.

Pienza, the Utopian city with which he glorified his humble birthplace, Corsignano, is the first modern example of considered town planning. This joyous little Renaissance New Town is a celebration of the bracing winds of change that blew from every direction through the culture of 15thC Italy.

It is a meeting ground of the Gothic and Renaissance styles, of the German church architecture Pius had seen on his travels and the strict Classical principles laid down by Alberti, of Florentine and Sienese art, of the Tuscan countryside and the sophisticated urbanity of the Tuscan *quattrocento* spirit.

As soon as Pius was elected Pope, he commissioned Bernardo Rossellino to rebuild Corsignano. Work began in 1459. Three years later the piazza and street grid were complete and the new city was renamed Pienza by Papal bull. Pius left instructions that his cathedral, "the finest in all Italy," should never be altered in the smallest detail.

Pienza's remote location has ensured that his orders were carried out.

SIGHTS AND PLACES OF INTEREST
The central **Piazza Pio II** is like an open-air room looking s through the two window spaces on either side of the **cathedral**, which is flanked by the **Palazzo Piccolomini** on the right and the **Palazzo Vescovile** (Bishop's Palace) on the left. The N side is closed by the **Palazzo Comunale** and a wing of the **Ammannati Palace**, built by one of Pius' cardinals. The beautifully carved well-head (1462) was designed by Rossellino.

CATTEDRALE ▥ ✝

The travertine facade follows Alberti's Classical principles of organization. On the pediment is the papal coat of arms. The interior was inspired by the German *Hallenkirchen* that Pius admired.

He specially commissioned the **paintings** by illustrious Sienese artists: Giovanni di Paolo, Matteo di Giovanni, Vecchietta and Sano di Pietro. The Classical frames and the decorative carvings elsewhere in the church were executed by Sienese craftsmen. The Gothic **canons' stalls** (1462) in the central chapel are magnificent. In the crypt, below the apse, is a **baptismal font** by Rossellino.

The **Cathedral Museum**, located in the Canon's House, contains Sienese paintings, Flemish tapestries, illuminated choir-books and ecclesiastical vestments including, most notably, the **cope** embroidered for Pius II in England.

PALAZZO PICCOLOMINI ▥

The papal residence is a rougher version of Alberti's and Rossellino's RUCELLAI PALACE (see FLORENCE A TO Z), with the important addition of a three-tiered loggia on the s side. The elegant courtyard gives access to the hanging gardens below the palace.

PALAZZO VESCOVILE

Pius acquired for Rodrigo Borgia, the future Pope Alexander VI, the old Gothic Palazzo Pretorio, which Borgia adapted and later gave to the city.

PIEVE DI CORSIGNANO ✝

Below the town, 1km ($\frac{1}{2}$ mile) from the Porta al Ciglio. Pius II was baptized in the rough stone font that remains in this endearing little Romanesque church, which now stands alone in a sloping olive grove.

Il Prato *(Piazza Dante Alighieri 25* ☎*(0578) 748601* ▥ ▧ ▨ ▼ AE ▣ ▣ VISA *closed Wed)* serves excellent antipasti — and don't fail to sample the *vin santo.*

Also **Buca delle Fate** *(*☎*(0578) 748448* ▥ *closed Mon)* and **Dal Falco** *(Piazza Dante Alighieri 7* ☎*(0578) 748551* ▥ AE ▣ VISA *closed Fri).*

7.5km ($4\frac{1}{2}$ miles) NE, **La Saracina** *(*☎ *and* Fx *748002)* is a tiny, peaceful hotel in an old farmhouse.

See also MONTALCINO and MONTEFOLLONICO.

PIETRASANTA

Map 13D3. 104km (64 miles) NW of Florence, 35km (22 miles) N of Pisa. 55045. Lucca. Population: 25,722.

The main town of the Versilia and center of marbleworking is 3.5km (2 miles) inland from the coastal resort of Marina di Pietrasanta. The imposing 13th-14thC **Duomo** is much restored.

Event ✝ An exhibition of marblework by local artisans is held in the Consorzio Artigiani from July to September.

Peralta, 3km (2 miles) SE of Camaiore at Pieve di Camaiore *(*☎*(0584) 951230* ▥ *closed Nov-Mar)* is a small, secluded rural hotel with a mainly English staff. A good base for walking.

Bernadone ❀ *(Via Nocchi 110* ☎*(0584) 951118* ▥ *to* ▥ AE ▣ VISA *closed Wed, Nov)* is located within an 18thC mill. Try also **La Dogana** at Capezzano Pianore *(Via Sarzanese 442* ☎*(0584) 913143* ▥ AE ▣ ▣ VISA *closed Wed, Nov);* **Emilio e Bona** at Candalla *(Via Lombricese 22* ☎*(0584) 989289* ▥ AE *closed Mon);* **Mulin del Rancone** *(*❀*)* at Rancone *(*☎*(0583)*

618670 ▢ *open daily in summer, weekends only in winter; closed Nov);* **Il Vignaccio** at Santa Lucia *(Piazza della Chiesa 5* ☎*(0584) 914200* ▢ *closed Wed, Thurs lunch).*

🍽 **Il Gatto Nero** *(Piazza Carducci 32* ☎*(0584) 70135* ▦ 👥 ▤ AE ◐ ◑ VISA *closed Mon; Sun dinner in winter; Oct)* is a family-run restaurant with bohemian personality; **Sci** *(Vicolo di Porta a Lucca* ▢ *open lunch only, closed Sun),* a minute trattoria favored by stone workers and sculptors.

🍽 See also FORTE DEI MARMI, LUCCA, MASSA and VIAREGGIO.

PISA ★

*Map **13**E3. 91km (56 miles) w of Florence, 3km (2 miles) n of Galileo Galilei international airport at S. Giusto. 56100. Pisa. Population: 103,400* **i** *Piazza Duomo* ☎*(050) 560464 and Piazza Stazione* ☎*(050) 42291.*

The golden age of Pisa was the 12thC, when the Duomo was completed and the Baptistry and campanile were begun. Pisa had enjoyed a modest maritime economy even during the Dark Ages, thanks to its natural harbor at the mouth of the Arno, and it was favored by successive Emperors who needed the support of its strong navy. In 1162 the Emperor Federico Barbarossa granted to the commune the control of a large coastal territory that stretched to the N and S beyond the borders of modern Tuscany.

The **Duomo**, a mix of the Italian and Oriental styles familiar to Pisan sailor merchants, was widely copied, and it infused Tuscan Romanesque architecture with new vigor. In sculpture, too, Pisa led the way, producing in Nicola and Giovanni Pisano the first great modern figure sculptors.

After the destruction of its fleet by the Genoese at the battle of Meloria in 1284, the communal government, distracted by internal conflict, neglected the shallow harbor, which began gradually to silt up. The city fell to Florence in 1406, the port in 1421. There was one final bid for independence in 1495 when Pisa, under the protection of Charles VIII, revolted, not to be retaken by Florence until 1509.

The Florentines paid special attention to the welfare of their prize conquest, which remained commercially active even after the harbor had finally silted up in the 16thC. The University, which is today one of the most respected in Italy, was revived in 1472 by Lorenzo de' Medici, who temporarily forbade Florentines to study elsewhere, and in 1561 Cosimo I made Pisa the headquarters of his new Crusading Order of St Stephen.

Pisa's most illustrious son was Galileo, who taught at the University (which has had a strong science faculty ever since). In the 19thC, when Walter Savage Landor, Shelley, Byron and later the Brownings all made their homes in Pisa for short periods, the city was a brooding backwater shrouded in the mists of its Maremma, where the rich grazing lands had once been a source of its republican prosperity. Elizabeth Barrett Browning found it "very beautiful and full of repose"; but to Shelley's more feverish imagination Pisa sometimes seemed "a desolation of a city, which was the cradle, and is now the grave of an extinguished people."

In the last years of World War II, some of Pisa's greatest monuments were severely damaged.

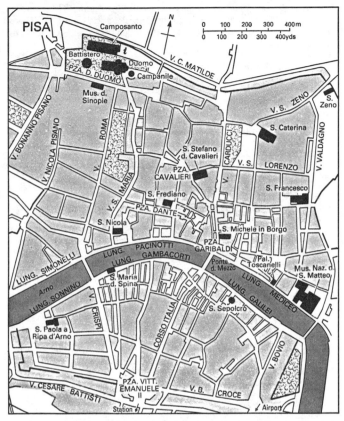

Events ‡ The annual Regatta di San Ranieri, a race among the city's four historic quarters, is held on the evening of June 17. ‡ The *Gioco del Ponte*, a mock battle in 16thC costume between residents of the Mezzogiorno (s of the Arno) and Tramontana (N of the Arno), takes place on June 28. ‡ Concerts are given in the Palazzo dei Cavalieri, from December to May.

SIGHTS AND PLACES OF INTEREST

The center of the modern city is **Piazza Garibaldi**. Immediately to the s is the **Ponte di Mezzo**, the city's oldest bridge, which gives the best view of the elegant palaces lining the Arno.

The religious center is the **Piazza del Duomo** on the N edge of the city, where the famous quartet of buildings — the **Baptistry**, **Campanile**, **Camposanto** and **Duomo** — are placed on their emerald lawn

245

like carved ivory pieces in a great ecclesiastical game. The complex, which also embraces the **Museo delle Sinopie** and **Museo dell'Opera del Duomo**, is enclosed on the W and N sides by sections of the 13thC city walls.

BAPTISTRY ▥ † ★

Begun in 1152 by Diotisalvi and carried forward from 1260-84 by Nicola and Giovanni Pisano, the Baptistry was completed by its extraordinary oriental-turban of a dome in the 14thC. Of the four portals, the most elaborate is the one facing the Duomo; the *Madonna* in the lunette is a copy of Giovanni Pisano's original, now in the Museo dell'Opera del Duomo.

Inside, to the left of Guido da Como's octagonal **baptismal font** (1246), is Nicola Pisano's **pulpit (★)**, the artist's earliest known work (1260) and the first to break with the more rigid formulae of Tuscan Romanesque sculpture. The style of his relief carvings was affected by the Roman sarcophagi which, in the 13thC, were used as the tombs of Christian Pisans buried around the Duomo. The handsome figure of *Fortitude,* a direct imitation of a Roman Hercules, has been called the first heroic nude sculpture in Italian art. The panels illustrate the *Nativity, Epiphany, Presentation at the Temple, Crucifixion* and *Last Judgment.*

BOTANICAL GARDEN (Orto Botanico)

Via L. Ghini ☎ *561795. Open Mon-Fri 8am-1pm, 2-5.30pm; Sat 8am-1pm. Closed Sun.*

Founded in the 1540s, and now part of the University of Pisa, this is one of the oldest and most richly-stocked botanical gardens in Europe. Some 1,600 species from all over the world — including important collections of *liliaceae, amaryllidaceae,* herbs, and palms — are cultivated in an area of about 6 acres.

CAMPANILE ▥ † ★

Closed indefinitely for consolidation.

The circular bell tower of Pisa is perhaps even more famous for leaning 4.5m (15ft) out of plumb than for its architectural elegance, and, interestingly, it has recently begun to straighten as a result of soil erosion on the opposite side. Begun in 1173, its foundations were tilted by a subsidence of the soil when the third story was half built. After a pause of 100 years, the tower was completed in the mid-14thC. It was, of course, from this tower that Galileo is said to have dropped the three metal balls of different masses that disproved Aristotle's theories about the acceleration of falling bodies.

A spiral staircase of 294 steps leads to the top, although the closure for restoration work makes an inside visit out of the question at the present time.

CAMPOSANTO (Cemetery)

Open summer 8am-8pm, winter 9am-5pm ▧

The legend has it that earth for the cemetery of Pisa was brought in shiploads from the Holy Land early in the 13thC. This sacred ground was enclosed by a rectangular building begun in 1277 and completed in the 15thC. The walls of the interior portico were frescoed by leading Italian artists including Taddeo Gaddi, Spinello Aretino and Benozzo Gozzoli. Over the centuries, a precious collection of antique sarcophagi was assembled here.

What could be salvaged from wartime damage has been painstakingly pieced together; but the ghostly frescoes speak more eloquently through their sinopie, now in the **Museo delle Sinopie**.

The most famous of the frescoes, now detached and hung in the Cappella Ammannati, is the *Triumph of Death* by an unknown late 14thC master, which inspired Liszt's *Totentanz.*

DUOMO ▥ † ★

Open summer 7.45am-12.45pm, 3-5pm; winter 9am-5pm.

The most influential Romanesque building in Tuscany and the first to be dressed in black and white horizontal stripes, the Duomo was begun in 1064 by Buscheto;

its tiered facade was added in the 12thC by Rainaldo. Entrance is normally by the Porta di San Ranieri on the s transept.

The crudely energetic and touching bronze doors (1180) by Bonanno represent *Scenes from the Life of Christ.*

The grandly proportioned **interior** consists of a nave with double aisles crossed by unusually deep transepts. The interior was heavily restored in the early 16thC after a devastating fire. At the bottom of the left side of the nave is Giovanni Pisano's **pulpit** (1302-10) (★). It bears an inscription suggesting that this extremely complex work caused the artist considerable worry. The result was one of the most personal and dramatic sculptural masterpieces of its own or indeed any time.

The relief panels, divided by figures of prophets and saints, depict scenes from the New Testament beginning with the *Birth of the Baptist,* facing the column. The sequence continues with the *Annunciation, Visitation, Nativity, Adoration of the Magi, Presentation at the Temple, Flight into Egypt, Slaughter of the Innocents, Kiss of Judas* and *Passion, Crucifixion, The Elect,* and *The Damned.*

In the E corner of the right transept is a reconstruction of Tino di Camaino's **tomb of Emperor Henry VII,** commissioned when the sculptor was made Head of Works of the Cathedral in 1315. On the balustrade flanking the entrance to the chancel are two **bronze angels** by Giambologna, who also made the *Crucifix* over the high altar. On the right as one enters the chancel is Andrea del Sarto's charming *St Agnes.* More paintings by Andrea hang below the choral galleries.

The 13thC mosaics of the *Redeemer in Glory* in the vault of the apse were completed with the head of *St John the Evangelist* by Cimabue in 1302. Below hang good canvases by Beccafumi.

MUSEO NAZIONALE DI SAN MATTEO ★
Lungarno Mediceo. Open Tues-Sat 9am-7pm; Sun, hols 9am-1pm. Closed Mon.

The national museum of Pisan art is housed in the former convent of the church of San Matteo, which was once a prison and is still a gloomy place to visit. The fine collection of sculpture and paintings includes some masterpieces, but it is ill-served by poor labeling and a distractingly over-ingenious provisional arrangement. After years of partial closure, not all of the museum's holdings are yet on view.

Highlights include the following. A polyptych of the *Madonna and Child with Saints* (1319-21), signed by Simone Martini, and opposite it, a polyptych of *St Dominic* with stories of his life, signed by Francesco Traini. The intensely beautiful *Madonna of the Milk* by Andrea and Nino Pisano from Santa Maria della Spina is the prize piece in a room of sculpture that also has the charming *Virgin Annunciate and Angel* by Francesco di Valdambrino.

In the galleries overlooking the cloister are Masaccio's *St Paul,* which was part of a polyptych of which the other sections are now scattered or lost. It is full of assured character despite being the artist's first major work. There is also the gilded bronze reliquary bust of St Rossore, which is attributed to Donatello.

Nearby on the Lungarno Mediceo is the **Toscanelli** palace where Byron lived in 1821-22.

MUSEO DELL'OPERA DEL DUOMO ★
Piazza Arcivescovedo 6. Open summer 9am-1pm, 3-7.30pm; winter 9am-1pm, 3-5pm ■■

A well-designed museum in the former chapter house of the cathedral displays works of art brought in from the Duomo, Baptistry and Camposanto. The cathedral treasury, in rooms 9-10, has a beautiful ivory statuette of the *Madonna and Child* by Giovanni Pisano. On the 1st floor there are paintings, intarsia panels and church vestments, plus an interesting collection of early 19thC copies of the frescoes of the Camposanto before their destruction in World War II. Finally, in the portico on the ground floor are the huge half-figures (1269-79) (★) of Evangelists, Prophets and a *Madonna and Child* by Nicola and Giovanni Pisano, taken from the exterior of the Baptistry.

247

MUSEO DELLE SINOPIE ✫
Piazza del Duomo. Open summer 9am-1pm, 3-7pm; winter 9am-1pm, 3-5pm 🈳

Opposite the s side of the piazza, in the Ospedale Nuovo della Misericordia, is this fascinating display of preparatory drawings, revealed by the destruction of the Camposanto frescoes, a unique opportunity to study the technique of some of the leading artists of the 13th-15thC. They include the *Triumph of Death* and Gozzoli's *Scenes from the Old Testament* and *Annunciation.*

PIAZZA DEI CAVALIERI ✫
Five minutes' walk from the Duomo is the central square of medieval Pisa, rebuilt in the 16thC by Vasari as headquarters of the Knights of the Order of St Stephen. The **Palazzo dei Cavalieri** (1562) is decorated with splendid and fantastic *sgraffiti* and incorporates niches containing sculpted busts of six Medici grand dukes. It is now the seat of the Scuola Normale Superiore, one of the most respected university colleges in Italy. In front of the palace stands an over-life-sized statue (1596) of Cosimo I, founder of the Order of St Stephen.

To its right is the church of **S. Stefano dei Cavalieri** (1569), also designed by Vasari but with a dull later facade. The **Palazzo dell'Orologio**, on the N end of the square, was built in 1607 around the remains of the medieval tower in which Count Ugolino della Gherardesca and his male heirs were starved to death by their political rivals in 1288; this episode, grimly described by Dante in *Inferno, XXXIII*, inspired Shelley's poem *The Tower of Famine.*

SANTA MARIA DELLA SPINA 🏛 ✝ ✫
Lungarno Gambacorti.

Named after a thorn from Christ's crown brought from the Holy Land by a Pisan merchant, this beautiful church was the swan-song of the Pisan Gothic style. The last of the great Pisan churches and perhaps the loveliest, it assumed its present size in the 1320s. The building originally stood closer to the Arno; in 1871 it was moved, stone by stone, to its present drier site.

SAN PAOLO A RIPA D'ARNO
Lungarno Sonnino.

This beautiful 11th-12thC church suffered both a bombardment in 1943 and a harsh restoration that deprived the facade of its charm. But the bare interior retains a solemn purity and contains a magnificent Roman sarcophagus decorated with lions' heads.

HOTELS

Pisa is well-supplied with hotels in all price categories, mostly clustered around the Campo dei Miracoli and around the station.

🕿 ≕ DEI CAVALIERI
Piazza della Stazione 2 ☎(050) 43290 📠590663 📠(050) 502242 🎟 *102 rms, all with* bathrm 🎴 ▣ 🚗 ≕ 🆎 ⊙ ⓪ 🎴 ✱ ☐ 🎴 ⚒ ⅄

Conveniently located near the station and air terminal, this well-managed modern hotel has an elegant and tranquil restaurant.

🕿 The **Ariston** *(Via Maffi 42* ☎*(050) 561834* ☐ *)*, which is rather basic, is situated near the Duomo.

≕ SERGIO
Lungarno Pacinotti 1 ☎(050) 48245 🎟 ▭ ◼◼ ≕ 🎴 🆎 ⊙ ⓪ 🎴 *Closed Sun, Mon lunch.*

The grand, expense-account restaurant of Pisa offers a large choice of traditional and more elaborate dishes. Service is attentive and practiced.

≕ VECCHI MACELLI
Via Volturno 49 ☎(050) 20424 🎟 *to* 🎟 ≕ 🎴 🆎 ⊙ ⓪ 🎴 *Closed Sun lunch, Wed.*

An appealing small restaurant (be sure to reserve ahead) which serves light, exquisite dishes based on fresh fish, seafood and game delicately flavored with herbs and seasonal vegetables. The desserts, too, are homemade and excellent.

Also **Da Bruno** *(Via Luigi Bianchi 12* ☎*(050) 560818* ▥ ▤ ☿ ◉ 𝗔𝗘 ◙ ◙ 𝗩𝗜𝗦𝗔 *closed Mon dinner, Tues);* **Taverna Kostas** *(Via del Borghetto 39* ☎*(050) 571467* ▥ *closed Mon, Aug),* a simple students' taverna which serves delicious Greek and Tuscan food; and **Lo Schiacciandoci** *(Via Vespucci 104* ☎*(050) 21024* ▥ ◙ *closed Sun dinner, also Sun lunch in summer, Mon, Aug)*

See also EXCURSIONS, below.

EXCURSIONS

There are two very worthwhile side trips within easy reach of Pisa.

S. PIERO A GRADO †

6km (4 miles) sw of Pisa is a Romanesque basilica dating from the mid-11thC. It was built on the site where St Peter is thought to have landed, on his way from Antioch to Rome.

There is a good choice of fish restaurants on the coast near S. Piero. At Marina di Pisa, try **L'Arsella** *(Via Padre Agostino* ☎*(050) 36615* ▥ 𝗔𝗘 ◙ 𝗩𝗜𝗦𝗔 *closed Tues dinner, Wed).*

TENUTA DI SAN ROSSORE

The area to the w of Pisa, from the mouth of the Arno to Lake Massaciuccoli, is designated as national park. The **Tenuta di San Rossore** *(* ☎*(050)27272; open Sun: summer 8.30am-7.30pm, winter 8.30am-5.50pm; open weekdays by appointment only)* is a protected littoral wood between the mouths of the Arno and the Serchio, with bird and animal sanctuaries. Formerly a royal estate and a summer estate of the President of the Republic, the land was given to the State in 1988.

Shelley's body was washed ashore in 1822 on the beach of Il Gombo, N of the mouth of the Arno.

See also CASCINA.

PISTOIA ★

*Map **14**D5. 37km (23 miles) NW of Florence. 51100. Pistoia. Population: 94,637*
i Piazza del Duomo ☎*(0573) 21622.*

In 63BC the Roman revolutionary Catiline was cornered by Roman legions near Pistoia; facing defeat, he plunged through the enemy ranks to his death. Dante considered the Pistoiesi to be even more dangerous than Catiline; and certainly their past is deeply scarred by factional conspiracy and violence. It was in Pistoia, as Dante recounts in the *Inferno, XXIV,* that the fierce political contest between Blacks and Whites originated.

For at least 200 years after the commune had surrendered to Florence in 1329, its citizens retained their reputation for rude manners and rough justice. Machiavelli described them as "brought up to slaughter and war"; and when the first pistols were made in Germany in the 16thC, they were named after the vicious little daggers worn by Pistoiesi and known as "*pistolese.*" Today Pistoia is a peaceful provincial capital surrounded by the orchards and nursery gardens that are the basis of its economy. Its main attraction for tourists is the wealth of Romanesque sculpture, especially the three pulpits in **S. Bartolomeo, S. Giovanni Fuorcivitas** and **S. Andrea**, which, if seen in that order, will enable one to follow the first "renaissance" of Tuscan sculpture as it evolved from 1250-1300.

SIGHTS AND PLACES OF INTEREST

The early 14thC walls, still partly intact, were later strengthened with bastions by the Medici. But the main historic monuments of the town lie within the earlier walls, the outline of which is traced in part by Corso Gramsci.

BAPTISTRY † ▥

Opposite the cathedral is the tall, hexagonal Gothic Baptistry (1338-1359), by Cellino de Nese to a design by Andrea Pisano. The interior is bare except for the original font, rediscovered during a restoration.

DUOMO ▥ †

The marble porch, which gives the cathedral the appearance of crouching ready to pounce, was added in the mid-14thC to the 12th-13thC Pisan-style facade. The terra cottas (1505) over the central portal and in the vault above are by Andrea della Robbia. The detached **campanile** was originally a watch tower.

The interior walls are decorated with fragments of 13th-14thC frescoes. At the top of the right aisle is the 14thC **tomb of Cino da Pistoia**, who was Dante's friend. In the Cappella di San Jacopo, off the right aisle, is the extraordinary silver **St James Altar**, one of the supreme examples of the Italian goldsmiths' art and crowded with many endearing details. It was created from 1287-1456 by a succession of Tuscan sculptors including Brunelleschi, who made the two **figures** on the left side. In the chapel to the left of the high altar is a *Madonna and Saints* (1485) by Lorenzo di Credi, possibly begun by Verrocchio; also the bust of *Archbishop Donato de'Medici* by A. Rossellino or Verrocchio.

The **Bishop's Palace** has a museum of other works made for the cathedral.

OSPEDALE DEL CEPPO ▥

Piazza Giovanni XII. Not open to the public.

The startling frieze over the porch of the hospital looks at first glance like the work of a Russian social realist. It was executed in the early 16thC by members of Andrea della Robbia's workshop and illustrates the *Seven Works of Mercy*, a fascinating picture of poverty and illness in the 16thC. The lovely Verrocchiesque tondas over the columns are by Giovanni della Robbia. The hospital is still in use.

PALAZZO DEL COMUNE ▥

The town hall, a very fine example of Gothic civic architecture, was founded in 1294 by the enlightened Florentine governor Giano della Bella, but building was delayed by political upheavals and not completed until 1355. Over the central door and on the corners are the crests of Medici Popes. The aerial corridor from the Sala Maggiore to the Duomo was added in 1637.

The **Marino Marini Center** (the sculptor was born in Pistoia in 1901) is off the courtyard; among the works on display are portraits of *Thomas Mann*, *Henry Miller* and *Chagall*. The **Museo Civico** occupies rooms on the first and second floors.

PALAZZO DEL PODESTÀ

This 14thC building is still the city's tribunal. Left of the entrance is the old court, with judge's seat, table of justice and bench of the accused.

SANT'ANDREA ▥ †

The 12thC church has an enchanting but unfinished facade. The reliefs (1166) of the *Journey and Adoration of the Magi* over the central portal are by the brothers Gruamonte and Adeodato. The blonde, barn-like interior is dominated by the city's outstanding work of art, the **pulpit** (★) by Giovanni Pisano (1298-1301). This pulpit was finished a year before Giovanni started work on the pulpit of the **Duomo** in PISA . These carvings are so intensely dynamic that one can scarcely believe they were created two centuries before the age of Michelangelo. Their subject is the *Life of Christ* and the *Last Judgment*. Opposite the pulpit is a wooden *Crucifix*, also by Giovanni, in a fine 15thC tabernacle frame.

SAN BARTOLOMEO IN PANTANO †
Piazza S. Bartolomeo.
A 12thC church, with a reconstructed **pulpit** (1250) by Guido da Como.

SAN GIOVANNI FUORCIVITAS †
Via Francesco Crispi.
The name refers to the original 8thC church that stood outside the city walls. The building was erected from the mid-12th to 14thC and restored after damage during World War II. The entrance is by the decoratively vivid but scarred N flank. Inside, the **holy water stoup** in the center is notable for the four busts of cardinals by the young Giovanni Pisano.

On the right wall is the **pulpit** (1270) by Guglielmo da Pisa, a follower of Nicola Pisano; the reliefs illustrate *Scenes from the New Testament.* On the left wall are the glazed terra-cotta figures of the *Visitation,* a moving work attributed to Luca della Robbia. Left of the altar is a large polyptych (1353-55) by T. Gaddi.

OTHER SIGHTS

Visitors with leisure time should also look at the churches of **S. Francesco**, **S. Domenico** and **S. Paolo**; also at **S. Maria delle Grazie**, which was designed by Michelozzo, and the **Cappella Tau**, which is decorated with 14th-15thC frescoes.

There is an attractively planned modern **zoo** *(Via Pieve a Celle 160)* just 4km (2½ miles) to the SW. And at Santomato, off the high road to Prato, the privately owned **Villa Gori** has interesting modern paintings and an outstanding collection of modern sculpture beautifully set out in the garden. Visits can be arranged, by appointment *(☎ (055) 8876321 or (0573) 479907).*

☜ ARCOBALENO
Via Valdi e Collina 37, Sanmommè, 51020 Pistoia ☎(0573) 470030 ⊠(0573) 470147 ▥ *29 rms, all with bathrm* ═ 🛏 *in summer* AE 🔘 🔘 ▥ 🖃 & 🖂 ⛟ ≪ ≋ ♒ 👟 ⚓ 🏊 ☶ ☎ ⊙
15km (9 miles) to the N at Sanmommè, this tourist hotel in the mountains is popular with children for its sports facilities and disco.

☜ VILLA OMBROSA
30km (19 miles) NW at Via M. D'Azeglio, 51028 San Marcello Pistoiese ☎(0573) 630156. Map 14D4 ▥ *27 rms* ═ ⚓ AE 🖂 ⛟ ✿ *Open July to mid-Sept only.*
Atmospherically furnished with antiques and set in a cool, shady garden.

☜ ═ RESIDENCE IL CONVENTO
Via S. Quirico 33, 51030 Santomato ☎(0573) 452651 ⊠(0573) 453578 ▥ *24 rms, all with bathrm* ⚓ ═ ▥ 🖂 ☐ 🖃 ✿ ⛟ ≪ ≋ ♈ *Restaurant closed mid-Jan to end Mar.*
5km (3 miles) to the NE near Ponte Nuovo, this peaceful retreat is in an 18thC former convent overlooking Pistoia.

☜   10km (6 miles) N at Piteccio is **Villa Vannini** *(Via Villa 6, 51030 Piteccio* ☎*(0573) 42031* ▥ AE *)*, which is a peaceful and refined private hotel in a Neoclassical villa.

═   There is nothing special in the historic center. But you can eat decently and inexpensively at the kiosk **Frisco** *(Piazza San Francesco 58a, open 10am-8pm,* *closed Tues)* and at **Da Loriano** *(Via Dalmazia 69* ☎ *(0573) 32937, closed Mon, Aug).*

🍽 **Osteria**, at Agliana 9km (5½ miles) E on the low road to Prato *(Via Provinciale Pratese 58* ☎ *(0574) 718450* Ⅲ *closed Mon, Tues and Wed dinner, Aug),* has simple country food and excellent wines.

🍽 See also MONTECATINI TERME and PRATO.

PITIGLIANO
Map **8***J7. 218km (134 miles) S of Florence, 74km (46 miles) SE of Grosseto. 58017. Grosseto. Population: 4,443.*

From a distance, Pitigliano is one of the most amazing sights in Tuscany. Carved out of a rock escarpment above a natural moat formed by three deep ravines, this was the seat of the Roman Orsini barons when they took control of the area in 1293. It retains the dour, impressive stamp of a warlord's headquarters — remarkably intact, charmless but fascinating.

The main square, Piazza della Repubblica, is dominated by the 14th-15thC **Palazzo Orsini**, modified in the 16thC by Giuliano da Sangallo. The strongly atmospheric medieval *borgo* straddles the escarpment beyond the Duomo.

The remains of the **Orsini Park** stretch along the Poggio Strozzoni, a vast promontory opposite the town. Begun in the 1560s by Niccolò IV, the park is now a romantic wilderness studded with crumbling statues and seats carved from the living rock.

🐌 🍽 **Guastini** *(Piazza Petruccioli 4 and 8* ☎ *(0564) 616065* Ⓕ *(0564) 616652* Ⅲ *Restaurant closed Fri).*

POGGIO A CAIANO
Map **14***E5. 17km (10 miles) W of Florence. 50046. Firenze. Population: 5,892.*

VILLA MEDICEA DI POGGIO A CAIANO 🏛 ★
☎877012 *Villa open Tues-Sat 9am-4pm, Sun 9am-1.30pm; gardens open 9am until 1hr before sunset. Closed Mon* ◀€

The most innovative and influential of all Medici country houses is distinguished from its predecessors by its formal grandeur. It was built for Lorenzo de' Medici in the 1480s, and is the only important surviving building for which he was personally responsible. He and his architect, Giuliano da Sangallo adapted the antique Roman villa type to the requirements of Renaissance country life.

> The cypress stands robust against the sky;
> Safely within, the storm tossed bird can lie...
> And as the wind moves up the slope unseen,
> The olive's leaves flick now from white to green.
> (Lorenzo de' Medici, c.1480)

Like the Medici villa at FIESOLE, Poggio a Caiano takes the form of a simple cube, and is situated on a hill commanding an extensive panorama from which it can also be viewed. But here the villa is further raised above an arcaded ground floor that housed service functions and provided a promenade around the piano nobile. And the temple-like portico serves to proclaim the importance and dignity of the inhabitants. The curved flights of stairs leading to the promenade are 17thC

replacements of the original perpendicular pair that can be seen in Giusto Utens painting of the villa.

The majestic two-story-high **salone** was frescoed by Andrea del Sarto (until 1512), Franciabigio (until 1520), Pontormo (until 1532) and completed by A. Allori (1582). The Classical subjects refer to events in Medici history. The high point is Pontormo's fresco in the lunette of the right wall of *Vertumnus and Pomona* (1521), an idyllic and graceful picture of a Tuscan summer's day and a masterpiece of design.

There is a good view of Poggio a Caiano from the neighboring Medici villa at ARTIMINO.

See ARTIMINO and LASTRA A SIGNA.

PONTASSIEVE
Map 15E6. 18km (11 miles) E of Florence. 50065. Firenze. Population: 19,752.
A commercial wine town. The Rufina wine zone (see TUSCAN WINES on page 178) is just to the N, and there are pretty roads into the Pratomagno hills to the E. The Wednesday market is good for shoes.

CASTELLO DI SAMMEZZANO
50067 Leccio-Rignano Sull'Arno, Firenze ☎(055) 8657911 ⊠573078 ⊠(055) 8657610
▥ 15 rms, all with bathrm ⬛ ═ AE ⊕ ⊙ VISA ⬜ ♨ ☐ ⬜ ❦ ❧ ⟨ ♨ ❦ ♨ ⟨ ♨ ♨ ♨
A 17thC castle stupendously decorated in 19thC Moorish style, near the Incisa autostrada exit from Florence.

Moderno (*Via Londra 5* ☎ *(055) 8315541* ⊠ *(055) 8315542* ▥ AE ⊕ VISA) is situated in the town.

Archimede (*N of Regello* ☎ *(055) 869055/868182* ▥ *closed Wed)* is pleasant in summer, and also has rooms.

See also SAN GIOVANNI VALDARNO and VALLOMBROSA.

PONTREMOLI
Map 13B2. 164km (102 miles) NW of Florence. 53km (33 miles) NW of Massa. 54027. Massa-Carrara. Population: 10,335.
The principal town of the Lunigiana, named after the Etruscan city of Luni (which is now in Liguria). A 19thC Neoclassical facade has been added to the Baroque **cathedral**. The town boasts a pretty oval Rococo church, the **Madonna del Ponte** (1738).

OTHER SIGHTS
In the **Castello** on the hill of Piagnaro is a museum exhibiting the strange, totemic *stele* statues and other pre-Etruscan material from the area.

1.5km (1 mile) to the SE of the center, the church of SS Annunziata has a fine 16thC interior, with a marble *tempietto* (1527) attributed to Jacopo Sansovino.

Golf (*Via Pineta 32* ☎ *(0187) 831573* ⊠ *(0187) 831591* ▥ *to* ▥ AE ⊕ ⊙ VISA ✿ ▤ ❦).

🍴 **Da Bussè** *(Piazza Duomo 31* ☎ *(0187) 831371* ☐ *open Mon-Thurs lunch only, Sat and Sun dinner; closed Fri, July)* is an old-fashioned rustic trattoria.

POPPI
Map 11E7. 53km (33 miles) SE of Florence, 38km (24 miles) N of Arezzo. 52014. Arezzo. Population: 5,790.
Poppi is the starting point for the beautiful drive to CAMALDOLI. It is worth pausing here to admire the arcaded old streets.

SIGHTS AND PLACES OF INTEREST

PALAZZO PRETORIO 🏛
Originally the castle of the Guidi lords, the palace was rebuilt in 1274 and extended in 1291. Its resemblance to the PALAZZO DELLA SIGNORIA (see page 126) suggests that Arnolfo di Cambio may have had a hand in the design.
PRIMO PARCO ZOO
🎦 ♿
Just outside the town, in a ravishing setting, this is the first zoo in Europe to be devoted exclusively to European animals.

🍴 See CAMALDOLI.

POPULONIA
Map 9H3. 149km (93 miles) SW of Florence, 89km (55 miles) NW of Grosseto. 57020. Livorno. Population: 122.
The only Etruscan town built on a coastal site, Populonia was inhabited from the 9thC BC and in the 7thC BC became a rich industrial city — the blast furnace of the ancient world. Iron ore imported from ELBA was smelted here in such quantities that the necropolis was buried in slag and the beaches are still streaked with black. The inhabitants may have been the first Etruscans to mint coins in the 5thC BC.

Populonia fell under the influence of Rome in the 3rdC BC, and by the 4thC AD was nearly empty.

The village is dominated by its restored medieval **rocca**. A privately owned **Etruscan museum** in the main street *(apply to custodian at #11)* houses an interesting collection of small, sacred and domestic objects from the necropolis.

NECROPOLIS ☆
3km (2 miles) E of village ✗ compulsory (tours roughly on the hour).
This complex comprises tombs of the 9th-3rdC BC.

🐚 🍴 See SAN VINCENZO.

PORT'ERCOLE
Map 7J5. 190km (118 miles) S of Florence, 50km (31 miles) S of Grosseto. 58018. Grosseto. Population: 3,400.
A fashionable sailing resort on the E coast of Monte Argentario, which has attracted a faithful English summer colony. The Etruscans gave it the name of Port of Hercules. The three fortresses that guard it testify to its strategic importance; there is nowhere outside Malta where one can

see Renaissance principles of fortification so well defined.

The Cala Galera, built next to the harbor in 1975, is one of the best-equipped marinas in the Mediterranean.

SIGHTS AND PLACES OF INTEREST

FORTE FILIPPO 血血

✗ (on Wed) compulsory.

The best demonstration of late Renaissance fortification in the Mediterranean. Mathematically and technically flawless, this fortress is in an excellent state of preservation. It has been converted into private apartments.

FORTE STELLA 血血

South of the harbor, this now abandoned hexagonal fort on a four-sided bastion base was built by the Spanish in the 17thC.

ROCCA SPAGNOLA 血血

Permission necessary from mayor's office (easily obtained).

The Rocca Spagnola is the original nucleus of the medieval fortress, refined and extended in the 15th-16thC, which dominates the historic center of the town, Piazza Santa Barbara. It forms a complete village.

On the Tombolo di Feniglia is a protected pine forest and a sandy beach where Caravaggio died in 1610.

⬱ DON PEDRO

Via Panoramica 23, 58018 Port'Ercole, Grosseto ☎ and ☒(0564) 833914 ▥ 45 rms, all with bathrm ➡ ⇶ ⬛ ▦ ✦ ⬜ ⅏ ⅏ Closed Nov to Mar.

The best medium-priced hotel in the area.

⬱ VILLA LETIZIA

1km (½ mile) to the N ☎ and ☒(0564) 834181 ▥ 19 rms ➡ ⬛ ⬛ ⬛ ⬛ ▦ ⬜ ⅏ ⅏ ⅏ ⅏ ⬜ ⬜ Closed Nov-Easter.

A simple but comfortable hotel overlooking the Cala Galera Marina.

⬱ ⇶ IL PELLICANO ⬛

Cala dei Santi, 58018 Port'Ercole, Grosseto ☎(0564) 833801 ☒500131 ☒(0564) 833418 ▥ 34 rms, all with bathrm ⬛ ⬛ ⬛ ⬛ ⬛ ⬛ ▦ ⬜ ⬜ ⅏ ⅏ ⅏ ⅏ ⅏ ⅏ ⅏ ⅏ ⅏ ⬱ ⅏ ⅏ Closed Nov-Easter.

The most attractive luxury hotel on the Argentario. Peace and quiet, attentive service, American country-house decor, a heated sea-water pool and a good restaurant. A beauty center opens in 1993.

⇶ **La Lanterna** is a restaurant and pizzeria on the harbor next door to (and better value than) the **Gambero Rosso**.

There is a better choice of restaurants at PORTO SANTO STEFANO.

EXCURSION

THE ISLAND OF GIANNUTRI

23km (14 miles) to the S, the island of Giannutri *(map 7K5)* is reached from Port'Ercole. Near Cala Maestra is a 1stC AD Roman villa. There is good underwater fishing in the clear waters of the Cala dei Grottoni.

PORTO SANTO STEFANO

Map 7J5. 193km (121 miles) s of Florence, 53km (33 miles) s of Siena. 58019. Grosseto. Population: 10,100.

This active fishing port on the N coast of Monte Argentario retains some of its charm; and the fish caught off the rocky coastline has a particularly fine flavor. Boats depart frequently for GIGLIO.

▬◪ **Armando** *(Via Marconi 1/3* ☎*(0564) 812568* ▥▥ ▣ ▣ *closed Wed, Dec)* is the best fish restaurant in the town; **La Fontanina** *(at S. Pietro above the town* ☎*(0564) 825261* ▥▥ *to* ▥▥ ▣ ▣ ▣ ▣ *closed Wed, Jan)* has a vine-covered terrace; **Dal Greco** *(Via del Molo 1* ☎*(0564) 814885* ▥▥ ▣ ▣ ▣ ▣ *closed Tues, Jan)* is a fish restaurant with a terrace overlooking the old harbor; or try **Orlando** *(Via Breschi 3* ☎*(0564) 812788* ▥▥ *closed Thurs, Nov-Feb).*

PRATO ★
Map **14**D5. *19km (11 miles)* NW *of Florence. 50047. Firenze. Population: 166,000* i *Via Cairoli 48/52* ☎*(0574) 24112 and Piazza S. Maria delle Carceri 15.*

Florentines say that if you listen closely in Prato late at night, when the textile factories are closed, you will hear a whirring: it is the sound of the inhabitants spinning in their back parlors, for 75 percent of the manufactured wool exported from Italy comes from Prato, and most of it is produced by small, privately-owned firms. Its population has doubled in 30 years and is now the fourth largest and one of the most affluent in central Italy. Florentines have often had reason to call Prato the tail that tries to wag the dog.

The first cloth mills on the banks of the Bisenzio were in operation in 1108, half a century earlier than the first in Florence. But the prosperous city that grew up around a meadow *(prato)* was no more successful than most Tuscan communes at self-government. Unable to control its political factions, Prato placed itself under the protection of the Anjou rulers of Naples in 1313.

In 1351, the Queen of Naples sold her rights to the city to Florence for 17,500 florins. The commercial fortunes of Prato were given an enormous boost later in the 14thC by the business operations of Francesco di Marco Datini, subject of Iris Origo's admirable biography, *The Merchant of Prato.*

But although Prato enjoyed a greater economic and political autonomy than many Florentine-dominated cities, it rebelled on several occasions, and in the 16thC Florence punished it by rationing its permitted production of wool.

Apart from its distinctive green and white striped churches, there are two artistic masterpieces, both by Florentines, which compel a visit to Prato: Filippo Lippi's frescoes in the Duomo and Giuliano da Sangallo's church Santa Maria delle Carceri.

Events ‡ The Teatro Metastasio *(Via Verdi* ☎*(0574) 605340)* is the home of one of Italy's most enterprising experimental companies. Concerts and plays are given at many venues including the Luigi Pecci Center. ‡ The *Ostensione del Sacro Cingolo*, the ceremonial display of the Virgin's Holy Girdle from the external pulpit of the Duomo, takes place on Easter Day, May 1, August 15, September 8 and December 25.

SIGHTS AND PLACES OF INTEREST

The old town sits within a partly intact hexagon of 13thC walls on the sw bank of the River Bisenzio.

CASTELLO DELL'IMPERATORE

Piazza S. Maria delle Carceri. Open Tues-Sat 9am-noon, 3-6pm; Sun 9am-noon. Closed Mon ◀€

For a good orienting view, walk around the battlements of this castle, built in the 13thC for the Emperor Frederick II.

Opposite the Castello is **Santa Maria delle Carceri** (see page 258).

CENTRO PER L'ARTE CONTEMPORANEA LUIGI PECCI ★

Viale della Repubblica 277 ☎*(0574) 570620. Open 9am-7pm. Closed Tues.*

The architecture of the Luigi Pecci museum, purpose-built in the late 1980s to house one of the most important collections of contemporary art in Italy, as well as a computerized information center of modern art, is exciting and therefore controversial. The temporary exhibitions are also of outstanding interest.

DUOMO ▥ † ★

The striped facade was applied to the Romanesque building in 1384-1457. The glazed terra-cotta lunette of the *Madonna with Sts Stephen and Lawrence* (1489) over the portal is by Andrea della Robbia. Projecting from the right corner is the covered **pulpit of the Holy Girdle** (1428-38) by Donatello and Michelozzo. The originals of Donatello's carvings of *Dancing Putti* have been removed to the Cathedral Museum.

The sturdy green and blonde interior conserves remarkable works of art, but the nave is bare except for the pulpit (1473) by Mino da Fiesole and A. Rossellino. Left of the entrance is the **chapel of the Holy Girdle** (1385-95), where the legend of the Holy Girdle is illustrated by Agnolo Gaddi's frescoes (1392-95). The Holy Girdle was brought from the Holy Land to Prato in the 12thC, and its story is still popular in Tuscany. Over the altar is a *Madonna and Child* (c.1317) by Giovanni Pisano.

Behind the high altar of the cathedral, in the choir, are Filippo Lippi's frescoes (1452-66) (★) of *The Martyrdom of St John the Baptist,* on the right wall, and of *St Stephen,* on the left (a coin-operated light switch is on the left of the last chapel in the left transept).

Filippo labored over these frescoes for 14 years, during which he was tried for fraud and fathered a child by the nun Lucrezia (who may be the model for the dancing Salome). They are the considered masterpieces of his troubled maturity, and yet they glow with a clear-eyed vivacity and apparently spontaneous grace that make them among the most immediately pleasing of Renaissance paintings.

The chapel to the right of the altar is frescoed with scenes from the *Lives of the Virgin and of St Stephen,* begun by Paolo Uccello or a disciple, and completed, still in the early 15thC, in a strange quasi-Mannerist style by Andrea di Giusto. In the right transept is a tabernacle of the *Madonna of the Olive* (1480) by all three Maiano brothers; also a panel painting of the *Death of St Jerome* by Filippo Lippi.

GALLERIA COMUNALE

Piazza Comune ☎*(0574) 452302. Open Mon, Wed-Sat 9.30am-12.30pm, 3-6.30pm, Sun 9.30am-12.30pm. Closed Tues.*

The gallery occupies three floors of the 13th-14thC Palazzo Pretorio. The large collection includes minor 14th-15thC altarpieces in good condition, two panels by Filippo Lippi, Neapolitan fruit paintings, and plaster models by L. Bartolini.

MUSEO DELL'OPERA DEL DUOMO (Cathedral Museum)

Mon, Wed-Sat 9.30am-12.30pm, 3-6.30pm; Sun 9.30am-12.30pm. Closed Tues.

The museum is located in the Bishop's Palace to the left of the Duomo. The main attractions are Donatello's reliefs of *Dancing Putti* from the exterior pulpit, but they are less good than the miniature frieze of dancing putti on the exquisite **reliquary of the Holy Girdle** (1446) by Maso di Bartolomeo.

257

SANTA MARIA DELLE CARCERI ▥ ✝ ★

Giuliano da Sangallo's harmoniously proportioned cruciform interior, begun 1485, is a masterpiece of Italian Renaissance architecture, a perfect restatement of Brunelleschi's principles. The blue and white terra-cotta decorations and medallions are by Andrea Della Robbia.

OTHER SIGHTS

Palazzo Datini *(Via Ser Lapo Mazzei* ☎ *(0574) 26064; open Mon, Tues, Thurs, Fri 9am-noon, 3-6pm, Sat 9am-noon; closed Wed, Sun),* which Francesco di Marco Datini had built for himself in the late 14th-early 15thC; **Datini's tomb** in the nearby church of **San Francesco**; and the late 14thC frescoes in the chapter room off the cloister, which include a picture of *St Matthew as a Money Changer* — a rare, but in Prato appropriate, genre subject.

▆ IL PIRAÑA

Via Valentini 110 ☎(0574) 25746 ▥ ▭ ▤ ▣ ◉ ▣ *Closed Sat and Mon lunch; Sun.*
Do not be deterred by the location of this restaurant, which is 10 minutes' drive from the center and opposite a string of factories. Even the Florentines will tell you that this is now one of the best fish restaurants in Italy, although the decor is an excessively fussy attempt to be ultramodern.

▆ **Tonio** *(Piazza Mercatale 161* ☎ *(0574) 21266* ▥ to ▥ ▣ ◉ ▣ ▥ *closed Sun, Mon, Aug)* has good pictures on the walls, a small varied menu with an emphasis on fish, and a loyal business clientele. **Villa Santa Cristina** *(Via Poggio Secco 58* ☎*(0574) 595951* ▣*(0574) 572623* ▥ ▣ ◉ ▣ ▥ *closed Sun dinner, Mon)* is in a handsome 18thC building with pool and rooms.

PRATOLINO

Map 11E6. 12km (7 miles) N of Florence. Firenze.

PARK OF VILLA DEMIDOFF

Open May-Sept, Fri-Sun 10am-8pm ▆
This vast, cool, hauntingly beautiful park was laid out in the 16thC for Grand Duke Francesco I and became the favorite residence of his second wife Bianca Cappello. Buontalenti's villa and most of the water-powered mechanical grottoes that were famous throughout Europe in their day, were demolished in the 19thC when the park was redesigned in the informal English style and planted with specimen trees.

A chapel by Buontalenti and the Grotto of Cupid have survived from the 16thC. But the most astonishing feature from the original garden is Giambologna's craggy, colossal *Appennino* (★), a grotto surmounted by a head in which you can stand upright and survey the park through the eyes. There is a stupendous view of the valleys of the Mugello from the **Convent of Monte Senario** above Pratolino.

▆ **Zocchi** *(* ☎ *(055) 409202* ▥ *closed Mon),* which overlooks the park, is a big, sunny restaurant offering a huge array of antipasti and charcoal-grilled meats.

▆ **La Botteghina** on the Via Bolognese at Montorsoli *(* ☎*(055) 401433)* ▥ ◉ ▥ *closed Tues)* is a fish restaurant with a garden. It offers panoramic views of the mountains.

PUNTA ALA

Map 9I4. 150km (93 miles) SW of Florence, 40km (25 miles) W of Grosseto. 58040. Grosseto. Population: 190.
This luxurious resort on a headland overlooking the island of ELBA was

founded in 1960. It offers golf, sailing, riding, polo, tennis and sandy beaches and is near the Etruscan sites.

❧ CALA DEL PORTO
Via del Porto, 58040 Punta Ala, Grosseto ☎(0564) 922455 ▦590652 ▦(0564) 920716 ▦ 42 rms, all with bathrm ▦ ● *Closed Oct-Apr.*
Comfortably appointed hotel overlooking the sea.

❧ PICCOLO HOTEL ALLELUJA
Via del Porto, 58040 Punta Ala, Grosseto ☎(0564) 922050 ▦500449 ▦(0564) 920734 ▦ 42 rms, all with bathrm ▦
The most attractive of the hotels, which preserves something of the mood of the old Tuscan farmhouse that was the nucleus of the original estate.

❧ ▤ GALLIA PALACE HOTEL
Via delle Sughere, 58040 Punta Ala, Grosseto ☎(0564) 922022 ▦590454 ▦(0564) 920229 ▦ to ▦ 98 rms, all with bathrm ▦ *Closed Oct-May.*
The modern luxury hotel of Punta Ala is an architecturally impersonal building set in a splendid garden. Good service and the best restaurant in Punta Ala. Conference facilities being introduced.

❧ ▤   Restaurants on the port include a reasonable self-service. See also CASTIGLIONE DELLA PESCAIA.

RADDA IN CHIANTI
Map 11F6. 58km (36 miles) s of Florence, 34km (21 miles) N of Siena. 53017. Siena. Population: 1,588.
A little hill village that became headquarters of the Chianti League in 1415. The medieval street plan and sections of the fortifications survive. 3km (1¾ miles) N is **Volpaia**, a pretty, restored medieval village.

❧ ▤ RELAIS FATTORIA VIGNALE
Via Pianigiani 15, 53017 Radda in Chianti ☎(0577) 738300 ▦(0577) 738592 ▦ to ▦ 26 rms, all with bathrm ▦ ▦ ▦ ▦ ▦ ▦ ▦ ▦ ▦ *Closed Nov to Mar.*
A charming and sophisticated small hotel in the 18thC manor house of a wine-making estate.

Save the restaurant *(Via XX Settembre 23* ☎*(0577) 738094)* for a rainy day: it is exceptionally pleasant and deserves its Michelin star, but has no tables outdoors.

▤   **Le Vigne**, at Podere Le Vigne *(* ☎*(0577) 738640* ▦ ▦ ▦ ▦ ▦ *closed Tues, mid-Jan to late Feb).*

ROSELLE
Map 10I5. 131km (81 miles) s of Florence, 10km (6 miles) NE of Grosseto. Grosseto.
Etruscan Roselle, like VETULONIA, was an island dominating the waters of the gulf that then filled part of the Grosseto Maremma. Excavations

have revealed layers of civilization stretching back to the Neolithic age. The Etruscan city, one of the federation of 12, was taken over by Rome early in the 3rdC BC. All the portable material that was uncovered is now in GROSSETO.

The **ruins (★)** are in a remarkably complete state of preservation, surrounded by a nearly intact ring of Etruscan- and Roman-built walls. Remains of the Roman city include the Forum, a stretch of paved street, basilicas, villas, amphitheater and baths. Etruscan remains include rare artisans' cottages of the 7th-6thC BC.

SAN CASCIANO IN VAL DI PESA

Map 10E5. 17km (11 miles) s of Florence. 50026. Firenze. Population: 14,522.
A busy agricultural-industrial town graced by the church of the **Misericordia** (which possesses several fine Sienese paintings including a *Crucifixion* on panel by Simone Martini).

The town is surrounded by good restaurants in all price bands.

NEARBY SIGHT

3km (1¾ miles) to the N is the one-street hamlet of **Sant'Andrea in Percussina** *(map14E5)*, where Machiavelli spent 15 years in exile from Florence during which he wrote his six great works, including *The Prince*. His house is privately owned but sometimes (irregularly) open to the public.

CIRRI IL FOCOLARE

At Montagnana, 12km (7½ miles) w ☎(0571) 671132 ▥ ▣ ◉ ◎ ▨ ♨ *Closed Mon dinner, Tues.*
A pleasant country restaurant which has a nice garden. It specializes in roasted, grilled and boiled meats.

LA TENDA ROSSA

5km (3 miles) nw at Cerbaia. Piazza del Monumento 9 ☎(055) 826132 ▥ ▬ ▦ *Closed Wed, Thurs lunch.*
The cooking is unusually ambitious for Tuscany, but so professional that it rarely falls short of excellence. Specialties include *carpaccio tiepido di spigola, raviolone di fiori di zucca e gamberi rossi al fungo, ventaglio di petto di piccione al fegato grasso.* Reservations essential.

TRATTORIA DEL PESCE

At Bargino, 5km (3 miles) s ☎(055) 8249045 ▥ ▣ ◉ ♨ *Closed Wed, Aug.*
Good, fresh fish and seafood to be enjoyed here, including an enormous selection of fish antipasti.

▬ Other recommended restaurants in and near San Casciano: **Il Fedino** *(Via Borromeo 9 ☎(055) 828612* ▯ *to* ▥ ▨ *closed Mon, Aug, lunch except Sun);* **Matteuzzi** *(Via Certaldese 8 ☎(055) 8288090* ▯ *open lunch only; closed Tues);* **Taverna del Cacciatore** at Falciani, 5km (3 miles) N *(☎(055) 2020432, closed Wed);* **Il Salotto del Chianti**, 5km (3 miles) SE at Mercatale *(Via Sonnino 92 ☎(055)8218016* ▯ *to* ▥ ▣ ◉ ◎ ▨ *closed Wed).*

▬ And S toward POGGIBONSI and COLLE DI VAL D'ELSA: **La Fattoria**, at Tavarnelle 12km (7½ miles) s *(Via del Cerro 11 ☎(055) 8070000* ▯ *to* ▥ ▣ ▨ *closed Mon lunch, Tues, Oct, Jan);* and **La Scuderia**, 15km (9½ miles) s above Sambuca at Passignano *(☎(055) 8071623* ▯ *to* ▥ ▣ ◉ *closed Wed, Jan, Feb).*

SAN GALGANO 血 † ★
Map 10G5. 101km (63 miles) sw of Florence, 33km (20 miles) sw of Siena.
The ruined church of San Galgano is one of the most moving sights in Tuscany. Although meadow grass now grows in the roofless nave, the magnificence of the once-powerful Cistercian foundation is still apparent. Built between 1218-80, the church introduced French Gothic architecture to Tuscany.

On a hill above is the domed chapel built in 1182 over San Galgano's tomb, with 14thC frescoes by A. Lorenzetti.

≈ ⇌ See BAGNI DI PETRIOLO.

SAN GIMIGNANO ★
Map 10F5. 55km (34 miles) sw of Florence, 38km (24 miles) NW of Siena.
53037. Siena. Population: 7,501.
San Gimignano *"delle belle torri"* (of the beautiful towers) is the best-preserved medieval town in Tuscany. Its defense system once involved more than 70 towers, of which 13 survive. Warring factions dropped rocks and burning pitch on their enemies from these towers, which were also important status symbols. Height meant prestige for medieval Tuscan noblemen, just as for 20thC American tycoons, and from a distance San Gimignano bears an eerie resemblance to a tipsy, miniature New York.

Most Italian cities looked very like San Gimignano in the 12th-13thC. The skyline of medieval Siena bristled with more than 50 such towers, and that of Florence with more than 100. E. M. Forster's early novel *Where Angels Fear to Tread,* is set in San Gimignano, which he calls "Monteriano."

> What has become of the soul of San Gimignano, who shall say?
> — but, of a genial modern Sunday, it is as if the heroic skeleton, risen from the dust, were in high activity, officious for your entertainment and your detention, clattering and changing plates at the informal, friendly inn, personally conducting you to the sight of the admirable Santa Fina of Ghirlandaio... in a dim chapel of the Collegiata church.
> (Henry James, *Other Tuscan Cities,* an essay from *Italian Hours,* 1894)

The narrative painter Benozzo Gozzoli was born here. His charming frescoes in the Collegiata and the church of San Agostino are not great art, but are easy to enjoy.
Events ‡ Colorful masked processions take place on the first and last Sunday of the carnival period before Lent. ‡ Operas are performed in summer in Piazza del Duomo.

SIGHTS AND PLACES OF INTEREST
Porta San Giovanni (1262), the finest of the town gates, is the main entrance; there is a parking lot nearby. The town is in any case best toured on foot.

261

Via S. Matteo, which runs NW from Piazza del Duomo, is the best street, lined with good medieval buildings, notably the Romanesque church of S. Bartolo, and the Pesciolini tower house *(#32)*.

There are marvelous views from the 13thC town **walls** and from the **Rocca**, built by the Florentines in 1353.

PIAZZA DELLA CISTERNA

The main square is actually triangular, and retains at its center the original 13thC cistern. The buildings are 13th-14thC, of which the finest is the 14thC **Palazzo Tortoli** *(#7)*, built in the Sienese style.

PIAZZA DEL DUOMO

The monumental buildings and seven towers of the Piazza del Duomo are all pre-1400. On the w of the square is the Collegiata. The Palazzo del Popolo is on the s side and the Palazzo del Podestà on the E.

The Romanesque facade of the **Collegiata** (✝) was enlarged by Giuliano da Maiano in the 15thC, but has been often restored since. The interior is notable for its 14th-15thC frescoes. On the interior facade the frescoes include the *Martyrdom of St Sebastian* (1465) by Gozzoli; the painted wooden statues of the *Annunciation* (1421) are by Jacopo della Quercia. On the right wall, the *New Testament Scenes* (c.mid-14thC) may be from the studio of Simone Martini.

Off the right nave is the **Cappella di Santa Fina** (★), one of the high points of Renaissance architecture, built in 1468 by Giuliano da Maiano with an altar by Benedetto da Maiano. The beautiful frescoes (1475) by Domenico Ghirlandaio and assistants depict two *Scenes from the Life of Santa Fina;* according to the legend, wallflowers sprang from the towers on the day she died.

In the chancel, the ciborium over the high altar is by Benedetto da Maiano. The choir stalls in the apse are by Antonio da Colle. On the left nave wall are frescoes of the *Old Testament* (c.1367) by Bartolo di Fredi. To the left of the church, in the 14thC Baptistry loggia, is a fresco of the *Annunciation* by Domenico Ghirlandaio.

The **Museo d'Arte Sacra** and **Museo Etrusco** *(opening hours as Museo Civico, see below)* entered here, display small collections of 13th-18thC art and church furnishings, and locally excavated Etruscan material.

The 13thC **Palazzo del Podestà** (🏛) on the E side of the square was enlarged in the 14thC. Its imposing Torre dell Ragnosa at 51m (167ft) was meant to set the maximum legal height for towers, but tower-building rivalry continued.

The **Palazzo del Popolo**, on the s side of the square, houses the Civic Museum and offers a spectacular view from the top of its tower, the **Torre Grossa**. Inside, on the first floor, the Sala di Dante, so called as the poet spoke here in 1300 in favor of an alliance with Florence, contains an important *Maestà* (1317) by Lippo Memmo. The **Museo Civico** *(open Tues-Sun, Apr-Sept 9.30am-12.30pm, 3.30-6.30pm; Oct-Mar 9.30am-12.30pm, 2.30-5.30pm; closed Mon 🎫)*, on the next floor, has a collection of 13th-15thC Sienese and Florentine paintings, including a profoundly moving painted *Crucifix* (late 13thC) by Coppo di Marcovaldo.

SANT'AGOSTINO ✝

A Romanesque-Gothic church (1290-98) in the NW corner of the town is of impressive simplicity. In the Cappella di S. Bartolo, right of the main entrance, is a marble altar (1494) by B. da Maiano. Over the high altar, the *Coronation of the Virgin* (1483) is a major work by Piero del Pollaiuolo. In the choir is Gozzoli's *Life Story of St Augustine* in 17 frescoed scenes (1464). In the left nave is Gozzoli's *St Sebastian* (1464).

Outside the walls, 4½ km (3 miles) from Porta San Matteo, is the Romanesque **Pieve di Cellole** (1237).

🛏 Two quiet, well-equipped hotels without restaurants are the **Relais Santa**

Chiara *(Via Matteotti 15* ☎ *(0577) 940701* 🅵🅰 *942096* 🎨 🅰🅴 💳 💳 💳 *closed Jan to mid-Feb)*, which has a pool; and **Villa San Paolo**, 4km (2½ miles) N on the Certaldo road *(*☎ *(0577) 955100* 🎨 🅰🅴 💳 💳 💳 *closed mid-Jan to mid-Feb)*.

☜ ☰ BEL SOGGIORNO 🏛
Via San Giovanni 91, 53037 San Gimignano, Siena ☎*(0577) 940375* 🅵🅰*(0577) 940375* 🎨 *to* 🎨 *22 rms, all with bathrm* 🅰🅴 💳 💳 💳 🔲 🔲 ⚡ ⬛ 📷 ⚓ ☕ *Restaurant closed Mon.*
Wonderful views of the town from this 13thC house.

☜ ☰ LA CISTERNA 🏛
Piazza della Cisterna 24, 53037 San Gimignano, Siena ☎*(0577) 940328* 🅵🅰*575152* 🅵🅰*(0577) 942080* 🎨 *50 rms, all with bathrm* ⬛ 🅰🅴 💳 💳 💳 🔲 ⚡ ♿ 📷 ☕ ⚓ *Closed mid-Nov to Mar.*
Huge rooms in a 13thC palace with an Edwardian atmosphere. The restaurant, **Le Terrazze** *(*🎨 *closed Tues, Wed lunch)*, offers splendid views from spacious rooms with low ceilings with exposed beams. The pastries are especially delicious.

☜ ☰ PESCILLE
4½ km (3 miles) s, near San Donato ☎*(0577) 940186* 🅵🅰*(0577) 940375* 🎨 *32 rms, all with bathrm* 🅰🅴 💳 💳 💳 🔲 📷 ⚡ ⚓ 🌙 ♪○ *Closed Nov-Apr.*
A modest, peaceful hotel with a restaurant, **I Cinque Gilli** *(closed Wed)*.

☜ ☰ LE RENAIE
6km (4 miles) N at Pancole ☎*(0577) 955072* 🅵🅰*(0577) 955044* 🎨 *to* 🎨 *26 rms, all with bathrm* ⬛ 🅰🅴 💳 💳 💳 🔲 📷 ⚡ ⚓ 🏮 ☕ 🐎 *Closed Nov. Restaurant closed Tues.*
A pleasant country inn with its own restaurant, **Leonetto**.

☰ **Delle Catene** ♣ *(Via Mainardi 18* ☎ *(0577) 941966* 🎨 🅰🅴 💳 *closed Wed)* is an unpretentious trattoria specializing in seasonal local produce.

SAN GIOVANNI VALDARNO
Map **10**F6. *45km (28 miles)* SE *of Florence, 37km (23 miles)* W *of Arezzo. 52027. Arezzo. Population: 19,908.*
The birthplace of the painters Masaccio and Giovanni da San Giovanni is now the chief industrial and market town of the Valdarno. The market is held on Saturday.

2km (1¼ miles) to the s, in the church of the convent of Montecarlo, is one of Fra Angelico's masterpieces, an *Annunciation* (c.1440), with a fine predella. 13km (8 miles) to the NE, near Loro Ciuffenna, is the tiny farming hamlet of Gropina (map **10**F7). Its Romanesque church, **S. Pietro**, has unusual capitals and primitive carvings on its pulpit. The area is rich in Etruscan and Roman remains and Romanesque churches, and there are fine views from the foothills of the Pratomagno.

☰ VICOLO DEL CONTENTO
Loc. Mandri 38, 52020 Castelfranco di Sopra, Arezzo ☎*(055) 9149277* 🎨 *Map* **11**F7 🔲 ⬛ ☰ 🏮 ⬛ 🅰🅴 💳 💳 *Closed Mon, Tues, Aug.*
One of the most interesting and attractive restaurants in the Valdarno. Local clients appreciate the refined international cooking. Tuscan meals are also outstanding but must be ordered in advance.

☰ **Castelucci** *(*☎*941679* 🎨 🅰🅴 💳 💳 *closed Sat lunch, Sun, mid-July to mid Aug)* is a pleasant, solid restaurant in the center which does splendid Roman-style antipasti and an outstanding *bistecca* grilled over an open fire; 20km (12½ miles) NW at Poggio alla Croce is **Becattini** *(Via dei Crocino 41 ☎(055) 8337813, closed Wed)*, which serves typically hearty Tuscan specialties and has a glassed-in terrace commanding nice views.

SAN MINIATO

Map 14E4. 44km (27 miles) W of Florence, 39km (24 miles) E of Pisa. 56027. Pisa. Population: 24,701.

Medieval San Miniato was the seat of the Lombard Imperial Vicariate in Tuscany and therefore known as S. Miniato al Tedesco ("of the German"). The fortifications, of which only two towers remain, were rebuilt in 1240 by Frederick II.

SIGHTS AND PLACES OF INTEREST

The 13thC **Duomo** has been rebuilt and restored many times; its pompous interior decorations are 18th-19thC. Its bell tower, the **Torre di Matilde**, pre-dates the Duomo and was built as a defense tower.

The **Museo Diocesano**, to the left of the Duomo, retains sacred art from the region including works by Filippo Lippi, Neri di Bicci, Fra Bartolommeo, Empoli and Verrocchio.

A short, stiff climb from the Prato del Duomo brings one to the tower which is the last surviving reminder of Frederick II's **Rocca**, a reconstruction of the original that was destroyed during World War II. On a clear day the view embraces the whole of the Arno plain. Below the Prato del Duomo is **Piazza della Repubblica**, the most picturesque in the town. The Seminario retains 14thC shop-fronts and 17thC *sgraffiti.*

▄═ **Omero** ♣ at La Scala *(Via Tosco Romagnola Est ☎(0571) 464320* ▢ *closed Sat, mid-Aug).*

♈ ═ **Miravalle**, at Piazza Castello 3 *(☎(0571) 418075* ▣*(0571) 419681* ▢ ▣ ▣ ▣ ▣ *).*

SAN QUIRICO D'ORCIA

Map 7H6. 111km (64 miles) SE of Florence, 43km (29 miles) SE of Siena. 53027. Siena. Population: 2,231.

A village overlooking the Orcia and Asso valleys.

COLLEGIATA ✝

The Romanesque-Gothic Collegiata has three magnificent **portals**: on the facade (1080); on the right flank (late 13thC), adorned with lions and caryatids by a follower of Giovanni Pisano; and at the head of the right transept (1298). Inside is an unusually fine triptych by Sano di Pietro and good choir stalls (1502) by A. Barili.

NEARBY SIGHTS

San Giovanni d'Asso, 15km (9 miles) N, dominated by its 12thC Castello; and **Castiglione d'Orcia**, 5km (3 miles) S, home town of the artist Vecchietta, which is near the atmospheric medieval village of **Rocca d'Orcia**. 6km (4 miles) SE is the little spa town of **Bagno Vignoni** whose thermal baths, now rather run down, were used by St. Catherine of Siena and Lorenzo the Magnificent.

♈ ═ **POSTA-MARCUCCI** ♣

Via Ara Urcea 43, 53027 Bagno Vignoni, S. Quirico d'Orcia, Siena ☎(0577) 887112

☎580117 ℻(0577) 887119 ▭ 49 rms, all with bathrm ⚏ ▣ ▣ ▥ ⌂ & ❤ ✻ ☐
▱ ➡ ≋ ♪ 🎿 ♈ Closed mid-Jan to mid-Feb.

Located 6km (4 miles) s, off the Via Cassia, this comfortably homely hotel is popular with the Sienese as a restful place to take the waters.

SANSEPOLCRO

*Map **12**F8. 114km (71 miles) se of Florence, 39km (24 miles) ne of Arezzo. 52037. Arezzo. Population: 15,695.*

In this somewhat mournful town close to the Umbrian border, Piero della Francesca was born after 1420 and spent the last 14 years of his life writing his treatises on *Perspective* and the *Five Regular Bodies*. It was probably in the early 1460s that he executed his masterpiece, the *Resurrection,* in his native town.

MUSEO CIVICO
Via Aggiunti 65.

Piero's hypnotic *Resurrection*(★) has been called the greatest picture in the world. Kenneth Clark describes the spell it casts:

"Before Piero's Risen Christ we are suddenly conscious of values for which no rational statement is adequate; we are struck with a feeling of awe, older and less reasonable than that inspired by the Blessed Angelico. This country god, who arises in the grey light while humanity is asleep, has been worshipped ever since man first knew that the seed is not dead in the winter earth, but will force its way upward through an iron crust. Later He will become a god of rejoicing, but His first emergence is painful and involuntary. He seems to be part of the dream which lies so heavily on the sleeping soldiers..."

Opposite is Piero's early polyptych, the *Madonna della Misericordia* (1446-c.1458) (★). Like the *Madonna del Parto* at Monterchi (see next page), this Madonna of Mercy is both a pretty, young peasant girl and icy goddess, whose state of spiritual detachment has been likened to that evoked by Buddhist and African sculpture. The whole polyptych is in uneven condition, and other sections were painted by assistants. Also by Piero are the frescoes of *St Julian* and *St Louis of Toulouse.*

Notable among other works in the museum are a processional flag representing the *Crucifixion* by Signorelli; Pontormo's *St Quentin;* and battered but fine 15thC choir stalls which demonstrate the influence of Piero on perspective intarsia work.

OTHER SIGHTS

In the Romanesque-Gothic **Duomo**, paintings include two panels by Matteo di Giovanni, part of a polyptych of which the central panel, the *Baptism of Christ* by Piero, was purchased for the London National Gallery in 1861 — for £241.

The church of **San Francesco** retains its Gothic high altar (1304) for which Sassetta painted his *St Francis* altarpiece, an early influence on Piero, now scattered, parts being in London and Paris.

In the 16thC church of **San Lorenzo** is a dramatic *Deposition* (c.1528-30) by Rosso Fiorentino.

❧ ▭ **La Balestra** at Via dei Montefeltro 29 (☎(0575)735151 ℻(0575) 740282 ▭ to ▥ ⚏ ▣ ▣ ▥ restaurant closed Sun dinner, Mon); or **Il Fiorentino** ♣ at Via L. Pacioli 60 (☎(0575) 740370/740350 ▭ to ▥ ▣ ▣ ▥ restaurant closed Fri) is a friendly and unpretentious hotel in the center. The restaurant takes great pride in serving the traditional food of the region, prepared with fresh, seasonal ingredients.

▆ OROSCOPO

1km (½ mile) nw at Pieve Vecchia, Via Togliatti 66 ☎(0575) 734875 ▥ ▭ ▆ ➡ AE ◉
Open dinner only; closed Sun, Tues, Nov. Also has 9 rms.

A carefully restored farmhouse owned by a young couple who take their cooking very seriously. If you choose the *menu de degustazione* you can sample a different wine by the glass with each course.

▆   **Dal Calisti** ❖ *(Via Luca Pacioli 50* ☎(0575) 76017 ▥ *closed Mon)* is a homely old trattoria in the center. At Badia Tedalda, 30km (18½ miles) N by way of the Viamaggio pass is **Il Sotto Bosco** ❖ *(* ☎(0575) 714031/714240 ▥ *closed Wed),* where you can sample a delicious variety of antipasti and pastas, accompanied by good Brunello wines.

See also ANGHIARI.

EXCURSION

17km (11 miles) S of Sansepolcro, in the tiny cemetery chapel on the edge of the village of **Monterchi**, is another masterpiece by Piero, the *Madonna del Parto* (★) *(custodian always on duty).* Pointing proudly to her pregnant womb, she is revealed to us by two triumphant angels, reverse images of the same cartoon.

SAN VINCENZO

Map 9H3. 146km (91 miles) sw of Florence. 57027 Livorno. Population: 7,188.
One of the most attractive small coastal resorts of the fashionable Pisan Maremma, San Vincenzo has 3km (2 miles) of irregularly sloping beach dominated by a tower built by the Pisans in the early 14thC.

The beautiful inland country to the N was ruled in the Middle Ages by the Gherardesca lords. The hilltops are studded with the remains of their castles, and their descendants now breed race-horses and grow some of the most ambitious Tuscan wines.

The pretty walled hill village of **Castagneto Carducci**, 6km (4 miles) N of San Vincenzo, incorporates a restored Gherardesca castle; it is named for the 19thC poet Giosuè Carducci, who lived in the area as a child. A few kilometers farther N, the famous **viale a cipressi**, the longest cypress *allée* in Italy, runs for 5km (3 miles) inland, from San Guido to the charming little village of Bolgheri. It was planted in 1801 by Camillo della Gherardesca and is the subject of one of Carducci's poems.

✎➤ ▆ PARK HOTEL I LECCI

Via della Principessa 114 ☎70411 ▣501536 ▣703224 ▥ *74 rms, all with bathrm*
▤ AE ◉ ◉ ▨ ▨ ➽ ✦ ▢ ▱ ᕕ ⅏ ⚓ ⚲

A well-managed and peaceful hotel set in a large park.

▆ IL BAMBOLO

On the Strada Aurelia at Bambolo, near Donoratico ☎(0565) 775055 ▥ *35 rms* AE ◉
◉ ▨ *Closed Mon in winter; Jan, Feb.*

An unpretentious restaurant on the coast road below Castagneto Carducci, where you can enjoy some Emilian dishes (the proprietor is a native of Parma) as well as local specialties. A good place to taste first-press local olive oils, which are at their best in mid-winter.

▆ GAMBERO ROSSO

15km (9 miles) N at San Vincenzo, Piazza della Vittoria 13 ☎(0565) 701021 ▥ ▭ ▆

◼▬🚗▦🆎▣◉💳⬜ *Closed Tues, Nov.*
One of the fashionable venues of the Pisan Maremma. The cuisine has flair but the excellent local ingredients can be overwhelmed by rich and fussy sauces.

▭ LO SCACCIAPENSIERI
At Cecina, 23km (14 miles) N of San Vincenzo. Via Verdi 22 ☎(0586) 680900 ⬜ *to* ⬜
🆎 ◉ 💳 *Closed Mon.*
A tiny, elegant and locally popular restaurant (so be sure to reserve ahead) which is famous for its warm seafood salad and refined pastas dressed with fish or seafood.

▭   Also: **Da Ugo** at Via Pari 3/A Castagneto Carducci *(☎ (0565) 763746 ⬜ closed Mon).*

SATURNIA
Map 7I6. 215km (134 miles) S of Florence, 57km (35 miles) SE of Grosseto. 58050. Grosseto. Population: 631.
The Etruscan town on this site was called Aurinia. The Romans named it Saturnia because they believed it had been founded by Jupiter's father. The walls, built by the Sienese in the 15thC, incorporate Etruscan and Roman sections.

The Etruscan necropolis lies to the N of the walls, the most interesting tombs being in the Puntone area.

The spa of **Terme di Saturnia**, where sulfurous water springs at a constant temperature of 37°C (99°F), is 3km (2 miles) to the S. The road N to MONTE AMIATA passes through a beautiful, sparsely populated landscape dotted with medieval castles and villages.

✿ TERME DI SATURNIA
Via della Follonata, 58050 Saturnia, Grosseto ☎(0564) 601061 ▥500172 ▣(0564) 601266 ⬜ *88 rms, all with bathrm* ▦ ▣ ⌂ ▭ 🆎 ◉ 💳 ⬜ ⌂ ✦ ♿ ▢ ▭ ❧ ♨
♨ ⚲ 🏋 ⬅ ⛳ ♉
A serious and fashionable but rather impersonal first-class spa hotel offering a wide range of treatments.

✿ VILLA CLODIA
Via Italia 43, 58050 Saturnia ☎(0564) 601212 ⬜ *to* ⬜ *10 rms, all with bathrm* ▦ 💳
⌂ ♿ ▢ ▭ ❧ ⚲ ♉ ♨ ♬ ♉ *Closed Feb.)*
Views of the spas and the beautiful countryside, from a turn-of-the century building.

✿ ▭   **Laudomia** is a welcoming traditional rustic hotel and restaurant 9km (6 miles) to the S at Poderi di Montemerano *(☎ (0564) 620062/620013 ⬜ 12 rms, 8 with bathrm* ▬ 🆎 ◉ 💳 💳 *restaurant closed Tues)..*

▭ MICHELE AI DUE CIPPI
In the main square ☎(0564) 601074 ⬜ 🆎 ◉ 💳 💳 *Closed Tues.*
This excellent restaurant is one of the most popular in the Maremma. Be sure to reserve ahead.

SESTO FIORENTINO
Map 5B2-3. 9km (6 miles) NW of Florence. 50019. Firenze. Bus 28 from Florence station. Population: 44,458.
An important center of the porcelain and ceramics industry. In the central square, Piazza Ginori, is the 15thC Palazzo Pretorio.

MUSEO DELLE PORCELLANE DI DOCCIA
Via Pratese 31 ☎(055) 4210453. Open Tues, Thurs, Sat 9.30am-1pm, 3.30-6.30pm 🔳
A superb collection of 18th-20thC porcelains from the Doccia factory, founded in 1737 by Carlo Ginori and still producing some of Italy's finest porcelain.

VILLA CORSI-SALVIATI
Via Gramsci. May be visited with Agriturist (see GARDENS on page 52) or on request to the Conti Corsi-Salviati.
A refreshing surprise in an otherwise dreary area. The villa and garden have been altered over four centuries, to suit the tastes of succeeding generations. The Smithsonian Institute holds a lecture program here in summer, and the University of Michigan houses its Florence course in the villa.

At Quinto, just to the E of Sesto, are two exceptionally interesting **Etruscan tombs** *(☎(055) 44961 for information about visiting hours)*. The most impressive is **La Montagnola** *(Via Fratelli Rosselli 95)* rediscovered in 1959; the other is **La Mula** *(Via della Mula 2)*.

♘ VILLA VILLORESI
Via Ciampi 2, 50019 Sesto Fiorentino, Firenze ☎(055) 4489032 🔤580567 📠(055) 442063 ▥ *28 rms, all with bathrm* 🛋 🍽 🆎 💷 🎮 🔟 🚪 🏊 ♿ ☐ ☙ 🍸 🐾 ♨ ♚
A beautifully maintained old villa 8km (5 miles) from the center of Florence in its own large park.

SETTIGNANO
Map 6D5. 8km (5 miles) E of Florence. Bus 10 from Piazza San Marco, Florence. 50135. Firenze. Population: 1,563.
A Florentine suburb in the Fiesolan hills, graced by cypresses, olive groves and fine old villas. Renaissance sculptors who were born or made their home for a time in the area near the *pietra serena* quarries of Monte Ceceri include Desiderio, the Rossellino brothers, the Maiano brothers, Benedetto da Rovezzano and Michelangelo. Boccaccio set the *Decameron* in these hills, and D'Annunzio lived here in the Villa Capponcina during his love affair with Eleanora Duse.

One of the many foreign literary residents was Walter Savage Landor, author of *Imaginary Conversations*, who lived in the 15thC Villa Gherardesca in the 1820s; another was the art historian Bernard Berenson, whose **Villa I Tatti** *(☎603251, open by appointment Tues pm)* is now run by Harvard University as a center for Renaissance Studies. The English attachment to this countryside reached a peak late in the 19thC when Queen Victoria visited the Castle of **Vincigliata** (see below). The gushing sensibilities of English esthetes were satirized by Anatole France in his novel *Le Lys Rouge*.

See also FIESOLE.

SIGHTS AND PLACES OF INTEREST
Approaching from central Florence, the Via G. D'Annunzio leads past Nervi's concrete **Stadium** in the Campo di Marte to Ponte a Mensola, where the church of **S. Martino a Mensola** *(ring for entrance)* has an elegant quattrocento interior with a triptych by Taddeo Gaddi. The Via D'Annunzio then climbs to the village of Settignano. There is a good view of Florence from Piazza Desiderio and, in the 16thC church of the

Assunta, a pulpit by Buontalenti and a Della Robbia *Madonna*.

To the NE is Montebeni, Berenson's favorite walking country and still unexpectedly rural. A left turn off the Montebeni road leads to the Castle of **Vincigliata**, which was Victorianized in 1855 by John Temple Leader.

GAMBERAIA
Open when owner not in residence.
One of the loveliest of all Tuscan gardens. The villa was destroyed in World War II, but the 1.2ha (3-acre) garden, with its architectural clipped yews planted when it was laid out in the 17thC, is well maintained. "But description faints and fails before the enchanting reality," wrote Harold Acton. "Perhaps the best way to evoke its atmosphere is to listen to Mozart's *Eine Kleine Nachtmusik*"

❧ The **Villa Linda** *(Poggio Gherardo 5 ☎(055) 603913 ▢)* is a simple *pensione* run by Benedictine nuns.

⚌ LE CAVE
Via delle Cave 16, Maiano ☎(055) 59133 ▯▯ ▭ ■■ ⊕ ⊰ ▣ ⊕ ⊕ ▣ Closed Thurs, Sun dinner, Aug.
An old *bottega* that once served the quarry workers. The food is variable; but the situation is magical.

⚌ **Osvaldo** *(Via G.D'Annunzio 51 ☎(055) 602168 ▢ to ▯▯ ▭ ⊕ ▣ ⊕ ▣ closed Tues dinner, Wed, Aug),* a favorite with fellows of **I Tatti**, takes pride in its antipasti.

❧⚌ See also FIESOLE.

SIENA ★
Map 10G6. 68km (42 miles) s of Florence, 53100. Siena. Population: 53, 100
i Piazza del Campo 56 ☎(0577) 280551. There is a frequent and punctual bus service on the SITA line from Florence, Via Santa Caterina da Siena 15
☎211487, to the stop near San Domenico. The fastest buses take 1¼ hours. There is also an efficient train service from Florence, but the Siena station is 1½ km (1 mile) N of the center. Private cars are strictly excluded from the center; there is free parking just outside the city gates.

Soft Siena, City of the Virgin, stands on her pedestal of three hills, vain of her beauty, absorbed in her past. She is the other half of Tuscany, feminine counterpart of the hard-headed masculinity of Florence. According to a persistent legend, Siena was founded by Senius, son of Remus; hence the wolf, one of the city's most prominent emblems. There is evidence of a modest Etruscan settlement, but the earliest certain knowledge we have of Siena is of the Roman colony Sena Julia.

During the early Middle Ages, Siena enjoyed a privileged relationship with the Hohenstaufen emperors. As a free republic from the early 12thC she attained a precocious pre-eminence in banking and trade, and became the leading Ghibelline center in Tuscany and the natural rival of Guelf Florence. Although the defeat of Florence at the Battle of Montaperti in 1260 is still celebrated in Siena as a glorious event, it was less significant than the Florentine victory 9 years later at Colle di Val d'Elsa. Then Siena joined the Guelf alliance and from 1287 was governed as an oligarchy by a Council of Nine "Good Men" chosen from the middle classes. The Republic flourished under the balanced, methodical rule of the Nine; the late 13th and early 14thC was an age of stability, prosperity and artistic achievement. But the turmoil and discontent following famines and the Black Death of 1348 led to the overthrow in 1355 of the Nine by the nobles assisted by the working class.

> There is nothing in the world quite like Siena;
> it is a medieval city that might be likened to a rare beast,
> with heart, arteries, tail, paws and teeth. Only the skeleton
> is left, intact, and it is enough to astound us.
> (Bernard Berenson)

Spiritually Siena was guided through the turbulent post-plague period by two remarkable religious reformers, Caterina Benincasa (1347-80) canonized in 1461 as St Catherine of Siena, whose mystical visions are the subject of so much Sienese art, and the more pragmatic Franciscan preacher St Bernardino of Siena (1380-1444).

Politically, the two centuries between 1355 and 1559 were marked by fruitless wars, voluntary submission to foreign control, and periods of unstable independence, when the power of the nobility became increasingly stronger. There were struggles against Charles IV from 1355. Giangaleazzo Visconti took over the government from 1399-1404. Under the pontificate of Pius II (1458-63) Siena became virtually a papal dependency; from 1487-1524 she was ruled by the autocratic Pandolfo Petrucci. In 1530 Siena was occupied by a garrison of the Emperor Charles V.

The city rebelled against the Spanish occupation in 1552, but 2 years later the combined forces of Charles V and Duke Cosimo I of Florence advanced on Siena and laid siege for 18 months, during which the population was halved and the countryside devastated. In 1557 Charles sold the city outright to Cosimo, and in 1559 Siena and her territories were officially annexed to the Tuscan grand duchy by the Peace of Cateau-Cambrésis.

As the unwilling bride of Florence, Siena was treated as a second-class member of the Tuscan empire. No public banks were permitted to operate until 1622; the wool industry collapsed in the mid-17thC and by the mid-18thC most Sienese noble families were deeply in debt. "Cracking, peeling, fading, crumbling, rotting", Henry James wrote of the city in 1909.

Siena, like all Tuscan cities, found new prosperity in the 1960s; and it is today a reasonably lively and well-run if deeply provincial town that nevertheless manages the annual influx of tourism with better grace than its old rival and master Florence.

SIENESE ART

Siena is a Gothic city. Its most prominent buildings — the Duomo and Palazzo Pubblico — and best-known pictures — Duccio's *Maestà,* Simone Martini's *Maestà* and Ambrogio Lorenzetti's *Good and Bad Government* — were created in the late 13th and early 14thC. In the early 15thC the Sienese by and large ignored the Florentine Renaissance. They continued to build ogival palaces; even their major painters, Giovanni di Paolo and Sassetta, set their figures against gold backgrounds in intuitively realized space. Not until the early 16thC did Renaissance painting arrive, with the Lombard-born Sodoma and Domenico Beccafumi (c.1486-1551), who was one of the greatest Italian Mannerists.

Most important works of art were commissioned by the government or religious bodies, powerful, conservative groups who knew exactly what they wanted as to style and subject matter. Over half the pictures commissioned between 1350-1550 were of the Virgin, Queen of Siena; collaborative projects were more common than in Florence.

Sienese sculpture advanced earlier and farther than its sister arts, thanks partly to the influence of Giovanni Pisano, whose figures for the facade of the Duomo are among the most important examples of Gothic sculpture in Italy. The later example of Donatello, who worked in Siena, was also a strong influence. The greatest native Sienese sculptors, Jacopo della Quercia and Vecchietta, effected the transition to the Renaissance.

Events ‡ The Palio, the bare-backed horse races around the Campo on July 2 and August 16, are the central events of the Sienese calendar and the focal points of every Sienese citizen's life. It is one of the strangest and most magnificent of all public spectacles: a mixture of pomp, licensed violence and corruption, skill, courage, luck, history, and fantasy. Ten of the city's 17 *contrade* (wards) are chosen by lot to participate in the race, which is preceded by a spectacular procession. The *palio,* or banner, is the prize. The second and more important Palio on August 16 is in honor of the Assumption of the Virgin. Tickets are scarce and expensive, but the trial races on the previous days can be viewed for a more reasonable price from a seat at one of the restaurants in the Campo. ‡ Siena enjoys a very rich musical life. Concerts and recitals, often of a very high international standard, are performed from November to April at the Accademia Musicale Chigiana *(Via di Città 89 ☎ (0577) 46152);* and in July and August, the Accademia holds master classes. ‡ In winter and early spring there are performances of opera and ballet in the charming Teatro dei Rinnovati in the Palazzo Pubblico *(for information and bookings ☎ (0577) 292265).* ‡ A weekly market is held on Wednesday mornings in the park La Lizza.

SIGHTS AND PLACES OF INTEREST

Siena is built on three hills, which form the most westerly spur of the Chiana mountains. Since the early 13thC the city has been divided into three districts, or *terzi:* Città, San Martino and Camollia.

The essential civic unit is the *contrada,* or ward, of which there are 17. Each has its own church, club and museum. Their fantastic names (Caterpillar, Eagle, Dragon, etc.) derive from allegorical carts paraded at the Palio. Every Sienese is a member of the *contrada* in which he is born and remains loyal to it for life.

The old city is surrounded by 7km (4.5 miles) of intact walls, entered through eight gates. The main streets are the Via di Città, Banchi di Sotto and Banchi di Sopra, which meet just above the Campo, the hub of the

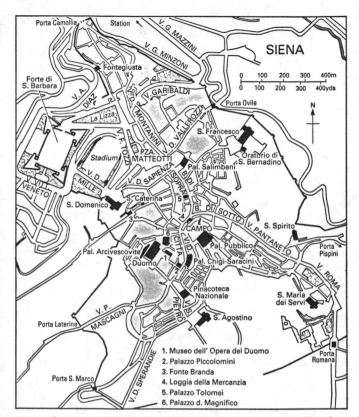

1. Museo dell' Opera del Duomo
2. Palazzo Piccolomini
3. Fonte Branda
4. Loggia della Mercanzia
5. Palazzo Tolomei
6. Palazzo d. Magnifico

city, at the Croce del Travaglio. Although the city is very small — less than 3km (1.25 miles) from the longest axis between Porta Camollia and Porta Romana — the streets are sinuous and often steep, and its parts are divided by deep valleys.

ACCADEMIA DEI FISIOCRITICI (Academy of Natural Sciences)

Piazza S. Agostino 4 ☒ *Open 9am-1pm, 3-6pm; closed Thurs pm, Sat, Sun, hols.*
Founded in the late 17thC, the Accademia dei Fisiocritici was one of the most active and respected of the Italian academies that proliferated in the age of science.

It now contains three museums — Zoological, Geomineralogical and Paleontological — which are full of instructive oddities donated in the late 19th and early 20thC. Exhibits include a collection of stuffed exotic birds, samples of a shower of meteorites which fell near Siena in 1794, an important collection of Foraminifers, and a unique display of more than 1,800 terra-cotta mushrooms.

BOTANICAL GARDEN (Orto Botanico)
Via P.A Mattioli 4 (near S. Agostino) ☎*298874* 📷 ✗ *Open Mon-Fri 8am-5pm, Sat 8am-noon; closed Sun, hols.*

The Botanical Garden of the University of Siena occupies about four acres of the south-facing slope of a valley where the sub-Mediterranean climate permits cultivation of a wide range of species, from dwarf palms to beech and firs. All plants are carefully and clearly labeled.

THE CAMPO ★

The central square of Siena, one of the most magical public spaces in Europe, lies on the site of the Roman Forum at the confluence of the three hills on which the city is built. Its sloping, semicircular shape often elicits comparisons: to a fan, or shell, or amphitheater. For the Sienese it is a cloak — the cloak of the Madonna spread out to protect her favored city. The perimeter of the cloak is trimmed with lacy palaces of which the most striking is the curved **Sansedoni**, originally a group of 13 palaces, which was extended in the 14thC and restructured again in the early 18thC.

The brick paving is divided into nine sections, each of which symbolizes the government of the Nine Good Men, who were responsible for the systematic development of the Campo from the late 13thC.

At the center of the curve is the monumental **Fonti Gaia**, fed by a 25km/16-mile-long mid-14thC aqueduct. The relief carvings are dull mid-19thC reproductions of the early 15thC originals by Jacopo della Quercia, the fragmentary remains of which are now inside the Palazzo Pubblico. They were the sculptor's masterpieces in Siena: affected by antique examples, they were in their turn to have an influence on Michelangelo.

PALAZZO PUBBLICO 🏛 ★

The structure of the Palazzo — the most graceful Gothic civic building in Tuscany — reflects that of the communal government for which it was erected from 1297-1342. The wings (raised by one story in 1681) were occupied respectively by the Podestà, responsible for justice, and

the Nine, responsible for administration, and separated by the central body housing the Biccherna, or treasury, and the General Council.

The black and white communal shield, the *balzana*, decorates all the openings of the facade. From the left corner, the bell tower (1325-48), known as the *Mangia* after the nickname ("wastrel") of its first bell-ringer, leaps — in William Dean Howells' vivid words — "like a rocket into the starlit air."

The Cappella di Piazza at the base of the Mangia was built from 1352-76 and modified in 1468. To its right is the entrance to the Cortile del Podestà, which gives access to the sections of the palace that are open to the public. For a stunning view, climb the 503 steps to the top of the Mangia.

MUSEO CIVICO ★
On the first floor of the Palazzo Pubblico. Open mid-Mar to mid-Nov Mon-Sat 9.30am-7.45pm, Sun 9.30am-1.45pm; winter daily 9.30am-1.45pm 🈂

The communal museum, one of the most important in Italy, is located in the frescoed state rooms of the palace.

Room 1: Sienese ceramics.

Room 2: 16th-18thC non-Italian paintings.

Rooms 3 and 4: 16th-17thC Sienese paintings including frescoes and sinopie by Sodoma from the Cappella di Piazza.

Room 5: 17th-18thC Sienese paintings and church silver.

Room 6: This is the entrance to the tower.

Room 7, Sala del Risorgimento: The six hyper-realistic frescoes in the lunettes, by the best late 19thC Sienese artists, relate episodes from the life of Victor Emmanuel II; on the ceiling are allegories celebrating the regions of united Italy.

Rooms 8 and 9: In the loggia at the top of the stairs are the remains of Jacopo della Quercia's original very ruined carvings for the **Fonte Gaia** (1409-19), the fountain that commemorated the bringing of water to the Campo. The carvings were replaced by copies and brought inside in the 19thC.

Room 10, Sala di Balia: The only room in the palace decorated by non-Sienese artists. The frescoes (1407) by Spinello Aretino and his son Parri di Spinello depict the life of the Sienese Pope Alexander III.

Room 11, Anticamera del Concistoro: This room contains detached frescoes and sculptures by followers of Jacopo della Quercia.

Room 12, Sala del Concistoro: The portal (1448) is by B. Rossellino. The frescoes (★) of the ceiling and vault (1529-36) by Beccafumi, which illustrate scenes from Roman history and political virtues, were the last great pictorial representations of good government before Siena lost its independence to Florence later in the century. Michelangelo singled out the figure of Justice for special praise. The walls are hung with Gobelin and 16thC Florentine tapestries.

Room 13, Vestibule: The damaged fresco of the *Madonna* is by Ambrogio Lorenzetti; the 15thC gilded bronze she-wolf, part of the city's coat of arms, is from the exterior of the palace where it has been replaced by a copy.

Room 14, Antichapel: The frescoes (1414), illustrating virtues and illustrious ancient heroes and divinities, are by Taddeo di Bartolo. The huge *St Christopher* symbolizes the commune's duty to care for the weak.

Room 15, Chapel: The elegant iron gate (1437) may have been designed by Jacopo della Quercia. The intarsiaed Gothic choir stalls (1428) illustrate the Nicene Creed. The frescoes of *Scenes from the Life of the Virgin* (1407) are by Taddeo di Bartolo. Over the altar is the *Sacred Family with St Leonard* by Sodoma.

Room 16, Sala del Mappamondo: The room where the city council met. The painted map after which the room was named no longer exists. The famous and now controversial fresco, known as *Guidoriccio da Fogliano after the Conquests of Montemassi and Sassoferrato,* was until recently attributed to Simone Martini and thought to be part of a cycle of frescoes celebrating castles conquered by Siena after 1314 that ran round three walls of the room. However, some experts now believe that much of the paint of the Guidoriccio was applied centuries later.

The 14thC fresco uncovered below it in 1980 is attributed by some to Duccio. The 16thC frescoes of saints on either side are by Sodoma. On the wall to the right the fresco of *St Bernardino* is also by Sodoma, that of *St Catherine of Siena* (1461) by Vecchietta.

On the wall facing the Guidoriccio is the *Maestà* (1315) (★), signed "Siena had me painted by the hand of Simone (Martini)." It was first restored by the artist himself in 1321. The enthroned Virgin is represented as the Queen of Heaven and Siena.

Room 17, Sala della Pace: The Sienese dedication to law and order received its most complete and vivid pictorial expression with Ambrogio Lorenzetti's *Allegory of Good and Bad Government* (★), painted in 1338-40 for the council chamber as a reminder of the Augustinian and Thomist teachings that justice and common good are the first aims of good government. On the wall opposite the windows, Good Government is represented by a king wearing the colors of the *balzana* and surrounded by symbolic virtues and attributes. On the right wall, we see the *Effects of Good Government in the City and Country,* a precise portrayal of trecento Siena, its activities and its surrounding country. This picture, perhaps the earliest accurate topographical record in Western art, may still be enjoyed in the spirit in which St Bernardino described it in the 15thC: "I see merchants buying and selling, I see dancing, the houses being repaired, the workers busy in the vineyards or sowing the fields..."

On the left wall is the badly damaged fresco of *Bad Government and its Effects*. The frescoes were restored in 1983-88.

Room 18, Sala dei Pilastri: The most important of the 13th-15thC Sienese panel paintings is Guido da Siena's *Maestà.*

CHIGI-SARACINI PALACE ▥

Via di Città 89. Visits on request ☎(0577) 46152.

Built in the 14thC for one of the great Sienese banking families, this fine stone and brick palace was enlarged in the Renaissance by the Piccolomini family and restored in Gothic style in the 18th and 19thC. It now houses the distinguished Accademia Musicale Chigiana, which holds some of its summer concerts here (see page 271), a small museum of musical instruments and an exceptionally good collection of 14th-17thC Sienese and other Tuscan paintings owned by the Monte dei Paschi bank.

Across the Via di Città *(#126),* is the **Palazzo Piccolomini delle Papesse** (1460-95), designed by B. Rossellino in the Florentine Renaissance style favored by his patron the Piccolomini Pope Pius II.

DUOMO ▥ ✝ ★

Open mid-Mar to end Oct 7.30am-7.30pm, Nov to mid-Mar 7.30am-1.30pm, 2.30pm-sunset.

The cathedral of Santa Maria dell'Assunta was the most expensive and carefully considered building project of Siena's golden age. Its construction, over nearly two centuries, was at first supervised by committees of Sienese citizens, and there was no Sienese artist or craftsman of any distinction who did not work at some time on the cathedral.

The site chosen for the building, which began in the late 12thC, was the Castelvecchio, the earliest inhabited part of the city. The basic structure was complete in 1215, the hexagonal cupola in 1264, and the facade was begun in 1284. In 1339 an extraordinary and hopelessly ambitious decision was taken: Siena would build a new and greater cathedral, rivaling those of Florence and Orvieto, for which the old cathedral would serve as transept. This unwieldy, prohibitively expensive scheme was abandoned after the 1348 plague, and the old cathedral was finally completed in 1382.

The skeletal remains of the new cathedral (Duomo Nuovo), now housing the Cathedral Museum (see page 278), stand to the right of the Duomo, behind Buontalenti's **Palazzo della Prefettura**.

The polychrome marble facade of the Duomo is best studied from the far right corner of the square. The lower section (1284-96), the first building project in Tuscany to reflect the Gothic influence of SAN GALGANO, was designed by Giovanni Pisano. The statues are copies of the originals, by Giovanni or assistants, now in the Cathedral Museum. The central bronze door dates from 1958, and the gabled upper section in the high Gothic style was begun in 1376; the mosaics are 19thC. From the right transept rises the Romanesque **campanile** (1313).

The **interior** is most immediately striking for the giddy optical effect of the black and white stripes. The floor (★) is paved in marble; its 56 designs were produced by more than 40 leading Sienese artists and executed by craftsmen in *sgraffiti* or intarsia. This remarkable collaborative work was carried out between 1369-1547. Beccafumi created 35 of the designs. Notice especially his *Old Testament Scenes* between the cupola and high altar.

The **Libreria Piccolomini** (★) *(open mid-Mar to end Oct 9am-7.30pm; Nov 1 to mid-Mar 10am-1pm, 2.30-5pm* 🕮*)*, located off the left aisle, is the most brilliantly decorative room in Tuscany. It was built in the 1490s by Francesco Todeschini Piccolomini (Pope Pius III) to house the library of his uncle, Aeneas Silvius Piccolomini (Pope Pius II). The vividly charming frescoes (1502-05) by Pinturicchio depict ten *Scenes from the Life of Pius II*. In the center of the room is the beautiful and influential *Three Graces*, a 3rdC Roman copy of an original by Praxiteles. Fine illuminated choir-books are displayed on late 15thC benches.

To the w of the library is the **Piccolomini Altar** (1485), designed by the Lombard sculptor Andrea Bregno. The statues of *Sts Peter and Pius and Sts Gregory and Paul* are by the young Michelangelo.

Left transept: The pulpit (1266-68) (★) is by Nicola Pisano, assisted by his son Giovanni and pupils including Arnolfo di Cambio; created six years later than the great Baptistry pulpit at PISA, this work is freer and more innovatory. The seven panels, separated by figures of prophets and angels, depict *Scenes from the Life of Christ*. The staircase was added by Riccio in 1570.

The **chapel of St John the Baptist** (1481-98), designed by Giovanni di Stefano, is entered through an elegant marble portal. Frescoes include Pinturicchio's two portraits of *Alberto Aringhieri,* in youth and old age. The vigorously spiritual bronze statue of the *Baptist* (1457) is a late work by Donatello which greatly influenced local sculptors. The statue of *St Ansanus* is by Giovanni di Stefano; that of *St Catherine of Alexandria* (1487) is by Neroccio.

The **chapel of St Ansano** contains a monument to Cardinal Petroni (1317-18) by Tino di Camaino, which was much imitated throughout the rest of the century; and, in the pavement, the slab tomb of Bishop Giovanni Pecci (1426) is signed by Donatello.

Chancel: The high altar (1532) by Peruzzi bears a huge ciborium (1462-72) by Vecchietta. The two higher flanking *Angels* (1489) are by Giovanni di Stefano; those placed lower down (1499) by Francesco di Giorgio Martini. Eight serenely beautiful candelabra-angels (1548-50) on the nave pilasters are by Beccafumi; they are perhaps his masterpieces as a sculptor.

The frescoes and two stucco figures of Victories in the apse are also by Beccafumi. The finely carved choir stalls are 14th-16thC. The window above (1288) is one of the earliest examples of Italian stained glass, made from cartoons by Duccio.

Right transept: The **Chigi chapel** (1661) was designed by Bernini for the morbidly pious Fabio Chigi, Pope as Alexander VII, to house the 13thC fresco of the *Madonna del Voto* over the altar. The statues of *St Jerome* and the *Magdalen* placed in niches on the entrance wall are by Bernini.

The **Baptistry** (★), facing its own Piazza San Giovanni, is situated beneath the apse of the cathedral and is reached by a steep flight of steps to its right. The impressive Gothic facade (1317-82) is incomplete in the upper section. The interior is frescoed by Vecchietta and his School. Although overpainted in the 19thC, the frescoes merit attention, particularly the bold and successful architectural setting of the *Washing of the Feet* by Pietro Orioli.

At the center is Jacopo della Quercia's hexagonal marble **font** (★) (1411-30), a masterpiece of collaboration between Florentine and Sienese sculptors. Two of the statues around the basin, *Faith* and *Hope,* are by Donatello.

The six gilded bronze relief panels include Jacopo della Quercia's powerful *Zacharias Expelled from the Temple,* Ghiberti's *Baptism of Christ* and Donatello's *Herod's Feast,* which was made in Florence after Jacopo had failed to meet his agreed deadline.

The **Cripta delle Statue** (*open Mar-Oct 10am-1pm, 2.30-6pm* 📷) is entered from the steps leading to the Baptistry. It contains statues from the Duomo by Giovanni Pisano and followers, fresco fragments (1270-80) which are the earliest known Sienese wall paintings.

To the E of the Baptistry is the **Palazzo del Magnifico** (1504-08), designed by G. Cozzarelli for Pandolfo Petrucci, autocratic political leader of Siena from 1487-1524. The beautifully wrought bronzes on the handsome facade have been replaced by copies.

MUSEO DELL'OPERA DEL DUOMO (Cathedral Museum) ★
Open daily summer 9am-7.30pm, winter 9am-1pm 📷

This is one of the greatest Italian cathedral museums. Sculptures, paintings and reliquaries from the Duomo and other Sienese churches are
on show on three floors in the right nave of the Duomo Nuovo (see above).

Ground floor: Among the carvings from the cathedral facade, the ten
figures (1284-96) (★) by Giovanni Pisano are among the most important
Gothic sculptures in Italy. In the center is a bas-relief of the *Madonna
and Child with St Anthony Abbot and Cardinal Antonio Casini*, a late
work by Jacopo della Quercia.

First floor, Sala di Duccio: Duccio's *Maestà* (1308-11) (★), the
inaugural work of the great period of Sienese painting, was carried to the
Duomo in a magnificent candlelit procession, while the bells of Siena
pealed the *Gloria* and the citizens offered prayers and alms to the poor.
It bears the inscription: "O Holy Mother of God, grant peace to Siena and
life to Duccio, who has painted you thus." It stood over the high altar of
the cathedral until removed to a side chapel in 1505. Originally painted
on both sides, the panel was split and dismantled in the 18thC. The
Madonna Enthroned now faces the 26 *Scenes from the Passion*. On the
left wall are 19 panels from the predella and upper section (others are in
London, Washington and New York). On the right wall are Pietro
Lorenzetti's triptych of the *Birth of the Virgin* (1342) and a *Madonna and
Child* attributed to the young Duccio.

Second floor: This floor comprises Sienese paintings including *The
Madonna of the Large Eyes* (c.1200) by an unknown artist, the image of
the Virgin to which the city was dedicated on the eve of the battle of
Montaperti; *The Blessed Agostino Novello and Four of his Miracles*
(c.1330) (★) by Simone Martini, from the church of S. Agostino; Beccafumi's *St Paul*. In the **Sala del Tesoro** the finest treasures are Giovanni
Pisano's tiny wooden *Crucifix*, F. da Valdambrino's polychrome wood
busts of saints (1409), and the late 13thC *Reliquary of St Galgano*.

From the last room, a staircase climbs to the rim of the facade of the
Duomo Nuovo, which gives stunning views of the city and countryside.

SANTA MARIA DELLA SCALA (Hospital of Santa Maria della Scala)
Piazza Duomo. For visits to the Sala del Pelegrinaio (Pilgrims' Hall) ☎*299410. For
information about the Archeological Museum* ☎*49153* 📷

The hospital building, which dates from the late 13th-14thC, was used
for the care of the sick until recently, and is now gradually being
opened as a museum complex. The old **Pilgrims' Hall** of the hospital
is decorated with a fascinating and unique cycle of 15thC frescoes by
Domenico di Bartolo, which illustrate the care of the sick in an em-
phatically realistic style.

The **Archeological Museum** (Museo Archeologico Etrusco), recently
installed in the hospital, displays coins, jewelry, vases and other material
from Etruscan sites in the Province of Siena.

Over the high altar of the adjoining church of **Santa Maria della
Scala**, built in 1252 and enlarged in 1466, is Vecchietta's bronze *Risen
Christ* (★) (1476); influenced by Donatello's late work, it is one of the
great masterpieces of Italian Renaissance sculpture.

FONTEGIUSTA †
Via Fontegiusta, off Via Camollia.
The church of the Madonna of Fontegiusta was built in 1482-84 as an expression of gratitude for a Sienese victory over the Florentines. The elegant portico was added in 1489. The unusual square interior contains 16thC Sienese frescoes and paintings and a large tabernacle by Marrina.

Via Camollia ends at the **Porta Camollia**, the most northerly of the Sienese gates opening onto the Florence road. The famous Sienese welcome *Cor magis tibi Sena pandit* (Siena opens wide its heart to you) was inscribed in 1604 when the 14thC gate was rebuilt in honor of a visit by Grandduke Ferdinand I.

FORTE DI SANTA BARBARA 血
Built in 1560 by Cosimo I de' Medici, the fortress now houses the Enoteca Italiana Permanente (see TUSCAN WINES on pages 176-7). The tasting bar is open from 3pm-midnight, and the views from the ramparts are best at sunset. To the NE is the **Lizza**, Siena's triangular public park where the Wednesday market is held.

LOGGIA DELLA MERCANZIA
Erected in the early 15thC where the three principal streets of Siena meet above the Campo, this loggia sheltered a commercial tribunal famed for its impartiality even outside Siena. The statues of *Saints Peter* and *Paul* (1462) are by Vecchietta, inspired by Donatello who had worked in Siena in the late 1450s. Vecchietta studied the drapery from real cloth dipped in plaster and arranged on a lay figure. Their physical and psychological realism opened a new era in Sienese art. The other statues are by Antonio Federighi.

The upper story is 17thC. A restoration of the loggia was completed in 1991.

PICCOLOMINI PALACE 血 ☆
Via Banchi di Sotto 52 ☻ Open Mon-Sat 9am-1pm; closed Sun, hols.
The palace, begun in 1469 for the Piccolomini family, was very likely designed by the Florentine architect Bernardo Rossellino, who was the favorite of the Piccolomini Pope, Pius II.

It resembles his RUCELLAI PALACE (see FLORENCE A TO Z) and Piccolomini Palace at PIENZA. With the nearby **Logge del Papa** (1462), designed by A. Federighi, this constitutes the most important Renaissance building complex in Siena.

The palace houses the **State Archives**, which may be freely consulted by the public. The most interesting objects that are on view in the museum of the archives are the covers of the registers of the *Biccherna* (the Treasury), which were painted by leading Sienese artists from 1258 into the 18thC.

The 16thC ex-monastery opposite the palace is the seat of the University of Siena. Via San Vigilio leads to the **Corte del Castellare degli Ugurgieri**, an atmospheric complex of medieval buildings.

PINACOTECA NAZIONALE ▥ ★
Via San Pietro 29. Open Mon-Sat 8.30am-2pm, Sun 8.30am-1pm ▱

The outstanding collection of Sienese paintings is housed in the hand-some early 15thC Gothic Palazzo Buonsignori. The display is hung chronologically, beginning on the 2nd floor with the primitives and early Renaissance artists. 16thC pictures, notably masterpieces by So-doma and the great Sienese Mannerist Beccafumi are on the 1st floor.

The galleries are gradually being rearranged and many of the pictures are either recently restored or removed for restoration. The following is a selective tour of some of the outstanding works.

Second floor: Altar frontal of *Christ the Redeemer* with symbols of the Evangelists and scenes from the Passion (1215), the earliest dated Sienese painting. Works by Guido da Siena (13thC) the first of the great named Sienese masters and by his school. Duccio — note especially the tiny, finely executed but damaged *Madonna dei Francescani* (c. 1285), and school of Duccio. Simone Martini, *Madonna and Child.*

Works by Ambrogio and Pietro Lorenzetti: the two small views of *A City by the Sea* and *A Castle by a Lake* are traditionally attributed to A. Lorenzetti, but some scholars now give them to Sassetta and believe they may be fragments of his dismembered altarpiece for the Arte della Lana (the wool-merchant guild). By A. Lorenzetti: *Madonna with Saints and Angels* and *Annunciation* (1344). P. Lorenzetti: *Madonna and Child* (1328-29), originally in the center of an altarpiece of which the superb *Stories of the Carmelite Order* formed the predella. *Birth of the Virgin* (c.1380-90) by Paolo di Giovanni Fei. Notice also the remarkable and profoundly moving wooden torso of the *Crucified Christ* (c. 1300).

Works by Giovanni di Paolo, who was with Sassetta one of the two greatest early 15thC Sienese masters: *St Nicholas of Bari and other saints* (1453), the *Crucifixion* (1440), *Last Judgment,* and delightful *Madonna of Humility.* The *Institution of the Eucharist* and *St Anthony Beaten by Devils* are predella panels by Sassetta from the Arte della Lana altarpiece, of which the half-figure of *The Prophet Elijah,* the four *Patron Saints of Siena* and four *Church Fathers* were also parts. Neroccio di Bartolomeo Landi, *Madonna and Saints* (c.1475); Francesco di Giorgio's small *Annunciation* and dazzling, turbulent *Coronation of the Virgin;* Matteo di Giovanni's *Madonna and Child with Angels* (1470). Works by Sano di Pietro, including *The Virgin Commending the City of Siena to Pope Calixtus III* (1456). Vecchietta's *Madonna and Child with Saints.*

First floor: Sodoma: the impressive *Deposition,* recently cleaned; *Nativity; Scourging of Christ,* a fresco from the cloister of S. Francesco; *Descent into Hell; Gethsemane.* Beccafumi: *Casting of the Rebel Angels from Heaven, Descent into Hell, St Catherine Receiving the Stigmata, Birth of the Virgin;* and Beccafumi's cartoons for the pavement of the Duomo.

The *Portrait of Queen Elizabeth I* is usually attributed to Federico Zuccari. Also paintings by Pinturicchio, B. Fungaí, Rutilio Manetti.

Third floor: Small paintings by non-Sienese artists from the Spannoc-chi collection, formed in the 17thC, include Dürer's *St Jerome,* Lorenzo Lotto's *Nativity,* Paris Bordone's *Annunciation.*

SALIMBENI PALACE ⌂
Piazza Salimbeni.
This beautiful 14thC palace is the headquarters of the Monte dei Paschi bank, which was founded in the 17thC. The Renaissance **Spannocchi Palace** (designed by G. da Maiano in 1470, completed in 1880) on the right, and 16thC **Tantucci Palace** on the left are also owned by the Monte dei Paschi.

SANT'AGOSTINO †
If closed ring for the custodian at #1 in the piazza.
The 13thC church has an attractive 18thC interior by Vanvitelli and a number of important paintings. Over the second altar on the right is a *Crucifixion* (1506) by Perugino. In the **Piccolomini Chapel** (✩) are three good Sienese works: a lunette fresco of the *Madonna and Saints* by Ambrogio Lorenzetti, Matteo di Giovanni's *Slaughter of the Innocents* (1482) and an *Epiphany* by Sodoma.

The **Bichi Chapel** in the right transept has a late 15thC majolica pavement; the two monochrome frescoes of the *Birth of the Virgin* and *Nativity* are by Francesco di Giorgio with additions by Pietro Orioli.

ST CATHERINE'S HOUSE AND SANCTUARY (Casa e Santuario di S. Caterina) †
Costa di S. Antonio. Open daily 9am-12.30pm, 3-6pm 📷
This was the family home of the eloquent mystic Caterina Benincasa, whose father was a dyer. After she was canonized in 1461, a complex of chapels was created in and around the house. The **Oratorio della Cucina**, in the family kitchen, is decorated with 16thC frescoes and paintings.

The Baroque **Oratorio del Crocifisso** contains the 13thC *Crucifix* before which the saint received the stigmata in 1375. The **Oratorio della Camera** is built over St Catherine's cell. The **Oratorio Superiore** has a ceiling by Riccio, and a 17thC tiled floor.

The **Oratory of St Catherine** is below the house facing via S. Caterina on the site of the dyer's workshop. It is the parish church of the *contrada* of Fontebranda, but is alas rarely open. Inside is a beautiful polychrome wooden statue of *St Catherine* (1474) by Neroccio de' Landi, and five frescoed *Angels* by Sodoma.

The **Fonte Branda**, one of the oldest of the many Sienese wells — recorded from 1081 and arched over with brick vaults in 1246 — is at the bottom of a steep street leading downhill from Vicolo dei Tiratori. The church of **San Domenico** is on the hill of Camporeggio above the house.

SAN DOMENICO †
The stark red-brick Dominican preaching church crowns the hill above **St Catherine's House** and the Fonte Branda. The present building, incorporating the original early 13thC church, dates from the 14th-15thC. The campanile was completed in 1340. The only authentic portrait of *St Catherine*, who assumed the Dominican habit in this church, is that by her friend Andrea Vanni, in a chapel at the w end.

In the Chapel of St Catherine on the right of the nave are frescoes by

Sodoma (1526) of *St Catherine in Mystical Ecstasy.* Also in the right nave is an *Adoration of the Shepherds* designed by Francesco di Giorgio at the end of his career and largely painted by assistants. The tabernacle with two angels (c. 1475) over the high altar is by Benedetto da Maiano.

SAN FRANCESCO †

As in Florence, the Franciscan preaching church stands across the city from that built by the Dominicans. An earlier church here was begun at once after the death of St Francis. The present building (1326-1475) was altered after a fire in the 17thC and again in the late 19thC. The Neo-Gothic facade was applied in 1913. In the N transept are detached frescoes (1331) by P. Lorenzetti of the *Crucifixion* and by A. Lorenzetti of *St Louis of Anjou before Pope Boniface VII* and the *Martyrdom of the Franciscans.*

On the piazza's S side is the **Oratorio di San Bernardino** *(apply to custodian or ☎ (0577) 287416).* This oratory was built in the 15thC on the site where the Franciscan St Bernardino had preached. The upper chapel has elegant 15thC stuccowork, carvings and frescoes by Sodoma, Girolamo del Pacchia and Beccafumi. The Via del Comune descends to the 14thC Porta Ovile.

SANTA MARIA DEI SERVI †

Piazza Alessandro Manzoni.

The building dates from the 13th-15thC; the interior naves and aisles were reworked in 1471-1528. Most important of the Sienese school pictures are: right aisle, Coppo di Marcovaldo's *Madonna* (1261); right transept, P. Lorenzetti's fresco of *The Slaughter of the Innocents;* left transept, Lippo Memmi's *Madonna.* Nearby is the imposing **Porta Romana** (1327), from which the Via Cassia leads to Rome.

SANTO SPIRITO †

Via dei Pispini.

The brick Church of the Holy Spirit dates from 1498. The portal is attributed to Peruzzi and the cupola (1508) to Cozzarelli. Inside are works by Sodoma, Cozzarelli and Beccafumi. At the end of Via dei Pispini is the 14thC **Porta Pispini**, with the remains of a fresco of the *Nativity* (1531) by Sodoma.

TOLOMEI PALACE 🏛

11 Via Banchi di Sopra.

The oldest private palace in Siena, now occupied by the Florentine Savings Bank, was built in 1208 and altered in c.1267.

OTHER SIGHTS OUTSIDE THE CITY WALLS

DIAVOLI PALACE 🏛

Just beyond Porta Camollia in Via Fiorentina, this palace, a medieval building rebuilt in 1460 by A. Federighi, is one of the first and most original pieces of Sienese Renaissance architecture.

OSSERVANZA 血 †

$2\frac{1}{2}$ km ($1\frac{1}{2}$ miles) from Porta Ovile, beyond the railway crossing, is the most interesting church near Siena, founded by St Bernardino in 1423 and rebuilt, after damage in World War II, to the original designs (1474-90) of Francesco di Giorgio and Giacomo Cozzarelli. It contains, most notably, a white-glazed terra-cotta group of the *Annunciation* and a blue-and-white enamelled terra-cotta altarpiece of the *Coronation of the Virgin,* both by Andrea della Robbia; the sinopia of a fresco of the *Madonna and Child with Saints* by Pietro Orioli, which demonstrates the artist's mastery of perspective; and, in the sacristy, a group of seven polychrome terra-cotta figures representing the *Pietà* by Cozzarelli.

GARDENS

Some of Tuscany's most beautiful old gardens are near Siena. Two that are open to the public on request are: **Vicobello** *(apply to Marchesa Chigi-Bonnelli, Via Vicobello 12)* and **Villa Palazzina** *(apply to Signor Gianneschi, Strada di Ventena 28).*

HOTELS

CERTOSA DI MAGGIANO 血

Via Certosa 82, 53100 Siena ☎*(0577) 288180* ✆*574221* ℻*(0577) 288189* 🛏 *14 rms including 9 suites, all with bathrm* 🖥 🔌 🖼 🛋 🍽 🔲 🔘 🎛 🖥 ♿ 🛋 🔲 🔌 → 🖼 ♨ ⚓ ⛳ 🏋 ♀

An exceptionally civilized hotel around the cloister and church of a 14thC monastery above the city, just a 15-minute walk E of the center. Clients are treated like privileged guests in a private house. The only disappointment is the food in the very pretty restaurant.

PALAZZO RAVIZZA

Pian dei Mantellini 34, 53100 Siena ☎*(0577) 280462* ✆*570252* ℻*(0577) 271370* 🛏 *to* 🛏 *30 rms, 21 with bathrm* 🔌 🛋 🍽 🅰🅴 🔘 🔲 🎛 ‡ ⚓ 🖼 ♨ ⛳ 🏋 ♀ 🏋

Only 5 minutes' walk from the Duomo and Campo, this attractive first-class *pensione* in a 17thC villa with a pretty garden is now part of a chain, but has kept its old-fashioned character better than most.

PARK HOTEL 血

Via Marciano 16, 53100 Siena ☎*(0577) 44803* ✆*571005* ℻*(0577) 49020* 🛏 *69 rms, all with bathrm* 🖥 🛋 🍽 🅰🅴 🔘 🔲 🎛 🛋 ‡ 🔲 🖼 ♨ ⚓ ⛳ 🏋

The luxury hotel of Siena, now under the same ownership as the excellent Helvetia & Bristol in Florence, occupies a modernized 15thC villa surrounded by a large park, 2km ($1\frac{1}{4}$ miles) to NW of the town. Bedrooms, all decorated in the same business-like dark chintz, are smallish but comfortably fitted out; those facing s overlook the historic center. The restaurants, **L'Olivo** and **La Magnolia,** serve above-average food.

SANTA CATERINA

Via Piccolomini 7, 53100 Siena ☎*(0577) 221105* ✆*575304* ℻*(0577) 271087* 🛏 *19 rms, all with bathrm* 🖥 🅰🅴 🔘 🔲 🎛 🖼 ♿ ‡ ♨ ♀ Closed mid-Jan to early Mar.

A charming small hotel opened in 1986 in a late 18thC villa surrounded by a large garden just outside Porta Romana.

VILLA SCACCIAPENSIERI

Via di Scacciapensieri, 53100 Siena ☎*(0577) 41441* ✆*573390* ℻*(0577) 270854* 🛏

29 rms, all with bathrm 🖳 🛏 🍽 AE ⊙ ⬤ VISA ⬡ ♿ ⬆ □ ⬛ 🌿 🔥 💈 ⚏ ♨ ☕

Closed Jan to mid-Mar.

A big, comfortable country villa, 3km (2 miles) to the N of Siena, it is set in a large garden with wonderful views of the town. The generous breakfasts are a rare treat in Tuscany. A good base for hiking or riding expeditions. Conference facilities are being added for 1993.

⚑   The youth hostel, **Ostello della Gioventù**, is at Via Fiorentina 89 *(☎(0577) 52212* Ex*(0577) 52480).*

RESTAURANTS

One explanation for the boring food served in most Sienese restaurants may be that the Sienese themselves prefer to eat in the clubs of their *contrade*. The food is not very good there either, but it is fun to join them for a special feast. Most *contrade* will sell tickets for celebration dinners *(information from the tourist office, see page 269).*

Another alternative to eating in restaurants would be to buy a picnic from the delicatessen **Morbidi** *(Via Banchi di Sotto 27, closed Wed pm).*

Dining in the Campo on a summer's evening is such a magical experience that the quality of the food scarcely matters. The best, and most expensive, of the restaurants in the Campo is **Il Campo** *(at #50* ☎*(0577) 280725* AE ⊙ ⬤ VISA 🍽 *closed Tues, Jan).* Otherwise, three simple, decent and locally popular restaurants in the streets behind the Palazzo Pubblico would be **Il Carroccio** *(Via Casato di Sotto 32* ☎*(0577) 41165, closed Wed, Feb);* **Le Logge** *(Via del Porrione 33* ☎*(0577) 48013* ▥ *closed Sun);* and **La Torre** *(Via Salicotto 7-9* ☎*(0577) 287548* ▥ *no cards; closed Thurs).*

RESTAURANTS OUTSIDE SIENA

🍽   Of the restaurants immediately to the N, a first choice for atmosphere, traditional Tuscan cooking based on fresh ingredients, and good Chianti wines would be **Antica Trattoria Botteganova** *(Strada Chiantigiana 29* ☎*(0577) 284230* 🖳 ▥ AE ⊙ ⬤ VISA *closed Sun; Mon lunch).*

Otherwise, **Il Molino delle Bagnaie**, off the SS408 at Pianella *(☎(0577) 747062; closed Mon, Jan)* is set in an attractively renovated old mill; **La Taverna** *(Via del Sergente 5, Vagliagli* ☎*(0577) 322532* ▥ ⬤ VISA *closed Mon);* and **Taverna do Solimano** *(SS 222, Querciagrossa* ☎*(0577) 51144* ▥ AE ⊙ ⬤ VISA *closed Mon, Jan).*

13km (8 miles) w of Siena at Stigliano, near Sovicille, is **Le Torri di Stigliano** *(Piazza Grande* ☎*(0577) 342029* ▥ *to* ▥ *closed Mon, Oct).*

⚑ 🍽   See also CASTELLINA IN CHIANTI, CASTELNUOVO BERARDENGA, GAIOLE IN CHIANTI, RADDA IN CHIANTI and MONTERIGGIONI.

SINALUNGA

Map 11G7. 103km (64 miles) SE of Florence, 45km (28 miles) SE of Siena. 53048.
Hill town in the heart of the Valdichiana near the entrance to the autostrada A1. Above the center, the church of **San Bernardino**, re-built in the 18thC, preserves some interesting Sienese Renaissance pictures, notably an *Annunciation* (1470) by Benvenuto di Giovanni, and a *Madonna and Child* by Sano di Pietro.

❦ ⇌ LOCANDA DELL'AMOROSA

2km (1¼ miles) s ☎*(0577) 679497* 📠*580047* 📠*(0577) 678216 15 rms, all with bathrm* 🎦 ☎ ■ ≣ ≣ 🅰 ⊙ 🄌 🖾 ⌂ ☐ 🖾 ✿ ✦ ⚞ ⚟ ⚑ *Closed mid-Jan to end Feb.*
Restaurant closed Mon, Tues lunch.
The hotel, in the converted brick stables of a wine-growing estate, is charming. But the food and service in the restaurant are unnecessarily fussy.

⇌ **Delle Grotte** *(Viale Matteotti 33* ☎ *(0577) 630269* 🎦 *closed Wed),* in the center, has tables outside in the summer.

SOVANA

Map 8I7. 226km (141 miles) s *of Florence, 82km (51 miles)* SE *of Grosseto. 58010. Grosseto.*
A solitary, semi-abandoned village with Etruscan-Roman foundations, on a plateau 8km (5 miles) NW of PITIGLIANO. The **Rocca** was built by the Aldobrandeschi lords in the 13thC.

The main street is flanked by medieval houses. At one end is the 13thC **Palazzo Pretorio**, modified in the 15thC, and the Romanesque church of **S. Maria**, with its **ciborium** (c.8th-9thC), a rare example of pre-Romanesque sculpture. At the far end is the splendid, dramatically situated Romanesque **Duomo**, with a beautiful, austere interior, which gave one writer "the overall sense that one day soon this cathedral, already looking impossibly ancient in experience and wisdom, will shrug its stone shoulders and amble off into the countryside, never to be seen again."

The **Etruscan necropolis** (✩) is in cool birch woods 1½km (1 mile) below the town *(a guide can be found at the Taverna Etrusca: allow a minimum of 1hr).* The architectonic tomb fronts are carved from the rock face of the gorge with burial grottoes beneath. The most sophisticated is the 2ndC BC Tomba Ildebranda in the form of a temple facade.

❦ ⇌ **Taverna Etrusca** *(Piazza Pretorio* ☎*(0564) 616183* 📠*(0454) 614193* 🎦 🅰 ⊙ 🄌 🖾 *restaurant closed Mon).*

STIA

Map 11E7. 49km (30 miles) E *of Florence. 52017. Arezzo. Population: 3,023.*
At the head of the Casentino just below **Monte Falterona**, where the Arno has its source. Its central Piazza Tanucci is a piece of first-class town planning, and the Romanesque church preserves a *Madonna and Child* (1437) by Andrea della Robbia and an *Annunciation* (1414) by Bicci di Lorenzo.

In the late Middle Ages, Stia was closely surrounded by the castles of the Guidi lords who ruled the upper Casentino and with whom the exiled Dante took refuge. The noblest of the ruined castles is the **Castello di Romena**, 3km (2 miles) to the s. Nearby, on a parallel road, is the 10th-12thC **Pieve di Romena** *(custodian in house next door),* the finest Romanesque church in the Casentino but over-restored. A magnificent 4-hour walk N from Stia will take one to the summit of Monte Falterona via the source of the Arno.

⇌ **La Buca** *(Via Fiorentina 2* ☎*(0575) 58797).*

TALAMONE
Map 7J5. 164km (102 miles) s of Florence, 24km (15 miles) s of Grosseto. 58010. Grosseto. Population: 485.

A fishing village and tourist harbor guarded by a grim medieval fortress on a headland s of MONTI DELL'UCCELLINA overlooking Monte Argentario.

The Sienese purchased Talamone from the Abbey of San Salvatore in 1303; their intention to make it into a port rivaling Pisa and Genoa was derided by Dante *(Purgatorio, XIII)*. It became part of the Spanish Garrison States in 1556.

☙ CORTE DEI BUTTERI
58010 Fonte Blanda, Grosseto ☎*(0564) 885546* ▦*580103* ▣*(0564) 886282* ▥ *87 rms, all with bathrm* ▤ ▣ ☎ ⬛ ▥ ▦ ▣ ⬥ & ▣ ☙ ⬰ ◆ ◴ ➤ *Closed mid-Oct to Apr.*
A modern luxury hotel at Fonte Blanda, 4km (2½ miles) to the NE.

☙ On the promontory is the **Capo d'Uomo** *(Via Cala di Forno 7* ☎*(0564) 887077* ▥ *closed Oct to Mar).*

⬛ **La Buca** *(* ☎*(0564) 887067* ▥ *to* ▥ *closed lunch except weekends, Mon, Jan-Feb, July).*

TORRE DEL LAGO PUCCINI
Map 13E3. 95km (59 miles) w of Florence, 16km (10 miles) N of Pisa. 55048. Lucca. Population: 5,450.

Just to the E of the dull little village of Torre del Lago Puccini is **Lake Massaciuccoli**, the largest of the few lakes in Tuscany. The opera composer Giacomo Puccini, who settled here in 1891, once described this place as his "supreme joy, paradise, Eden, the Empyrean, *turris eburnea, vas spiritualis,* kingdom." He built himself a house on the shore of the lake, where he lived until shortly before his death in 1924.

Event ‡ A festival of Puccini operas is held in early August *(for information and bookings contact Segreteria del Festival Pucciniano, Piazza Puccini, 55048 Torre del Lago, Lucca* ☎*(0584) 342006).*

VILLA PUCCINI ✭
The villa is preserved as it was in Puccini's lifetime, and he is buried here in a mausoleum built, appropriately, between his piano and his gunroom. The house is a shrine as well as a vivid testimony to this likeable genius.

⬛ Next to the villa are **Butterfly** *(* ☎*(0584) 341024* ▥ *closed Thurs)* which has rooms; and **Da Cecco** *(* ☎*(0584) 341022* ▥ *closed Mon).*

VALLOMBROSA
Map 11E6. 33km (20 miles) SE of Florence. 50060. Firenze.

In the NE Pratomagno Hills, reached by beautiful twisting roads, is the monastery of Vallombrosa, mother house of the order founded in the early 11thC by the Florentine religious reformer San Giovanni Gualberto.

The imposing **monastery (▥)**, like a finely designed symmetrical castle, has a facade (1635-40) by G. Silvani. The campanile is 13thC, and the tower 15thC; the church itself is mainly 17thC. A plaque records that the poet Milton stayed here in 1638.

All around is the magnificent deciduous forest that inspired Milton's description of the gathering devils in *Paradise Lost*.

"Thick as autumnal leaves that strow the brooks
In Vallombrosa, where th'Etrurian shades,
High-overarch'd, imbower."

9km (6 miles) above, near the summit of **Monte Secchieta** at 1,449m (4,216ft), is fine walking country, also equipped for skiing. **Saltino**, a modern summer and winter sports resort, is 2km (1¼ miles) W, and **Consuma**, another holiday resort, is 10km (6 miles) NE.

☙ ═ VILLA RIGACCI
15km (9½ miles) S at Vaggio, Via Manzoni 76, Vaggio 50066 Reggello ☎(055) 8656718 ☒(055) 8656537 ▥ to ▥ 18 rms, all with bathrm ⌂ ▤ ═ ▣ ⊡ ▣ ▦ ⌂ ⚡ ⟨⟨ ≋ ⚲ ♨ ☕ Closed Jan.
A country house situated high on a hill and surrounded by mature trees. The stylish restaurant **Le Vieux Pressoir** *(closed Tues in winter)* serves French provincial cooking prepared with unusual technical skill.

☙ ═ **Croce di Savoia**, at Saltino Vallombrosa, 1km (½ mile) W *(☎ and* ☒ *(055) 862035-6* ▥ ▣ *open mid-June to mid-Sept). Comfortable wooded retreat.*

☙ ═ **Sbaragli**, at Montemignaio *(Via Casentinese 3-4 ☎ (055) 8306500* ▥ ▦ *closed mid-Nov to mid-Mar; restaurant closed Tues).*

VETULONIA
Map 10I5. 141km (87 miles) SW of Florence, 29km (18 miles) NW of Grosseto. 58040. Grosseto. Population: 615.
Vetulonia is the most enigmatic of the great Etruscan city states. Like ROSELLE, Etruscan Vetulonia was a maritime city situated on an island rising from the navigable waters of the gulf that then filled part of the Grosseto plain. Its culture flourished from the 8th-6thC BC and then seems to have died with mysterious suddenness. The Roman symbol of power, the *fasces,* was borrowed from archaic Vetulonia.

SIGHTS AND PLACES OF INTEREST

MUSEO ARCHEOLOGICO
This small, interesting museum occupies the site of the acropolis at the entrance to the village. Above are remains of the **walls** (6thC BC), built of huge polygonal blocks of stone and commanding a magnificent view.

NECROPOLIS ☆
3km (1¾ miles) to NE ✗ compulsory (inquire about tours at museum).
The most important tombs are the **tumulo della Pietrera**, domed in the manner of Mycenaean tombs, and, 400m (¼ mile) below, the **tumolo del Diavolino**; both are probably late 7thC BC.

VIAREGGIO
Map 13D3. 97km (60 miles) W of Florence, 27km (17 miles) W of Lucca. 55049. Lucca. Population: 59,460 i Viale Carducci 10 ☎(0584) 962233.
The capital of the Versilia Riviera is one of the oldest seaside resorts in

Italy. The climate is healthy and mild in winter, but the atmosphere today is that of a tough, citified seaside strip masking a sleazy but more congenial port area. Stately Liberty buildings and palm-fringed avenues were laid out in the 19thC in strict parallel roads where the medieval King's Highway *(Via Regia)* once ran through the pine woods. The fine-sand beach is over 100m (325ft) wide and is divided into well-equipped and expensive bathing establishments. The harbor is lively with fishing and tourist boats.

To the N, Viareggio merges with the modern and less expensive **Lido di Camaiore**. To the S, a protected pine wood stretches as far as TORRE DEL LAGO, and there are free beaches.

The monument to Shelley in Piazza Shelley records that the poet's body was washed up on the beach in 1822.

Event   ‡ Viareggio Carnival, the most elaborate in Tuscany, takes place throughout the month before Lent. Festivities include processions of allegorical floats, masked balls, fireworks and a football tournament.

ASTOR
Viale Carducci 54, 55049 Viareggio, Lucca ☎(0584) 50301 ▣501031 ▣(0584) 55181
▥ 68 rms, all with bathrm ▤ ▣ ▥ ▤ ▣ ▣ ▣ ▣ ‡ ▣ ▣ ▣ ▣ ◟ ▣ ▣ ▣ ▣
This attractive ultramodern luxury hotel offers every possible comfort and convenience, including a health center, solarium and heated indoor swimming pool. There are also 14 service apartments with private roof terraces.

IL PATRIARCA
Viale Carducci 79 ☎(0584) 53126 ▥ to ▥ ▣ ▣ ▣ ▣ ▣ ▣ ▣ ▣ ▣ ▣ ▣ ▣ ▣
Closed Wed in winter.
One of the super-smart restaurants of the Versilia. Good soups, risottos, *baccalà*.

ROMANO
Via Mazzini 120 ☎(0584) 31382 ▥ ▣ ▣ ▣ ▣ ▣ ▣ ▣ ▣ *Closed Mon.*
Already a pilgrimage restaurant for connoisseurs of fish, Romano seems to get better and better. Specialties include *zuppa di calamaretti* and *rombo al forno con patate*. But everything is simply, although often unexpectedly, prepared and elegantly presented.

▣   Restaurants also suggested: **Margherita** *(Lungomare Margherita 30* ☎*(0584) 962553* ▥ ▣ ▣ ▣ ▣ *closed Wed);* **Montecatini** *(Viale Manin 8* ☎*(0584) 962129* ▣ ▥ ▣ ▣ ▣ ▣ *closed Mon).* And there are two less expensive wine bars: **La Taverna dell'Assassino** *(Viale Manin 1* ☎*(0584) 45001, closed Wed)* and **Il Punto di Vino** *(Via Mazzini 229* ☎*(0584)43357, closed Mon, Nov).*

VINCI
Map **14E5**. *43km (27 miles) w of Florence. 55009. Firenze. Population: 13,577.*
Leonardo's birthplace is on Monte Albano, N of EMPOLI.

MUSEO LEONARDIANO
Open daily 9.30am-noon, 2.30-6pm ▣
The town has dedicated rooms in its restored 13thC *castello* to a small museum about its famous son, displaying models made from his designs.

NEARBY SIGHTS

At **Anchiano**, 3km (2 miles) to the N, is the farmhouse where Leonardo may have spent his childhood *(open 9.30am-noon, 2.30-6pm; closed Wed)*. It is in a ravishing setting amid olive groves.

Beyond Lamporecchio, 7km (4½ miles) NW, is the unfinished **Villa Rospigliosi**, designed by Bernini in 1669 for Pope Clement IX. 7km (4½ miles) SW at Cerreto Guidi is the 16thC **Villa Medicea** *(open summer 9am-6pm, winter 9am-5pm; Sun 9am-1pm; closed Mon)*, which houses a museum and is approached by impressive ramps designed by Buontalenti.

The drive N from Vinci over Monte Albano to PISTOIA is spectacularly beautiful.

See ARTIMINO and LASTRA A SIGNA.

VOLTERRA ★

Map 9F4. 81km (50 miles) SW of Florence, 57km (35 miles) W of Siena. 56048. Pisa. Population: 14,911 i *Via Turazza 2* ☎*(0588) 86150.*

Volterra was the northernmost and one of the most powerful of the federated Etruscan city states. Its name was Velathri, it was three times the size of the present town, and it controlled a territory stretching from Pisa to Populonia and from the sea inland as far as the Pesa valley. 522m (1,712ft) above sea-level and protected by 7km (4½ miles) of walls that were in places 12m (39ft) high, it became a prosperous Roman municipality in the 4thC BC, but supported Marius against Sulla in the civil war and was conquered by the latter in 82-80BC.

During the Middle Ages, Volterra's struggle against the ecclesiastic lords for communal independence was bitter and protracted but, in the 13thC, successful. Although taken under the "protection" of Florence from the mid-14thC the Republic of Volterra remained technically independent until 1470. This was when Lorenzo de' Medici, desperate to safeguard the crucial Florentine rights to alum mining in Volterra's territory, hired the Duke of Urbino to invade the city. The brutality of the siege remained one of the few blots on Lorenzo's diplomatic career; one of his would-be assassins in the Pazzi Conspiracy 8 years later was Volterran.

Lorenzo built a new fortress, known as the Fortezza Nuova or *"Il Maschio"* (now a prison) and fortified the old 14thC tower, the Fortezza Vecchia or *"La Femmina"*. The city waited in the shadow of these loathed symbols of foreign domination until the final and futile rebellion of 1530, which was quickly subdued by the Florentine general Federigo Ferrucci.

Many travelers have remarked on the uncanny atmosphere of Volterra, where a chill wind can spring up from nowhere on the balmiest summer day, and where the hill on which the town stands has sheered off, forming the cliffs, the *Balze,* to the NE, and carrying parts of the Etruscan city with them. D.H. Lawrence saw the city "that gets all the wind and sees all the world" as "a sort of inland island, still curiously isolated, and grim."

It is certainly very much its own place. Unlike its neighbor and traditional enemy SAN GIMIGNANO, Volterra does not primp for tourists. The inhabitants are courteous, but there is about them an air of brooding energy that can prompt the fancy, especially when the wind is high, that Volterra is still waiting, and for something more important than tourists.

Meanwhile, the town is economically if not politically independent.

The quarrying and carving of alabaster is the chief occupation. There are dozens of shops selling objects made of alabaster. The central outlet and information center is the **Cooperativa Artieri Alabastro** *(Piazza dei Priori 2* ☎ *(0588) 87590).*

SIGHTS AND PLACES OF INTEREST

The medieval city is contained within 13thC walls. The views, on a clear day, extend to the mountains below CARRARA, to Corsica and inland to MONTE AMIATA and the Casentino.

The parking lot nearest the central Piazza dei Priori, the main square, is in Piazza Martiri della Libertà, the s entrance to the town. The following itineraries assume a day's visit, half devoted to the medieval town and half to the remains of the Etruscan city and to visiting the *Balze.*

DUOMO ▥ †

The simple facade is 12thC, adapted to the Pisan style in the 13thC. The interior, altered in the 16thC, has an attractive painted wooden ceiling. In the right transept is a polychrome wooden *Deposition* (1228), an unusual larger-than-life-size folk-Romanesque scene made by Pisan sculptors, more religious theater than art. Over the high altar is Mino da Fiesole's exquisite **ciborium** (1471), flanked by his two charming *Angels* resting on 12thC twisted columns. In the left aisle is the **pulpit**, remade from 12thC carvings, and an *Annunciation* (1497) by Albertinelli.

In the chapel off the entrance to the nave, two niches contain 15thC polychrome terra-cotta groups by Zacchi Zaccaria of the *Epiphany* (right) and *Nativity* (left). The background to the *Nativity* is Gozzoli's delightful panoramic fresco of the *Magi.* Inside the 13thC **Baptistry** is a **baptismal font** (1502) by A. Sansovino.

MUSEO DI ARTE SACRA

Via Roma.

A display of architectural fragments, sculptures, reliquaries and paintings, next to the Duomo. Notice particularly A. della Robbia's bust of *St Linus,* the silver bust of *St Octavian* by A. Pollaiuolo, and a gilded bronze *Crucifix* by Giambologna.

MUSEO ETRUSCO GUARNACCI ★

Via Don Minzoni 15 ▨ *Open daily summer 9.30am-6.30pm; winter 9am-2pm.*

This is one of the largest and most important Etruscan collections outside Florence and Rome. There are some 600 cinerary urns in tufa, alabaster or terra cotta, dating from the 6th-1stC BC. For D.H. Lawrence these urns were like "an open book of life;" for scholars they show Etruscan beliefs about the afterlife. They are arranged according to subject matter of the carvings. In Rm. 24 on the first floor is the tiny Giacometti-like *Ombra della Sera* and other Etruscan bronze votives.

PIAZZA DEI PRIORI ★

The central square retains its character thanks partly to some modern imitations of the medieval architecture. On the sw side is the **Palazzo dei Priori** (1208-54), now the town hall and the oldest civic building in Tuscany; on its lower facade are the terra-cotta emblems of the 15-16thC Florentine commissioners. The **Bishop's Palace** next to it was originally the town granary. The **Palazzo Pretorio**, on the NE side, is a 13thC complex but much restored; its crenelated tower, adapted in the early 16thC, is known as the *porcellino* (piglet).

PINACOTECA CIVICA

Via Sarti ▨ *Open daily summer 9.30am-6.30pm; winter 9.30am-1pm.*

The 15thC Palazzo Minucci-Sarti houses a collection of 14th-17thC Florentine and Sienese pictures by, among others, D. Ghirlandaio and Signorelli; but the museum is worth visiting if only for Rosso Fiorentino's vivid, whirling *Deposition* (1521) (★).

QUADRIVIO DEI BUOMPARENTI

The intersection of Via Roma with Via Ricciarelli and Buomparenti is the most picturesque corner of the town. The 13thC tower-houses have remained remarkably intact.

SAN FRANCESCO †

The **Cappella della Croce di Giorno** is entirely covered with frescoes of the *Legend of the True Cross* (1410) by Cenni di Francesco Cenni.

✿ NAZIONALE

Via dei Marchesi 11, 56048 Volterra, Pisa ☎(0588) 86284 ▢ *36 rms, all with bathrm* ⌂
🚅 🔳 🔳 🈁 ⌂ ⟨⟨ ⟨ ⟩ 🖂 ⚓ ⟨⟨

"The hotel is simple and somewhat rough, but quite friendly, pleasant in its haphazard way." D.H. Lawrence's description of 1927 still fits.

✿   **Villa Nencini** (*Borgo S. Stefano 55* ☎(0588) 86386 ▢ 🔳 🈁 ⟨⟨ ⚓).

🚅   A local favorite is **Da Badò** (*Borgo S. Lazzero 9* ☎(0588) 86477; *open lunch only; closed Wed, mid July-mid Sept*). Also **Da Beppino** (*Via delle Prigioni 15-19* ☎(0588) 86051 ▢ 🔳 🔳 🔳 🈁 *closed Wed*). Or try **Etruria** (*Piazza dei Priori 8* ☎(0588) 86064 ▢ 🔳 🔳 🔳 🈁 *closed Thurs, mid-June, Nov*), which is on the main square.

SUGGESTED WALKS

WALK 1: ETRUSCAN AND ROMAN VOLTERRA

Just to the w of Piazza Martiri della Libertà is the **Arco Etrusco**, the s entrance to the Etruscan city. The uprights and bases on the inner side are Etruscan; the archivolt was rebuilt by the Romans who reincorporated the three Etruscan heads. Via Porto dell'Arco lies on the cardinal axis of the Etruscan-Roman city which continues with Via Matteotti, lined with medieval tower-houses, and into Via Guarnacci, which was the site of part of the Roman Forum.

Turn left into Via Lungo le Mura del Mandorlo, which overlooks the **Roman Theater** (1stC BC) and **Baths** (3rdC BC). Beyond the Porta Fiorentina, the pretty Via Diana leads to the Porta Diana, the N Etruscan gate of which only fragments survive. Beyond is the site of the **Necropoli del Portone**. The empty underground tombs are mostly unmarked, but some, in the middle of a farm, are signposted *Ipogei dei Marmini.*

WALK 2: TO THE BALZE

Start at the church of San Francesco; the *Balze* are 2km (1¼ miles) by foot from Porta S. Francesco. Taking Borgo S. Stefano, turn left under Vicolo della Penera, then sharp right behind the hand railings. You will find a path running along the base of the stretch of the **Etruscan walls** known as the Mura Etrusche di S. Chiara, which in summer are festooned with flowering capers, to the **Balze**, the cliffs formed by repeated landslides.

The views to the w are superb, and on a peaceful summer midday when the scent of broom is sweet and strong, one may wonder at Augustus Hare's description of the Balze as "an arid and ghastly desert." But if you go just before sunset you could share his vertiginous apprehension "that the flowery surface on which you are standing may be hurled into destruction tomorrow."

Words and phrases

A guide to Italian

This glossary covers the basic language needs of the traveler: for essential vocabulary and simple conversation, finding accommodations, visiting the bank, shopping and using public transportation or a car. There is also a special menu decoder, explaining all the most common descriptions of food terms.

REFERENCE WORDS

Monday	*lunedì*	Friday	*venerdì*
Tuesday	*martedì*	Saturday	*sabato*
Wednesday	*mercoledì*	Sunday	*domenica*
Thursday	*giovedì*		

January	*gennaio*	July	*luglio*
February	*febbraio*	August	*agosto*
March	*marzo*	September	*settembre*
April	*aprile*	October	*ottobre*
May	*maggio*	November	*novembre*
June	*giugno*	December	*dicembre*

1	*uno*	12	*dodici*	30	*trenta*
2	*due*	13	*tredici*	40	*quaranta*
3	*tre*	14	*quattordici*	50	*cincuanta*
4	*quattro*	15	*quindici*	60	*sessanta*
5	*cinque*	16	*sedici*	70	*settanta*
6	*sei*	17	*diciassette*	80	*ottanta*
7	*sette*	18	*diciotto*	90	*novanta*
8	*otto*	19	*diciannove*	100	*cento*
9	*nove*	20	*venti*	200	*duecento*
10	*dieci*	21	*ventuno*	1,000	*mille*
11	*undici*	22	*ventidue*	2,000	*duemila*

1992/93/94   *millenovecento novantadue/tre/quattro*

First	*primo, -a*	Fourth	*quarto, -a*
Second	*secondo, -a*	One o'clock	*l'una*
Third	*terzo, -a*	Six o'clock	*le sei*

Quarter-past....	....*e un quarto*	Quarter to....	....*meno un quarto*
Half-past....	....*e mezzo*		

Mr	*signor(e)*	Ladies	*signore, donne*
Mrs	*signora*	Gents	*signori, uomini*
Miss	*signorina*		

BASIC COMMUNICATION

Yes *sì*
No *no*
Please *per favore/per piacere*
Thank you *grazie*
I'm very sorry *mi dispiace molto/mi scusi*
Excuse me *senta!* (to attract attention), *permesso!* (on bus, train, etc.), *mi scusi*
Not at all/you're welcome *prego*
Hello *ciao* (familiar), *pronto* (on telephone)
Good morning *buon giorno*
Good afternoon *buona sera*
Good evening *buona sera*
Good night *buona notte*
Goodbye *ciao* (familiar), *addio* (final or familiar), *arrivederci*
Morning *mattino*
Afternoon *pomeriggio*
Evening *sera*
Night *notte* (f)
Yesterday *ieri*
Today *oggi*
Tomorrow *domani*
Next week *la settimana prossima*
Last week *la settimana scorsa*
....days ago ....*giorni fa*
Month *mese* (m)
Year *anno*
Here *qui*
There *lì*
Big *grande*
Small *piccolo, -a*
Hot *caldo, -a*
Cold *freddo, -a*
Good *buono, -a*

Bad *cattivo, -a*
Beautiful *bello, -a*
Well *bene*
Badly *male*
With *con*
And *e, ed*
But *ma*
Very *molto*
All *tutto, -a*
Open *aperto*
Closed *chiuso*
Entrance *entrata*
Exit *uscita*
Free *libero*
On the left *a sinistra*
On the right *a destra*
Straight ahead *diritto*
Near *vicino*
Far *lontano*
Up *su*
Down *giù*
Early *presto*
Late *tardi*
Quickly *presto*
Pleased to meet you. *Molto lieto/piacere.*
How are you? *Come sta?*
Very well, thank you. *Benissimo, grazie.*
Do you speak English? *Parla inglese?*
I don't understand. *Non capisco.*
I don't know. *Non lo so.*
Please explain. *Può spiegare per favore.*
Please speak more slowly. *Parli più lentamente per favore.*
My name is.... *Mi chiamo....*

293

I am American/English. *Sono americano/inglese, -a.*

Where is/are....? *Dov'e/dove si trova/dove sono....?*

Is there a....? *C'è un, una....?*

What? *Cosa?*

When? *Quando?*

How much? *Quanto?*

That's too much. *È troppo caro.*

Expensive *caro*

Cheap *a buon mercato*

I would like.... *Vorrei....*

Do you have....? *Avete....?*

Just a minute. *Un momento.*

That's fine/OK. *Va bene/benissimo/OK*

What time is it? *Che ore sono?*

I don't feel well. *Non mi sento bene/sto male.*

ACCOMMODATIONS

Making a reservation by letter

Dear Sir/Madam, *Egregio Signore/Signora,*
I would like to reserve one double room *Vorrei prenotare una camera doppia* (with bathroom) *(con bagno)* — a twin-bedded room *una camera con due letti* — and one single room (with shower) *e una camera singola (con doccia)* for 7 nights from August 12 *per 7 notti dal 12 agosto.*

We would like bed and breakfast/half board/full board *Vorremmo una camera con colazione/mezza pensione/ pensione completa* and would prefer rooms with a sea view. *e possibilmente camere con vista sul mare.*

Please send me details of your terms with the confirmation. *Sarei lieto di ricevere dettagli del prezzo e la conferma.*

Yours sincerely, *Cordi ali saluti,*

Arriving at the hotel

I have a reservation. My name is....
Ho già prenotato. Sono il signor/la signora....
A quiet room with bath/shower/WC/wash basin
Una camera tranquilla con bagno/doccia/WC/lavandino
....overlooking the sea/park/street/the back.
....con vista sul mare/sul parco/sulla strada/sul retro
Does the price include breakfast/tax/service?
E'tutto compreso/colazione/tasse/servizio?
This room is too large/small/cold/hot/noisy.
Questa camera è troppo grande/piccola/fredda/calda/rumorosa.
That's too expensive. Have you anything cheaper?
Costa troppo. Avete qualcosa meno caro?

Floor/story *piano*
Dining room/restaurant *sala da pranzo/ristorante* (m)
Manager *direttore, -trice*
Porter *portiere*

Have you got a room? *Avete una camera?*
What time is breakfast/dinner? *A che ora è la prima colazione/la cena?*
Is there a laundry service? *C'e il servizio lavanderia?*
What time does the hotel close? *A che ora chiude l'albergo?*
Will I need a key? *Avrò bisogno della chiave?*
Is there a night porter? *C'è un portiere di notte?*
I'll be leaving tomorrow morning. *Parto domani mattina.*
Please give me a call at.... *Mi può chiamare alle....*
Come in! *Avanti!*

SHOPPING (LA SPESA)

Where is the nearest/a good....? *Dov'è il più vicino/la più vicina....? Dov'è un buon/una buona....?*
Can you help me/show me....? *Mi può aiutare/Può mostrarmi....?*
I'm just looking. *Sto soltanto guardando.*
Do you accept credit cards/travelers checks? *Accettate carte di credito/travelers checks?*
Can you deliver to....? *Può consegnare a....?*
I'll take it. *Lo prendo.*
I'll leave it. *Lo lascio.*
Can I have it tax-free for export? *Posso averlo senza tasse per l'esportazione?*
This is faulty. Can I have a replacement/refund? *C'è difetto. Me lo potrebbe cambiare/rimborsare?*
I don't want to spend more than.... *Non voglio spendere più di....*
Can I have a stamp for....? *Vorrei un francobollo per....*

Shops

Antique store *negozio di antiquariato*
Art gallery *galleria d'arte*
Bakery *panificio, forno*
Bank *banca*
Beauty parlor *istituto di bellezza*
Bookstore *libreria*
Butcher *macelleria*
Cake shop *pasticceria*
Clothes store *negozio di abbigliamento, di confezioni*
Dairy *latteria*
Delicatessen *salumeria, pizzicheria*
Fish store *pescheria*
Florist *fioraio*

Greengrocer *ortolano, erbivendolo, fruttivendolo*
Grocer *drogheria*
Haberdasher *merciaio*
Hairdresser *parrucchiere, -a*
Jeweler *gioielleria*
Market *mercato*
Newsstand *giornalaio, edicola (kiosk)*
Optician *ottico*
Perfumery *profumeria*
Pharmacy/drugstore *farmacia*
Photographic store *negozio fotografico*
Post office *ufficio postale*
Shoe store *negozio di calzature*
Stationers *cartoleria*
Supermarket *supermercato*

Tailor   *sarto*
Tobacconist   *tabaccheria* (also sells stamps)

Tourist office   *ente del turismo*
Toy store   *negozio di giocattoli*
Travel agent   *agenzia di viaggio*

At the bank
I would like to change some dollars/pounds/travelers checks
Vorrei cambiare dei dollari/delle sterline/dei travelers checks
What is the exchange rate?
Com'è il cambio?
Can you cash a personal check?
Può cambiare un assegno?
Can I obtain cash with this charge/credit card?
Posso avere soldi in contanti con questa carta di credito?
Do you need to see my passport?
Ha bisogno del mio passaporto?

From the pharmacy
Antiseptic cream   *crema antisettica*
Aspirin   *aspirina*
Bandages   *fasciature*
Band-Aid, sticking plaster   *cerotto*
Cotton (wool)   *cotone idrofilo* (m)
Diarrhea/upset stomach pills   *pillole anti-coliche*
Indigestion tablets   *pillole per l'indigestione*
Insect repellant   *insettifugo*
Laxative   *lassativo*
Sanitary napkins   *assorbenti igienici*

Shampoo   *shampoo*
Shaving cream   *crema da barba*
Soap   *sapone* (m)
Sunburn cream   *crema antisolare*
Sunglasses   *occhiali da sole*
Suntan cream/oil   *crema/olio solare*
Tampons   *tamponi*
Tissues   *fazzoletti di carta*
Toothbrush   *spazzolino da denti*
Toothpaste   *dentifricio*
Travel sickness pills   *pillole contro il mal di viaggio*

Clothing
Bra   *reggiseno*
Coat   *cappotto*
Dress   *vestito*
Jacket   *giacca*
Pullover   *maglione* (m)
Shirt   *camicia*
Shoes   *scarpe*

Skirt   *gonna*
Stockings/tights   *calze/collants*
Swimsuit   *costume da bagno* (m)
Trousers   *pantaloni*
Underpants   *mutande*

Miscellanous goods
Film   *pellicola*
Letter   *lettera*
Money order   *vaglia*

Postcard   *cartolina*
Stamp   *francobollo*
Telegram   *telegramma* (m)

DRIVING

Service station   *stazione di rifornimento* (f), *distributore* (m)
Fill it up.   *Faccia il pieno, per favore.*
Give me.... lire worth.   *Mi dia.... lire.*
I would like.... liters of gasoline.   *Vorrei.... litri di benzina.*
Can you check the....?   *Può controllare....?*
There is something wrong with the....   *C'e un difetto nel/nella....*

Accelerator *acceleratore* (m)	Gear box *la scatola del cambio*
Axle *l'asse* (m)	Lights *fanali, fari, luci*
Battery *batteria*	Oil *olio*
Brakes *freni*	Spares *i pezzi di ricambio*
Exhaust *lo scarico,* *scappamento*	Spark plugs *le candele*
	Tires *gomme*
Fan belt *la cinghia del* *ventilatore*	Water *acqua*
	Windshield *parabrezza* (m)

My car won't start.   *La mia macchina non s'accende.*
My car has broken down/had a flat tire.   *La macchina è guasta/la gomma è forata.*
The engine is overheating.   *Il motore si scalda.*
How long will it take to repair?   *Quanto tempo ci vorrà per la riparazione?*
I need it as soon as possible.   *Ne ho bisogno il più presto possibile.*

Car rental

Where can I rent a car?   *Dove posso noleggiare una macchina?*
Is full/comprehensive insurance included?   *E'completamente assicurata?*
Is it insured for another driver?   *E'assicurata per un altro guidatore?*
Does the price include mileage?   *Il kilometraggio è compreso?*
Unlimited mileage   *kilometraggio illimitato*
Deposit   *deposito*
By what time must I return it?   *A che ora devo consegnarla?*
Can I return it to another depot?   *Posso riportarla ad un altro deposito?*
Is the gas tank full?   *E'il serbatoio pieno?*

Road signs

Accendere le luci in galleria lights on in tunnel
Autostrada 4-lane highway, motorway
Caduta di massi falling stones
Casello toll gate
Dare la precedenza yield, give way

Divieto di accesso, senso vietato no entry
Divieto di parcheggio no parking
Divieto di sorpasso no passing
Divieto di sosta no stopping
Lavori in corso road repairs ahead

297

Passaggio a livello   level crossing
Pedaggio   toll road
Raccordo anulare   beltway, ring road
Rallentare   slow down

Senso unico   one-way street
Tangenziale   bypass
Tenersi in corsia   keep in lane
Uscita (autocarri)   exit (for trucks)

OTHER METHODS OF TRANSPORTATION

Aircraft   *aeroplano*
Airport   *aeroporto*
Bus   *autobus* (m)
Bus stop   *fermata*
Coach   *corriera*
Ferry/boat   *traghetto*
Ferry port   *porto*
Hovercraft   *aliscafo*
Station   *stazione* (f)
Train   *treno*

ticket   *biglietto*
Ticket office   *biglietteria*
One-way, single   *andata*
Round trip, return   *andata e ritorno*
Half fare   *metà prezzo*
First/second/economy   *prima classe/seconda classe/turistico*
Sleeper/couchette   *cuccetta*

When is the next.... for....?   *Quando parte il prossimo.... per....?*
What time does it arrive?   *A che ora arriva?*
What time does the last.... for.... leave?   *Quando parte l'ultimo.... per....?*
Which track (platform)/quay/gate?   *Quale binario/molo/uscita?*
Is this the.... for....?   *E'questo il.... per....?*
Is it direct? Where does it stop?   *E'diretto? Dove si ferma?*
Do I need to change anywhere?   *Devo cambiare?*
Please tell me where to get off.   *Mi può dire dove devo scendere.*
Take me to....   *Mi vuol portare a....*
Is there a dining car?   *C'è un vagone ristorante?*

FOOD AND DRINK

Have you a table for....?   *Avete un tavolo per....?*
I want to reserve a table for...., at....   *Vorrei prenotare un tavolo per.... alle....*
A quiet table.   *Un tavolo tranquillo.*
A table near the window.   *Un tavolo vicino alla finestra.*
Could we have another table?   *Potremmo spostarci?*
I did not order this.   *Non ho ordinato questo.*
Breakfast/lunch/dinner   *prima colazione/pranzo/cena*
Bring me another.... please.   *Un altro.... per favore.*
The bill please.   *Il conto per favore.*
Is service included?   *Il servizio è incluso?*

Hot   *caldo*
Cold   *freddo*
Glass   *bicchiere* (m)
Bottle   *bottiglia*

Half-bottle   *mezza bottiglia*
Beer/lager (draft)   *birra (alla spina)*
Fruit juice   *succo di frutta*

Mineral water   *acqua minerale*
Orangeade/lemonade
  aranciata/ limonata
Carbonated/noncarbonated
  gassata/non gassata
Flask/carafe   *fiasco/caraffa*
Red wine   *vino rosso, vino nero*
White wine   *vino bianco*
Rosé wine   *vino rosé*
Vintage   *di annata*
Dry   *secco*
Sweet   *dolce, amabile*
Salt   *sale* (m)
Pepper   *pepe* (m)
Oil   *olio*

Vinegar   *aceto*
Mustard   *senape* (f)
Bread   *pane* (m)
Butter   *burro*
Cheese   *formaggio*
Milk   *latte* (m)
Coffee   *caffè* (m)
Tea   *tè* (m)
Chocolate   *cioccolato*
Sugar   *zucchero*
Steak   *bistecca*
  well done   *ben cotto*
  medium   *medio*
  rare   *al sangue*

Menu decoder

Abbacchio   baby lamb
Acciughe   anchovies
Acqua cotta   thick bread and
  vegetable soup with egg
Affettati   sliced cold meats
Affumicato   smoked
Aglio   garlic
Agnello   lamb
Agnolotti   pasta envelopes
Agro   sour
Albicocche   apricots
Amaro   bitter
Ananas   pineapple
Anatra/anitra   duck
Anguilla   eel
Animelle   sweetbreads
Antipasto   hors d'oeuvre
Aragosta   langouste,
  lobster
Arancia   orange
Aringa   herring
Arrosto   roast meat
Arselle   baby clams
Asparagi   asparagus
Baccalà   dried salt cod
Basilico   basil
Bianchetti   whitebait
Bianco   plain, boiled
Bietola   Swiss chard
Biscottini di Prato   small, hard
  almond biscuits

Bistecca alla fiorentina   grilled
  T-bone steak
Bollito misto   boiled meats
Brace (alla)   charcoal grilled
Braciola   chop
Branzino   sea bass
Bresaola   dried salt beef
Brodetto   fish soup
Brodo   consommé
Bruschetta   garlic bread
Burrida   fish stew
Burro (al)   (cooked in) butter
Cacciagione   game
Cacciucco   fish stew
Calamaretti   baby squid
Calamari   squid
Calzone   half-moon-shaped
  pizza
Cannelloni   stuffed pasta tubes
Capitone   large conger eel
Cappelletti   stuffed pasta hats
Capperi   capers
Cappe sante   scallops
Capretto   kid
Carciofi alla giudia   artichokes
  fried in oil and lemon
Carne   meat
Carote   carrots
Carpa   carp
Carpaccio   raw lean beef fillet
Carrello (al)   from the trolley

299

Casa (della) of the restaurant
Cassalingo, -a homemade
Castagnaccio chestnut cake
Castagne chestnuts
Castrato mutton
Cavolfiore cauliflower
Cavolini di Bruxelles sprouts
Cavolo cabbage
Ceci chick peas
Cenci fried pastry twists
Cervella brains
Cervo venison
Cetriolo cucumber
Cicoria chicory
Ciliege cherries
Cima cold stuffed veal
Cinghiale wild boar
Cipolle onions
Cocomero watermelon
Coda di bue oxtail
Coniglio rabbit
Contorno vegetable side-dish
Controfiletto sirloin steak
Coppa cooked pressed neck of pork or an ice cream sundae
Cosciotto di agnello leg of lamb
Costata di bue entrecôte steak
Costolette cutlets
Cotto cooked
Cozze mussels
Crema custard, cream soup
Crespolini savory pancakes
Crostacei shellfish
Crostini small savory toasts
Crudo raw
Diavola (alla) in a spicy sauce
Dolci desserts, sweets
Espresso small black coffee
Fagiano pheasant
Fagioli all'uccelletto beans with tomatoes and garlic
Fagiolini French beans
Faraona guinea fowl
Farcito stuffed
Fatto in casa homemade
Fave broad beans
Fegatini chicken livers
Fegato liver
Ferri (ai) grilled

Fesa di vitello leg of veal
Fettina slice
Fettuccine thin flat pasta
Fettunta garlic bread
Fichi figs
Filetto fillet
Finocchio fennel
Finocchiona fennel-flavored salami
Focaccia dimpled savory bread
Formaggio cheese
Forno (al) cooked in the oven
Fragole strawberries
Fresco fresh
Frittata omelet
Frittelle fritters
Fritto fried
Frutta fruit
Frutti di mare shellfish
Funghi mushrooms
Gamberetti shrimps
Gamberi big prawns
Gelato ice cream
Giorno (del) of the day
Girarrosto (al) spit-roasted
Girello topside of beef
Gnocchi small pasta dumplings
Grana Parmesan cheese
Granchio crab
Granita water ice
Gran'pezzo roast sirloin of young beef
Graticola (alla) grilled
Griglia (alla) grilled
Indivia endive
Insalata salad
Involtini skewered veal and ham
Lamponi raspberries
Lampreda lamprey
Lasagne baked flat pasta
Lenticchie lentils
Lepre hare
Lesso boiled (meat)
Limone lemon
Lingua di bue ox tongue
Lombata, -ina loin, loin chop
Lonza cured fillet of pork
Luccio pike

Lumache snails
Macedonia di frutta fruit salad
Magro lean
Maiale pork
Mandorle almonds
Manzo beef
Marmellata jam
Medaglioni rounds of meat
Mela apple
Melagrana pomegranate
Melanzane eggplant, aubergine
Melone melon
Merluzzo cod
Miele honey
Minestra soup
Minestrone vegetable soup
Misto mixed
Mostarda pickle
Muscolo alla fiorentina beef casserole with beans
Naturale (al) plain
Nocciole hazelnuts
Noci nuts
Nodino di vitello veal chop
Nostrale, nostrano local
Oca goose
Orata gilt-head bream
Osso buco veal knuckle
Ostriche oysters
Paglia e fieno green and white tagliatelle
Paillard thin grilled steak
Palombo dogfish
Panforte di Siena hard cake with honey, fruit and almonds
Panino imbottito roll
Panna cream
Panzanella salad of soaked bread and fresh vegetables
Pappa al pomodoro thick tomato and bread soup
Pappardelle long flat pasta
Passato purée
Pasta e fagioli bean and pasta soup
Pasticcio layered pasta pie
Pasto meal
Patate potatoes

Pecorino hard ewes' milk cheese
Penne all'arrabbiata short pasta tubes with a fiery sauce
Peperoni sweet peppers
Pera pear
Pernice partridge
Pesca peach
Pesce fish
Pesce persico perch
Pesce spada swordfish
Pesciolini small fry
Pesto green basil sauce
Petto di pollo chicken breast
Pezzo piece
Piacere according to taste
Piatto del giorno today's dish
Piccante spicy, piquant
Piccata thin escalope
Piccione pigeon
Pinzimonio oily vegetable dip
Piselli peas
Polenta maize porridge
Pollame poultry
Pollo chicken
Polpette meatballs
Polpettone meatloaf
Polpo octopus
Pomodoro tomato
Pompelmo grapefruit
Porchetta roast sucking pig
Primizie spring vegetables
Prosciutto ham
Prugne plums
Quaglie quails
Radicchio red bitter lettuce
Ragù meat and tomato sauce
Rane frogs
Ravanelli radishes
Ravioli stuffed pasta squares
Razza skate
Ribollita thick vegetable soup
Ricciarelli almond biscuits
Ricotta cheese — similar to cottage cheese
Rigatoni ridged pasta tubes
Ripieno stuffed
Risi e bisi pea and rice soup
Riso rice

Risotto   savory rice dish
Rognoni   kidneys
Rombo maggiore   turbot
Rosmarino   rosemary
Rospo (coda di)   (tail of) angler fish
Salsa (verde)   (green) sauce
Salsiccia   sausage
Saltimbocca alla romana   veal escalopes with ham and sage
Salumi   cold cuts
Salvia   sage
Sarde   sardines
Scaloppine   escalopes
Scelta (a)   of your choice
Schiacciata alla fiorentina   unleavened Lenten cake
Scottadito   grilled lamb cutlets
Selvaggina   game, venison
Semifreddo   frozen dessert
Semplice   plain
Seppie   cuttlefish
Sgombro   mackerel
Sogliola   sole
Sottaceti   pickled vegetables
Spaghetti all'amatriciana   spaghetti with bacon and tomatoes
   alla bolognese   with *ragù*
   alla carbonara   with bacon and eggs
   alla napoletana   with tomato
Spezzatino   meat stew
Spiedini   skewers, kebabs
Spiedo (allo)   on the spit
Spigola   sea bass
Spinaci   spinach
Squadro   anglerfish, monkfish
Stagionato   hung, well-aged
Stagione (di)   in season

Stoccafisso   stockfish
Stracciatella   clear egg soup
Stracotto   beef in red wine
Stufato   braised, stew(ed)
Sugo   sauce
Supplì   rice croquettes
Susina   plum
Tacchino   turkey
Tagliatelle   thin flat pasta
Tartufi   truffles
Tegame (al)   fried or baked
Telline   cockles
Timballo   savory pasta pie
Tinca   tench
Tonno   tuna
Tordi   thrushes
Torta   flan, tart
Tortellini   small stuffed pasta
Tost   toasted sandwich
Totano   squid
Tramezzino   sandwich
Trancia   slice
Trenette   flat, thinnish pasta
Trifolato   fried in garlic
Triglia   red mullet
Trippa   tripe
Trota   trout
Uccelletti   grilled beef on skewers
Umido (in)   stewed
Uova   eggs
Uva   grapes
Verdure   green vegetables
Vitello   veal
Vongole   clams
Zabaglione   egg yolks and Marsala whip
Zucchini   courgette
Zuccotto   ice cream liqueur cake
Zuppa   soup
Zuppa inglese   trifle

Index

Page numbers in **bold** refer to main entries. *Italic* numbers refer to illustrations and maps. The GENERAL INDEX begins on page 306.

INDEX OF PLACE NAMES

List of Florence street names

All streets mentioned in this book that fall within the area covered by our maps of Florence are listed below. Map numbers are printed in **bold** type. Some smaller streets are not named on the maps, but the map reference given here will help you locate the correct neighborhood.

Acciaioli, Lung., **3D3**
Albizi, Borgo d., **4C5-6**
Alfani, V. d., **4A5-B6**
Alfieri, V. V., **2B5-C5**
Amerigo Vespucci, Lung., **1C2-3**
Antinori, Pza., **3C3**
Aprile, XXVII, V., **2B4**
Archibusieri, Lung., **4D4**
Ardiglione, V. d., **1D3**
Arte della Lana, V. d., **4C4**
Azeglio, Pza. M. d', **2C5**

Barbadori, V., **3E3**
Bardi, V. d., **3E3-4F4**
Bartolini, V., **1C2**
Beccaria, Pza., **2C6**
Belle Donne, V. d., **3B2-C3**
Benci, V. d., **4E5-D5**
Bolognese, V., **6C4**
Borgognissanti, **3C1-2**

Caldaie, V. d., **3E1**
Calimala, V., **4C4**
Calzaiuoli, V. d., **4C4**
Campidoglio, V., **3C3**
Canto dei Nelli, V. d., **2C4**
Carmine, Pza. d., **1D2**
Cavalleggeri, Pza., **2D5**
Cavour, V., **2C4-A5**
Cerretani, V. d., **3B3**
Cesare Battisti, V., **2B4**
Cimatori, Pza. d., **4C4**
Cimatori, V. d., **4C4**
Ciompi, Pza. d., **2C5**
Colonna, V., **2B5-C5**
Condotta, V., **4D4**
Corsini, Lung., **3C2-D2**
Corso, V. d., **4C4**
Coverelli, V. d., **3D2**

Dante Alighieri, V., **4C4**
Davanzati, Pza., **3D3**
Donatello, Pza., **2B4**
Duomo, Pza. d., **4B4-C4**

Erta Canina, V. d., **2E4**

Farine, V. d., **4D4**
Farini, L.C., V., **2C5**
Ferrucci, Pza., **2D6-E6**
Fiesolana, V., **2C5**
Filippo Strozzi, V., **1B3**
Fonderia, V. d., **1C1-2**
Fossi, V. d., **3C2**
Fratelli Rosselli, V., **1B2**
Frescobaldi, Pza., **3D2**

Galileo, Pza., **1F3**
Galileo Galilei, V., **2F4-E5**
Generale Diaz, Lung., **4E4-5**
Ghibellina, V., **4C5-D6**
Ginori, V. d., **4B4-A4**
Girolami, Volta d., **4D4**
Giudici, Pza. d., **4E4**
Giusti, V., **2B5-C5**
Goldoni, Pza., **3C2**
Gondi, V. d., **4D4**
Greci, Borgo d., **4D5**
Guelfa, V., **1B3-2B4**
Guicciardini, Lung., **3D2**
Guicciardini, V., **1D3**
Giuseppe Poggi, Pza., **2D5**

Il Prato, V., **1B2-C2**
Indipendenza, Pza., **2B4**
Isola delle Stinche, V., **4D5**
Italia, Corso, **1C2**

Jacopo da Diacceto, V., **1B2-B3**

Lambertesca, V., **4D4**
Lamberti, V. d., **3C3-4C4**
Laura, V., **2B5-C5**
La Pira, V., **2B4**
Libertà, Pza., **2A5**
Limbo, Pza. d., **3D3**
Lorenzo Ghiberti, Pza., **2C5**

Macci, V. d., **2D5**
Machiavelli, V., **1E2-F3**
Maggio, V., **3E2-D2**
Mantellate, V. d., **2A4**
Manzoni, V., **2C5-6**
Martelli, V. d., **4B4**
Mentana, Pza., **4E4-5**
Mercato Centrale, Pza., **2B4**
Mercato Nuovo, Pza. d., **4D4**
Mezzo, V. d., **2C5**
Michelangelo, Pza., **2E5**
Michelangelo, V., **2E5-6**
Michele di Lando, V., **1F3-E3**
Micheli, V., **2B4-5**
Mille, V., **6D4-5**
Montebello, V., **1B2-C2**
Monte alle Croci, V. d., **2E5**
Moro, V. d., **3C2**
Mozzi, Pza. d., **4F5-E5**

Nazionale, V., **3A3**
Neri, V. d., **4D4-5**

Oche, V. d., **4C4**
Ognissanti, Pza., **1C3**
Olio, Pza d., **3B3**
Oriuolo, V. d., **4C5**
Oro, Pza. d., **3D3**
Orsanmichele, V., **4C4**
Orti Oricellari, V. d., **1C2-B3**
Orto, V. d., **1D2**
Ottaviani, Pza., **3C2**

American Express Travel Guides

spanning the globe....

EUROPE
Amsterdam, Rotterdam
  & The Hague
Athens and the
  Classical Sites ‡
Barcelona & Madrid ‡
Berlin ‡
Brussels #
Dublin and Cork #
Florence and Tuscany
London #
Moscow & St Petersburg *
Paris #
Prague *
Provence and the
  Côte d'Azur *
Rome
Venice ‡
Vienna & Budapest

NORTH AMERICA
Boston and New
  England *
Los Angeles & San
  Diego #
Mexico ‡
New York #
San Francisco and
  the Wine Regions
Toronto, Montréal and
  Québec City ‡
Washington, DC

THE PACIFIC
Cities of Australia
Hong Kong & Taiwan
Singapore &
  Bangkok ‡
Tokyo #

*   Paperbacks in preparation   #   Paperbacks appearing January 1993
‡   Hardback pocket guides (in paperback 1993)

Clarity and quality of information, combined with outstanding maps — the ultimate in travelers' guides

Medici Chapel
(San Lorenzo)

Uffizi

S. Maria Novella